The Objectivist Nexus

See the Acknowledgments for a continuation of the copyright page.

1 2 3 4 5 6 7 8 9 / 07 06 05 04 03 02 01 00 99

∞
The paper on which this book is printed meets the minimum requirements of American National Standard for Information Science-Permanence of Paper for Printed Library Materials, ANSI Z39.48-1984.

Library of Congress Cataloging-in-Publication Data

The objectivist nexus : essays in cultural poetics / edited by
Rachel Blau DuPlessis and Peter Quartermain.
p. cm. — (Modern and contemporary poetics)
Includes bibliographical references (p.) and index.

ISBN 0-8173-0974-8 (alk. paper)
ISBN 0-8173-0973-X (paper : alk. paper)
1. American poetry—20th century—History and criticism.
2. Social problems in literature. 3. English poetry—20th century—History and criticism. 4. Literature and society—History—20th century. 5. Marginality, Social, in literature. 6. Objectivism (Philosophy) 7. Modernism (Literature) 8. Poetics. I. DuPlessis, Rachel Blau. II. Quartermain, Peter. III. Series.
PS310.S7 035 1999
811′.509—dc21 98-58047

The cover photo is of an oil painting by Kay Sage, *A Little Later* (1938). Gift of the Estate of Kay Sage Tanguy, Denver Art Museum Collection.

Contents

Acknowledgments vii

Introduction 1
Rachel Blau DuPlessis and Peter Quartermain

I. "We Said / *Objectivist*": Optics, Objectification, Sincerity, Seriality

1. The Objectivist Tradition 25
Charles Altieri

2. A Poetics of Marginality and Resistance: The Objectivist Poets in Context 37
Burton Hatlen

3. Be Aware of "the Medusa's Glance": The Objectivist Lens and Carl Rakosi's Poetics of Strabismal Seeing 56
Ming-Qian Ma

4. George Oppen's Serial Poems 84
Alan Golding

II. Politics, Class, and Ideology

5. Communists and Objectivists 107
Eric Homberger

6. Irrelevant Objects: Basil Bunting's Poetry of the 1930s 126
John Seed

7. Objectivists in the Thirties: Utopocalyptic Moments 144
Michael Heller

8. Lorine Niedecker's "Folk Base" and Her Challenge to the American Avant-Garde 160
Peter Middleton

III. Ethics and Religious Culture

9. Tradition and Modernity, Judaism and Objectivism: The Poetry of Charles Reznikoff 191
Norman Finkelstein

10. Reznikoff's Nearness 210
Charles Bernstein

11. Of Being Ethical: Reflections on George Oppen 240
Peter Nicholls

IV. Affiliations

12. Reading Reznikoff: Zukofsky, Oppen, and Niedecker 257
Robert Franciosi

13. Zukofsky's List 275
Andrew Crozier

14. "And All Now Is War": George Oppen, Charles Olson, and the Problem of Literary Generations 286
Stephen Fredman

15. Land's End 294
Yves di Manno

16. The Transformations of Objectivism: An Afterword 301
Charles Altieri

Notes 319

Works Cited 343

Contributors 361

Index 365

Acknowledgments

Peter Quartermain and Rachel Blau DuPlessis would like to thank each other for intense, collegial, and mutually supportive work on the poets to whom we are both committed. We would also like to thank Meredith Quartermain and Robert and Koré DuPlessis for their tolerance during our transcontinental and transfixing phone calls, Curtis Clark and Mindy Wilson of The University of Alabama Press for their forthright professionalism, Hank Lazer and an anonymous reader for incisive and helpful reports, our copy editor Jonathan Lawrence for his keen eye, Cynthia Nakamura of the Denver Art Museum for her cover photograph, and all our distinguished contributors for their perseverance and expertise.

Rachel Blau DuPlessis and Peter Quartermain

Permissions

From Basil Bunting, unpublished correspondence. Copyright © 1999 by the Estate of Basil Bunting. Material from the Basil Bunting Poetry Archive, Durham University Library is quoted by permission of the University Library.

From *The Collected Poems of Robert Creeley, 1945–1975.* Copyright © 1983, The Regents of the University of California. Reprinted by permission of University of California Press.

From Jean Day, *The Literal World,* Atelos Press, 1998. Copyright © 1998 by Jean Day. Used by permission of the author; all rights reserved.

From Lyn Hejinian, *The Cell,* Sun & Moon, 1992. Copyright © 1992 by Lyn Hejinian. Used by permission of the author; all rights reserved.

Unpublished Lorine Niedecker materials. Copyright © 1999 by Cid Corman, Literary Executor of Lorine Niedecker. Clayton Eshleman Papers, Fales Library, New York University.

Unpublished Niedecker materials. Copyright © 1999 by Cid Corman, Literary Executor of Lorine Niedecker. Charles Reznikoff Papers. Mandeville Special Collections Library, University of California at San Diego.

Poetry from *Collected Poems of George Oppen.* Copyright © 1975 by George Oppen. Reprinted by permission of New Directions Publishing Corporation.

"Foreword" and back cover citation by George Oppen. Copyright © 1999 by Linda Oppen. In *Charles Reznikoff, Poems 1937–1975.* Reprinted by permission of Black Sparrow Press.

Poetry from *Primitive.* Copyright © 1978 by George Oppen. Citation from p. 20. Reprinted by permission of Black Sparrow Press.

From *The Selected Letters of George Oppen,* ed. Rachel Blau DuPlessis. Copyright © 1990 by Duke University Press.

Uncollected Oppen poem (Alternative version of "A Morality Play: Preface"). Copyright © 1999, by Linda Oppen, Literary Executor of George Oppen. Used by permission; all rights reserved.

Unpublished Oppen materials. Copyright © 1999 by Linda Oppen, Literary Executor of George Oppen. Used by permission. George Oppen Papers. MSS 16. Mandeville Special Collections Library, University of California at San Diego.

Unpublished Oppen materials. Copyright © 1999 by Linda Oppen, Literary Executor of George Oppen. Used by permission. Charles Reznikoff Papers.

MSS 9. Mandeville Special Collections Library, University of California at San Diego.

From *Collected Poems of Charles Olson—Excluding Maximus Poems.* Edited by George Butterick. Copyright © 1987, Estate of Charles Olson, previously published poetry, © 1987 University of Connecticut, previously unpublished poetry. Reprinted by permission of the University of California Press.

From *The Palm at the End of the Mind: Selected Poems and a Play by Wallace Stevens,* edited by Holly Stevens. Copyright © 1971 by Holly Stevens. Citations from pp. 363 and 364. Reprinted by permission of Alfred A. Knopf, Incorporated and Random House, Inc.

From *The Collected Poems of Carl Rakosi.* Copyright © 1986 by Callman Rawley. Citations from pp. 42, 44, 46, 47, 49, 50, 53, 55, 237–38, 380. Reprinted by permission of The National Poetry Foundation, University of Maine.

From *Holocaust* by Charles Reznikoff. Copyright © 1975 by Charles Reznikoff. Citations from pp. 46, 75. Reprinted by permission of Black Sparrow Press.

From *Poems 1918–1936, Volume I of The Complete Poems of Charles Reznikoff,* ed. Seamus Cooney. Copyright © 1976 by Charles Reznikoff. Citations from pp. 45, 72, 115, 116, 121, 174–75. Reprinted by permission of Black Sparrow Press.

From *Poems 1937–1975, Volume II of The Complete Poems of Charles Reznikoff,* ed. Seamus Cooney. Copyright © 1977 by Marie Syrkin Reznikoff. Citations from pp. 30, 62, 69, 75, 76, 80, 81, 86, 136, 167, 171, 176. Reprinted by permission of Black Sparrow Press.

From *Selected Letters of Charles Reznikoff, 1917–1976,* ed. Milton Hindus. Copyright © 1997, The Estate of Charles Reznikoff. Editing, Introduction and Notes Copyright © 1997 by Milton Hindus. Citation from p. 201. Reprinted by permission of Black Sparrow Press.

Unpublished Reznikoff materials. Copyright © 1999 by the Literary Estate of Charles Reznikoff. Permission granted by David Bodansky. Material held in George Oppen Papers. MSS 16. Mandeville Special Collections Library, University of California at San Diego.

From Walt Whitman, *Complete Poetry and Collected Prose,* edited by Justin Kaplan. Published in 1982 by Library of America.

Unpublished letter from William Carlos Williams to Louis Zukofsky. Copyright © 1999 by Paul H. Williams and The Estate of William Eric Williams. Used by permission of New Directions Publishing Corporation, agents.

Unpublished letter from William Carlos Williams to Louis Zukofsky (7 May 1929). Louis Zukofsky collection. Credit line: Harry Ransom Humanities Research Center, The University of Texas at Austin.

From *"A"* by Louis Zukofsky. Copyright © 1978 Celia Zukofsky and Louis Zukofsky. From pp. 17 and 210 and as well from the version of *"A"-6* published in *The "Objectivists" Anthology.* Reprinted by permission of Johns Hopkins University Press.

From *Complete Short Poetry* by Louis Zukofsky. Copyright © 1991 by Paul Zukofsky. From pp. 17, 48–49, 66, 69, 70, 72, 73. Reprinted by permission of the Johns Hopkins University Press.

Certain chapters are copyrighted as follows:

"Reznikoff's Nearness" by Charles Bernstein. Copyright © 1999 by Charles Bernstein. All rights reserved.

"Zukofsky's List" by Andrew Crozier. Copyright © 1999 by Andrew Crozier.

"Land's End" ("Finistère"). Copyright © 1995 by Yves di Manno and *Java.* Translation of di Manno into English © 1999 by Rachel Blau DuPlessis.

Certain chapters were published as follows, sometimes in earlier versions, in periodicals and with presses to whom grateful acknowledgment is made:

Robert Franciosi, "Reading Reznikoff, Zukofsky and Oppen," *North Dakota Quarterly* 55 (Fall 1987): 283–95.

Alan Golding. "George Oppen's Serial Poems" appeared in an earlier version in *Contemporary Literature* 29. 2 (Summer 1988): 221–40. Copyright © 1988. Reprinted by permission of The University of Wisconsin Press.

Eric Homberger, Chapter 7 (revised) from Homberger, *American Writers and Radical Politics, 1900–1939.* Copyright © 1986. Reprinted by permission of Macmillan Press Ltd.

Peter Middleton. "Folk Poetry and the American Avant-Garde: Placing Lorine Niedecker," appeared in *Journal of American Studies* 31. 2 (1997): 203–18, published by Cambridge University Press, to whom acknowledgments are made.

Peter Nicholls. "Of Being Ethical: Reflections of George Oppen," *Journal of American Studies,* 31. 2 (1997): 153–70, published by Cambridge University Press, to whom acknowledgments are made.

The Objectivist Nexus

Introduction

Rachel Blau DuPlessis and Peter Quartermain

Tamalpais in cloud

One is conscious also of the farmlands

Place names unrecorded   local knowledge
Of the heavy hills

It is not that one means to bring home
A moral to an audience

We are those selfish travellers
Happiest in foreign streets

Insomuch as we are not travellers
We are afraid

Courage of the traveller
Piety

We said
Objectivist

—George Oppen, "*Morality Play*"[1]

Resistant to definition, "Objectivist," uppercase, with or without quotation marks, is a notably unstable term. Originating with Louis Zukofsky's "Objectivist" issue of *Poetry* (February 1931), "Objectivist" has historically and metonymically been applied to poets affiliated with that issue, yet not necessarily included in it or in the follow-up *An "Objectivists" Anthology* of 1932. Indeed, some of those included resisted the label, and Zukofsky himself came to view it with a fond ambivalence.[2] As George Oppen observed in October 1966, "none of the poets who have regarded themselves to any degree as Objectivists have resembled each other in their surfaces, their manner, their lives or in their ultimate concerns as men [*sic*]" ("Three Oppen Letters" 84). Nevertheless, we affirm that these writers were indeed conjoined through a variety of personal, ideological, and literary-historical links. Genealogically, they can be regarded as those who identified with and extended the practices of Pound, Williams, and, in some cases, Stein, Stevens, and Moore. Situationally, they are poets reading each other with special attentiveness, who challenged, spurred, and occasionally exasperated and annoyed each other, however intermittently, for the rest of their lives. In reception, they can be identified as a set of persistently underknown and undervalued late-modernist and early contemporary writers who, to read their peers and to identify their own poetics, kept the rubric "Objectivist" as a conceptual, variable "historic and contemporary particular," self-reflexively inflected with that suspicion that sometimes occasioned the ironic quotation marks (Zukofsky, "Program: 'Objectivists' 1931" 268; also *Prepositions* 12).[3]

This anthology focuses on Basil Bunting, Lorine Niedecker, George Oppen, Carl Rakosi, Charles Reznikoff, and Louis Zukofsky as Objectivist writers, treating them as a nexus for poetic production and for critical and poetic reception. It is our purpose to claim for them a central place in twentieth-century poetry and poetics. Several forces have cumulated to bring attention at this point to these writers. Their own later careers filled with an exploratory formal breadth, including Basil Bunting's, George Oppen's, and Carl Rakosi's return to the writing of poetry after silence. The trade publication of Zukofsky's work after long neglect called attention to his notable theorizing of poetry. And the later publication of Oppen's letters and daybooks/working papers and Niedecker's letters had a similar effect in another decade. This theorizing in poetics within the Objectivist nexus, combined with the credibility and interest of poststructuralist theory in general, has made more legible the philosophic and ethical emphases inside their poetry and poetics. The critical work of Charles Altieri (1973, 1979), David Antin (1972), L. S. Dembo (1969, 1972), Burton Hatlen (1978, 1982), Michael Heller (1985, 1993), Hugh Kenner (1975), Marjorie Perloff (1981, 1991), and Charles Tomlinson (1975, 1981), as well as the National Poetry Foundation (editors Hatlen and Carroll Terrell) with its considerable volumes of assessments and documents, all played significant and provocative roles.

Since about 1970, the widening of what had been a somewhat specialized audience for Objectivist writing, along with the retrieval of such work, has had appreciable and identifiable effect upon later generations of poets, and has offered a way of reading or folding back over modernism through what Michael

Davidson calls "an Objectivist continuum" (*Ghostlier Demarcations* 23). There is arguably an Objectivist source in the most recent contemporary American poetry, one with at least two branches: those loosely grouped and customarily labeled as Language poets, and an even looser unlabeled affinity, as yet less articulated, but palpable—a neo-Objectivist branch. All writers absorbing the Objectivist example consider the praxis of the poem to be a mode of thought, cognition, investigation—even epistemology; most of these writers are, in an enlarged sense, realists and materialists—people as various as Norma Cole, Cid Corman, Michael Davidson, Kathleen Fraser, Lyn Hejinian, Michael Palmer, Ron Silliman, Rosmarie Waldrop, and Barrett Watten, among a host of others.[4] Thus the term "Objectivist" has come to mean a non-symbolist, post-imagist poetics, characterized by a historical, realist, antimythological worldview, one in which "the detail, not mirage" calls attention to the materiality of both the world and the word (Zukofsky, *Prepositions,* 12).

I

In his *Autobiography,* William Carlos Williams suggested that in 1931 Objectivists agreed that "the poem, like every other form of art, is an object, an object that in itself formally presents its case and its meaning by the very form it assumes" (264). But the implications are hardly as formalist as Williams's words suggest; his own quarrel here, similar to Pound's in the early 1920s, is with a loosened and permissive, vatic imagism. Pound's quarrel ended with both a formalist and intellectual *rappel à l'ordre,* a calling to traditionalist (and masculinist) attention, an archetypal evocation of certain organic principles, however heteroclite his diction. The Objectivists, instead, worked out a dialectical, materialist, and situational accountability to this notion of "order," as (in Charles Altieri's words in his first essay in this book) "the mind's act brought to objective form." Zukofsky emphasized equally the formalist and historical aspects of this poetics by insisting that the poem be shaped by specific necessities of the particular historical moment in which it is written, what he called "inextricably the direction of historic and contemporary particulars" ("Preface" 15; also *Prepositions* 12, 15). Any given particular is both historic and contemporary, and may, considering the Marxist connotation of "inextricably the direction," resonate with teleological overtones. A poem was also to be a mode of social observation, connecting a variety of basic, essential phenomena, as our epigraph from George Oppen says.

These goals have analogues with the view of the poetic text set forth by Ernst Bloch in his 1935 essay "Marxism and Poetry." Concerned to defend poetry from being a token of pure, ungrounded imagination, and to integrate poetry into a materialist practice, Bloch proposed the still somewhat idealist sense that poetry—"an elucidated waking dream of the essential"—intuits latent and almost invisible tendencies in the social, and communicates them in texts (88). Good poetry for Bloch cannot help being accurate to society now or in the future; it is news that has a predictive value: "reality plus the future within it." But Bloch's formulation does not guarantee attention to the specific rhetorics of poetry as a literary text: his discussion modulates from "poetry" in general to poetic drama in particular as best able to reveal social conflicts and processes through characters exposed in their fundamental drives and motives (90). In his picture of the social meaning of poetry, the poetry these characters speak is a rhetorical wrapping that heightens the conflicts and contradictions being bared. So Bloch implicitly proposes narrativity and performativity as more decisively able to encode social materials. In contrast, and from the beginning, the Objectivists, with their decided sense of the line and their inventive serial organization, use the basic nature of poetry—its "segmentivity"—to articulate social meanings (DuPlessis, "Manifests" 51).

The first Objectivist practice occurred from 1927 to 1935, across the time of an economic crisis, with its profound political and social disruptions, including a rise in fascist movements for totalitarian social control and in Left and working-class movements for social justice. In the wake of the 1917 Russian Revolution and its sense of hope, many people, including all the Objectivists, were committed to (inter alia) a radical vision of social justice, Marxist analyses, or socialist/communist allegiances. All six poets—Bunting, Niedecker, Oppen, Rakosi, Reznikoff, and Zukofsky—were productive in this eight-year period, though they did not all know each other. For a variety of reasons, not all of them appeared in the 1931 issue of *Poetry* which named the nexus (or in the 1932 anthology) and about which Kenneth Rexroth quipped resistantly: "Almost all the people that Zukofsky picked as Objectivists didn't agree with him, didn't write like him or like one another, and didn't want to be called Objectivists"—one might delicately claim resistance *to* nexus as part of the construction *of* nexus (*American Poetry* 111). Many other poets appeared in these publications—including Rexroth himself, T. S. Eliot, Mary Butts, and Whittaker Chambers. Indeed, during this time Niedecker was engaged in surrealist experiment. The period before 1935 is also marked by the interested scrutiny, support, and ambivalence of Ezra Pound, by a fascination with the work of Gertrude Stein on the part of Oppen, Zukofsky, and Williams, and by the general influence of Objectivist poetics, and especially of Zukofsky, on William Carlos Williams.[5]

After 1935, Objectivist practice is marked by absences and silences; a variety of career and publication gaps among the poets makes this a poetics gone underground, or dormant. This career interruption was curiously consistent, though specific to each poet: there are gaps of approximately twenty-five years in the careers of Oppen, Rakosi, Bunting, and even (intermittently) Zukofsky. For example, Oppen, characterizing himself as callow, sought a deeper grounding in political activism on the Communist Left; he finally had to come to terms both with Stalinism and its depredations and with the persecutions of right-wing McCarthyite purges. These career gaps are in some cases related to the definition, within the Communist Party's cultural blueprint, of a simplistic but very influential program for art: so-called "socialist realism," its absolutist, melodramatic, and inflexible agendas ending the earlier "great epoch of [Marxist] cultural experiment" (Eagleton, in Eagleton and Milne 10). The career gap in Zukofsky's case was also abetted by tensions between a genteel Jewish assimilationist stance (rejected by Zukofsky) and the sharp-edged avant-garde modernism with which Zukofsky identified but which was increasingly anti-Semitic (Finkelstein, "Jewish-American Modernism"). The narratives differ for each poet, but in each case their career gaps acted emphatically to hinder and thwart their critical reception.

Furthermore, the Objectivists also positioned themselves as outsiders in degrees of negotiation with a mainstream literary and political culture, and they may be outright nonhegemonic and resistant. Bunting as a Northumbrian found himself in political and cultural disagreement with the cultural metropole defined by London, and spent many of his years in more or less voluntary exile. Niedecker was fairly isolated both economically and geographically, living in semirural Wisconsin for most of her life. Oppen was in political exile in Mexico for a number of years. Zukofsky claimed a mid- and late-career interior exile.[6] It is worth recalling that three (Zukofsky, Rakosi, Reznikoff) learned English as a second or even third language (as did Stein and Williams) and that these three, plus Oppen, were differently, but markedly, urban and Jewish. One—Oppen—concertedly, and mainly successfully, resisted his social class of origin—"upper class of '29," he jokes in a letter (Oppen, "Letters to Rachel Blau DuPlessis" 130). There are factors in each case that made marginalization, even exile, central to the existence, and to the poetry, of each.

In the late 1950s and after—that is, in the postwar, post-Holocaust period—these poets started writing and publishing again, and began to be accorded some critical recognition. This recent period in reception/production has been characterized by Ron Silliman as "third phase Objectivism," a "renaissance phase" that mingled "resurgence of interest in existing texts with the production of new writings," a mix that is exactly our sense of "nexus"—in which the linear, ideal literary historical narrative from production to reception gets disturbed, torqued, or folded upon itself ("Third Phase" 85). Nevertheless, Objectivist work remains largely unrecognized and unacknowledged, despite the fact that from the 1960s on—for almost forty years—it has been increasingly significant for a growing and diverse number of practicing poets in the anglophone world and in France. The newest edition of the *Heath Anthology of American Literature* (third edition, 1998) includes a section entitled "Charles Reznikoff, Louis Zukofsky, and Objectivist Poetry," and both the fourth and the fifth editions of the *Norton Anthology of American Literature* include selections of poetry by George Oppen and Lorine Niedecker—but in the longer versions of the anthology only.

II

Each of the four sections in this anthology bears on the sociocultural and historical reading of the authors and Objectivist poetics and practices. Discussing poetics and form, the essays in the first section insist on poetry as a mode of thought; those in the second analyze and evaluate a generally left-wing Objectivist politics of the thirties and a concomitant skepticism of capitalist distortions of the humanist tradition. The third section focuses on the ethical, spiritual, and religious issues raised, mainly in the post-Holocaust fifties and sixties, by Objectivists' affiliations with Judaism and their own Judaic ancestry and cultural practice. The final section explores the sense of nexus directly: as George Oppen put it, "I believe I thought of these poets simply as the poets I found revelatory" (*Selected Letters* 284). Running through all four sections are two related threads: Objectivist writing as aware of its own historical contingency and situatedness, and Objectivist poetics as a site of complexity, contestation, interrogation, and disagreement.

The opening section insists, as Burton Hatlen's essay articulates, that these poets are concerned to fashion "objective" (not subjective) poetic positionalities and to construct poetic forms and modes adequate to, or in effective tension with, both the politics and the ethics they professed. Hatlen's essay also offers the rubrics of politics, religious culture, and social location and affiliation that this anthology favors. In characterizing the Objectivist statement in toto as a "poetics of resistance," this essay links to Michael Palmer's characterization of the poets (in *Sulfur*) as manifesting "the poetic values of resistance, social awareness and exploratory integrity" ("On Objectivism" 117).

Charles Altieri's classic statement on Objectivist poetics discusses how the compositional acts themselves articulate a relational ethics which, in avoiding or finessing the "interpretive will" of symbolist practice, actuates a poetics that is anti-sublime, anti-transcendent, anti-universalizing. The links among form, poetics, and ethics are traced in the "strabismal" form which is the outcome of mutual respect between speaking subject and seen object, as Ming-Qian Ma articulates. Seriality is a central strategy of the Objectivist poetry of thought and of its constructivist debate with a poetics of presence and transcendence. The formal "problem of connection" is played out structurally and thematically in the work of Oppen, as the relation between fragment and series parallels the thematics of individual and community. Alan Golding further proposes that the nature of Robert Creeley's concept of "writing" as well as of Oppen's serial works challenges the received commonplaces on the nature of poems, and positions Creeley in the Objectivist nexus.

There are two relations of this section to the definition of "nexus," our title word. First, it is interesting to remark that some of the formal, aesthetic, and generic modes of the Objectivist writers—seriality, "discrete series," anacoluthon, collage, ideogrammic or vectored structures, refusal of closure—are consistent with the term "nexus," for "nexus" means ligatures joining items serially, or a set of crossings that may proceed outward in a variety of directions from a nodule of importance.

Speaking not only formally, but for the literary history of an idea in poetics, the notion of a nexus tries precisely to address the fact that once the rubric "Objectivist" was set into play by Zukofsky, it took on, magnetized, and got attributed to it a set of historical responsibilities that one may track and assess. As the first section shows, the poets and critics in this book recur to the Zukofskian topoi of sincerity, objectification, and lens/rays/optics. When Zukofsky, somewhat unwillingly, undertook to write a justificatory essay for *Poetry*—"Sincerity and Objectification with Special Reference to the Work of Charles Reznikoff"—he proposed two key terms essential to this poetics, terms to which, for example, Oppen and Niedecker return repeatedly. It is no surprise then, that although "Objectivist" as a term has some clear meanings, it is nevertheless unstable, first since the proportion of such key concepts as "sincerity" and "objectification" varies in each narrating of the issues by the poets, and second since each writer constructs those concepts differently, and may add others to the mix. There may be a shared vocabulary, but its applications and gloss differ from writer to writer. In short, the term "Objectivist" has situated meanings, not an absolute one.

At various moments in Zukofsky's essay, "objectification" seems to mean, first, the ability to focus many factors into one unit—this seems like an early version of "composition by field," or the Poundean ideogram, but miniaturized in scale. Second, the elucidation of a new object, or an old one stripped so one could see it freshly, is parallel to Williams's much repeated term "cleansing." Third, "objectification" has always brought in its wake the notion of objectivity in its philosophic sense: "of or having to do with a material object as distinguished from a mental concept, idea, or belief." But in Zukofsky's essay, objectification essentially proposed "rested totality," the poise of a finished art object ("Sincerity and Objectification" 274; also *Prepositions* 13). Objectification was originally formalist because it meant a perception of form, and, since the analogy Zukofsky uses most often is music, the term even had symbolist implications: form as "the totality of perfect rest" ("Sincerity and Objectification" 276; also *Prepositions* 13). Indeed, Zukofsky's emphases left his essay open to the charge that there was nothing new in this poetics—charges duly presented as a response to the 1931 statement in subsequent issues of *Poetry* by Harriet Monroe and others.

The rhetorical function of that equalizing "and" of Zukofsky's title, "Sincerity and Objectification," suggests that perfection-rest-totality-music, which is to say "directing [things as they exist] along a line of melody," are all "inextricably" related to a particular focus on "thinking with the things as they exist," which is to say "the detail, not mirage, of seeing" (*Prepositions* 12). Zukofsky's title thus balances a set of formalist terms with a set of imagist/realist and historical terms. And his rhetoric presents paratactic equivalences in a concertedly hypotactic structure balanced on that decided word "inextricably." The essay itself is somewhat equivocal, and even indecisive about its propositions, a fact that may have made it (perhaps paradoxically) productive. Arguing that objectification is the primary Objectivist practice, Zukofsky nevertheless finds it quite rare in Reznikoff, whose works are "actually almost constant examples of sincerity" ("Sincerity and Objectification" 278), and he even suggests that "objectification" may not be as central to the denomination "Objectivist" as is sincerity: "It is questionable, however, whether the state of rest achieved by objectification is more pertinent to the mind than presentation in detail" (278).

For Oppen, too, "'Objectivist['] meant, not an objective viewpoint, but to objectify the poem, to make the poem an object" (*Selected Letters* 47). But even more formative for him is the fact that writing was described by Zukofsky "as the arrangement, into one apprehended unit, of minor units of sincerity" ("Sincerity and Objectification" 274). As a result both of reading Zukofsky's essay in the "Objectivist" issue of *Poetry* and of his strong personal/intellectual bond with him, Oppen made a compact with poetry. Oppen seems, thus, to have constituted his early practice as a proving ground for Zukofsky's ideas, with special emphasis on the compression, the "veracity," the idea of "sincerity" which constitutes "accuracy of detail" (Zukofsky, "Sincerity and Objectification" 280). In writing *Discrete Series*, he took Zukofsky's notions, especially about sincerity, as axiomatic.[7] Political critique, suspicion of symbolism, and the analytic framing of selected particulars in a language unusually mobile both in syntax and reference all animate Oppen as Objectivist.

For Oppen, sincerity is above all an ethical term. The potential he saw in "historic and contemporary particulars" was a sense of social purpose without agitprop posturing. Indeed, his aesthetic concerns again recall those of Ernst Bloch, who, in "Marxism and Poetry," avers that Marxism appears in poetry as "genuine realistic" impulses, concerned with facts, "imagination without lie," and "process." Most strikingly, Bloch insists that "the true poetic aura" potential in Marxism "remains as clarity" (86). "Clarity" was a term that became central for Oppen. When L. S. Dembo interviewed Oppen in 1968, the poet reviewed his own first book as embodying the epistemological and ethical potential of that Zukofsky essay. Oppen's poetics of sincerity—"you construct a meaning from . . . moments of conviction"—necessitates (objectified) form (Oppen in Dembo, "The 'Objectivist' Poet" 161). The objectification of the poem is the joining of discrete sincere statements of that conviction; both the statements and the poem thereby have the force of empirical fact.

Oppen's one essay—"The Mind's Own Place" (1962)—can be viewed as an extension and renewal of the materials in the Zukofsky essay of 1931, giving fullest weight, however, to the criterion of sincerity. Such ideas as "a test of truth," "clarity," and "the image is encountered, not found" all emphasize a practice of existential honesty ("The Mind's Own Place" 133). Indeed, the image as encountered, not found, works against the trouvaille—the hyperwrought and ingenious literary turn. Hence Oppen follows Zukofsky's essay, but importantly did not follow what he saw as the ingenuities of Zukofsky's poetry. In Oppen's view, with "Mantis" Zukofsky had committed himself to the arcaneness of trobar clus. To reestablish Objectivist practice, Oppen was separating one part of Zukofsky from another, and shifting the emphasis.

What did other Objectivists think either of these terms or of Zukofsky's foundational essay? In asking for "information which is itself action," in his conviction that the function of literature "is to explore the resources of language and make language available for all existing or potential thoughts," and in his poetic practice, Bunting's connection to both the nexus and to Pound is apparent, though he himself scorned the label "Objectivist," or any presumably "abstract" label: "I don't believe," he wrote to Zukofsky in 1934, that "abstract words correspond to anything except the noise made in pronouncing them" (Letter to Zukofsky, 27 April 1934). Although the status of Bunting is discussed in several of the essays here (Crozier situates him in a localist, anti-metropole set of British poetries), he represents a post-Poundean political modernism that is obscured, denied, and even erased: as John Seed shows, Bunting's oeuvre also contests current interpretations of British modernism in the thirties.

Zukofsky's foundational essay is also very much in key with Rakosi's view of Objectivism as the opposite of "subjectivism." In a 1969 statement synthesizing and summarizing the poetics he understood as Objectivist, Rakosi wrote: "For myself, I found the term Objectivist useful. It conveyed a meaning which was, in fact, my objective: to present objects in their most essential reality, to make of each poem an object . . . meaning, by this, obviously, the opposite of a subject; the opposite, that is, of all forms of personal vagueness" ("A Note" 36). In the 1930s Rakosi published no critical or theoretical statements, but he conducted an intense, brief correspondence with Zukofsky between November 1930 and January 1933. When Zukofsky asked him whether he objected to the label "Objectivist," Rakosi recalls (from the vantage of the 1990s) a pragmatic motivation: "I didn't care what he called us so long as we got published in *Poetry,* the only magazine in this country then willing to take some risks with new poetry" ("A Word" 63). In fact, Rakosi's early work was strongly under the influence of Wallace Stevens, who thus becomes another player in the nexus. In the mid-thirties, in his prose poem "Equations," which functions as a statement in poetics, Rakosi carefully separates himself from work by Eliot, Tate, MacLeish, and Winters, praising instead work by Moore, Zukofsky, Cocteau, and Williams (Rakosi, "A Word" 149–50). These studied affinities seem to be representative of all writers in the Objectivist nexus.

Lorine Niedecker's considerations and reconsiderations of the term "Objectivist" are singularly destabilizing and lively. Niedecker differs from the other Objectivists in that her work has a distinct, liberatory, pre-Objectivist phase of surreal writing, a phase on which she draws and with which she negotiates throughout her career. Jenny Penberthy's criticism and textual studies have been especially fruitful in foregrounding Niedecker's surrealist aspects. Niedecker is an exemplary case in the later manifestations of the Objectivist nexus because of her own distinctly ambivalent relationship to what she came to see as "Objectivism"—which she speaks of as an identifiable and defined literary movement. The 1931 "Objectivist" issue of *Poetry* seems to have induced in her a conversion experience (she said: "here was the center of literature in this country and in the world"); at around the same time, in about 1932, she heard Zukofsky read "in a kind of chant with soft-voiced—as you say, certainty—utter, deep sincerity" (Letter of 11 June 1969 in Niedecker, "Extracts" 37). That last word as an ethical criterion is a direct allusion—articulated thirty-eight years later—to Zukofsky's "Program" of 1931.

Niedecker's dialogue with Objectivist poetics can be tracked in two sets of letters, probably thirty years apart, one (speculatively) about 1935–36 and the second clustering around 1966–68. In a letter from the mid-thirties sent to Mary Hoard, she proposes some kind of fusion or dialectical correction of Objectivism through surrealism: "Thank god for the Surrealist tendency running side by side with Objectivism and toward the monologue tongue. It is my conviction that no one yet, has talked to himself. And until then, what is art?" (Penberthy, *Lorine Niedecker* 87). The letter reflects her connection with "Louis Zukofsky and the Objectivist Movement," but, influenced by the book *Foundations of Modern Art* (Amedée Ozenfant, trans. John Rodker), parses "objectivist" as "Objects, objects," and asks, "Why are people, artists above all, so terrifically afraid of themselves?"[8] This suggests that one of her early views of Objectivist proposals were that they functioned as veils to expressive, frank, energized feelings. "It is my belief objects are needed only to supplement our nervous systems," she wrote Hoard. This statement shows that at least then she interpreted Objectivist practice as having to focus on the materiality of objects in the real world to express intensities of interior feeling.

Niedecker had apparently discussed these ideas with Zukofsky, who was fairly resistant to them. Her positive use of the term "surrealist" can be juxtaposed against Zukofsky's entirely dismissive observation, in his 1931 essay in *Poetry,* that "surrealism in 1928 was not essentially novel, and that for [Reznikoff] at least, ten years earlier [1918], it was not worth doing" ("Sincerity and Objectification" 273). Niedecker's aim to privilege the subjective and her desire to create a new psychosocial subjectivity through cultural work is also seen in her remark, "I conceive poetry as the folk-tales of the mind and us creating our own remembering" (Penberthy, *Lorine Niedecker* 88). The linkage of psychological/mental phenomena and folk materials is a sophisticated fusion of two strands of thought in the 1930s (tracked in parallel ways by Peter Middleton here): populism, Popular Front subjects, and the intellectual movements of abstraction and psychoanalysis. Niedecker's word for all this seems to have been "surrealism," a term that was, of course, very damaged goods in the Objectivist context. Niedecker's distinction also raises the considerable question of the different positionality a poet gendered female would have to negotiate.

In the early 1960s she hints clearly to Zukofsky that she is "trembling on the verge of" a new "form of poetic thinking": it seems to be "What we feel, see, inside us and outside us melted together absolutely" (Penberthy, *Niedecker Correspondence* 343, 327). That blending of inside and out is never far from certain Objectivist work. For example, in 1974 Oppen made one of his repeated reconsiderations of the meaning of "Objectivism." His revisionary meaning—that "consciousness in itself, of itself carries the principle of actualness" (*Selected Letters* 290)—puts in circulation two terms that parallel Niedecker's concern—"consciousness" and "actualness." But she takes this integrated fusion of inside and out as impossible or unlikely under the Objectivist banner. In 1967, Niedecker continued to articulate her suspicion, or judgment, of "Objectivism": "I went to school to Objectivism but now I often say *There is something more*" (Letter to Clayton Eshleman, 18 November 1967).

Writing to Kenneth Cox on 10 December 1966, Niedecker begins to build another (not exclusively Zukofskian) genealogy for herself, indicating that her double heritage, however contradictory, had always been there: "Well—there was an influence (from *transition* and from surrealistes that has always seemed to want to ride right along with the direct, hard, objective kind of writing" ("Extracts" 36). Time and again in the 1960s till her death at the end of 1970, she bluntly proposes this two-pronged heritage; would it be oversimple to speculate that gender difference, or difference of social circumstance, was in a dialogic relation with her repeated emphasis on her further difference in poetics? In an important letter to Gail Roub of 20 June 1967 she writes:

> Much taken up with how to define a way of writing poetry which is not Imagist nor Objectivist fundamentally nor Surrealism alone . . . I loosely called it 'reflections' or as I think it over now, reflective, maybe. The basis is direct and clear—what has been seen or heard etc. . . . —but something gets in, overlays all that to make a state of consciousness. . . . The visual form is there in the background and the words convey what the visual form gives off after it's felt in the mind. . . . And [there is] awareness of everything influencing everything. . . . I used to feel that I was goofing off unless I held only to the hard, clear image, the thing you could put your hand on but now I dare do this reflection. (in *Origin* 42)

It is clear that Niedecker continues to take Objectivist poetics as meaning a resistance to association, to any "streaming" of the mind at all levels, to any concentration on an emotional "afterimage." One might risk the surmise that she placed this emotional resonance in language in opposition to Zukofskian language play or wit, and possibly as opposed to the anti-female undercurrent in all the Poundean pronouncements about the "hard," but at any event it aligns her own particular revision of the Objectivist nexus with late Oppen.

III

Burton Hatlen has discussed the invention of an alternative to socialist realism that Zukofsky initiated with his issue of *Poetry.* There is a strong political dimension in Zukofsky's editing and writing in the 1930s: Zukofsky included work by proletarian poet Herman Spector, for instance, in the issue of *Poetry;* Hatlen suggests that up to at least 1940, Zukofsky was "explicitly and consistently a political poet" ("Art and/as Labor" 206) who had written a eulogy to Lenin in 1925, "Constellation: In Memory of V. I. Ulianov"; "During the Passaic Strike of 1926"; and a poem "D.R." dedicated to Diego Rivera in early

1929. As both Hatlen and Mark Scroggins argue elsewhere, Zukofsky had a serious knowledge of and some commitment to Marxism by the late 1920s (Scroggins 45, 215–16).

However, Zukofsky's apparently thematic demand for the poem to be political (exemplified in these titles and allusions) is in fact an epistemological and structural move, for he sees "the necessity of a strictly objective estimate of all the class forces and their inter-relation in every political action." In thus quoting Lenin in a letter to the editor of *Poetry* in 1933 to defend *An "Objectivists" Anthology* against the charge of cultural elitism, he implicitly conflates the political with the poetic. He proposes that the poem is the "strictly objective estimate" of social forces and "historic and contemporary particulars," and at the same time that the poem is a complex linguistic "inter-relation" (117). Such a poem, in its concentrated complexity, will have the force of a political statement and will potentially infuse and inspire political vision. For Zukofsky this is a structural matter, for in presenting such complexities of interrelationship across modes he achieves a simultaneity of address to history, values, and rhetoric, and makes a poem synthesize and contain "entire aspects of thought: economics, beliefs, literary analytics, etc." ("Sincerity and Objectification" 273). Just as Pound saw himself as the poetic embodiment of Mussolini's social program, so Zukofsky here makes a similar claim for himself in relation to Marx and Lenin.

In 1934, Zukofsky was writing his tour de force "Mantis," a sestina about the poor and his resistance to them, in an elaborate form following his "thought's torsion." The most brilliant cultural move of "Mantis" is the relationship of the initial poem and the series of reflective notes in "Mantis, An Interpretation," the companion poem: analysis of its origin, rough draft, a formulation of the principles of his choices, an allusive history of other practitioners of the sestina, a gloss, a scholia, and a "curriculum" as well. (Amazingly, Zukofsky wrote the interpretation because Williams asked him to; see Quartermain, *Disjunctive Poetics* 91.) Completing "Mantis" with a poem-essay called "An Interpretation" lays bare the device of the sestina in a Brechtian "estrangement effect"; it places modernism and all its poetics of presence, represented by the sestina, in a subversive role generated by a discursive meditation on praxis. As Michael Davidson remarks, "The dialogue between formalism and critique (the 'Mantis' sestina and its interpretation) involves intellectual labor in which a new kind of subject is born" (*Ghostlier Demarcations* 134). Davidson discusses this poem within a generally Marxist field in an informing chapter in *Ghostlier Demarcations* (116–34). The Objectivists "regard their formalism as a material agent within the social" (239).

Basil Bunting was deeply skeptical of Zukofsky's intentions in some of his political moves, and through the 1930s conducted a running argument in his correspondence with him, objecting so strongly to Zukofsky's "Program: 'Objectivists' 1931" that he composed a series of essays and letters, not all specifically addressed to Zukofsky, but each, in a different way, pointing to the materiality of language and hence of the poem, and each, more or less, forcibly reminding Zukofsky of the sheer ineffectualness of poetry in direct political action. Nonetheless, poetry contributed to the capacity of individuals to act. Bunting's "Observations on Left-Wing Papers," sent to Zukofsky in 1935, is a mine of practical advice on the relation of language to politics, stressing the local, the immediate, and the concrete as the ground of all political and poetical action: "the effect of turning people's eyes away from their own surroundings is invariably to dissipate their attention, and thus to paralyse the sources of effective action" (44). "A word like sincerity seems to me to be almost without any assignable meaning at all," he would say some forty years later (Bunting, "Basil Bunting" 75), and his sheer exasperation at the abstractness of Zukofsky's language was often accompanied by solid Popular Front advice to say it "so the bum on the bridge can understand it" (Letter to Zukofsky, 27 April 1934).

IV

There is a clear ancestry to the Objectivist nexus, particularly in Pound, Stein, and Williams. But it is striking that when Louis Zukofsky wrote the introduction to the 1931 issue of *Poetry,* instead of acknowledging these connections, he chose to eulogize Charles Reznikoff, his senior by ten years and an extremely unknown writer, in an essay whose title bears those crucial terms "Sincerity and Objectification." This strategy managed to leave the question of ancestry open while proposing an unanticipated and unfashionable Yiddish and Jewish one. Indeed, the quondam Jewishness of four of the Objectivist poets (with the obvious exceptions of Bunting and Niedecker) might also have contributed to their overall neglect. This seems especially likely when we recollect an unstated and often unconscious anti-Semitism, as witnessed in the career of such a figure as Lionel Trilling, in the mainstream literary and university worlds.

Zukofsky's honed poetic ambition, his elegant, somewhat brooding, occasionally crabbed, but certainly witty practice, and his well-educated mind were grounded on a particular Jewish terrain: assimilation, secularization, and the response to anti-Semitism. His "Poem beginning 'The'" (1926) tricks and trumps *The Waste Land* (1922) in part by an angry affirmation of his Yiddishkeit and Jewish learning in the face of a mainstream (that is, Christian) modernist literary culture.[9] At its close he offers a seethingly disdainful program of overcompensation, offering to beat hegemonic culture on its own terms. Hence, going to the very heart of Western anti-Semitism, he cites and reiterates Shylock's speech in *The Merchant of Venice:* "The villainy you teach me, I will execute, and it shall go hard but I will better the instruction" (III.i). This moment is talismanic for his career as a whole.

As senior, Reznikoff was source and symbolic figure for both Oppen and Zukofsky. If we think of him as a Yiddish poet writing in the American language, the Objectivist nexus becomes a site where the materials, poetics, and ethics of Yiddish poetry came into modern American writing. From the 1890s to the 1930s and beyond, there thrived in the United States a poetry in modern Yiddish (a diasporic Germanic language of Jews, written in the Hebrew alphabet), compounded of folk lyric and social satire, often from socialist, anarchist, and proletarian roots, and using Jewish ritual, custom, history, and scripture within the texts. Of the several generations of Yiddish poetry in this period, the third (the In Zich poets) had a serious appeal to and impact on Reznikoff and Zukofsky in particular.[10]

Indeed, the so-called "introspectivist" In Zich manifesto of 1920 prefigures certain aspects of Zukofsky's program of 1931: "we introspectivists want, first of all, to present life as it actually is, with precision," and this in a language devoid of ready-made images and used poeticisms (Howe and Greenberg 41). There are other analogues and motifs in the work of the Objectivists and Yiddish poets. Their social vision, their concern for the marginalized, their tender and ironized introspective self-debate, and such motifs as the "quarrel with God (*krign zich mit Got*), a quarrel undertaken with intimacy, affection, and harshness"—all are trackable within the Objectivist nexus, pointing as they do to the criterion of sincerity and the high spiritual stakes (Howe and Greenberg 16). On these grounds, later to be encapsulated in the title of his first book to be published by the Objectivist Press, *Testimony* (1934), Reznikoff is representative of Objectivist writing. It is certainly plausible to suggest that Zukofsky's "Sincerity and Objectification" may in Reznikoff's eyes have consolidated his own focus on testimony while at the same time the impulse to testimony in his work may have inflected Zukofsky's formulation of an Objectivist program. Yet, though Zukofsky may be said to have studied with Reznikoff, the impulse to testimony also derives from one of the enabling documents of Objectivist writing, Pound's "A Few Don'ts" (1913, reprinted in "A Retrospect" [1918]), which eschews language "that does not contribute to the presentation" (Pound, *Literary Essays* 3).

From his own legal training, Reznikoff had found that the examination of language, standards of clarity, and lack of the superfluous must carry over into poetry. He had been deeply affected by the persecution of Jews in late-nineteenth-century Russia—his grandfather's poems were destroyed by his grandfather's wife lest they be accused of anti-czarist subversion—and his major works of "testimony" (whether from the late-nineteenth-century U.S. court records or, later, from the court records of the Nuremberg trials after the Holocaust) are, inter alia, documents from a Jewish subject position. Not only meaning evidence, or declarations of truth under oath—swearing by one's very "testes," in etymological frankness—"testimony" is also a word that comes out of a religious discourse, and may indeed be said to be a word marking the spot where legal and religious discourses meet.[11]

"Testimony" is also by dictionary definition a public declaration of a religious experience. One might ask, what possible "religious" experience could be claimed from Reznikoff's relentless rhizomic anti-teleological accumulation of documents in verse from factory, home, and street about profound injustice, social spite, grim accident, casual violence, hatred, callous and killing practices, implacable meanness, and generally the disgraceful disregard (in profit-making businesses and elsewhere) for ethics and justice. One could equally well ask what similar "religious" experience could be claimed from Oppen's poems. The use could be ironic, atheistic—a testimony without God, made in his astonishing absence, that "God of my unbelief" who also motivated Jacob Glatshteyn. Or one might say that Reznikoff is offering these carefully, "artlessly" selected and focused works-in-facts as that which must be reckoned with, in the interests of undercutting the whole realm of imaginative literature—presenting motives, characters, narratives, and outcomes as they really are, objectively. And there is a political agenda in simply confronting readers with the record of hurt and wounding, a general defense of the chumps and "churls" from which his English name came.

But more, this record of the suffering and social martyrdom of the most common people (*dos klayne menshele*) may be made in the spirit of reporting to God, for his book of the Last Day, the day when such powerless suffering will, it is said, be avenged. The personal humility that distinguishes Reznikoff veils this ferocious vocation of recording angel. The omniscient narrator, the impersonal tone, the (almost always) nonsentimental, the sense that the soul of the writer is nowhere and everywhere, and the assumption that "the truth" is an ascertainable datum, recordable in real language—all contribute to this kind of angelic subjectivity. Even if he worked without the hope of a Last Day, this implacable record stands as such, the recording angel in spite of the institutionalized consolations of official Judaism, and possibly in spite of such formulations as "God." This is very much in keeping with both Zukofsky's and Oppen's goals, and indeed with those of writers in the Objectivist nexus generally.

V

Oppen summarizes the sense of nexus directly when he writes, "I believe I thought of these poets simply as the poets I found revelatory," a remark that nicely points to the suggestive fluidity of that term (*Selected Letters* 284). "Nexus" embraces contradiction, variousness, and dispute; the final section of this book treats dissemination and the vagaries of reception through a foregrounding of some critical tasks and debates about affiliations as self-conscious aspects of cultural poetics. As is evident from the history of poetry, poets themselves initiate the processes of reception by pronouncements of various sorts, and the first two essays in this section suggest some ways the Objectivist poets began their own self-scrutiny and reception. A non-Bloomian reading of the Objectivist nexus takes shape in a narrative of affiliation proposed by Christopher Beach based on bonding around an exemplary figure rather than on strong-weak Oedipal contestation: Robert Franciosi shows how Reznikoff as example helped to link, if not unify, the poets with a sense of their responsibilities to the poetic task. Reznikoff's struggles, and his integrity, are reflected in textual allusions and transformative borrowings. Franciosi also notes the ways poets structure a literary career by affiliative relations and gift exchange.

Since the "Objectivists," in contradistinction to both modernists (Pound, Williams, Eliot) and "New American" poets (Olson, Creeley, Duncan), were chary and irregular with critical writings, "Zukofsky's list" importantly defined the poets' allegiances. Examining this list, Andrew Crozier isolates a specific and telling moment in the formation of the modernist canon, and his contention that the Objectivists "disturb" our "ordinary understanding of history as chronology," and his argument that Zukofsky intervened, with this list, in a specific historical situation, both evince attention to poetics as a historical product and refine our formulation of "nexus."

In a similar vein, the next two essays in this volume recast and extend the Objectivist moment by cutting across the way we have constructed the nexus in most of this anthology. Several counter-narratives of placement and literary historical arrangement may then be constituted and put into consideration. In linking Olson and Oppen (as did Altieri in the first essay here), although neither had personal nor poetic fondness for the other, Stephen Fredman finds they are joined by their professing "the objective" in particularly existential ways, shaped by experiences in and of World War II. The evocation of that war and its aftermath in the recognition that the twentieth century was the century of genocides links Oppen to such postwar European writers of meditation as Paul Celan and Edmund Jabès. Yves di Manno, in a polemical intervention into contemporary French poetry, proposes that it is structured by a debate between

Pound and Mallarmé. His essay, written in 1989, avers that Poundean practices influenced by the Objectivist emphasis on the "real, real world" have "recentered and revitalized" French poetry. He thus evokes the cultural functions of translation and attempts to see how and why influence crosses national borders.

Other counter-narratives are possible and plausible. Horace Gregory's view of Reznikoff's "plaintive undertone of Yiddish American speech, of the same quality and tonal dimension of the Negro spiritual"—however motivated, and whether true or not—raises the issue of race as an absent presence in American literature in general and in this literature in particular (Gregory 383; source courtesy of Stephen Fredman). In other ways, A. L. Nielsen's critique of Oppen and Rakosi for certain patronizing poems involving racial representations, and John Shoptaw's penetrating suggestion that Langston Hughes could be considered a contributor to the poetics of realism and seriality in the Objectivist nexus, show the analytic dimensions of the question of racial discourses, depictions of racially marked persons, and the to-date missing question of the construction of whiteness in these poets.

Given the current discussions of mobility and mixage in the construction of gender, and of masculinity as an ideology, and as well, the studies of specifically Jewish maleness, it would be likely that such discussions, along with the concomitant question of the representation of gender in various works, will be raised in the future (see Middleton and Boyarin). The relative lack of such discussions is a mark of the unevenness of reception of these poets; such discussions usually follow, rather than precede, the increased canonicity of writers.

Finally, Charles Altieri expands his original definitional essay in poetics by extending, first, the concept of sincerity to indeterminacy, and, second, the concept of objectification and the poem as material object to the anti-representational constructions of several contemporary investigative poets—Lyn Hejinian, Charles Bernstein, and Jean Day among them. Though the Language poets have claimed a particular affinity with the Objectivists, a claim tested and analyzed by Altieri's afterword, the affinity is by no means exclusively theirs, and extends to a number of other writers who follow quite different compositional practices, those who generally fall into what Kathleen Fraser has called a "tradition of marginality" (52) and what Michael Palmer has called "an enduring counter-tradition" ("Active Boundaries" 265). With this section on the making of dissemination and reception, the self-reflexive issues in our own literary historical and poetic practices are foregrounded, and we see once more that a nexus is a continuous and continuing construction, according to the accidents of historical moment and critical location.

Our cover, a 1938 oil painting by Kay Sage, illustrates some of these considerations by showing distinct objects—of organic, worked, and machine-made matter—poised against and with each other. Like these poets, they are certainly grouped, but they are also, like these poets, separate and individuated. Sage's title *A Little Later* may be taken, in this context, as a comment both on the belated reception of Objectivists and on the continuing temporalities of reception to which our term "nexus" points.

The word "nexus" itself is a past participle, from the Latin *nectere,* meaning to bind, join, or connect. It means, first, the link already existing between members of a group or a series, and, as well, a means of connection between things that creates a connected series or group. The term thus expresses tension between past and present, between the prior existence of and the intended construction of linkage among certain items, and invites engagement in cultural poetics as practice. In this particular case, a nexus is made of some writers once designated "Objectivist," who continued, from a variety of motives, to "say Objectivist"—who continued, that is, to focus on that term and the pressures it put on them for the whole of their literary careers. Nexus is affirmed, and reaffirmed, then, through a series of choices, accidents, debates, and critical inquiries and redefinitions that this book examines and exemplifies.

"Nexus" is a term useful for resisting definitive fixity while encouraging a continuing discussion of cohorts and groups, over such questions as: What is an Objectivist at any moment during the poetic and critical history of the use of the term? What are the issues and models that certain poetics propose, and how do those intersect with other models simultaneous to a historical moment or contiguous in some way? Are there analogues to this poetics in the visual arts, in architecture, or in music? What do the personal/biographical shifts of affiliation and connection among the poets tell us? What are recurrent issues, and what are the disparities of answer or proposition? Are there contradictions among poet, poem, and poetics? For any particular writer in a nexus, does any other affiliation or formation rival this one in importance? What benefits are accrued and what disadvantages are suffered if, as a writer, one starts, and then continues to "say Objectivist"? Most of these questions are repeatedly addressed in this book.

We have chosen this term because we want to distinguish literary "nexus" from literary "generation," literary "movement," and the like, and because it changes the conceptualization of a literary "group." Indeed, we would suggest that the ideas animating the term "nexus" could contribute to new ways of narrating literary history. Seeing literary works, in Jerome McGann's terms, as "particular forms of transmissive interaction" leads to a discussion not only of the "materialist hermeneutics" of textual transmission involving bibliographical codes, editions, and their material and intellectual meanings, but as well proposes any investigation "along the double helix of a work's reception history and its production history" (*Textual Condition* 11, 15, 16). The construction and reconstruction, configuration and reconfiguration of a literary "group" to assist production, and then to encourage reception, offers one such area for a cultural poetics.

One aim of this book, then, is to offer culturalist interpretations of poetry, readings inflected with sociopolitical concerns—an activity framed by what, adapting Stephen Greenblatt, we have been calling "cultural poetics" (5). Cultural poetics assumes the critical task of "investigating both the social presence to the world of the literary text and the social presence of the world in the literary text" (Greenblatt 5). This in turn involves the understanding that a literary product is always, as George Levine puts it, "participating in a culture-wide system of signs and thus always implicated in other discourses," including, of course, those systems through and in which the reader-critic reads and responds (8). In continuing yet modifying Greenblatt's call, Levine challenges critics who want to achieve a cultural poetics to articulate "the relation between aesthetics and ideology" in such a way as neither to lose the distinctive sense of the literary text nor to lose the palimpsests of understanding generated when one situates a work amid the social debates that surround it (9). Recently, Barrett Watten has rearticulated his commitment to "cultural poetics," calling for a faceted debate on its potential as a paradigmatic probe of contextual readings and writings of texts with attention to any "specific history of difference" from which texts originate and "the particular contexts" for their use ("Bride" 4, 7, 6).

Those social debates, it hardly needs to be added, are deeply inflected by the actual existing situation of the critic. As Page duBois has commented, if we see rhetoric as "a language in which social conflicts are being staged, contested, negotiated, and managed," then we shall see "discourse about rhetoric as itself bearing social-historical weight, . . . working in culture, doing cultural labor, providing pleasures, reinforcing and negotiating relations of powers" (167–68). Cultural poetics, then, necessarily includes in its purview a recognition of the critic's own position as gazer.

There is, however, a further torque to this question. As the call for a "cultural poetics" has begun to reverberate, it appears that very few of the academic critics who engage in the analytic tasks prompted by cultural poetics talk about (nondramatic) poetry. Poetry has most often been exempt from this kind of contextual analysis, since there is a long critical tradition of viewing the "textiness" of a poetic text as engaged only with the aesthetic realm, with the rich history of its own genre, and with the nuanced intermingling of philosophy and language practice that go by the name of "poetics." Formal analysis and formal concerns, its own intertextualities, its own vibrant genres, are constituted for poetry as an autonomous realm of practice. Therefore, in attempting culturalist readings of poetry, critics are struggling with and against accepted institutionalized paradigms for the analysis of that genre.

In framing this anthology, we thus offer a double, and productive, use of the term "poetics." The term "cultural poetics" is used by Greenblatt to mean a systematic way of articulating the working assumptions, the premises, the ideologies of practice of any discursive system that gives rise to texts, whether poetry or not. But "poetics" is used generally by poets and critics of poetry to mean the working assumptions, the premises, and the ideologies of practice lying behind the creation of poetic texts. Poetics generally includes discussions of the vocation of the poet, the functions ascribed to poetry, the explicit or implicit reading list of worthwhile practitioners, the motivated defenses of poetic technique, form, and diction, the constitution of an audience, and the puncturing or harrying of an opponent poetics: these are the kinds of activities one may see *passim* in such texts as Olson's "Projective Verse" and Bernstein's "Artifice of Absorption" (not to mention Shelley's "A Defense of Poetry"). When we say we want to study Objectivist poets via a cultural poetics, we are, at one and the same time, trying to present culturalist readings—that is, readings alert to the material world, politics, society, and history, and readings concerned with the production, dissemination, and reception of poetic texts—and, as well, readings analyzing the poetic assumptions and textual choices that animate a set of practitioners. In this regard, then, this anthology tries specifically to consider the cultural poetics of Objectivist poetics, and more generally to open up the consideration of a cultural poetics for poetry. It is here, we believe, that the concept of nexus is especially useful.

While we certainly agree in general with critics who suggest that it is mostly fruitless to try to unify the writers once called "Objectivist" under some common rubric of aesthetic practice or philosophy ("movement," "common project"), nonetheless the term "objectivist" is provocative because it is more than some bad habit or ex post facto critical genuflection. The term "nexus" refers to a confluence of interests cutting across notions of movement, period, and even era, but most interestingly, as McGann's analysis suggested, it proposes a linkage among production and transmission, including critical transmission. Such linkages, to which the concept of nexus emphatically draws attention, perhaps lead writers and readers away from instruments of dominance in a competitive canonical marketplace. Nexus declines to establish those quasi-impermeable boundaries by means of which cultural power seeks permanent and central installation and through which critical intervention is rendered invisible.

To talk in terms of a literary movement is, for literary production, to identify boundaries of time or location, to examine manifesto, meetings and membership, marks of solidarity, a specific lexicon of debate, and, in reception or consumption, to stress questions of conformity to or variation from some extractable or centralized norm of aesthetics or practice. Critical perception will indeed tend to invoke, or produce, uniformity, self-consistency, sameness, and orthodoxy as identifying markers and even as virtues in a movement (and in its criticism). Literary history written from this standpoint can function as a celebration of a group, as customs officer or patrol of the borders of a group, can exaggerate debates with others, can burnish bonds, dialogues, and excommunications among its members. Thinking in terms of a nexus does not deny this complex of generative ideas, practices, and ways of seeing, or undercut the shared interests, anguishes, and delights that also distinguish literary groups or movements. However, when writers think of themselves as a nexus, or when critics proceed with this formation in mind, they no longer demand conformity of the literary materials or producers, nor a temporal and philosophical consistency of application, but rather a continued interest in the grounds for debate.

Hence, "nexus" could be a term for a literary history written under the rubric of Foucault's observation that the problem in the study of literature "is no longer one of tradition, of tracing a line, but one of division, of limits; it is no longer one of lasting foundations but of transformations that serve as new foundations"—a literary history that remains a shifting place of dialogue, debate, and reconfiguration (5). Thinking of a literary nexus offers a three-dimensional model of participation, production, and reception over time. It includes the critical acts that form reception: what are the investments any critic or poet-critic may have in the term "Objectivist" and its perpetuation? Thinking about writers in a nexus allows one to appreciate difference and disparity among them, to pinpoint perhaps radical disagreements, to attend to rupture as well as continuity, and to dispersion as well as origin. The term "nexus" is useful because it describes a relationship among writers based on their shared meditations, but not necessarily shared conclusions or even practices, about the particulars of their writing life and their historical position. It engages the actual material, social, psychological, and aesthetic circumstances of literary production and transmission.

1
"We Said / *Objectivist*": Optics, Objectification, Sincerity, Seriality

1

The Objectivist Tradition

Charles Altieri

> An objective; (Optics)—The lens bringing the rays from an object to a focus. (Military use)—That which is aimed at. (Use extended to poetry)—Desire for what is objectively perfect, inextricably the direction of historic and contemporary particulars.
>
> —Louis Zukofsky, "Sincerity and Objectification," 1931

> In any given instance, because there is a choice of words, the choice, if a man is in there, will be, spontaneously, the obedience of his ear to the syllables. The fineness, and the practice, lie here, at the minimum and source of speech.
>
> O western wynd, when wilt thou blow
And the small rain down shall rain
O Christ that my love were in my arms
And I in my bed again.
>
> —Charles Olson, "Projective Verse," 1950

> Then for nine reigns there was no literary production! None at all; because there was neither consciousness of the "objectively perfect" nor an interest in clear or vital "particulars." Nothing—neither a new object nor the stripping of an old to the light—was "aimed at."
>
> —Zukofsky, "Sincerity and Objectification," 1931

I

Poetic traditions make their mark less by virtue of themes or doctrinal values than through the modes of relatedness whose power and scope they demonstrate. By "modes of relatedness" I mean the ways in which the basic elements of poetic form, the signs of how intelligence and craft shape materials and focus energies, offer models for the mind's means of adjusting its dynamic properties to features of experience. In commenting on "Western Wynd," Olson at once celebrates the power of its dynamic interplay between mind and world and testifies to the enduring effects of its energies liberated out of history by their capacity to create an enduring objective field. He teaches us to read a poem as new by opening himself to the relational lines of force that embody the qualities and scope of feelings constituting a distinctive attitude toward craft, and, through craft, toward a world worth attending to. Olson's testimony, in turn, celebrates and continues the efforts of his immediate objectivist masters, whose capacity to create a tradition is measured by the distinctiveness of the energies Olson has available to bring to his critical act.

On the most general level, there are probably two basic modes of lyric relatedness—symbolist and objectivist styles. The former stress in various ways the mind's powers to interpret concrete events or to use the event to inquire into the nature or grounds of interpretive energies, while objectivist strategies aim to "compose" a distinct perceptual field which brings "the rays from an object to a focus." Where objectivist poets seek an artifact presenting the modality of things seen or felt as immediate structure of relations, symbolist poets typically strive to see beyond the seeing by rendering in their work a process of meditating upon what the immediate relations in perception reflect. Louis Zukofsky provides one index of this distinction by defining two properties as basic to objectivist poetry:

> In sincerity shapes appear concomitants of word combinations, precursors of . . . completed sound or structure, melody or form. Writing occurs which is the detail, not mirage, of seeing, of thinking with the things as they exist, and of directing them along a line of melody. Shapes suggest themselves, and the mind senses and receives awareness. . . .
>
> This rested totality might be called objectification—the apprehension satisfied completely as to the appearance of the art form as an object. . . . [Its] character may be simply described as the arrangement, into one apprehended unit, of minor units of sincerity—in other words, the resolving of words and their ideation into structure. ("Sincerity and Objectification" 273–74)

Where a symbolist poet would concentrate on relations that dramatize meanings beyond the event, the poet in "Western Wynd" wants to make relational forces intensify "the detail, not mirage, of seeing." To do so articulates a field where one can think with things as they exist. The primary relations here are denotative (in an imaginary world) rather than connotative or metaphoric. In order to keep the denotations intensely resonant, the poet marks his or her field—perceptually and musically—by a dense interplay of direct perceptions standing toward one another as planes in an abstract painting. The poetry is in the parallels between forms of desire and energy held together in a perceptual space. Wind and desire are less metaphors for feeling than its direct equivalent in physical fact, so that nature and person's nature are adequate vehicles for one another, echoed again in the overt energies of the writing where the desire for concepts is constrained and directed into the plosive play of alliterating syllables and of strong vowels modulating the kinetic energies of speech from back to front of the mouth. Desire here takes form, not by being mastered, but by achieving full expression in each of the overlapping energy fields—perception, memory, projected future, and act of writing. Desire becomes a condition of energy at rest in itself, and the theological analogues in Zukofsky's poetic statement find here a perfectly adequate secular ground. The literal will suffice, provided one has learned the craft of the letter.

This model of poetic art needs to be continually reinvented because as soon as perceptual and compositional energies grow slack or seem inadequate to the mind's needs, writers seek to supplement concrete detail by symbolic generalization. Consider now the state of wind and syllable during the nine reigns when for Zukofsky there was no literary production. Here are Shelley—the beginning and ending of "Ode to the West Wind"—and Coleridge—from "Dejection: An Ode," the seventh stanza:

> O wild West Wind, thou breath of Autumn's being,
> Thou, from whose unseen presence the leaves dead
> Are driven, like ghosts from an enchanter fleeing,
>
> Yellow, and black, and pale, and hectic red,
> Pestilence-stricken multitudes . . .
>
> . . . .
> Scatter, as from an unextinguished hearth
> Ashes and sparks, my words among mankind!
> Be through my lips to unawakened earth
>
> The trumpet of a prophecy! O Wind,
> If Winter comes, can Spring be far behind?

> Hence, viper thoughts, that coil around my mind,
>   Reality's dark dream!
> I turn from you, and listen to the wind,

> Which long has raved unnoticed. What a scream
> Of agony by torture lengthened out
> That lute sent forth! . . .
> . . . .
> What tell'st thou now about?
> 'Tis of the rushing of a host in rout.

These are very different poetic acts of mind. They are not the only form of romanticism, nor do they warrant careless modernist charges of egotism and vagueness. Shelley and Coleridge introduce new sources of perceptual and philosophical energy into English poetry. But in making the act of the interpretive mind, rather than the measuring mind, the poem's central focus, they also make central and inescapable some very serious problems. In their pursuit of dialectical symbolic structures capable of reconciling discordant elements into satisfying conceptual wholes, these poems simultaneously produce too little and too much meaning. On the one hand, the mind enacts only a mirage of seeing because it thinks about, rather than with, things. The wind has little objective status: what details the poet attends to are significant only as tenors for stories or spiritual metaphors like "pestilence-stricken multitudes." And, on the other hand, as the mind moves over, rather than among, the particulars of its world, it leaves itself no place to rest that is not dependent upon the "trumpet" of a prophetic ego whose metaphors are its only authority. The pursuit of abstract synthesis through metaphoric processes is at best tenuous; the mind is always threatened by the possible return of self-consciousness insisting on the merely conceptual and fictive grounds for its orders and driving the self back into a despondent and passive relation to the natural energies its interpretations displace. Unseen presences, nature become metaphoric words, and story-telling winds all too easily become again only the deadness of seen presences that resist only mirages in reality's dark dream. Moreover, by so insistently dramatizing the efforts of mind locked into a single lyric space, the poem's craft is subject to the same alternations as its desire for meaning. At one extreme, lyric exaltation becomes the melodramatic tone poem of Shelley's opening trumpets, while at the other the verse slackens into prosaic analogues whining the poet's passive surrender to external forces. Composition verges on losing its ground in composure, and poetic modes of relatedness come dangerously close to echoing the frenetic dualities of the culture they try to resist.

Shelley and Coleridge are great poets, but the modes of relatedness on which their greatness is based may be no longer accessible, or desirable, for our culture. Threatened by Enlightenment intellectual and social forces calling into question all they treasured, these poets' only line of defense was to make the sublime serve metaphysical purposes. The sublime enabled them to accept rationalist critiques of the limits of empirical propositions while creating a space in which the empirically unreal could remain imaginatively real, albeit indefinable except through the vehicle of symbolic imaginative dialectics. And by increasing the distance between the empirical and a realm of imaginative values, these poets purchased a Miltonic exaltation and tragic intensity no Objectivist poet but Pound can rival. But the price of this nobility—in the psychic torments it creates no less than in the poetic postures it encourages—may be too high. And even this question may be irrelevant because the sublime too is a faith that may have died. The symbolist vision may not be one we can make new without the various ironies of Wallace Stevens and of John Ashbery.

II

> I do believe that consciousness exists and that it is consciousness of something, and that is a fairly complete but not very detailed theology.
>
> —Oppen in Dembo, "The 'Objectivist' Poet" 1969

> The poet wonders why so many today have raised up the word "myth," finding the lack of so-called "myths" in our time a crisis the poet must overcome or die from, as it were, having become too radioactive, when instead a case can be made out for the poet giving some of his life to the use of the words *the* and *a:* both of which are weighted with as much epos and historical destiny as one man can perhaps resolve.
>
> —Zukofsky, "Poetry/For My Son When He Can Read," 1946, *Prepositions*

> For a man's problem, the moment he takes speech up in all its fullness, is to give his work his seriousness, a seriousness sufficient to cause the thing he makes to try to take its place alongside the things of nature. . . . [He must work] in that area where nature has given him size, projective size.
>
> —Olson, "Projective Verse," 1950, *Collected Prose*

The Objectivists repeatedly insist that theirs is not a doctrinal movement: there are objectivists but no Objectivism because the poets share only a sense of the necessity and value of sincerity and a concern for the attention to craft, for the poem as machine made of words or the poem as thing in which ideas inhere. It is possible, nonetheless, to sketch a general definition of their poetic, that is, of the discursive ways that they articulate forms of relatedness explored in poetry and speculate about the psychological and cultural significance of these forms.

As is the case with most abstract statements about poetics, objectivist theory is clearest and most widely shared in its accounts of the evils it opposes. Here Eliot and Pound are the significant figures. They developed the basic catalogue of the evils attendant upon the pursuit of the sublime as means of smuggling religion past Enlightenment customs. With the sublime, Dante's precise vision and disciplined dream give way to poetry that purchases transcendence by muddying perception with generalizations and thus cannot rest with objects until they have been transformed by metaphor into explicit analogues for psychic life. In pursuit of this "semi-allegorical gleam" ("Sincerity and Objectification" 273), Zukofsky tells us, "Poets put on singing robes to lose themselves in the universal" (*Prepositions* 147). Because of this quest for transcending specific objective conditions, poets lose any sense of firm ground on which the mind can rest and poetry achieve resolution. There is left only the triumph of will singing its own incoherence, the louder for every self-conscious reminder of the fictive status of its half-believed mythic substitutes for religion. And this uneasy will creates the range of evils Eliot would find both in his culture and in the poetry unable to escape cultural pressures—dissociated sensibility with its vacillations between abstract rumination and uncontrolled flights of feeling, and sentimental faith in progress and technology which might compensate for poets' discomfort with their craft and with their confused transcendental beliefs. Only the dream of progress could justify the bad faith of poets desperately convincing themselves that their devices were compatible with truths and that there were authorities to which they might submit the uneasy self-consciousness that dogged their efforts to dramatize sensibilities on a scale large enough to give content to the sublime.

Objectivism, then, is first of all a discipline of the poetic will and a critique of prophetic roles assumed by nineteenth-century poets. Again Zukofsky is a precise spokesman: "no predatory manifestation," no imposition of a will not completely responsible in the poem for its acts—"Yet a manifestation making the mind more temperate because the poem exists and has perhaps recorded both state and individual" (*Prepositions* 16). Objectivism, then, is not merely attention to objects: it entails the construction of aesthetic objects in such a way that the conditions of desire are themselves dramatized and forced to take responsibility for their productions. This demand for lucidity, however, creates serious constraints on the poet. As the imagist phase of Objectivism makes clear, the impulse to avoid romantic tendencies to let reason pander the will can tempt poets to discipline the will virtually out of existence. Insisting on objectivity threatens reducing poetic craft to the merely descriptive function of making perceptual images—thus trapping poetic energies within scientistic reductions of the psyche which, in turn, encourage other poets (like Yeats, Eliot, and Crane) to court the comfortable evasions of the sublime. And fear of prophetic role-playing can create the tension between poetic discourse and political commitment that silenced Reznikoff and Oppen in the thirties and forties. Similar distrust of ideas in poetry leads to the enervated satiric evasiveness of "Hugh Selwyn Mauberley," where self-consciousness once again collapses into self-pity. The central task, the imperative for Pound, Williams, Zukofsky, and Olson, must be to use imagist techniques in such a way as to escape the limits of description and satire. As George Oppen put it, Objectivist poets "attempt to construct meaning, to construct a method of thought from the imagist technique of poetry—from the imagist intensity of vision" (Oppen in Dembo, "The 'Objectivist' Poet" 161). Construction, not description, would be the basic source of models of relatedness, and these would find their roots in the collagist techniques whose implications for poetry have been described by David Antin.

The basic principle of collage construction in poetry was once described by Ron Loewinsohn as "the layering of frames of reference." This layering can consist of elaborate cultural units, as in the *Cantos,* in the organization of discursive thought units characteristic of Olson, or in the delicate alignment of perceptual and syntactic units we have observed in objectivist nature poetry. In all these cases, collage allows a direct series of discrete objective notations fused into complex dimensions of interrelatedness not dependent on the interpretive will for dialectical synthesis. Consequently, poets need not submit to principles of dramatic order that encourage the pursuit of intensity by theatricalizing the poet's self-conscious stances in quest of sublimity. We have terms for meeting the challenges Eliot and Pound defined as basic to modernism because we have a framework for exploring fresh ways of articulating emotions and acts of mind. Thus it becomes possible to justify Oppen's equation of a phenomenological poetics with theology and Zukofsky's attacks on the epic sensibility. Poets can emphasize the significance of emotions intrinsic to complex acts of perception, rather than to the dramatic process of attributing meanings to perception by means of metaphors and symbols. "The accomplished fact," as Zukofsky put it, might carry "the maximum of the real." And, most important, by defining "the maximum of the real" in terms of perception in discrete yet intensive relations dependent upon compositional acts, the poets reinterpret the nobility of acts of mind. Nobility inheres not in transcending facts but in constructing their relations into immediately satisfying wholes. Because the real is "accomplished," not simply given in perception, acts of disclosure and formal composition demand all those energies which romantic poets often felt could only be expressed either in apocalyptic vision or in dramatizing one's awareness of the dilemmas inherent in pursuing that vision. The real can be sufficient.

Collage construction enables images to become a form of thinking. Two closely related principles—field and measure—define the nature and value of that thinking. These concepts evade both description and symbolic interpretation by exhibiting meaning as itself dependent upon collage principles, upon the dynamics of relationship in a distinct field. In Oppen's terms, "things explain each other, / Not themselves" (*Collected Poems* 134). And "measure" is the term for describing the values created by discrete relations within a field. We can then consider the same principles at work in the ways objectivist poets handle the romantic bogey of self-consciousness. So long as language remains essentially denotative and the energies of mind can be maintained within the compositional lines of force that the field establishes among the layered references in the poem, there need be no residue of unnameable desire or shaping will behind the poem, and no need for universals beyond it. There is nothing that can return in self-consciousness to haunt one with the fear that his or her fictions evade to transcend empirical conditions. The mind's act brought to objective form is as present to itself as are the objects it brings into relationship. The writer can be intensely personal; still the personal energies are at once exhausted and maintained within the composition. The measure of the self, and the measure of the mind, is what stands in what one makes, not what one desires or intends or glimpses of universals only provisionally shadowed in particulars. Self and mind require no myth: their being is the intensity of their power to focus the "the" as it takes form through hesitations of mind and melodic movements. Objectivist poetics creates an instrument sufficiently subtle to make attention and care—to the world and to the corresponding energies the world elicits—ends in themselves. Attention, care, and composition become testimony to levels of fit between the mind and the world in rhythmic interactions that require no supplementary justification in the form of abstract meaning.

III

The objectivist tradition has numerous sources, from Sappho to Flaubert to Zen. These formative influences and their transformations have been superbly documented by Herbert Schneidau and Hugh Kenner. But here, because our concern is with the continuing development of this tradition, attention must be focused on definition and on the exemplary presences that establish models for poetic practice and measures for other poets' imaginative achievements.

I define the objectivist tradition in American poetry as that body of work molded by freeing imagist techniques into methods of thought based on notions of field, measure, and "open form" in the service of principles of sincerity and objectification. Then, in order to keep from being hoist on my own definitions, I must be careful to recognize the many different ways the terms "sincerity" and "objectification" can be understood. Sincerity is usually not self-expression. Rather, it involves insistence on the surface of the poem as concerned primarily with direct acts of naming as signs of the poet's immediate engagement in the areas of experience made present by conceiving the act of writing as a mode of attention. Sincerity involves refusing the temptations of closure—both closure as fixed form and closure as writing in the service of idea, doctrine, or abstract aesthetic ideal. Sincerity can take the form of presenting any form of direct experience—perceptions, feeling, alogical or Olson's post-logical movements of thought—that is intensified in the act of writing. Objectification, then, pertains to various vehicles for bringing form and resolution to the energy fields elicited in pursuit of sincerity while concentrating on form as measure rather than controlling imposition. Objectification is a property of writing committed to composition rather than to interpretation. Techniques for objectification range from Denise Levertov's and Zukofsky's sense of expressive melodic pattern to Jackson MacLow's experiments with formal and aleatory models of invention which make structure the creative ground rather than the result of immediate poetic thinking.

The best way to structure these varying stresses within Objectivism is to recognize the field of possibilities created by the co-presence of three fully articulate stances—those of Williams, Zukofsky, and Olson. (Pound's long development stands as a kind of *summa* representing the interplay of all three modes.) In Williams the stress is on sincerity as a mode of attention that can be fully expressed only by insisting on the poet's dual role of antagonist-composer with respect to natural sciences. Poetry for Williams can be an intense form of disclosing the real because it is first of all an act of writing that remakes in order to recover perceptual energies. Attention becomes fully active only in reconstituting the forms of relatedness upon which it depends. Hence writing is the keenest instrument for disclosing modalities of voice, perspective, and structure as conditions of thinking in and with things. And conversely, writing aware of its exemplary status can be conceived less as a vehicle for imposing thoughts on the world than as a process of perception by composition. Zukofsky, on the other hand, emphasizes the freedom won in the act of writing: composition remains a mode of attention, but the activity of putting words together places the mind in a space where the forms constructed within perceptions are more significant than the immediate existential qualities disclosed by the poetic act. Adamantly opposed to *symboliste* displacements of objects into purely connotational relations, Zukofsky nonetheless tries to articulate Objectivist ways of recovering the import (in Mallarmé's sense) of the poem as artifact. Zukofsky's project is to insist on the transforming power of form while reinterpreting *symboliste* transcendences in their own right, capable of standing as emblems of the mind's place between natural and cultural energies.

Williams emphasizes the painterly qualities of poetic composition, Zukofsky the musical qualities. Olson's projectivist alternative does not so readily admit analogies from the other arts. The best I can do is to suggest as his ideal a synthesis of dance and prophetic philosophy—Nietzsche speaking from within the Dionysiac ritual. This stance, it goes without saying, threatens to destroy the objectivist poetics it desires to extend. Hence Olson's tensions with the original Objectivists. Yet these tensions are not surprising if we recognize how Olson comes to Objectivism, that is, in a very different fashion from the poets who developed it in the thirties. Where they went from poetry to political commitments that they could not reconcile with their forms of literary attention, Olson shifted from a political to a poetic career. As a consequence, he demanded from the start a model of poetry that could handle what he envisions as a revaluation of public values. He found in Fenollosa (buttressed by Whitehead) the principles for extending Objectivism into a speculative ontology. The transformations here get quite complicated. Fenollosa's *The Chinese Written Character as a Medium for Poetry* is itself a transitional text between symbolist and objectivist modes. For Mallarmé, a sense of activity in nature, of "the forest's shuddering," warranted a radical opposition between a descriptive poetry intended to represent "the actual and palpable wood of trees" (36) and a poetry stressing self-reflexive compositional acts that might capture the lines of relations between abstracted natural forces and the energies of a responding creative sensibility. The analogue to the forest's shuddering must be the delicate movement of energy between the poet's words, so that a poetry adequate to this analogical ground would have to conceive the self-contained book as its imaginative ideal. In order to render the subtlety of relations he saw, Mallarmé proposed to conjure up "the architecture of the ideal and only habitable place . . . else the book could not be properly closed" (36). For Fenollosa, on the other hand, a similar vision of the mind's relation to the trees' motion demands discovering ways of denying closure so that the book might stay open to continual interchange. Fenollosa conceived the "visibility of metaphor" as the vehicle for keeping poetic language "always vibrant with fold on fold of overtones and with natural affinities" (23). Metaphor could be objective and thus could ground Mallarmé's delicate sensations in physical fields of force.

With this as his context, Olson could propose "objectism" as an explicit metaphysical position combining the best of both worlds. Now a vision of sincerity was possible where the acts of perception and composition become measures of the human power to make oneself a dynamic presence equal in intensity to the powers of nature: "When men are not such jugglers, are not able to manage a means of expression the equal of their own or nature's intricacy, the flesh does choke" (*Collected Prose* 159). But with sincerity now asked to carry such a large burden, Olson can overcome the impersonality that limits Zukofsky and early Williams only by finding himself hard-pressed to preserve Objectivist constraints on the lyrical ego and unmeasured generalization. In theory, his position is exemplary: the true personal lies beneath the ego, because the "I" is only a limiting classification, reductive selection from energy fields where "any of us, at any instant, are juxtaposed to any experience . . . on several more planes than the arbitrary and discursive which we inherit can declare" (157). But ennobling man tempts Olson to risk once again mystifying the objects of attention proposed as the source of mystery. Olson's poetry vacillates between, on one hand, a somewhat private, anachronistic, and often pompous mythologizing of the self as the means for establishing projective size, and on the other, a complex interplay between the personal and the acts of a speculative mind discovering terms by which it is an extension of what it discloses. Yet at his best Olson expands notions of objectivity, field, and measure so that they articulate a fully speculative mode of objectivist sensibility.

In my view, Robert Duncan is the contemporary writer who most fully discloses the powers possible in the orientation Olson proposes. Duncan remains in spirit a romantic poet, but the example of Olson and Pound enables him to relocate the energies of romanticism within the dynamics of field poetics. Duncan's as yet unpublished *H.D. Book* may be the most interesting work of speculative imaginative play since the later writings of Yeats. Duncan, like Olson, flirts with the temptation of basing speculative poetry on the possibilities of a modern sublime. But precisely because Duncan's romanticism must be earned by intense struggles with Pound and Williams, his incursions into the sublime retain two distinct, "projective" objectivist features. First, Duncan preserves the immediacies called for in the doctrine of sincerity. He defines sincerity, however, in terms of the divinations that constitute the imaginative field for self-reflexive acts, and thus that open "distances in back of" appearances. Duncan's text becomes a model of "how consciousness moves" at the interfaces between the positions of an empirical self and the groundings of that self in a larger Self which is source and ultimate shape of his loves and creative acts. Poetic desire is "arousal . . . to some larger form or soul-self . . . in which I have my present/presence or womb of myself" ("H.D. Book" 61). Second, this vision of the desires informing composition provides passage to a larger model of objectivity, definable as a tension between "the actual real and the real of imagination" (58). On the one hand, this tension leads Duncan to a rich descriptive engagement with the oppositions that plague modern sensibilities as they struggle with models of the real that exclude and repress energies still present in imaginative traditions. On the other hand, Duncan tries to embody the interplay of relations contained in these traditions in order to show how the alternative to Pound's "clear edges" and Williams's "masculine voice" need not be the muddle of the romantic sublime. The opposite of enlightenment clarity is not some vague infinity or apocalyptic darkness but an alternative objectivity constituted by the matrix of images recurring in the hermetic tradition and creating analogues between Duncan, H.D., and the archaeology informing their pursuits of a feminine dimension in imaginative language. Duncan's field is the net and network offered not by the world but by "the imagination of the world." The power of this field resides not in mystery or in abstraction, but in the measure of the "objective" relations his analogies disclose. Duncan's field permits remarkably sharp descriptions of the claims to truth in art and of the basic impulses and contradictions of modernism, while also producing suggestive contexts for clarifying the sources of what is described in traditional allegorical tensions between the claims of paternal law and of maternal nature and nurture. Objectivism, for Duncan, need not be confined to objects because he understands, and exemplifies, how objectivity is ultimately not simply agreement about external conditions but about the possibility of locating what imaginative acts can share.

2

A Poetics of Marginality and Resistance: The Objectivist Poets in Context

Burton Hatlen

The group of poets that has come to be known as the Objectivists constellated themselves in the early 1930s around Louis Zukofsky. In 1930 Harriet Monroe, at the suggestion of Ezra Pound, invited Zukofsky to guest-edit a special issue of *Poetry* devoted to younger American poets—although when the issue was published in February 1931 it also included a British poet, Basil Bunting. Monroe told Zukofsky that he should give his poets a label, and he called them "Objectivists"—always in quotation marks, as Zukofsky used the term.[1] This term pointed back toward imagism as the wellspring of a new American poetics, while implicitly claiming that this new group of poets had gone beyond the image to re/discover the object itself. In the critical essays that he wrote for the special issue of *Poetry*, Zukofsky sketched a poetic theory to justify the practice of the young poets he had drawn together, and identified three older poets as forerunners of the new movement: Ezra Pound, William Carlos Williams, and (although she was clearly less important to him than the other two) Marianne Moore.[2] These three poets were all about two decades older than Zukofsky, who also reached out to a poet about a decade older than himself, Charles Reznikoff: in the special issue of *Poetry* Zukofsky discusses Reznikoff's work at length as an example of an objectivist poetics.[3]

In editing the special issue of *Poetry*, Zukofsky sought to draw together under the objectivist rubric a heterogeneous group of younger writers, including such unlikely candidates as Kenneth Rexroth and John Wheelwright. These and some of the other poets included in the special issue or in the follow-up *An "Objectivists" Anthology* resisted Zukofsky's tutelage or went off in their own directions.[4] But Reznikoff happily accepted the role of exemplary "Objectivist" to which Zukofsky nominated him, while Basil Bunting's dialogue with Zukofsky about matters both poetic and political would continue for many years. Two other poets included in these objectivist publications, George Oppen and Carl Rakosi, became essentially protégés of Zukofsky's. Oppen's early work, from 1928 to 1935, when he stopped writing to join the Communist Party, is clearly composed under the influence of his forceful friend. And throughout the 1930s, Rakosi continued to send his new poems to Zukofsky, who often aggressively rewrote them. Finally, and perhaps most significantly, Lorine Niedecker wrote to Zukofsky after reading the January 1931 issue of *Poetry;* there ensued a brief love affair, a much longer friendship, and an extended correspondence that profoundly shaped the work of both poets. Reznikoff, Zukofsky himself, Oppen, Rakosi, Bunting, and Niedecker—these, then, are the poets to whom I shall here apply the Objectivist label.[5]

What did the six Objectivist poets have in common? This question can be answered, I would propose, in at least three ways. First, we might look for some common ways of thinking that they shared. Or we might approach the issue historically, by focusing on common elements in their social situation and life experiences. Or third, we might foreground similarities in their poetic methods. Rather than choosing one of these approaches, however, I will explore the interrelationships among the philosophic assumptions, the historical situation, and the poetic methods of these six poets. For as I shall here argue, what distinguishes these poets is their determination to find or invent a poetic language that will, by remaining faithful to what Zukofsky called the "historic and contemporary particulars" of their experience, shatter the grand ideological abstractions of the dominant culture, and thus open up a new way of being-in-the-world. This project was at once linguistic, sociopolitical, and philosophic or even quasi-religious, and to focus only on one of these dimensions at the expense of the others will inevitably miss the point. Nevertheless, as a critic I must start somewhere, and so I shall here work from philosophic premises toward poetic method, with a visit to New York's Lower East Side along the way.

I

In the February 1931 issue of *Poetry*, under the title "Program: 'Objectivists' 1931," Zukofsky summed up, in emphatic italics but in characteristically elliptical language, the fundamental principles of an "Objectivist" poetics: "An Objective: (Optics)—The lens bringing the rays from an object to a focus. (Military use)—That which is aimed at. (Use extended to poetry)—Desire for what is objectively perfect, inextricably the direction of historic and contemporary particulars" (268).[6] Zukofsky begins with the act of seeing. We have, "out there," an object. Light rays bounce off the object. But we cannot see the object unless a lens brings these rays into focus: the lens of a camera, the lens of an eyeball—or, Zukofsky implies, the poem. Three explicit variables, then: object, light rays, lens. And a fourth, implicit variable: a mind that perceives the focused image and thereby apprehends the object. The second meaning of "an objective," the "military use," shifts our attention from the mind's more or less passive apprehension of images to seeing as an *act* that directs itself toward the object. The third, specifically poetic, definition picks up this emphasis. The poem is born out of *desire*—the mind *wants* to grasp "the direction of historic and contemporary particulars," to know the actual world as it unfolds before us. And the word "perfect" adds an ethical dimension to this project: insofar as we give ourselves over to the object before us, with what Zukofsky later calls "sincerity," the object offers itself to us as "perfect."

The poetics that Zukofsky here sketches out affirms the objective reality of a material world. Zukofsky carefully distances himself from all forms of philosophical idealism. Not the mental image but the physical object—this is the starting point for Zukofsky's poetics.[7] This emphatic materialism owes something to Marx—or perhaps more directly to Lenin, whom Zukofsky labels, in the special issue of *Poetry,* a "great writer" (272). It is important to recognize that most of the "Objectivist" poets were in or close to the Communist Party during the 1930s: Oppen and Rakosi both joined the party, Zukofsky called himself a "small c" communist and once applied for party membership, Niedecker was at the least a fellow traveler, and Reznikoff too read Marx and wrote with sympathy about the socialists of Vienna. Almost all of the "Objectivists" came out of the working class. They were for the most part poor Jews, *Jews Without Money,* in the title of Mike Gold's famous book. Oppen, whose father was a successful entrepreneur, is a partial exception here, but the parents of both Reznikoff and Zukofsky worked in New York's garment district, one of the principal seedbeds of American socialism, and both Bunting and Niedecker also experienced genuine poverty. The political orientation of these poets is apparent in the February 1931 issue of *Poetry,* which might well have been titled "New Poets of the American Left." If some of the poets included in the issue seem aesthetically distant from Zukofsky, their presence might be due to their Marxist politics: thus we find here John Wheelwright the Trotskyite and the Communists Whittaker Chambers and Norman Macleod, and I suspect that some of the other more obscure contributors (Howard Weeks, S. Theodore Hecht, Harry Roskolenkier, Henry Zolinsky, Jesse Loewenthal) were also party members. As communists or at least poets of the Left, all of our poets saw themselves as "revolutionaries." None of them threw any bombs, went off to fight in Spain, or *did* anything else that was especially revolutionary—although

Kenneth Rexroth apparently believed that Oppen was complicit in the murder of the anarchist Carlo Tresca. But from Marx and other thinkers of the Left, the "Objectivists" all absorbed certain "materialist" ways of thinking that defined their perspective on the world.

Marx rejected philosophical idealism as bourgeois and reactionary, and the Communist Party at least tried to inculcate in all its members the principles of dialectical materialism, as codified by Engels and Lenin. And while the materialism of the "Objectivist" poets was much more subtly nuanced than what quickly became a rigid and banal party dogma, they could and did attempt to see the world as matter extended in space. Zukofsky's search for a poetics grounded in direct apprehension of an objective world is clearly apparent in a "symposium" on surrealism appended to the special issue of *Poetry.* The symposium prints one poem each by Parker Tyler and Charles Henri Ford, both precocious—they were still teenagers at the time—American surrealists, along with comments by the authors and responses from Zukofsky himself. Zukofsky finds some admirable qualities in the poems of Tyler and Ford, but he objects to a strain of "hallucination" in their writing.[8] In a rebuttal, Ford and Tyler suggest that Pound's *Cantos,* an exemplary text for Zukofsky, might "qualify" as an example of "hallucination." Clearly we have a watershed moment here between two ways of reading Pound and between two poetic methods, one turning inward to explore possibilities of alternative modes of perception, and the other directed outward toward the physical world; and the "Objectivists" followed the second of these paths. Zukofsky recognizes some degree of what he called "objectification" in the poems of Tyler and Ford: the poems were interesting as objects, insofar as they displayed some degree of formal necessity. But he misses in the writings of the young surrealists what he elsewhere in the special issue calls "sincerity": "Writing . . . which is the detail, not mirage, of seeing, of thinking with the things as they exist, and of directing them along a line of melody" (273). Zukofsky finds this quality of sincerity especially in the poetry of Reznikoff: "There is to be noted in Reznikoff's lines the isolation of each noun so that in itself it is an image, the grouping of the nouns so that they partake of the quality of things being together without violence to their individual intact natures" (278). Or again: "The economy of presentation in this writing is a reassertion of faith that the combined letters—the words—are absolute symbols for objects, states, acts, interrelations, thoughts about them. If not, why use words?" (279).

The February 1931 issue of *Poetry* offers striking evidence that Zukofsky was here speaking not only for himself but also for a community of poets; for the issue includes a poem by Basil Bunting that echoes in verse the principles that Zukofsky lays out in prose. Here titled "The Word" but collected as Ode 15 in Bunting's *Complete Poems*, this poem celebrates

> the word spoken in shapeless night, the
> sharp tool paring away
> waste and the forms
> cut out of mystery!

The word, Bunting suggests, is born at the moment when

> thought's intricate polyphonic
> score dovetails with the tread
> sensuous things
> keep in our consciousness.

By articulating the moment when thought meets things, the word

> mimes clouds condensed
> and hewn hills and bristling forests,
> steadfast corn in its season
> and the seasons
> in their due array,
>
> life of man's own body
> and death . . . (*Complete Poems* 93)

The true "word," Bunting thus suggests, not only registers with precision the movements of the particulars that compose the world, but also locates us within and allows us to participate in the grand rhythms of the cosmos. Bunting's debt to Pound is audible not only in his cadences but also in the vision that animates them, and Bunting's neo-Poundian poetics here assumes a specifically objectivist form, as the poet affirms his faith in the existence of a real world that our senses—and our words—can lay hold upon.

I will limit myself to two additional examples of the objectivist commitment to the reality of a knowable world of objects. The first is a short poem by Lorine Niedecker titled "LZ's" ("LZ" is, of course, Louis Zukofsky):

> As you know mind
> aint what attracts me

nor the wingspread
of Renaissance man
but what was sensed
by them guys
and their minds still carry
the sensing (*From This Condensery* 152)[9]

Niedecker is not interested in the mind per se, nor in "the Renaissance world-picture." For her the poem is born at the moment when the mind meets a world of objects, to create what Pound called the "formèd trace." My second example is George Oppen's well-known "Psalm," from his book *This In Which* (1963). This poem takes its epigraph from Thomas Aquinas: "Veritas sequitur esse rerum," or "Truth follows from the existence of things." The poem salutes "The wild deer bedding down" in the forest: the miracle, Oppen asserts, is simply "That they are there!" And the poem goes on to affirm the power of

The small nouns
Crying faith
In this in which the wild deer
Startle, and stare out. (*Collected Poems* 78)

Here, as in Bunting's poem, "things" present themselves to us haloed in mystery: the greatest miracle is simply that something exists, rather than nothing at all.[10] And for Oppen too, language allows us to greet this miracle, if only with a cry of faith.

The objectivist poets were not, however, naive empiricists.[11] They did not see the mind simply as a mirror reflecting a world of objects "out there." In this respect Zukofsky and the other objectivists diverged from dialectical materialism, as this dogma evolved during the 1930s, to be enforced as "scientific" truth by various party hacks. For Lenin, the "materialist theory" is simply "the theory of the reflection of objects by our mind." And Lenin reduces this theory to three principles: "things exist outside us. Our perceptions and ideas are their images. Verification of these images, differentiation between true and false images, is given by practice" (119). Into this dangerously simplistic model of the relationship between the mind and the world,[12] Zukofsky introduced, as we have already seen, several additional variables. First, desire. Our minds, it seems, *want* to lay hold upon the things that make up the world, and any adequate record of the transactions between mind and world must acknowledge the force of this desire. Second, ethical responsibility. To know the world is to act upon it, and we have an obligation, Zukofsky suggests, to see clearly and accurately. We want the "objectively perfect," and this desire implies the existence of greater or lesser degrees of perfection. And third, a sense of historical process. "Things" are not static. They exist in motion and in relation—that is, in history. Thus the mind must come to terms with "the direction of historic and contemporary particulars." And finally—although this point remains implicit in his definition of "objective"—Zukofsky introduces a fourth variable: language itself. Lenin takes language for granted, as simply a neutral medium through which what is out there in the world imprints itself on the mind, and through which the contents of our minds in turn pass out again into the world. But Zukofsky, as a poet, wants to measure the weight and trajectory of every word he uses. And as we shall see more fully below, a poetic sense of language, conjoined with a Marxian materialism, leads all the objectivists to treat words not merely as symbols that stand in for things, but as things in their own right, "historic and contemporary particulars" among all the other such particulars that, collectively, make up the world.

Zukofsky's sense of what is at issue in the mind's engagement with the things of this world suggests why he and the other Objectivist poets had little interest in "socialist realism," the literary method that emerged out of Lenin's "mirror" theory of the mind. In practice, socialist realism always tended toward allegory: neither things nor people had any objective reality, except as personifications of larger sociopolitical forces. And Zukofsky and his friends really did want to find a poetics that would allow them to "think with the things as they exist." In the search for such a poetics, these poets turned for guidance not to Lenin (nor to Mike Gold, who became the literary commissar of the CPUSA) but to the modernist writers of the previous generation. In particular, Zukofsky adopted Pound as his mentor, as their extensive correspondence demonstrates; in large measure the theoretic principles of Objectivism emerge out of the dialogue between the two. There is, of course, a certain irony in the spectacle of a young poet of the Left taking as his mentor an older poet who was at this time moving toward a fascist politics. But to understand the Pound/Zukofsky relationship, we must bear in mind that Zukofsky was interested not in Pound's political or social views but in his poetic methods.[13] In particular, he saw in Pound's early *Cantos* a poetics of collage that acknowledged the force of the mind's desire (desire determines what objects the mind selects and how they are positioned within the collage), while at the same time keeping the focus on "the direction of historic and contemporary particulars" (the collage form places clear demarcation around each "particular," thus allowing it to retain its integrity and autonomy). In the first ten sections of *"A"*, written in the late 1920s and the 1930s, Zukofsky adapted Poundian collage to the services of a Marxist vision of art as a mode of labor and potentially an instrument of revolution, and in the process demonstrated that there is nothing inherently fascistic about the collage method. In their own formal experimentations, most of the other objectivist poets followed Zukofsky's example.[14] But before exploring in more detail the formal choices these poets made, I want to reflect for a time on the ways in which the work of Zukofsky and his friends emerges not only out of some shared ways of thinking, more or less "materialist" and "Marxist," but also out of certain common social and cultural circumstances.

II

Beyond the paradox of a left-wing poet adopting a fascist as his mentor, the Pound/Zukofsky relationship offers a second irony, in the spectacle of a young Jewish-American poet taking as his model an older poet who during the 1930s became an overt anti-Semite, who repeatedly declared that Jews were poisoning the well of Western culture by fomenting war-for-profit and by creating a usurious banking system that drained off the wealth generated by human creativity.[15] Nor was Zukofsky the only Jew among the Objectivists. Although they were at most minimally involved with organized Judaism, Reznikoff, Rakosi, and Oppen along with Zukofsky all thought of themselves as Jewish. Zukofsky grew up within a largely Yiddish-speaking family, and although he early ceased to be a practicing Jew he retained a powerful if ambivalent identification with Jews. Reznikoff also grew up in New York in a largely Yiddish-speaking family, and as an adult he wrote primarily for a Jewish audience, publishing much of his work in the *Menorah Journal*, a magazine that sought to define for Jews the possibility of a cultural as distinct from a religious identity. Reznikoff also took as one of his principal subjects the history of the Jewish people. Oppen grew up in an essentially secular family, but the rise of Nazism evoked within him a strong identification with Jews, which finds intermittent voice in his poetry. Rakosi also grew up in a largely secular family: in Hungary some of his uncles converted to Christianity to open up for themselves possibilities of career advancement. But his first published poem is about an aged Jew named Jacob Gold, who "worked and bore the burdens of his race" (*Poems, 1923–1941* 33), and Rakosi's work consistently speaks out of a consciously Jewish identity.

Thus all of the Objectivist poets were in varying senses and degrees Jewish, except for Bunting and Niedecker—and I will have more to say on them shortly. As Jews, Reznikoff, Zukofsky, Oppen, and Rakosi shared a heritage that placed strong emphasis on family bonds, on ethical responsibility for the community, and on the law. This heritage translated itself into certain characteristic patterns as immigrant Jews entered American society. The sense of the majesty of the law drew many Jews, both religious and secular, into the legal profession: thus Reznikoff trained as a lawyer, and, although his diffidence and scrupulous moral sense prevented him from ever practicing his profession, a sense of the power of the law informs all of his work, especially his epic *Testimony.* A sense of responsibility for the lives of others drew many Jews to medicine and related professions. Rakosi, for example, aspired to attend medical school, and when this ambition was frustrated he pursued a long and successful career as a psychiatric social worker, where he could work to repair damaged families. The Jewish tradition of ethical responsibility led secularizing Jews in New York to form the Ethical Culture Society; and this same impulse could assume a political form, as Jews joined the Communist and Socialist Parties in numbers radically disproportionate to their percentage of the American population. These parties, by inviting Americans to join in the struggle for a just and equitable society, offered secular Jews an opportunity to exercise their sense of responsibility not only toward other members of the Jewish community but toward all human beings. In gravitating toward the political Left, then, our four Jewish Objectivists were following the pattern of an entire generation of the children and grandchildren of Jewish immigrants.

We may also at least speculate on the possibility that a distinctively Jewish religious vision emerges from time to time in the writings of some of the objectivist poets: their insistence that we live within a real world, a world that presents itself to us as Other, may owe something to Marx, but it may also derive in part from the Torah. In Christianity, Jesus, at once God and man, bridges the distance between the two, so that God ceases to be unambiguously Other: that the joining of these realms requires a blood sacrifice suggests a tragic dimension to this process, but death here becomes finally a step on the way to resurrection, and through Jesus the Christian can become one with God, right now. In resisting the Christian concept of the redemptive God-man, Judaism preserves a tension between the human and the divine. God presents himself to us as holy. He demands that we come to terms with him, and invites us to enter into dialogue with him. But historically, Judaism has been deeply suspicious of Greek—and thus eventually Christian—aspirations to become one with the One. Caution is in order here, because there are as many different religious postures within Judaism as within Christianity. Nevertheless, I hear some distinctively Jewish overtones in the insistence of the Objectivists that the world is not only real but also Other—and inherently numinous. An example is Oppen's declaration that "The self is no mystery, the mystery is / That there is something for us to stand on" (*Collected Poems* 143). We stand on/in the presence of mystery, Oppen says. He does not label this mystery "holy," and to assume a posture of adoration would seem impertinent. But this mystery is clearly Other. The self does not share in and cannot lay hold upon the mystery. Yet, Oppen suggests, the mystery reveals itself to us and demands our attention.

My next hypothesis demands no less caution, but I would like to propose that we can also detect in the poetry of Reznikoff, Zukofsky, Oppen, and Rakosi a specifically Jewish sense of language. The Christian tradition is imbued with an originally Greek idea of the *logos:* "In the beginning was the Word, and the Word was with God, and the Word was God. . . . And the Word was made flesh, and dwelt among us." The opening of the Gospel of John announces the possibility of a word that enjoys absolute presence, a word that is God, and which can at the same time become flesh like us, so that we can know this word in our own flesh. Once again the Jewish tradition resists the attempts of the human mind to measure the absolute in our own terms.[16] The Jews are the original People of the Book, deeply, even obsessively engaged with language. And yet words are, in the Jewish tradition, also deeply problematic, for the Holy of Holies can*not* be captured in language. God's true name is unspeakable. Language can point toward or circle about God's presence, in commentary piled upon commentary; but he remains beyond all human words, and Truth is always already displaced. This complex relationship to language finds voice not only in Midrash but in Jewish humor, which constantly turns back on itself, to inflect toward irony words that we were prepared to hear as imbued with pathos. A similar engagement with language as a form of serious play or playful seriousness seems to me characteristic of the Objectivist poets. The specific varieties of language that we find in their work covers an enormous range, from the apparent transparency of Reznikoff's common speech to Zukofsky's baroque arabesques. Yet the works of all four of these Jewish poets are marked by an acute, self-reflexive awareness of—even anxiety about—the problematic character of language. In the works of all of them, we have a sense that the poet is speaking in a language that he has *chosen,* with a full awareness of the meaning of this choice.

And indeed, at least three of these poets, Reznikoff, Zukofsky, and Rakosi, *did* choose the language in which they wrote, for the circumstances of their childhood suggest that all three probably started their lives in languages other than English: Reznikoff and Zukofsky in the Yiddish spoken by their mothers, and Rakosi in Hungarian—although he probably also spoke German before he began to learn English, having spent most of his first nine years in Germany. These biographical details should remind us that the four Objectivist poets here under discussion were marginalized not only by their identities as Jews in a predominantly Christian society but also by their status as children of immigrants—with embarrassingly "foreign" accents and modes of behavior. In the New York of the 1920s you could choose to live entirely in a Jewish culture, as did the parents of Zukofsky and Reznikoff; or you could live at the interface between this culture and the larger secular-Christian world beyond. All of our poets chose the latter option, and thus they were reminded daily of their difference, their marginality. But Jewish marginality is itself "different" from some other marginalities, for it is not—or not only—imposed from without, by signs declaring NO JEWS ALLOWED. Rather it can be a freely, even proudly chosen, alternative.[17] Not without some self-doubts, our four Jewish-American Objectivists *chose* to locate themselves at once inside and outside American culture: to write in English, not in Yiddish, and to link up with secular political and literary cultures, while continuing to affirm a distinctively Jewish identity. And it is this decision to speak from the margin—not, or not primarily, in shame and/or anger, but with a pride, albeit liberally salted with irony, grounded in a rich cultural tradition—that gives the writings of Reznikoff, Zukofsky, Oppen, and Rakosi much of their distinctive flavor.

But what about Bunting and Niedecker? They were not Jews, and the generalizations I have laid out in the preceding paragraphs cannot apply to them. And yet I have identified these poets too as Objectivists. Indeed, there are some identifiable differences between these two poets and the four Jewish poets discussed above. In particular, the poetry of Bunting and Niedecker is rooted in the rhythms of rural life, in marked contrast to the more urban poetry of Reznikoff, Zukofsky, and Oppen—Rakosi, the Midwestern Jew, does not fit either pattern. And in the poetry of the ex-Quaker Bunting we can detect, as in the poetry of Pound, an emphasis on death-and-resurrection patterns that suggests a lingering Christian influence. Nevertheless, Bunting and Niedecker share one common quality with the Jewish Objectivists: a powerful sense of marginality. Bunting came by his marginality honestly: as a Quaker; as a Northumbrian deeply suspicious of London, the center of economic, cultural, and political power; as a pacifist during World War I; and as a self-chosen exile from Great Britain through most of the 1920s and 1930s. And Niedecker? A woman poet in America during the 1930s and 1940s was by definition marginal. In addition, she was visually challenged and divorced, and she generally lived on the edge of destitution—so poor that for several years she earned her livelihood as a cleaning woman in a hospital. I would propose that Zukofsky and the other Jewish Objectivists offered Bunting and Niedecker a model of marginality, not as a curse imposed by an indifferent society, but as a freely chosen destiny. The kind of poetry that Bunting and Niedecker wanted to write could be written *only* from the margins; and they looked to the Jewish poets, who had inherited centuries of cultural lore about surviving on the edges of dominant cultures, for guidance in how to live in this demanding but liberating space.

Why did the Objectivists find it necessary to move toward the margins if they were to survive as poets? As communists or in any case poets of the Left, the Objectivists were acutely aware of the injustices of capitalist society; all offer sharply critical, and in some cases bitterly satirical, views of that society—Rakosi's "Americana" series (*Collected Poems* 319–68) is a case in point. In particular, all these poets recognized the tendency of capitalism to reduce everything, including poems, into commodities. Here it is important to remember that the 1920s and 1930s represented a period of consolidation by the mass media, as the cultural arm of commodity capitalism. The mass-print media had been established for almost a century, and nineteenth-century poets like Whitman and Dickinson in America, the Pre-Raphaelites in England, and the symbolists in France had been forced to develop new strategies to maintain control over their work in spite of the power of the media. These strategies included self-publication (Whitman), the "fine" press (Morris), and the "little" magazine (*The Yellow Book*). Increasingly in the face of the mass media, poets organized themselves into a network of underground subcultures: thus the proliferation of movements, schools, and cenacles starting roughly in the 1870s. Pound and the other American modernists emerged out of this avant-garde underground; and if the Objectivists looked to Pound as a model, one reason was his insistence that if people interested only in enormous profits controlled publishing, the result would be the death of poetry, unless poets could create for themselves refuges on the margins.[18] The 1920s and 1930s saw the initial emergence of the new electronic media, movies and the radio. At first these media were curious novelties, and many poets responded with interest: Pound sought opportunities to take to the airwaves, Zukofsky admired Chaplin and wrote a film script of *Ulysses,* and Reznikoff went to Hollywood to try his hand at scriptwriting. But it quickly became apparent that the new media offered even less space than the mass-circulation print media for language used with care and precision, that language worked against the grain of the hypnotic clichés that increasingly controlled public discourse. Along with choosing marginality, therefore, the Objectivists also committed themselves to a *poetics of resistance:* resistance against centralizing cultural hegemonies, against the financial and media oligarchies that were and are steadily consolidating their control over our lives, against the pressure of a language that lulls the reader into a comfortable or despairing acquiescence to these powers. The Objectivists found precedents for such a poetics of resistance in the defiant aestheticism of high modernism. And so it was that, in the years around 1930, Jewish and modernist marginality came together, a marriage consummated in the midst of a worldwide political and economic crisis; and out of this marriage the Objectivist movement was born.

III

A poetry devoted to "the detail, not mirage, of seeing, of thinking with the things as they exist" might seem destined to issue in some kind of documentary realism, but in fact the writings of the Objectivists are generally less concerned with the thing seen than with the way we see, a process that becomes in their poetry profoundly problematic. In this respect the Objectivists take a significant step beyond the work of their modernist models. Pound and Williams were still haunted by the dream of a "natural" language, the word that will be "true" because it gives us, in effect, the thing itself. But the Objectivists, standing in the indeterminate territory between English and Yiddish, between a "Jewish" identity and an "American" identity, discovered that there is no natural language: and with this discovery they passed beyond modernism into postmodernism. All languages are, the Objectivists realized, codes, "made up." The signifier cannot, as we were told ad nauseam in the 1970s, touch the signified. No code can claim to be "truer" than any other code. The Objectivists themselves found this discovery disquieting: three of them—Oppen, Rakosi, and Bunting—gave up writing poetry for long periods, and the other three practiced their art more or less underground. But in the end they all found their way back to language, for they had discovered something of shattering importance, and they could not let go of this discovery. Their sense of the arbitrary character of all codes leads the Objectivists to look at words with the same "objectivity" that they bring to the perception of other "historic and contemporary particulars." The result is, first, a systematic destabilization of poetic language. "Poetry" had become, by the end of the nineteenth century, a safely encapsulated mode of discourse defined by the use of poetic diction (only in verse did the familiar pronouns "thee" and "thou" and sometimes even "ye" survive), "poetic license" (if you needed to put the verb before the subject to make the rhyme work out in a satisfactory way, that was OK), the reassuring pulse of the iambic beat, and the melodious chime of the assertively masculine rhyme.[19] All serious writing in our century has tried to break out of this prison, and in the first three decades of the century the modernists had proposed many alternatives to "poetic diction," from the mannerist ironies of Wallace Stevens to the plain speech poetics of William Carlos Williams, all of them claiming to be "a mirror to this modernity" (Williams, *Collected Poems* 1: 28). The Objectivists admired the experimental work of their predecessors and adapted to their own ends many of the strategies initiated by the modernists, but they refused to see *any* poetic idiom as offering a privileged "truth." Rather, they saw all modes of discourse as potentially available to them, and they deliberately played off various poetic idioms against one another, to initiate an interrogation not only of poetic discourse but of all the codes that compose our culture, and eventually of the "code of codes," language itself.

My first example comes from Zukofsky, unquestionably the central figure in the movement. Anyone reading the poetry of Zukofsky for the first time must be surprised that this presumed disciple of Pound and Williams relies so heavily on formal artifice, including rhyme and elaborately textured patterns of assonance and alliteration, as in the following poem from the early 1930s:

Crickets'
thickets

light,
delight:

sleeper's eyes,
keeper's;

    Plies!
lightning

frightening
whom . . . ?

doom
nowhere . . .

where eyes . . .
air,

are crickets'
air (*Complete Short Poetry* 48–49)

On the page, "Crickets' Thickets" looks like a typical Williams short-line poem ("so much depends / upon // a red wheel / barrow"), but Williams certainly never wrote anything remotely like this; for while Williams sought to exorcise rhyme, it here returns with a vengeance. The initial delight of this poem comes from a sense that the poet has given himself, in a spirit of sheer play, an apparently insuperable challenge: to write a poem in which *every word* will be a rhyme word. The semicolon after "keeper's," the abrupt drop down to "Plies," and the exclamation point after that word all draw us into the process, as the poet invites us to watch him hunt for one more rhyme—and then, to his (and our) relief, he finds it! The appetite for sheer formal elaboration evident in this poem might tempt us to place Zukofsky, not in the Pound/Williams tradition, but among the neoformalist poets who emerged at about the time he began writing. Zukofsky was only a little younger than John Crowe Ransom, and he was a contemporary of Hart Crane, Allen Tate, and Yvor Winters. These poets, members of what Winters called the "reactionary generation," orchestrated a return to traditional forms in the 1930s, and Zukofsky shared some of their antipathy to the presumed transparency of a plain English "that dogs and cats can read." Zukofsky even wrote an intricately elaborated sestina, "Mantis," and contributed several pieces to *Hound and Horn,* the principal journal of the new reactionaries. Yet to place Zukofsky among the reactionaries seems no less false than to see him as merely an heir of Pound and Williams. To Ransom, Tate, and Winters the return to form meant a return to tradition, to a moral and cultural order that they saw as threatened by a barbaric modernity: in this respect these poets are true conservatives. In contrast, cultural nostalgia never became the dominant note either in Zukofsky's life or in his poetry. Rather than reaffirming for us the eternal verities, for example, "Crickets' Thickets" delivers us over to a language that seems to have a will of its own, as form here serves, not to contain and control content, but rather to subvert and finally explode the very notion of "content" as something we might find "inside" a form.

I assume that the pleasures of Zukofsky's rhymes in "Crickets' Thickets" are obvious enough, but as soon as we ask what the poem might "mean" it becomes more problematic: as sound moves to the foreground, syntax must fare for itself, and the words here refuse to come together in readily decoded propositions. Is "light" a verb, with "thickets" as its subject and "delight" as its object? Thus, "Crickets' thickets light delight." Well, maybe, but why that comma after "light"? And maybe also the keepers are plying the sleeper's eyes—although the possessive "keeper's" tends to preclude such a reading. But the real focus of attention here is the isolated word, and the way sound can lead us from one word to another: from "light" to "delight" to "lightning" to "frightening"—at which point the tone has darkened, and we ("whom?") drift toward "doom." The ellipses, borrowed perhaps from Pound's Sappho poem, "Papyrus" ("Spring. . . . / Too long. . . . / Gongula. . . . "), support our sense of gaps opening up within the language—gaps so vertiginous that "meaning" threatens to leak away entirely. The puzzling last lines of the poem become a little clearer if we remember that for Zukofsky "air" almost always means the clear medium that sustains us with each breath, *and* a melody, *and* the way a stylish person comports him- or herself. But while syntax never evaporates completely, in general the poem's formal rigor systematically disrupts our attempts to construe sequences of words into meaningful assertions, while at the same time the music of the words opens up whole new ranges of extra-syntactic "meanings." In the process, Zukofsky also calls into question both the conventional social function of rhyme, which normally serves to reassure us that we all know what a poem is, and the claim to a superior directness and authenticity implicit in the "plain speech" poetics of Williams. In all of these ways, "Crickets' Thickets" is representative of Zukofsky's work, for almost every Zukofsky poem finds some way of ensuring that language never finds a point of equilibrium, in the presumed stability of a shared social consensus. Instead, his poems always direct us back to the material fact of language itself, forcing us to acknowledge that words are as opaque, impenetrable, mysterious, and resistant as all the other "historical and contemporary particulars" amid which we live.

While Zukofsky, as I have noted above, saluted Charles Reznikoff as the model of an Objectivist poet, the latter's poetry initially looks radically different from Zukofsky's:

> Hour after hour in a rocking-chair on the porch,
> hearing the wind in the shade trees.
>
> At times a storm comes up and the dust is blown in long curves along
> the street,
> over the carts driven slowly, drivers and horses nodding.
>
> Years are thrown away as if I were immortal,
> the nights spent in talking
> shining words, sometimes, like fireflies in the darkness—
> lighting and going out and after all no light. (*Poems, 1918–1936* 35–36)

"Crickets' Thickets" is nothing if not playful, while "Hour after hour" is dead serious. While Zukofsky seeks to subvert syntax as a structuring principle, this Reznikoff poem is structured in syntactic units, with each line a phrase, and with one sentence (although the first one is somewhat elliptical) per stanza. Whereas music largely displaces meaning in the Zukofsky poem, Reznikoff betrays no interest at all in rhyme, and his poem consists of a series of clear propositions. And Reznikoff, unlike Zukofsky, is clearly committed to a speech-based poetics: indeed, Reznikoff's austere refusal of rhetorical effects makes the poetry of Williams seem flamboyantly lyrical. But despite these differences, Reznikoff in fact problematizes language no less radically than does Zukofsky, by leveling it down to the point where it is almost prose—but the "almost" is the key word here, for we are constantly impelled to try to define the ways in which what we are reading *is not* prose. In the quoted poem, the simile in the penultimate line seems to be lifting us toward a rhetorical climax, but then the last line denies the gesture: there is, "after all no light." Does the last line allude to death as the ultimate absence of light, or does it simply invoke an image of the fireflies winking out as the night deepens? Characteristically, Reznikoff balances—more adroitly than any other poet I can think of—on the razor edge between the imagistic and the symbolic, and this indeterminacy constantly deflects us back toward the poet's language as irreducibly problematic.

Between the extremes of Zukofsky at one pole and Reznikoff at the other, and with the unity of the movement established by Zukofsky's admiration for Reznikoff, the other Objectivist poets worked out various individual strategies for pushing language to its limit-point. In addition to the intellectual and social commonalities I have discussed in the first two sections of this essay, all these poets shared a sense that language is always inadequate, insofar as it can never lay hold upon the absolute, but that it is nevertheless the only means we have to articulate our common humanity. Bunting and Rakosi are perhaps the least radical of the group, insofar as they still felt reasonably comfortable in certain traditional poetic modes. In his culminating work, *Briggflatts,* Bunting recovered the grand elegiac mode, and Rakosi found his characteristic voice in a series of witty introspective meditations and barbed epigrams. But despite their relative traditionalism, both Bunting and Rakosi had put themselves to school with Zukofsky, and they retained from this experience a habit of twisting language toward self-reflexivity. Oppen, more dangerously, perfected a poetry in which syntactic interruptions and suspensions open up abysses within which the unsayable resonates behind, around, and within what gets said. The title of Oppen's radically disjunctive sequence of the 1930s, *Discrete Series,* proclaims his desire simultaneously to honor the autonomy of each thing and to bring these things into a relationship neither logical nor chronological, but existential: what we stand on may be a mystery, but we *do* stand here, together. And after a return in his middle period to the relatively self-contained short poem, Oppen's later work abandons all punctuation and all but minimal vestiges of syntactic closure, allowing the gaps and fissures within language free play. In Niedecker's poetry too, the silences that surround the words are at least as important as the words themselves. Zukofsky's wit and musicality, the rigorous understatement of Reznikoff, Oppen's openness to the unsayable—all these come together in Niedecker's practice of condensation, or her "condensery":

There's a better shine
on the pendulum
than is on my hair
and many times

. . .

I've seen it there. (*Granite Pail* 3)

The row of periods that stands as the penultimate "line" in this poem opens up a space in which anything can happen. But whatever happens, the last line insists, we must remain faithful to what our eyes tell us. We do not know where the sway of the pendulum, the tick of time, may be carrying us, but there is a humble trust here that the rhymes will tell us where we must go.

In their systematic interrogation of language, the Objectivists, I would finally like to propose, constitute the chief link between the great American modernists, especially Pound, Williams, Stein, Moore, and Stevens, and our principal poetic avant-gardes of the postwar years, from the Black Mountain school to the Language poets. Among the Black Mountain school writers, while Olson showed no interest in the Objectivist poets, by 1950 both Robert Duncan and Robert Creeley had become enthusiastic readers of Zukofsky. "Will you," Duncan asked himself in a poem of the late 1950s, "give yourself airs / from that lute of Zukofsky?" (90). And late in his life Duncan told me in conversation that he felt closer to Oppen than to any other poet of our time. As for Creeley, his elliptical short line derives as much from Zukofsky as from Williams. In the early 1960s, as I have shown elsewhere, Denise Levertov entered into a complex dialogue with Oppen: the elder poet did most of the talking, but it seems clear that Levertov learned something important from this exchange. As editor of *Origin,* Cid Corman gave the Black Mountain poets their first hearing; and as a poet he has positioned himself explicitly within a neo-objectivist lineage, taking as his principal models Zukofsky and Niedecker. Under this neo-objectivist rubric I would also group such poets as Ted Enslin, Hugh Seidman, Michael Heller, Armand Schwerner, Rachel Blau DuPlessis, and Norman Finkelstein, all of whom have acknowledged a direct debt to the Objectivist poets. From their beginnings in the 1960s, the Language poets, our most influential current avant-garde, have also looked to the work of the Objectivists as a model and an inspiration. Barrett Watten names Williams, Zukofsky, and Stein "the American modernist masters of the 'word as such'" ("for *Change*" 485), and Ron Silliman sees Zukofsky's work as marking the first full emergence of the "modern eye and ear" (*New Sentence* 127). And Charles Bernstein, while obviously indebted in many ways to Zukofsky and Oppen, has also written more eloquently than any other recent critic on the work of Reznikoff. Almost invisible when L. S. Dembo edited his Objectivists issue of *Contemporary Literature* in 1969, Zukofsky and his friends now seem to stand at the center of the American poetic tradition as it has evolved in the middle and late years of this century. In various ways, these later avant-gardes have adapted and made their own the stances that I have here presented as characteristic of the Objectivists: a freely chosen marginality and a dogged resistance against the cultural—and at some point also inevitably political—tyranny of the media. For the problems that the Objectivists confronted in the 1930s are still our problems, though vastly compounded, as the century stumbles to a close. The Objectivist poets still have much to teach us, and we can be grateful to them, for the air out here on the margins is bracing. Indeed, who would want to stand anywhere else?

3

Be Aware of "the Medusa's Glance": The Objectivist Lens and Carl Rakosi's Poetics of Strabismal Seeing

Ming-Qian Ma

> We should keep our eyes on eyes themselves, eyes to see how they see.
>
> —Balthasar Gracian, *Arte de ingenio, tratado de Agudeza*

> The splinter in your eye is the best magnifying glass.
>
> —Theodor W. Adorno, *Minima Moralia*

> Strabismus: Squint; a failure of one of the visual axes to pass through the fixation-point (the point which is looked at).
>
> —*The Century Dictionary and Cyclopedia*

I

The Objectivist movement, more than any other poetic phenomenon in the twentieth-century American poetry scene, has exhibited the true character of an avant-garde almost in the literal sense of the word. While its forced and brief appearance in *Poetry* magazine in 1931, followed by *An "Objectivists" Anthology* the next year, for instance, shocked and angered the establishment with what Harriet Monroe describes as the "barbed-wired entanglements" ("Arrogance" 333), its "third or renaissance phase" after three decades of silence, as Ron Silliman points out, "restructured the entire field of American verse" ("Third Phase" 85, 89). Probably because of its avant-garde status, the experimental nature of this radical and oppositional movement, known as the New American Poetry, has presented a territory yet to be fully explored.[1] In her recent theorizing of the historical position of the Objectivists in the genealogy of American postmodernism, Marjorie Perloff captures a distinction crucial to one's understanding of the Objectivist experiment. Responding to the question of "In what sense was the work of these poets a departure from that of the 'once-revolutionary imagists,'" she argues that the Objectivists represent a "larger aesthetic," one that is articulated by way of a shift "from the modernist preoccupation with *form* in the sense of imagistic or symbolist structure, dominated by a lyric 'I,' to the questioning of *representation* itself" ("Barbed-Wire" 145, 147; emphasis in original). That being the case, the questioning of representation itself in the Objectivist poetics can be seen as having centered upon a specific focal point. What seems to have preoccupied these poets in their praxis is how to decenter the "I" as the organizing principle underpinning the scheme of mimesis. For the much vexed complication lies in that the "I" as such also puns on the "eye," an optical agency with a corresponding linguistic structure built in.

From its early inception, the Objectivist consciousness is plagued by self-questioning, and its poetic emphasis on a clear, impartial, physical eye is relentlessly shadowed by a distrust of language as its reading glass. A case in point is Zukofsky's "An Objective," the founding manifesto of the movement foregrounding the Objectivist vision: "An Objective: (Optics)—The lens bringing the rays from an object to a focus. That which is aimed at. (Use extended to poetry)—Desire for what is objectively perfect, inextricably the direction of historic and contemporary particulars. . . . Writing occurs which is the detail, not mirage, of seeing, of thinking with the things as they exist" (*Prepositions* 12). Two issues, more than others, take center stage in Zukofsky's "An Objective": epistemology (or desire to know) and perception (or the use of the eye). But to a great extent, it is neither the former nor the latter alone as an isolated issue that Zukofsky is considering here. Rather, his theorizing seems to have focused upon the rethinking of the nature of the relationship between the desire to know and the use of the eye, a relationship ordained by methodology, at once structured and sustained by language. Shadowing the statement, the implicit question that Zukofsky has put forth, for himself and for the Objectivist experiment, is how to present "[an] object unrelated to palpable or predatory intent" (*Prepositions* 16); how, that is, to see an object in and through language when language is itself predatory, with a formal structure that materializes and objectifies what is predatorily intended. As such, Zukofsky's "An Objective," though written as a manifesto, casts a concomitant questioning look at itself as a language act capable of expressing the desire for what is objectively perfect, a look betrayed, on the one hand, by the poet's rather self-conscious phrasing and, on the other, by his much-felt need to repeat and to emphasize.

In an awkward turn of phrase, for instance, Zukofsky begins "An Objective" by reconfiguring and redefining the Objectivist visual trajectory. Rather than "The lens bringing an object to a focus," which is more acceptable in terms of usage as well as logic, he specifies the act of seeing as "The lens bringing the rays from an object to a focus." With this seemingly redundant wording, Zukofsky disarms the predatorily "omniscient" agency traditionally attributed to "the lens" by foregrounding the autonomous, ontological Otherness of the object. For whereas the phrase "the rays from an object" clearly asserts the separateness of and the distance between the seeing subject and the seen object, the preposition "from," in particular, further problematizes the immediacy of the object, an immediacy rendered otherwise readily available by the more "appropriate" and more "logical" preposition "of," one that denotes a projected or intended relationship from the vantage point of the predator.[2] To press his argument further, Zukofsky, as if already sensing language's predacious appetite, wastes no time reiterating "the rays from an object." And "That which is aimed at," though an apposition dependent in grammar, is nevertheless presented, both emphatically and suggestively, as an independent unit.

The same concern then resurfaces later when Zukofsky comes to expound the Objectivist theorem of sincerity, where he identifies language, seeing, and thinking as synchronous, as mutually infiltrating in a joined epistemological campaign. In accord with his emphasis on "the detail" over the "mirage," the poet, in the same vein, chooses the preposition "with" (thinking with the things as they exist) over the predatory "of" to guide the Objectivist vision. For the word "with," meaning "alongside of," "as a member of," or "in the same terms as" (*Webster's*), demystifies thinking/vision as mirage-making generalization and reduces it to a particular, to a thing or an object itself, thus establishing a parallel, coexisting, and mutually respectful relationship between the subject and the object.[3]

Such labored, self-reflexive use of language in "An Objective," in this sense, seems to suggest an answer to the poet's question of how to see an object in and through language as a predatory mechanism. The Objectivist lens, according to the Zukofskian prescription, is one that sees but does not falsify or assassinate the object.[4] It is, in other words, a two-way language lens, so structured that to see is to be seen, the one and same movement in which the intent to prey upon the object is isolated from the mirage that "words remain absolutely faithful to 'things' in their sensory immediacy" (Hatlen, "Zukofsky" 66). Defined as "sincerity," this Objectivist lens, with its intense "care for the detail," as Zukofsky explains in the interview with L. S. Dembo (Dembo and Pondrom 222), resists the compulsion to absorb what it sees into a totalizing system. This particular property of the Objectivist lens receives an apt description from Charles Altieri, who thus posits in "The Objectivist Tradition": "Sincerity is usually not self-expression. Rather it involves insistence on the surface of the poem as concerned primarily with direct acts of naming as signs of the poet's immediate engagement in the areas of experience made present by conceiving the act of writing as a mode of attention. Sincerity involves refusing the temptations of closure—both closure as fixed form and closure as writing in the service of idea, doctrine, or abstract aesthetic ideal" (15).

As such, this lingu-optical configuration presents itself as an initial model of what Marjorie Perloff observes as "the questioning of representation itself." The Objectivist departure from modernism, as is signaled by Zukofsky's "An Objective," is then marked by a radical shift from the late-imagist "act of vision" that "implicitly legitimates the existence of these things" (Hatlen, "Zukofsky" 66) to the Objectivist act of attention that attempts to acknowledge and accept the object. In this sense, the Objectivist "larger aesthetic" is manifested not only in a rethinking but also in a thorough revision of a tradition far beyond the literary. It opened, to a great extent, a new area of inquiry in the early 1930s, the significance of which was to receive concentrated critical attention decades later. What Ron Silliman has designated as the "Objectivism's third or renaissance phase, from 1960 onward" ("Third Phase" 85), for instance, corresponds in particular to a surge of philosophical reflection of the Western culture as the culture of vision. With their emphasis on the "lens" in relation to the world, Objectivist poets find themselves joined by such thinkers as Theodor Adorno, Maurice Merleau-Ponty, Martin Heidegger, Michel Foucault, Jacques Derrida, and Luce Irigaray in their critique of the construction and function of the "I/eye." In this context, there is Carl Rakosi, in whose work the Objectivist lens brings into view a phenomenological landscape where the poet's "acknowledgment of the perceived arrangement of things," in Michael Heller's words (*Conviction's Net* 44), is articulated in a poetics of strabismal seeing.

II

"A thing can be described, but what it is can not be rendered except by variations of itself," observes Carl Rakosi in *Ex Cranium, Night;* "Man, however, is not satisfied with this. He is more obdurate than nature. Thus his own character is the mother of metaphysics and poetry" (131), a character manifested in a craving "to find something permanent behind changing appearances, some yet unknown form of a transcendent nature," by "assigning a habitat and a character to [its] form in the mind itself" (*Collected Prose* 38–39).

In an epigrammatic way, Rakosi sketches out the epistemological model underlying, since the ancient Greeks, what John Dewey describes as the "spectator theory of knowledge," one in which to see is to know (*Quest* 23, 214). But in this "vision-generated, vision-centered interpretation of knowledge, truth, and reality" (Levin 2), ocular vision is compromised. Particularly since Descartes, seeing becomes an auxiliary at the service of a higher entity. "The properties of the visible," as Dalia Judovitz argues, are in fact "transferred to the mental domain, whence they will illuminate metaphorically the powers of reason to attain certitude as clear and distinct ideas . . . [affirming] the arbitrary relation between the object of vision and the impression that object generates"; for what is at issue here, Judovitz continues, is "logic rather than mimesis. In other words the visible can only be addressed because its figurative character conforms to pre-given conventions" (63–64, 72).

Rakosi is clearly aware of this predatory "reduction of being to being-represented" (Levin 5). "Who is like man," he writes satirically in "Associations with a View from the House," "sitting in the cell / of referents, / whose eye / has never seen / a jungle, / yet looks in?" (*Collected Poems* 237). His choice of verbs in his statement above—"describe" versus "render"—pinpoints, for instance, the distinction between two kinds of seeing, ones that can be labeled, in Husserl's terminology, as "assertoric" and "apodeitic." Referring to a "perceptual awareness of things in the ordinary sense" (Macann 39–40), the assertoric constitutes a seeing *onto* the objects, thus foregrounding what Rakosi calls, citing Nicolai Akimov, "the expressiveness of things" (*Collected Prose* 19). By contrast, the apodeitic designates a conceptual seeing "*into* the essence of things" (Macann 40), a seeing that performs, via desire and intention, an anthropomorphic "transmutation" (*Collected Prose* 18). It is, more specifically, a transmutation "from matter to trope, into imago . . . the images as my way of knowing, of making matter conform to my mode of perception" (*Collected Prose* 18).

Of these two modes of seeing, Rakosi contends further, the apodeitic, dictated by one's epistemological craving, becomes in a sense *a priori*, subordinating the assertoric to its own hegemony.[5] "No sooner does a person feel something," says Rakosi, "than the mind butts in: looks, describes, interprets, denatures, absorbs, controls, encapsulates. Its wit and precision make it so complacent that it assumes it has improved on the original, or at the very least, made an even exchange," thus always turning, say, "the beauty of a tree" into "the result of what is thought about it" (*Collected Prose* 29, 73). Hence an "ocularcentric paradigm" (Levin 2), whereby the subject's access to truth and knowledge is rendered both direct and immediate by virtue of his or her visual trajectory, with desire and intention adjusting its focus on the object to extract the essence.

Rakosi's critical turn of mind here postulates a theoretical resonance with Theodor Adorno's critique of Edmund Husserl's so-called "pure phenomenology," a phenomenology armed, nevertheless, with an "epistemological inclination to ascertain how knowledge of objecthood is in general possible and how it may be identified in the structure of consciousness" (*Against Epistemology* 3,

125).[6] In its attempt to initiate "a radically new and original beginning" (125), a "first" seeing that purportedly presents the "object-in-itself," phenomenology, Adorno asserts, sets up its camera obscura in nowhere but the mind and resorts to epistemological methodology to secure the givenness of the world. Adorno writes:

> Since acts of thought as such may be immediate facts of consciousness just as much as impressions of sense-perception, then what for Husserl is in each case thought in acts of thought, is mediated by them, becomes for its part, immediacy. Givenness at the moment is identified in the sixth Logical Investigation with consciousness. Hence intentionality in the pregnant sense, which Husserl gave the term, would in the end be identical with givenness. Since the mediated, what is already thought through intention, should simply be assumed, the concept of immediate givenness becomes total. Perception becomes knowledge of something, this knowledge becomes the primary, irreducible factual state of consciousness and the perceived thing world becomes, so to speak, a radical first. (*Against Epistemology* 129–130)

It is one's consciousness that determines the existence of the object, which places itself on call and will present itself instantly and automatically in its original form the moment it becomes intended. Thus the password to the "thing world," as Adorno's diction explicitly indicates, is "identity" or "recovery" granted by consciousness, and the magic verb, "become," both conjuring up, in Mikel Dufrenne's terms, not so much "the actual presence of the thing" as "the presence itself" (101). Phenomenology in the Husserlian scheme of things, Adorno argues, is anything but innocent: it "falls into the fundamental position of transcendental subjectivity, or as the late Husserl called it, the ego" (*Against Epistemology* 193). In this sense, underlying Husserlian phenomenology one finds a different kind of optics with a corresponding methodology, one that brings the rays from the "eye/I" to a focus through a dialectical, circular movement from the ego back to the ego, bypassing, rather conveniently, the object itself: "The ego constitutes things by applying categories to the sensible. . . . [W]hat the subject knows is true, if it corresponds with what the subject itself is constituted. The subject's knowledge of the objective leads . . . right back to the subject and is thus in a certain sense tautological" (*Against Epistemology* 174).

Rakosi's Objectivist insight into the sense perception as always already mediated—that is, intentional in the sense that the consciousness "of" an object constitutes, in the same movement, the predatory capture of its essence—

evokes Adorno's metaphor of "the Medusa's glance of a sudden 'ray of vision'" (*Against Epistemology* 196).[7] Adorno's allusion to the Medusa's eye, together with his wording of the metaphor, offers a merciless, detailed dissection of the nature of vision in the Husserlian construction of objecthood. While the word "sudden," for instance, suggests the intensity as well as the violence of such a vision that disfigures the object, the indefinite article "a" explicitly qualifies it as whimsical and arbitrary. Furthermore, the intense vision as the desire to know demands, by logic, to be objectified into method, a method as a weapon to conquer the world.

Medusa's severed head, so the mythical story goes, is used as a strategic weapon, the eyes of which turn the adversary into stone by a fixed, penetrating staring. In Husserl's "hunt for the given" (*Against Epistemology* 140), this "Medusa's glance of a sudden 'ray of vision'" has a similar function: it is a deadly gaze that reduces what Adorno calls "the unformed manifold of the factical itself" to "the unified conceptual structures" (127).[8] By alluding to a visual construct from myth to illustrate the functional, administrative mechanism basic to all reduction of the "non-homonymous down to a common denominator" (125), Adorno succeeds in showing that such a mechanism per se is fictitious.

Rakosi's poem "The Romantic Eye" presents a kind of poetic gloss of this critique of Husserl's phenomenology. Gathered in the *Collected Poems* (1986) in a section titled, rather pointedly, "Adventures of the Head," the poem is what one might call a textbook example of the Medusa's glance, a parody of its working mechanism.[9]

> On the eight thousandth magnification
> the chromosome of the Chironomus fly
> stirred its microscopic nebulae into
> the figure of a Greek Orthodox cross. (44)

In these four lines, the Medusa's glance assumes, in Jeffrey Peterson's words, "the 'creative' character of microscopic vision" (162). Rakosi's unhesitating switch to the scientific discourse under the heading of "Romantic" makes a statement. Not only, for instance, does he thus define the nature of science as such but also implicates the nature of philosophy, which, as Adorno claims, "takes science as its model" (*Against Epistemology* 41).[10] As an intentional-objectivating act, the creative character of the microscopic vision (science) proves, in this sense, to be identical with the no less creative character of the macroscopic vision (metaphysics). For in both, as Adorno observes, "the schema of order imposed on objects by human consciousness . . . is handled as if the need indicated in this schema were the order of the objects themselves" (76).

The four lines of the poem designate the four components constitutive of such an imposition in the form of an apodeitic seeing: the gaze (magnification), the object (chromosome), the anthropomorphic transmutation (stirred . . . into), and the result or creation (a Greek Orthodox cross). Their sequential ordering outlines the logical steps in a methodological procedure facilitating a conceptual *seeing into* that first projects in and then extracts from the object a preestablished, hierarchical order at the sacrifice of that object. In addition, the power of the Medusa's glance to see into things so as to "magically [transform] all becoming into being" (*Against Epistemology* 152) is, as the first line suggests, entirely determined and adjusted by one's desire or intention measurable in percentile, and any change in the intensity of the former or the degree of the latter will alter the end result proportionally. From this perspective, the economy of the Medusa's glance lies in a circular movement, in its intentional and judgmental capacity to establish an identity by projecting, directly and immediately, from the eye ("the eight thousandth magnification") into its prey (the figure of a Greek Orthodox cross), across the materialist middle, in which the thing-object (chromosome), by virtue of being seen, is intimidated and subdued into servitude to the subject, becoming "the ultimate 'fulfillment' of intention," as Adorno argues, "the proof of the correctness of the judgment" (149, 206).

In this way, through its powerful image of the Medusa's glance at work, Rakosi's "The Romantic Eye" stages, rather self-consciously, "a closed system," as the poet himself puts it in a different context, a system "not related to what is going on outside: it assumes it is what is going on there" (*Collected Prose* 48). In such a system, assumptions take the form of methodology, whereby, as Harari and Bell point out, "a given type of knowledge [is illustrated] through the set of results that the method can produce" (xxxvi n. 48). Concurring with Rakosi in this regard, Adorno specifies further the anthropomorphic nature of "to see is to know" as mastery and closure: "Thus cognition does not linger over its object for the sake of elucidating it. It does not really refer to (*meinen*) its object at all, but rather degrades it to a mere function of the schema under which it is haughtily subsumed. The more objectively cognition poses and the more purified from all delusion and supplement from the observer, the more subjective it becomes in the totality of its procedure" (*Against Epistemology* 44). With "The Romantic Eye" as a reminder of the Medusa's glance at work, "Adventures of the Head," contrary to what the title seems to have suggested, assumes an ironic inversion. For the poems collected here do not indulge in portraying the epic adventures in hunting for knowledge; rather, they body forth a series of meditations foregrounding Rakosi's Objectivist adventures in breaking through this closed system, in resisting "the Medusa's glance of a sudden 'ray of vision.'" "We broke out of the romantic / gravitational field," Rakosi writes in "The Adventures of Varese," "The idea / was to reach *sui generis,* / a state of random mass / above sensitivity" (*Collected Poems* 53). At the points of departure of all these adventures, however, there persists this one haunting question: how to see with "the living eye / . . . / forever and ever / without bias or mercy, / without attrition or mystery" (*Collected Poems* 237); or, to put it differently, how to realize what Rakosi himself calls, in his interview with L. S. Dembo, the "fidelity to the object" (Dembo and Pondrom 202) through a lingu-optical construct which is itself not descriptive but prescriptive, "not 'about' the world," as Burton Hatlen observes, "but constitutive of it" ("Carl Rakosi" 129).

III

"I respect the external world," Rakosi states, "there is much in it that is beautiful if you look at it hard. I don't want to contaminate that; it has its own being; its own beauty and interest that should not be corrupted or distorted. But so does the poet have his own being" (Dembo and Pondrom 199).

The moral basis of Rakosi's Objectivist approach is laid, as he has emphasized here and elsewhere, in "integrity": the integrity of the object as the seen, and of the subject as the seer (Dembo and Pondrom 200).[11] But for the object to have any integrity at all, the subject must, first and foremost, assert his or her own integrity by abstaining from the apodeitic propensity, by "[fighting] against his own intellect," as Rakosi himself puts it (*Collected Prose* 44). For the integrity one accords the object originates, in actuality, only from the act of seeing that is based on respect or acknowledgment, one that resists any predatory intent. "Not to aggrandize a perception," Rakosi thus defines this moral concept, "not to inflate the lyric impulse, that seems to go counter to one's whole romantic thrust, the thrust of poetry itself, yet that is integrity" (32). Yet the impulse to aggrandize a perception, Rakosi also seems to suggest, has a psychological component, which he addresses, in a way as much metaphorical as literal, through the relational condition of this integrity between a hunter and a wolf in the poem "Riddle":

> In the dead of night
> the caribou slept.
>
> The possibility of not knowing
> what you are
> had not yet been conceived.

It is the original forest.
There is peace.

The wolf has eaten.
He goes into a long howl
to give his location.

If the hunter does not find him,
he'll live seven years.

A box is a box.
Integrity has been defined. (*Collected Poems* 49)

The poem depicts a fragile, transient moment temporarily balanced between two worlds: the world of objects, as is represented by the caribou and the wolf, and the world of knowledge, as is embodied by the hunter. What tips this balance in favor of the latter laden with potential violence, Rakosi seems to indicate here, is fear. In "The possibility of not knowing / what you are / had not yet been conceived," for instance, the construction of the verbal phrase, coupled with a tone not without a tinge of appreciation of that "not yet" moment, already foresees and anticipates a panic reaction once this possibility is conceived. While it points out, indeed, the necessary condition for the "peace" in "the original forest," it isolates, in one and the same gesture, the psychological cause of the inevitable disappearance of that condition. For the moment one conceives the possibility of not knowing what one is is also the moment that generates fear, a fear powerful enough to turn that possibility into impossibility; and with the knowing of what one is comes, as a result, the knowing of what the world is. Thus, fear, epistemology, and methodology work hand in hand, forming an intricate network of self-defense mechanism.[12] Rakosi's implicit psychological reading in this poem finds a more explicit and pertinent articulation in Roland Barthes, who, in his discussion of "The Image" in *The Rustle of Language,* offers the following diagnosis:

> At the origin of everything, Fear. (Of what? Of blows, of humiliations?) Parody of the *Cogito* as the fictive moment when, everything having been "razed," this *tabula rasa* will be reoccupied: "I'm afraid, therefore I'm alive." An observation: According to today's *mores* (we need an ethology of intellectuals), one never speaks of fear: it is foreclosed from discourse, and even from writing (could there be a writing of fear?). Posited at the origin,

> it has a value as *method;* from it leads an initiatic path. (350; emphasis in original)

And that "initiatic path," leading from fear, is the one that the hunter is to travel in his pursuit of the wolf. To achieve integrity, Rakosi announces clearly at the end of the poem, one has to overcome one's fear and let the object be, be it the wolf or the box. But the hunter, Rakosi also knows very well, is always on the move, exhorted by the fear of not knowing and, concomitantly, the desire to solve the riddle.

Viewed in this light, Rakosi's Objectivist sensibility in "Adventures of the Head" centers on the tension between two kinds of desires: the *unarmed* desire for what *is* objectively perfect on the one hand, and the *armed* desire for what *should be* objectively perfect on the other. Michael Heller, in his studies of Rakosi, thus defines the former when he writes, "In Objectivist formulations, desire is unarmed and, in a sense, has no preconceived notions of the nature of the encounter; its only givens are appearances, emotions aroused, intellectual stimulations, that is, elements in the occasion" (*Conviction's Net* 42). It is a desire with neither the literary "overtones of strained metaphorization" nor the modernist "slight flavor of encoding and reifying reality" (42). To put it in Rakosi's own words from "Riddle," it is a desire that does not concern itself with "the possibility of not knowing." By contrast, the armed desire, as is manifested in Husserlian epistemology, invokes its own fulfillment or satisfaction by turning the object into and then identifying it as its much-needed "evidence," evidence, as Adorno observes, "expected of the 'object'" as something given or present (*Against Epistemology* 149, 150); that is, it is a desire to know that secures its answer through a process of *re*covery, not *dis*covery.[13] Whereas Rakosi's poems, as Michael Heller asserts, "do not really attempt to capture an essence" (*Conviction's Net* 38), there exist, throughout his writing, both a keen awareness of and a concomitant vigilance against "the Medusa's glance of a sudden 'ray of vision.'" As such, the encounter between the subject and the object is articulated in Rakosi's work in an "implied interrogation of the self and of any stated position or system," as Rachel Blau DuPlessis argues ("Objectivist Poetics" 130): of the self as the epistemological hunter who knows the wolf-object by hunting it down, and of any stated position or system as ultimately the lingu-optical militarism which, as Roland Barthes asserts in terms of language's function in relation to any object, "attacks, surrounds, sizzles, hardens, and browns" (355).

Rakosi's Objectivist lens, through which this "implied interrogation" is implemented, takes the form of strabismal seeing. The model of Rakosi's optics, interestingly enough, can also be traced back to the same story Adorno alludes to; but while Adorno succeeds in revealing the predatory mechanisms of the Medusa's glance, Rakosi takes a step further by pointing out that embedded in the Medusa's glance is its own undoing. As Ovid's Perseus learns, the only means to render ineffective Medusa's fixed, one-way staring into the object is to return it a counter-look, a looking-back made possible by Perseus's bronze shield which defocuses the Medusa's glance by deflecting its deadly gaze, thus making it unable to lock on the target directly.[14]

Rakosi finds his bronze shield in strabismal seeing, in the inability of the axes of vision to be coincidentally directed to the same object, which simultaneously forces his attention back to the act of seeing itself. As a result, this dual attention both to seeing and to the act of seeing turns what was formerly a one-way vision into a two-way one: a seeing that also watches itself in action, questioning its own shaping and interpretative capacities and holding in check its own predatory intent. In other words, it is a seeing that resists the Medusa's glance as meaning, as the impulse or desire to project and to categorize. To be strabismal, then, is to break away from Medusa's one-way, self-fulfilling gaze, one in which "Judging and becoming aware of a judged state-of-affairs are equivalent expressions," as Adorno puts it, "or rather the second disguises the first in metaphor." In this sense, strabismal seeing is "becoming aware" without "the immediacy of the performance of judgment" (*Against Epistemology* 205). This Objectivist optics is mirrored, in particular, in Rakosi's use of language, which can be characterized as intransitive.

In discussing the Objectivist lens in Rakosi's work, one can hardly overlook one poem that could be considered as the twin piece of "The Romantic Eye." Although included in a section titled "*Droles de* Journal" in *Collected Poems,* a section that presents a highly parodic as well as ironic treatment of the pretentiousness and silliness of poetry in Horatian epigrams, "Objectivist Lamp" nevertheless deserves, indeed demands, one's critical attention. For one thing, in sharp contrast to other poems' exaggerated and affected mannerism that borders upon clownery, this poem seems oddly out of place with a guarded tone and serious subject matter. For another, while most of the poems in this section are written as monologues featuring a loud-mouthed "I" and sometimes a silent "you," as utterances of either imperatives, comments, rhetorical questions, or insults, this poem unfolds a careful observation of an object. Moreover, the title of the poem is too theoretically pertinent to the Objectivist poetics to be simply dismissed at that. In fact, it constitutes a powerful redefinition of the Objectivist vision by way of a critique of "The Romantic Eye" as the projector; for the word "Lamp," as the popular analogy in the romantic tradition for the perceiving mind fashioning its own experience by recovering "what it has itself partly made," alludes to M. H. Abrams's important study of romanticism and its poetics: *The Mirror and the Lamp* (58).[15] In this sense, "The Romantic Eye" and "Objectivist Lamp" are twin pieces in that, together, they form the two parts of Rakosi's Objectivist demonstration: the former dissecting the romantic eye as the Medusa's glance, and the latter showing the Objectivist lamp as strabismal seeing.

As is manifested by its title, "Objectivist Lamp" postulates a direct, word-for-word opposition to "The Romantic Eye." But the crucial difference that sets the tone for the Objectivist poetics from the outset lies in the absence of a definite article "The," denoting that which is mentioned, designated, identified, or recognized already or previously. To expand its grammatical as well as semantic parameters slightly, "The" can also be read and employed as an adjective designating the nature or the attribute of the modified as such. "The Romantic Eye," in this sense, is the eye that always sees what it already saw; that is, it only sees what it wants to see, what it is determined to see, or what it projects to see. It follows, then, that the absence of the definite article in "Objectivist Lamp" suggests an assertoric seeing, a seeing without any preconceived notions of the nature of the encounter between the eye and the object. Instead of "[imposing] forms . . . and categories on the 'sensuous manifold'" by "throwing its beams into the external world" (Abrams 58, 59), as the romantic mirror and lamp would do, "Objectivist Lamp" enacts a double negation of "The Romantic Eye": it sees itself, and it sees itself assertorically.

goddess,
    ivory carved
Japanese
    lady,
hands crossed
    over breast,
holding
    on her head
electric bulbs
    and batik
lamp shade. (*Collected Poems* 380)

Here the lamp is an object perceived but not, as Rakosi would say, aggrandized. The poem outlines a process in which language's transitive, nominating impulse is nullified at its inception, and the mirage of seeing is shattered at the moment of its suggestiveness and taken over by the detail of seeing. Rakosi's strabismal vision begins with a mythical figure, "goddess." But the apodictic projections otherwise associated with this word are immediately called into question due to the lack of an identifiable signification caused by the letter "g" in lowercase. What can be identified, then, is only the material out of which this "goddess" is made: "ivory carved." Although "goddess" is further specified by its apposition of "Japanese / lady," it is nothing more than the same physical substance that relates them, thus frustrating any attempt to see beyond the appearance. In a like manner, the ghost of a symbolic gesture suggestively promised in "hands crossed / over breast, / holding / on her head" is driven away by the rather banal "electric bulbs / and batik / lamp shade." The absence of any visionary posturing then helps to unveil a human figure as physical details carved *onto* the lamp, not as a mirage projected *into* it. With its focus on the detail of seeing, "Objectivist Lamp" sheds light exclusively on the object in its own variations, warning itself against what Michael Palmer terms "the dangers of posturing and verbal contrivance and . . . the 'large Romantic tone of greatness' " ("On Objectivism" 121).

In "Adventures of the Head," three poems present the most appropriate testing ground for Rakosi's strabismal shield in his adventures against the Medusa's glance: "Cenozoic Time," "Man Contemplating a Rock," and "How To Be with a Rock." Rakosi's choice of a rock as the object of vision in all three poems is significant on two counts. On the one hand, it gestures, as Marjorie Perloff avers earlier, to a radical departure from the modernist poetic tradition as is evidenced, in particular, in Wallace Stevens's poem "The Rock." Grounded in the tradition of "High Romantic, Wordsworthian-Whitmanian crisis-poems," "The Rock" is not a poem about matter; rather, argues Harold Bloom, it is "Stevens's major elegy for his own poetic self" (*Wallace Stevens* 3, 205). The "I" in the poem, tormented by a strong desire for transcendental beyonds, is eagerly merged in a transmutational vision of either an active beholding or a passive regarding. While to behold, for Stevens, is to "[possess] the object" through a "scrutiny" so as "to drive or to set [the object] in swift motion," Bloom points out, to regard is to "watch out for something" by looking at an object "attentively or closely" (57). In either case, the result is the same as that in Rakosi's "The Romantic Eye." The rock is a "high rock" (Stevens, *Collected Poems* 526) in the poem because, as Stevens himself writes,

> In this plenty, the poem makes meanings of the rock,
> Of such mixed motion and such imagery
> That its barrenness becomes a thousand things
>
> And so exists no more . . . (527)

A modernist icon, Stevens's "rock" thus bodies forth the site "where by apposition," observes Bloom, "the mind and the external realm are brought together as a dialectical alpha and omega" (*Wallace Stevens* 351); it is that which has already been transmuted, as Rakosi has aptly epitomized earlier, "from matter to trope, into imago . . . the images as my way of knowing, of making matter conform to my mode of perception." On the other hand, it signals Rakosi's Objectivist position as well as his strategy. For the "rock," while reminding one of the Medusa's glance that turns the object into stone, provides a dual perspective in each poem: that of the "rock" as an independent, ontological Otherness in its own process of becoming, and that of the "prey" as the captured, disfigured "stone" already processed into a categorized being. The juxtaposition of both perspectives, then, forces a moment of *re*vision.

The poem "Cenozoic Time," it seems, carries a message almost identical to what Rakosi once warned himself: "When I sit down to write, I must not forget that one does not strike an attitude in front of a mountain" (*Collected Prose* 19). Highly ironic is Rakosi's use of a geological term here. For the title of the poem refers to a time span following the Mesozoic all the way to the present, during which both the earth (rocks, mountains) and modern human culture have been in the active process of becoming (*Webster's*), a becoming as, one might hasten to add, historic and contemporaneous particulars. Yet as a scientific term, "Cenozoic" enacts the mirage of seeing by one into the other, the Medusa's glance that freezes the becoming into being, into what the scientist-philosopher would consider "the ultimate reality" (*Collected Prose* 46). Hence "Cenozoic Time" is a title from which the rock is absent, having been subsumed under a concept. Against such a deadly gaze, the poem, both in theme and in structure, dramatizes Rakosi's strabismal seeing:

A man looks
            at a rock.
The rock sits.
            Rock and man.
The rock is.
            What is being?

He has sensed
            his nature,
idea as idea
            and trembles
before the insoluble
                    art. (*Collected Poems* 42)

The first six lines, with exactly three words in each, display as a unit a marked terseness indicative of a conscious guard against the "vision-generated, vision-centered language" (Levin 14). Rather strategically, the line break that dismembers the first sentence occurs nowhere but between "looks" and "at." For, as an intransitive verb followed by a preposition to form a transitive verbal phrase, this linguistic collocation otherwise demands, in syntax as well as in grammar, the presence of a direct object; it thus establishes and enforces a hierarchical, military control based on subjection and subordination, imposing its apodeitic gaze upon the object as its captive. Rakosi's typographical layout here serves as a counter-look, in that it obstructs the intended, straight-line *seeing into* by demilitarizing language's mission from the transitive (look at something) to the intransitive (look, at).[16] "A man looks," then, suggests a man who looks in acknowledgment, who sees without magnifying the object into an immediate mirage. It signifies, in this sense, a happening as a particular, no more or less, among others; and "at a rock," read in this context, becomes an adverbial of place. Both lines claim, as such, a material moment in which intention is suspended and the detail of seeing becomes subsequently possible: "The rock sits," with the verb functioning descriptively rather than nominatively. The integrity of the rock, which is already indicated here not only by its dignified posture of sitting but by its status as a self-sufficient syntactical unit, is highlighted further in the next line, "Rock and man," where the former is seen, by way of juxtaposition, as a particular equal to, rather than as "the sheer function of" (Adorno, *Against Epistemology* 148), the latter. Hence a *with*-relationship between the two. Indeed, that "The rock sits," by virtue of its facticity, is itself, Rakosi seems to argue, enough proof to show that "The rock is."

In contrast to the clarity of seeing as a material moment, in which the rock is witnessed in its spatio-temporality, the question in the sixth line becomes ironically as well as rhetorically self-conscious. "What is being?" does not sound here so much as a meditation attempting a "Medusian" imposition upon the rock as a self-doubt on the part of the ego reminded of its transitive seeing. For what is in fact accidental or "supervenient" (Adorno, *Against Epistemology* 148, 149) is not the rock; but rather, as the word "being" suggests, the mirage of seeing contrived ideationally to project a so-called ultimate reality.

The "inability" to see *into* the object and capture its essence, as the first six lines exemplify, in turn redirects the rays of vision back to the act of seeing itself, which, already signaled by the question "What is being?", is executed in the next six lines. What occupies the subject's mind now is not how to answer the question, but rather why ask it in the first place. And the answer the subject has found is painfully revealing. "He has sensed / his nature," which, as the apposition defines it, is none other than "idea as idea," an objectivating circle in which the predatory intent "presupposes what, by its proper *raison d'être* it should have deduced" (Adorno, *Against Epistemology* 171). The Medusa's glance, therefore, becomes an "art" in a double sense: epistemologically it is "human ability to make things," "to execute a plan"; while methodologically it is "sly or cunning trick, wile" (*Webster's*). And the source of its deadly rays lies in the intensity of one's desire and intent. It is, in other words, a self-fulfilling promise, with a guaranteed winning strategy perfected to the point of transparent immediacy. To resist the Medusa's glance as such, the subject realizes, posits a formidable task: "and trembles / before the insoluble / art."

"Man Contemplating a Rock" continues this trend of thought by bringing to the fore just how formidable or "insoluble" this "art" could be. The poem can be read, to a great extent, as a philosophical rendition of "The Romantic Eye," but it is different from "The Romantic Eye," which shows, step by step, how "the immediate is also mediated" in scientific process (Adorno, *Against Epistemology* 129), "Man Contemplating a Rock" makes a caricature of the philosophical tradition that gives birth to the ultimate form of immediacy. And by doing so, it implicitly adds to the Objectivist integrity with Rakosi's statement that "The poet is more modest than the ancient philosopher: he doesn't claim that what he has thought out is the ultimate reality" (*Collected Prose* 46).

Incipit
        the first
Philosopher
                & *ad*
infinitum. (*Collected Poems* 47)

Here the Medusa's glance assumes the form of the transitive, philosophical discourse. As the object of apodeitic seeing, the rock, though still present in the title, is literally contemplated into oblivion in the poem, the brevity of which suggests a swift movement from the deadly gaze to its prey, an immediate slaughter. The five-line verse then presents a world that begins and exists forever only in Latin, the discourse of traditional philosophy that has magically conjured up a meaning-laden universe. Lording it at the center of this universe one finds "the first / philosopher," the origin of all origins, who authored the "*Incipit*" and authorized the "*ad / infinitum.*" Hence an *of*-relationship between the predator and its prey. Indeed, "the relation of metaphysics to knowledge, and the relation of the latter to domination come together in the same place," as Michel Serres contends, "at the outcome provided by death" (28). And the poem, itself a demonstration of the Medusa's glance at its most predatory, encircles the burial ground of the rock.

In contrast to "Cenozoic Time" and "Man Contemplating a Rock," "How To Be with a Rock," as its title states, seems to have been written as a manual in three parts, detailing and demonstrating the strabismal seeing in the form of language, a language demilitarized from saying something *of* the rock to saying something *with* it. Rakosi sets up his strabismal lens in the first part:

> The explicit ends here.
> Outer is inner.
> It is all manifest.
> Its character is durity.
> There lies its charisma.
> By nature it is Pangaea.
> It has its own face
> and its own tomb,
> the way it stands,
> unmoved by destiny,
> a model for the mind.
> We can only be spectators.
> All is day within. (*Collected Poems* 50)

For language to say something *with* the object is to say something *of* itself. In the first five lines there exists a pronounced self-reflexiveness of the word cautioning itself against its own propensity to see and say more than what is there. Conditioned as such, the conceptual trajectory of the word loses its predatory momentum the moment it touches the rock and becomes defocused—replaced, instead, by a bird's-eye view in which intention is kept at bay. "The explicit ends here," reads the first line, with "explicit" emphasizing the assertoric, not the apodeitic, nature of seeing. Further, while "here" refers to nothing but the rock in its physical entirety, "ends" means, perhaps, "completes," both providing what Burton Hatlen calls the "limit-point to the pretensions of the Ego" ("Carl Rakosi" 139). Hence the paraphrase: The rock, in its physical entirety, speaks for itself. In this sense, "The explicit ends here" suggests a language abstaining from its own Medusa's glance by acknowledging the rock's self-sufficiency, denying, as a result, any possible room for the "*Incipit*" of "the first / philosopher." It is more so also because "here" designates a dimension not only horizontal but, and more importantly, vertical: "Outer is inner," which announces the rock's material consistency and integrity that necessitate no projection or interpretation. "It is all manifest," as Rakosi writes—the rock in its corporeality, language in its superfluity. And the "character" of the rock, in which "There lies its charisma," is "durity," a hardness and endurance that testify to nothing but its own becoming.

Rakosi's strabismal lens, while bringing the rays from the rock to a focus, is turned in the next eight lines to its own consciousness, a consciousness engaged in a monologue, reminding itself of its own predatory desire. Already at work in "By nature it is Pangaea," for instance, is indeed the Medusa's glance, hypothesizing the rock into a category. But the nominating act via scientific-geological discourse therein is immediately negated in the following four lines. Not only does the repeated and emphatic use of the phrase "its own" ("It has its own face / and its own tomb") recognize a beginning-and-end independent from the "*Incipit* / . . . / & *ad* / *infinitum*" envisioned by the scientist-philosopher, it also accepts the rock's way of existence ("the way it stands, / unmoved by destiny") as transcending the human chain of logic and laws of determinacy. The result is the awareness of a mind lacking in integrity, easily and habitually seduced by old myths or armed desires, a mind that needs, therefore, to look to the rock as its example ("a model for the mind"). Through Rakosi's strabismal lens, the traditional "ocularcentric paradigm" is thus turned upside down. "We can only be spectators," Rakosi draws the line, spectators who see without taking an active part in the schemes of the Medusa's glance, and whose position as spectators is defined further by the phrase "can only." And this is so because "All is day within": the rock is most articulate and expressive in its own integrity.

A husband's speech to his wife, the second part of the poem, stages Rakosi's Objectivist belief that "Specificity pulls the most profound-looking ideas down to earth" (*Collected Prose* 46):

> "Go to the village,"
>   I tell my wife,
> "and bring back a chicken,
>   an onion, a goose
> and an apple
>   and we'll lie here
> and repopulate this Siberia." (*Collected Poems* 50)

Armed with irony, Rakosi's strabismal lens in the form of intransitive language works on three levels here. Discursively, the speech, voiced as an imperative ringing with a Genesis-sounding intention and purposefulness ("and repopulate this Siberia"), never receives any response. The result is a statement isolated from any mirage-generating context and, as such, reduced to a mere utterance, a vocal happening, or a physical particular. Syntactically, the excessive use of the conjunction "and" calls into question any possible causal relation that supposedly organizes the content of the speech. Why, for instance, does the speaker demand these particular food items (chicken, onion, goose, apple)? What is the connection between bringing back these foods and "lie here / and repopulate this Siberia"? Why "*re*populate"? And why, further, "Siberia"? Instead of setting up an explicit, logical scaffolding, "and" helps, on the contrary, to demilitarize the speech into a series of parallel specifics, displaying, rather, Zukofsky's "detail, not mirage, of seeing." Referentially, Rakosi's equally excessive use of the indefinite article "a/an" and his choice of the deictic "this" to designate "Siberia" create what might be called an "association-resist" effect. Connoting "a thing not previously noted or recognized," "a/an," in this sense, defamiliarizes whatever follows it by drawing attention to itself as a general, nonsequential each or any one. Similar in effect but reverse in function, the word "this" decontextualizes Siberia as a public domain by shrouding it in private, individual nuances inaccessible from any grand, universal perspectives. Each in its own way, both the indefinite article "a/an" and the deictic "this" foreground a life episode in concrete, even arbitrary particulars that constitute what Michael Heller terms "a salient aspect of the world" (*Conviction's Net* 18), not in the "profound-looking ideas" of them.

The last part of the poem articulates Rakosi's "Objectivist motto" as, in Hugh Kenner's words, "No myths" (*Homemade World* 187). It is a section where Rakosi returns to myth to announce the death of myth, where, through Rakosi's strabismal lens, the mythical figures are themselves seen just as dead as unearthed human mummies, as mere inventions or imaginations parasitic on death:

> It is in Genesis.
> A strange god,
>   all torso
> and without invention or audacity.
>
> It can be accused of both plutonism
> and the obvious.
>   The closest human thing to it
> is the novocained tooth,
>   its Medussa hair now fossilized.

> It can be bequeathed to one's heirs
> with the assurance that it will not depreciate
> or be found irrelevant. (*Collected Poems* 50)

Here, more than elsewhere, the strabismal lens proves most powerful, and the irony, most biting. It rereads the book of myth as an excavated tomb and reexamines its content as futile preservations of highly decomposed remains. Read in the context of this section, the first line presents a succinct critical review of the epistemological tradition as the Medusian language act, mythologized as well as mythologizing. Its form as a complete sentence that ends with the loaded term "Genesis" exemplifies the apodeitic "first seeing," outlining the predatory, self-referential circle already sketched in "Man Contemplating a Rock": to write (or, to use language) is to create or invoke, and whatever is created is always born complete. With the first line setting up the thematic backdrop, the following three constitute a critique of the romantic eye by demythicizing a god-figure as a language construct. While the letter "g" in "god" is seen through the strabismal lens as written in lowercase, signifying, perhaps, nothing more than a historical particular, "It is in Genesis," Rakosi seems to claim, that it becomes capitalized. For "Genesis" embodies armed desires manifested in a myth-making narrative, whose uppercase "G" invokes its own transcendent identity by projecting itself into the "G" in "God." Once demythicized, "god" turns ordinary and dead, seen as "strange," "without invention or audacity," whose headless trunk ("all torso") testifies further, by default of course, to the fact that its alleged "completeness" is no more than a language artifact.

The next five lines continue this demythicizing process in the form of an autopsy report. But it is a report that does more than just observe and record the state of the "torso": it also examines the demythicized "god" as the dead Medusa so as to reflect upon its forms of disguises and working mechanism. For Rakosi's choice of words with science and myth references highlights his strabismal lens wary of a culture in which the Medusa's eye is hard to close, and of a language in which, whatever its condition, is always embedded the predatory intent. In "It can be accused of both plutonism / and the obvious," for instance, the pronoun "It" clearly points to "A strange god" in the previous sentence. This "god," as Medusa with its eyes shut, is then identified immediately as the potential or would-be defendant by the verbal phrase "can be accused of." Apart from "the obvious," the crime this "god" can be specifically charged with is "plutonism." Derived from the scientific term "plutonium" and denoting in particular the action of intense heat and radioactive destruction (*OED*), the word "plutonism," as its suffix dictates, also signifies a practice, a conduct, a quality, a doctrine, a belief, or an abnormal condition. It names, in other words, a logical system armed with a destructive methodology. Hence science and/as philosophy, the intention as well as the intensity of both violently transforming all becoming (life) into being (death). At the same time, science and/as philosophy find their roots in myth, for both "plutonism" and "plutonium" are named after the planet Pluto, which in turn receives its name from Pluto, the god ruling over the lower world. In this sense, science and/as philosophy are recognized further through the strabismal lens as the "gods of death," as the Medusa's glance, in whose vision an object "lives" only in its death. Not only are myth and science and/as philosophy identical in operation, the autopsy report reads on, they are also reciprocal in relation. While myth provides science and/as philosophy with an origin, for instance, the latter offer to keep resurrecting and preserving the former as something *trans*human: "The closest human thing to it / is the novocained tooth." What they have failed to realize is that myth, as their epistemological cornerstone, is itself dead long since: "Its Medussa hair now fossilized."

Here, Rakosi's misspelling "Medussa" makes a brilliant point. Spelled with a double "s," "Medussa" suggests, with each "s" referring, perhaps, to "sight" or "seeing," a split vision, a lingu-optical disfigurement of what used to be an intensely focused, deadly penetrating apodeitic seeing. But to see all this in Medusa, Rakosi seems to indicate, the Objectivist poets have to look into Medusa's eye, in which they see their own. In this sense, the double "s" also reflects the structure of Rakosi's strabismal lens, a two-way seeing that enables the poet to see Medusa's hair fossilized without being turned into a stone. It is this extra "s" in the eye, rather ironically, that makes the eye see better. This Objectivist vision of strabismus is best captured in an aphorism by Adorno when he writes in *Minima Moralia*, "The splinter in your eye is the best magnifying glass" (50). For both Rakosi and Adorno, only when the apodeitic seeing *into* an object is troubled and defocused can the assertoric seeing *onto* it become possible. Indeed, if a normal eye always misses so much, an abnormal one with an additional "s / plinter" presents an alternative. Paradox thus constitutes each's position. The poem then ends with a statement of the Objectivist optics. What "can be bequeathed to one's heirs / with the assurance that it will not depreciate / or be found irrelevant," Rakosi argues, is the "torso" seen in detail as a historical particular, not a "god" projected into mirage as a transhistorical abstraction.

Michael Palmer, commenting on George Oppen's Objectivist position, makes the following observation: "He argues as well for a gaze turned outward, a responsibility of the self to find its realization, its form as thinking subject, in its relation to the visible and invisible things of the world. The understanding that such a realization is at best problematic is part of what informs the silences and ellipses of his lines with their particular resonance, or perhaps I mean content" ("On Objectivism" 123). This Objectivist understanding takes, of course, diverse forms. While it finds its expression in Oppen's emotionally charged silences and ellipses of his lines, it assumes the form of intense meditations in Rakosi, whose poetics of strabismal seeing underscores the tension between armed and unarmed desires, between a gaze turned outward and a gaze turned inward. Indeed, in Rakosi's poems, as in Reznikoff's, "Sight and directness of presentation have a priority" (Palmer, "On Objectivism" 125), but it is through a relentless vigilance against Medusa's ever greedy glance that such a priority is articulated. When asked if "there was something to the name Objectivist," Rakosi thus replies, in his interview with George Evans and August Kleinzahler: "There is if you stick to the word's core, *object*... in this case anything and everything outside one's self... and to its adjective, *objective*, which has meaning along a sliding scale in proportion to how much the poet's subjective is absorbed in it or kept out... a useful consideration against psychological slush and sentimentality in any period and against stereotypes" (222; emphasis in original). An Objectivist, in this sense, is a poet in a designated position, informed by both the necessity that "The work faces the world" (Palmer 121) and the problematic, as Barrett Watten points out in a different context, that "The mind that thinks its way into the world of things is the same mind that perceives things as having argued their way into existence. Exterior causality becomes the same as the [mind's] interior romance" (*Total Syntax* 59). It is a locale of intensely self-conscious negotiations, a scale measuring and adjusting the interactions between the internal and the external, between the Medusian imposition and the strabismal counter-vision, between the intellectual or psychological drive toward a rational apprehension of the world on the one hand and what Oppen calls "the life of the mind" as "an awareness of the world" (Dembo and Pondrom 177) on the other. Such, then, is the poem "The Indomitable," the title of which describes, perhaps, not only the obdurate nature of the Medusa's glance but also the very character of an Objectivist against psychological slush and sentimentality.

copulate
        < *copulare*
to join,
        to couple.
Says nothing
        of lust,

the iron master,
        sweaty,
breathless,
        fierce. (*Collected Poems* 55)

With "Says nothing / of lust" as the demarcation lines sounding a warning against the Medusa's glance, the poem falls into two parts: the mirage of seeing versus the detail of seeing; or, thinking *of* an object as it exists vis-à-vis thinking *with* it as it exists. It dramatizes a confrontation between the Medusa's glance and Rakosi's strabismal lens, a confrontation as a language act, in which the former's deadly gaze upon the object is defocused by the latter and the detail of seeing is restored.

The first part presents a dictionary entry on the verb "copulate," complete with its etymology and its current usage. While the word's denotative nuances are explicitly listed ("to join, / to couple"), its meaning of uniting, linking, or connecting is nevertheless extended from mere sexual intercourse to other semantic fields by the symbol "<," meaning "derived from" (*Webster's*). The word "copulare," for instance, from which "copulate" is derived, can itself be traced to the word "copula," which means something more than just a sexual activity. As any dictionary would show, "copula" refers, in grammar, to a form of "linking verb," like the verb "to be" "or any similar verb, as seem, appear, etc., which links a subject with a predicate complement"; in logic, it denotes the "connecting link between the subject and predicate of a proposition" (*Webster's*). Whatever its semantic field, the word prioritizes the subject, and its function is to substantiate the subject by assisting it to form, to engineer, to give birth; in other words, to project elements into a construct, to configure details into a mirage. Further, the nature of this linking, whether in language, logic, or biological function, is defined first by the word's attached symbol "<" and then by its part of speech. The verb "to derive," which the symbol "<" stands for, has three semantic branches apart from simply "to get or receive": it means, in logic, "to get by reasoning; deduce or infer"; in genealogy or etymology, "to trace from or to a source; show the derivation of"; and in chemistry, "to obtain or produce (a compound) from another compound by replacing one element with one or more other elements" (*Webster's*). Quite explicitly, both the symbol "<" and the verb "derive" as such highlight the gist of the handbook for the hunter of knowledge. Either in philosophy or in science, they thus prescribe, to get, to obtain, or to produce as a way of knowing invariably necessitates a step-by-step process, and its operational mechanism, as is indicated by the preposition "by," is methodology. What is more, it is a methodology at once aggressive and predatory, for "copulate" is a verb, a part of speech foregrounding not only an armed desire for a certain object by linking it into a mirage of complement or proposition, but also a single-minded drive or action toward its capturing. Through Rakosi's strabismal lens, Medusa's glance is revealed in this part as language, language as reasoned method and methodized reason.

The second part of this poem performs an ironic twist, in that the details listed therein contribute, rather tantalizingly, to the Medusa's glance dramatized as "copulate" in the first part only to tease out their own strabismal implications in keeping with the tenets of the Objectivist vision. In sharp contrast to the first part, which consists of one verb only, a part embodying Medusa's highly focused predatory intent, the second part lists a noun (the iron master) followed by three adjectives (sweaty, breathless, fierce), suggesting an observation, an assertoric awareness of an object. But the three adjectives, each with its rich sensualness, lend themselves psychologically and suggestively to the first part of the poem featuring "copulate," which in turn finds, rather appropriately and conveniently, all its physical, supportive manifestations in those adjectives. As such, the two parts of the poem present the Medusa's glance in action, staging a mirage of seeing in which the second part becomes what is projected into by the first. They portray a predatory language movement whereby there occurs a Medusian reduction of the manifold of an object to what Rakosi refers to as mere "psychological slush." Yet this Medusian imposition, Rakosi seems to argue, is rendered possible only when "the iron master" is entirely ignored or sacrificed, a step essential to all anthropomorphic transmutation of being to being-represented. For "sweaty, / breathless, / fierce" are in fact sensual details of seeing of "the iron master" at work, which is itself one of the particulars constitutive of an assertoric view of a concrete work scene. In other words, the three adjectives, descriptive of an object, have nothing to do with rendering an apodeitic mirage of a sexual frenzy. "Says nothing / of lust," Rakosi announces in the middle of the poem, referring to the first part to demilitarize language as the Medusa's glance bringing the rays from an "eye/I" to a focus, and pointing to the second to activate the Objectivist strabismal lens bringing to a focus the rays from an object. "The Indomitable," read in this context, is indeed a poem "free at last from psychology" (*Collected Prose* 49), not without, of course, a confrontation against the Medusa's glance.

The form of "The Indomitable," in this sense, makes an important statement. It demonstrates an Objectivist critique of traditional epistemology by "copulating," so to speak, two poems already discussed. Beginning, for instance, with "The Romantic Eye," the poem ends with "Objectivist Lamp," which outshines the former, releasing details from the grip of what Rakosi describes in the poem "Ground Breaking" as "the eye of abstraction" (*Collected*

Poems 46). For Rakosi's Objectivist strabismal lens, as Michael Heller points out in his discussion of Zukofsky's use of the word "Objectivist," "is not concerned with the reified objectification of knowledge into a science . . . but with an objectification of human instance, of witnessing (active) or being witnessed" (*Conviction's Net* 19). However, it is by no means a given—in fact, far from it—that poems can be simply witnessing, can be "only acts upon particulars, outside of them," as Zukofsky phrases it in the preface to *An "Objectivists" Anthology* (25). For to realize the assertoric seeing, the poet has to resist his or her own impulse to render, rather than to describe, an object. And this resistance, or tension, is also articulated through objectification, which, according to Altieri, "pertains to various vehicles for bringing form and resolution to the energy fields elicited in pursuit of sincerity" ("Objectivist Tradition" 15). Viewed from this perspective, Rakosi's strabismal lens, when enacted in "The Indomitable," as elsewhere, also sheds light on its own compositional strategy as a measure against the Medusa's glance. In other words, sincerity and objectification work hand in hand. For Objectivist poetics "is not merely attention to objects," as Altieri aptly recapitulates in "The Objectivist Tradition"; "it entails the construction of aesthetic objects in such a way that the conditions of desire are themselves dramatized and forced to take responsibility for their productions" (12).

IV

Rakosi's Objectivist sensibility is markedly informed by a paradox: to bring the rays from an object to a focus, one has to defocus simultaneously the authoritative rays from the "eye/I" as mediated by desire and intention. To do so, the Objectivist lens has to be so constructed as to defocus the "mirage of seeing" as a way to focus on the "detail of seeing." In Rakosi's poetics, this defocusing-as-focusing figuration is cast in a mode of counter-vision best described as strabismal, a seeing that also places itself under close surveillance against its own predatory instinct. Equipped with a "bronze shield" of demilitarized language, Rakosi's poetics of strabismal seeing runs counter to a culture of vision, venturing, as a result, into a hunting ground, a closed system, where "the Medusa's glance of a sudden 'ray of vision'" facilitates the acquisition of truth and knowledge by *re*covering its prey.

As such, Rakosi's Objectivist poetics has ramifications far beyond the parameters of the literary. His Objectivist critique of phenomenology as epistemology, in particular, finds its philosophical counterpart in Adorno's "metacritique" of Husserl. Both share the same concerns. Rakosi's belief in thinking with the things as they exist, for instance, and his sustained effort to maintain the fidelity to the object by refusing to aggrandize perception, espouse, in a way, Adorno's critique of the phenomenologist as "certainly incapable of thinking objects as other than subjectively constituted" (*Against Epistemology* 194). Similar to Rakosi's diagnosis of "The Romantic Eye" as a circular movement from the ego back to the same ego, motivated by one's desire and intention, there is Adorno's conclusive statement that "Phenomenology resembles a circle because it arises out of idealism and reproduces idealism at every one of its stages, as usual as a sublated moment" (193). While Rakosi considers the mirage of seeing as nothing but myth, Adorno treats the so-called "first seeing" as pure illusion. As much as Rakosi and Adorno see eye to eye in this regard, it is, however, their shared insight into methodology, into the essential role methodology plays in phenomenology as epistemology, that brings them together. To a great extent, Rakosi's poems such as "The Romantic Eye" and "Man Contemplating a Rock" exhibit the poet's remarkable understanding of methodology as a tautological construct, as a closed system, with preordained outcomes; and, viewed in this light, they present themselves as powerful and convincing examples or demonstrations supporting Adorno's theorem that "Methodologically, . . . epistemology presupposes what, by its proper *raison d'etre* it should have deduced" (*Against Epistemology* 171). This shared realization of the "eye/I" as living, walking methodology leads, then, to the shared interests in as well as efforts to search for the alternative, an alternative that describes, rather than renders, an object.

What is most revealing in Rakosi's and Adorno's choices of alternatives is the striking similarity between the two in terms of their own methodologies, methodologies that might be best specified with the prefix "counter-." Challenging the metaphysical foundation of a culture privileging the all-mighty "eye/I," whose "spirit [is] objectified (*versachlicht*) into method" and, concomitantly, whose "totality of consciousness, is the world" (*Against Epistemology* 15, 27), both Rakosi and Adorno find their counter-methods in optic abnormalities. Whereas Rakosi resorts to a strabismal seeing, for instance, Adorno favors the eye with a splinter in it ("The splinter in your eye is the best magnifying glass"). Against a cultural background of visionary clarity and immediacy of various kinds, this seeming absurdity of their alternatives itself makes, in fact, a powerful argument. For it is not only ironic but also paradoxical, and the aesthetic underlying both's methods, as the "Publisher's Note" in *Minima Moralia* makes it clear, lies in their use of "allusions [that] involve irony or inversion" (13); or rather, both. Capable of a two-way seeing that unmasks the nature of the centuries-old approach to the world through vision-generated, vision-centered interpretations of truth, knowledge, and reality, Rakosi's strabismal eye defocuses desire's deadly gaze from "Medusian" to "Medussian," turning upside down the established ocularcentric paradigm sanctioning its own mirage of seeing. Alluding to religious as well as epistemological conventions, Adorno's splintered vision not only makes a mockery of the biblical morals preaching the clarity of seeing by removing the plank from one's own eyes first,[17] but also invests Hegel's—and Husserl's, for that matter—phenomenological dictum from "The whole is the true" (Hegel 81) to "The whole is the false" (*Minima Moralia* 50).[18] Each in his own way, Rakosi and Adorno deploy optic abnormality as a metaphor, as a double-edged sword: it implicates the existing sociocultural formation as an abnormality, as largely the result of the affection of an ideologically mediated ocularcentrism, and it points to itself, rather paradoxically, as a radical alternative. With these optic abnormalities as their counter-methods, they attempt to break away from Medusa's glance as closure into the world where they can be *with* the world, where they can see things as what they *are* rather than what they *should* be. This being the case, these counter-methods are charged with emotions and unarmed desires, and the tension one witnesses or experiences in reading Rakosi and Adorno comes from a war of eye against eye: the strabismal eye or the splintered eye versus the Medusa's glance.

"Be aware of the Medusa's glance" thus becomes the motto that informs both the poetic and the theoretical discourses from various perspectives since the 1960s. In the postmodernist reflection upon issues of immediacy and transparency of language, the Objectivist concern with vision and its critical strategy of visual abnormality in its radical questioning of representation itself present a precursory model for later generations of avant-gardes, with the Language poets championing and leading the exploratory praxes into uncharted territories. In his project of "repossessing the word" stated in *The L=A=N=G=U=A=G=E Book* (ix), for instance, Charles Bernstein, for one, resorts to a linguistic "amblyopia" to reveal the "dysraphism" of language (*Sophist* 112, 44). Similar but less explicit examples can also be found in Lyn Hejinian's poetics of what might be called "no-match" between the word and the world ("Rejection," in *Poetics Journal* 143) and in Susan Howe's strategy of "the chance meeting of words" (*My Emily Dickinson* 24). Read within such a context, the Objectivist experiments in general and Rakosi's poetics of strabismal seeing in particular indeed have "historical implications," as Zukofsky rightly foresaw in 1961 (*Prepositions* 167), implications to be further explored, developed, and articulated in the decades to come.

4

George Oppen's Serial Poems

Alan Golding

George Oppen has often been discussed as if he were a kind of miniaturist, preoccupied with the small, the particular, the concrete detail. Even sympathetic readers note how modest his ambitions seem, how he writes mostly short poems capturing what he calls "moments of conviction" (Dembo and Pondrom 174), how he pays fiercely focused attention to, in his own words, "the small nouns." Certainly this view is not wrong, and Oppen himself, both in his poetry and in interviews, does much to invite it. He summarizes his ambitions as follows in "Route": "I have not and never did have any motive of poetry / But to achieve clarity" (*Collected Poems* 185)—"a limited, limiting clarity" of language and perception applied to what he calls in another poem "the lyric valuables" (29). In a 1968 interview he said, "all the little nouns are the ones that I like the most: the deer, the sun, and so on" (Dembo and Pondrom 175). In 1980 he explained his characteristic disruptions of syntax thus: "All along I've had a sense that the structure of the sentence closes off the little words. That's where the mysteries are, in the little words. 'The' and 'and' are the greatest mysteries of all" ("Poetry and Politics" 38). In "Song, the Winds of Downhill," "the words // *would with and* take on substantial // meaning handholds footholds // to dig in one's heels" (*Collected Poems* 213). And "Psalm" contains these often-quoted lines: "The small nouns / Crying faith / In this in which the wild deer / Startle, and stare out" (78).

But despite Oppen's genuine faith and interest in "the little words," "the small nouns," it's worth remembering a few things: that he won a Pulitzer for *Of Being Numerous*, a book dominated by the long serial poem of the same title; that this book contains a second serial poem, "Route"; that both *This In Which* and *Seascape: Needle's Eye* contain series ("A Language of New York" and "A Narrative" in the former book, "Some San Francisco Poems" in the latter); that Oppen began his career with a book-length serial poem, *Discrete Series;* and that some of his closest associates and poetic models—Zukofsky, Pound, Williams—did much of their major work in the long poem. I don't want to make a perversely revisionary case for Oppen as a writer of epics. Obviously, he never wrote anything on the scale of *"A"*, the *Cantos, Paterson, The Maximus Poems, Trilogy,* or *Helen in Egypt.* Nevertheless, Laszlo Géfin exaggerates only slightly in claiming that "from the beginning Oppen conceived of poetic creation in the form of series" (63); Marjorie Perloff also remarks that "from the beginning . . . Oppen has displayed a penchant for what we might call a poetic of 'discrete series'" ("Shape" 223). Oppen did distinguished work in the genre of the serial poem. My point, then, is this: that to overlook Oppen's series *as series*—to ignore *why* he works in this genre—is to misunderstand, by limiting, the nature of his achievement and to overlook a significant part of his impact on contemporary poetics. As Michael Davidson puts it, "it is as though we have focused only on the first word in the title to [Oppen's] first book, *Discrete Series,* to the exclusion of the second. By doing so we have reified the processual—and I would argue dialogical—nature of his thought in an ethos of the hard, objective artifact" (*Ghostlier Demarcations* 71).

One reason that Oppen has been overlooked as a writer of serial poems is that too many people still don't know how to read his work in that genre.[1] Except for Joseph Conte's approach in *Unending Design,* most paradigms for reading the American long poem or sequence cannot accommodate Oppen's work. I have in mind here the approaches proposed by Roy Harvey Pearce in *The Continuity of American Poetry;* by Michael Bernstein in *The Tale of the Tribe;* by James E. Miller in *The American Quest for a Supreme Fiction;* by Thomas Gardner in *Discovering Ourselves in Whitman;* and by M. L. Rosenthal and Sally Gall in *The Modern Poetic Sequence.* In none of these books does Oppen make so much as an index appearance. (Nor do the other Objectivists, beyond Miller's one mention of Zukofsky).[2] Pearce finds in the American long poem "an effort to wrest a hero from history" (133)—an effort on the poet's part to make him- or herself into that hero by pursuing through poetry a struggle for "self-identification and self-preservation," what Pearce calls "the epic struggle of modern times" (130). Oppen's series, however, are resolutely nonmythopoeic and nonheroic, and he suspects the ambition and large vision by which Pearce measures the success of the American epic. A similar scale or ambition is called for by Michael Bernstein in his discussion of Pound's, Williams's, and Olson's "modern verse epics." Bernstein implies in his title and proposes in his book the paradigm of a didactic cultural narrative addressed to the polis (14). This paradigm, however, has no place for Oppen, who is rarely didactic, has a modest sense of audience, and does not write poems "including history" in the same way that Bernstein's poets do.[3]

James Miller sees Whitman as the presence that presides over nearly all American long poems since *Leaves of Grass.* He calls such poems "personal epics" and summarizes their main characteristics as follows. First, "the new epic is written in a 'free' form, with a loose or an open structure, in a style that is familiar, colloquial, common, or earthy." Its action is "interior," frequently a spiritual quest, emphasizing mediation, rumination, contemplation. As regards character, "the hero of the new epic is created out of the poet's self," "an embodiment of his time and place"—a criterion that recalls Pearce. The setting is the poet's own locale, "and the time is his time, a continuous present." Subject and theme involve implied or direct social criticism, the sketching of an implied ideal order, the seeking and delineation of new myths (34–36). How useful is Miller's paradigm for discussing Oppen? Certainly Oppen uses "a loose or an open structure." But his style is hardly familiar—he openly disavowed Williams's faith in the vernacular ("Interview" 15)—and while the action of his serial poems may be interior or psychological, Oppen himself is not consistently their focus. He subdues his personal presence and does not use a strong central voice to organize his work in serial forms. Even in "A Language of New York" and "Some San Francisco Poems," his settings are barely determinable in either time or place. And finally, while he may offer social criticism, he is too much the skeptic to offer new myths or resuscitate old ones, as do Eliot, Crane, Williams, Pound, H. D., and Olson. As Oppen writes in "Philai Te Kou Philai," "the myths / Have been murderous, // Most murderous" (*Collected Poems* 76). Not surprisingly, then, since Whitman is the model, Miller's approach works best to describe Whitmanesque long poems or sequences.

The project of connecting American long poems to Whitman continues in Thomas Gardner's argument that "Whitman's creation of a self-portrait out of his indirect embrace of a medium can be used as a model for reading a number of important contemporary long poems" (21) by Berryman, Kinnell, Roethke, Duncan, Ashbery, and Merrill. For Gardner, "it was Whitman who most clearly identified and exploited the distance between an individual voice and the larger world . . . shaped, entered, and drawn from" (1). While Oppen (like many other poets) may share Whitman's concern with that distance, he is hardly the kind of poet—one "wrestling with and empowered by the problems of self-rendering" (2)—in whom Gardner is most interested and for whom Gardner's approach works best. A late allusion to Whitman, in *Primitive,* suggests that Oppen found his predecessor too self-involved to be an entirely useful model:

looking back over his own career, Oppen wonders if he has produced "images // of existence (or song // of myself?)" (20).[4]

At first glance, Rosenthal and Gall's approach looks more promising. They are interested in lyric sequences, and are not Oppen's serial poems best described that way? Certainly that is the term Perloff uses in her discussion of "Of Being Numerous." Rosenthal and Gall's late-romantic view of poetry, however, leads them to find in every poetic sequence a series of quasi-confessional lyrics. Following Poe, they see the poetic sequence as simply a series of intense local effects or expressive peaks. They characterize the modern sequence as "intimate, fragmented, self-analytical, open, emotionally volatile," driven by "a highly subjective impulse of lyrical energy at work" in "the poem's 'speaker' or 'protagonist'" (9). Their least convincing chapters concern those sequences where the sense of a central speaking subject is least stable, or those that do not place the poet in extremis on center stage, works such as "Notes toward a Supreme Fiction" or *The Maximus Poems.* Like Pearce, Bernstein, and Miller, Rosenthal and Gall do not even mention Oppen's sequences. If they did, it is hard to imagine how they could discuss satisfactorily the work of a writer who does not shape his serial poems around privileged centers of emotional intensity, who defines the self as "what I've seen and not myself" (*Collected Poems* 35), and who, at a time when confessional poetry was at its peak of popularity, published these lines:

> Soul-searchings, these prescriptions,
> Are a medical faddism, an attempt to escape,
> To lose oneself in the self.
> The self is no mystery, the mystery is
> That there is something for us to stand on. (*Collected Poems* 143)

As a 1975 letter to Harvey Shapiro suggests, Oppen found confessional poetry (as represented, in Oppen's own example, by Lowell's "Skunk Hour,") problematic because "it doesn't tell, it's locked in itself" and fails to acknowledge that which is outside the self, "the force of the given" (*Selected Letters* 313). One year earlier, writing to James Laughlin, Oppen seems to dismiss the confessional in asserting that "weakness is common" (and thus, implicitly, an inadequate basis for a poetics), and that while he himself has "put in the moments of extreme weakness, extreme error," he has stopped short of Lowell's notorious moment of voyeurism in "Skunk Hour": "Not the love-cars" (282).[5]

Joseph Conte offers a more useful framework for reading Oppen's serial poems in differentiating the "series" (which he sees as a distinctively postmodern form) from the modernist epic and "neoromantic sequence" (*Unending Design* 15). In doing so, he opens up considerably the canon of poets discussable under the (admittedly vague) "long poem" rubric.[6] Conte proposes a valuable contrast between the discontinuity, incompleteness, and "accumulation" of serial form and the impulse toward "encompassment, summation" of the modernist epic (37), with its underlying "organic theory of continuity and development" (15). He then goes on to distinguish between the infinite and the finite series, placing Oppen's *Discrete Series* in the latter category as a work that "emphasizes the separate validity of the individual poems," while the infinite series (Creeley's *Pieces,* Duncan's *Passages,* Blackburn's *Journals*) "emphasizes the continuous process and the multiplicity of poems which find their validity in that process" (130).[7] Conte's tendency to take *Discrete Series* as representative of all Oppen's work in serial form—it is the only work of Oppen's that he mentions—leads him to overlook differences within Oppen's career and thus to propose too sharp a distinction between Oppen and Creeley (later in this essay I shall argue for significant similarities between their serial poems). Nevertheless, Conte provides the most helpful paradigm and terminology available for distinguishing Oppen's series from the work of his modernist and late-modernist contemporaries.

Oppen is temperamentally suspicious of the large claims for poetry, of the expansive tone and form which in various ways characterize the modernist long poem. Not for him the rhetorical stance, derived from Whitman, that leads Jeffrey Walker to coin the term "bardic poem" for the *Cantos, The Bridge, Paterson,* and *Maximus.* As Walker rightly says, "the fundamental enterprise in which [these] modern poems participate is Whitmanesque. And because it is Whitmanesque, it is necessarily suasory as well. Pound, Crane, Williams, and Olson all want to constitute themselves, like Whitman, as an American epic bard," uttering a "polemical call . . . to alter and direct the national will" (xi). Oppen criticizes even the shorter poems of Ginsberg's *Kaddish* for having "too high and too declamatory a note" which results in too much "copiousness," "expansiveness," "declamatory form" ("Three Poets" 329). In "Route" he says, "If having come so far we shall have / Song // Let it be small enough" (*Collected Poems* 192). In "West" he waxes incredulous: "'We address the future?' // Unsure of the times / Unsure I can answer // To myself" (208). These are not the words of a poet likely to write the kind of long poem undertaken by a Zukofsky, a Pound, a Williams, an Olson.

Oppen's skepticism regarding epic claims left him with serious doubts about the longer poems of all these writers. Some sample comments: "I can make an awful lot of objections to parts of *A*"; "Pound's ego system, Pound's organization of the world around a character, a kind of masculine energy, is extremely foreign to me"; "I've always had reservations about *Paterson*"; "I don't really like the *Maximus Poems* nor accept them at all" (Dembo and Pondrom 183–84). While place—New York, San Francisco—affects Oppen's poetry, it does not lead him to write an epic identifying with a place as Olson and Williams did. Contrasting himself specifically with these poets, he says, "I have no theory of the need for a locality at all. It would rather frighten me to be too dependent on a locality" ("Interview" 9).[8] From among the works of these twentieth-century writers of long poems, rather, Oppen values the lyric poem or the lyric moment. Of Olson and Pound, for example, he remarks, "I think 'In Cold Hell, In Thicket' is a very fine poem"; "what I really read in Pound are passages and lines. Just about the time I'm beginning to consider Pound an idiot, I come to something like the little wasp in the *Pisan Cantos*, and I know that I'm reading a very great poet" (Dembo and Pondrom 184, 183).

Given these reservations and his own undoubted lyric talent, why did Oppen turn to serial form as often as he did? For Oppen, poetry is a form of thinking, and the serial poem allows him a different, a more extended and flexible form of thinking than is possible in the lyric. As John Taggart puts it, "the series permits any number of variations without forcing new beginnings and without losing sight of the object." It enables Oppen "to *think actively in his poetry*" ("Deep Jewels" 163, 162) without, on the one hand, having to formulate an inclusive philosophical system, or, on the other, having to begin over with a kind of self-imposed tabula rasa in each new poem, "out of poverty / to begin // again" (*Collected Poems* 213). As many of his readers have realized, and as one would expect of someone more affected by Hegel and Marx than he was by most poets, Oppen is a dialectical poet and thinker. The dialectic especially between particular and general, between individual and group, always occupied him. Oppen plays out this dialectic in his serial poems by foregrounding as a formal problem the relationship between individual piece and whole sequence.

Especially in a poet like Oppen, who pays such insistent attention to discrete particulars, the serial poem has a formal dialectic built into its very structure. Are Oppen's serial poems most usefully seen as a number of discrete pieces added together to make a whole? Or do they represent the remains of single, continuous poems that have been shattered into pieces? Serial organization in Oppen's poetry goes back to his first book, *Discrete Series* (1934), and his comments on that volume emphasize alternately the whole and the part, seriality and discreteness. Oppen's stated purpose in *Discrete Series* was "to construct meaning, to construct a method of thought from the imagist technique of poetry—from the imagist intensity of vision" (Dembo and Pondrom 174)—to build a larger worldview ("meaning") and an epistemology ("a method of thought") from the brief, closely scrutinized moments characteristic of the imagist lyric. Also implied in "intensity" is the need to maintain a sharp intellectual and perceptual focus: "One must not come to feel that he has a thousand threads in his hands, / He must somehow see the one thing; / This is the level of art" (*Collected Poems* 168). L. S. Dembo summarizes the poet's position by saying, "one can know only particulars and hope to build a meaning from them" ("Existential World" 68). Oppen himself further explains his thinking using Williams's dictum "no ideas but in things": "I have always wondered whether that expression didn't apply to the construction of meaning in a poem . . . that there would be in the poem no ideas but those which could be expressed through the description of things" (Dembo and Pondrom 183).

Oppen tends to talk of his poetic technique in ethical terms and in terms that try to reconcile the claims (and limitations) of the imagist poem/moment with the hope for a broader system of thought or belief. Thus in discussing *Discrete Series* he conflates terms of form and structure ("construct," "technique") with terms of content and value ("meaning," "intensity of vision"). "Intensity of vision" implies not only clear rendition of the image but also spiritual or moral insight and an emotional response: "The virtue of the mind // Is that emotion // Which causes / To see" (*Collected Poems* 87), as he writes in "Guest Room." Elsewhere in the interview from which his comments on *Discrete Series* derive, Oppen uses an ethical criterion to explain a formal feature of the book, saying that its disjointed structure results from his perceiving and writing in isolated "moments of conviction." The term "conviction" implies what most of Oppen's work makes clear, that he sees his poetry as an effort to formulate an ethic for living. In "Blood from the Stone" he asks, "What do we believe / To live with?" and answers "all / That verse attempts" (*Collected Poems* 31). He feels that he can formulate that ethic only in "moments of conviction"—that conviction is so fragile and fleeting as to be available only in moments. For Oppen, however, every moment is charged with potential material for poetry. At any given moment, to put it simply, there is a lot going on to write about. Hence Oppen speaks of "the moment's // Populace" and "The light, the volume / Of the moment" (22, 25). The richness and value of this material—of *The Materials,* to use one of Oppen's book titles—is, I take it, what Oppen means he is convinced *of* in his moments of conviction.

In the context of explicating Oppen's sense of the imagist moment and his effort to weld those moments into larger poetic structures, his well-known gloss on the title *Discrete Series* deserves repeating: "A discrete series is a series of terms each of which is empirically derived, each one of which is empirically true. . . . The poems are a series, yet each is separate" (Dembo and Pondrom 174). In this comment Oppen stresses not the cumulative effect of the "terms" or poems in his discrete series but their separate, self-contained quality. The construction of meaning involves forging or finding relationships among ideas and things; the very gesture of putting fragments of language into a series invites us to connect them in some way. At the same time, "meaning" remained something more sought after than achieved for a skeptic like Oppen, and something momentary: "meaning's // instant," "meaning / in the instant" (*Collected Poems* 237, 239). He uses in *Discrete Series* the least "constructed" form of connection possible—seriality, or, in his own words, "Successive / Happenings." Further, he defies traditional notions of progression or climax: "Not by growth / But the / Paper, turned, contains / This entire volume" (*Collected Poems* 14). Oppen tries to realize what one might have thought an unrealizable oxymoron—an imagist long poem.[9]

This strategy invites these questions: Do the particular empirical "truths" in fact add up to anything larger? What is the relationship of part to whole, in poetry and in society? Characteristically, Oppen explores these questions obliquely rather than answers them. Characteristically, too, that exploration moves by fits and starts, inconclusively. Seeing things in "moments of conviction," attending to words one by one, breaking up syntax, refusing full predication—when all these familiar Oppen techniques of disjunctiveness come together, inevitably a poem or series of poems will move fitfully. In the 1968 Dembo interview, Oppen says he "had trouble with syntax in this undertaking," and especially "trouble with verbs" (Dembo and Pondrom 174), the part of speech connecting the nouns that Oppen attends so closely to.[10] His refusal of any symmetrical structure and of emphatic closure for the series (a form that, by definition, resists closure), his questioning of traditional modes of connection, at the levels of both sentence and series, help make *Discrete Series* one of the first open-form serial poems. Eric Homberger has suggested that *Discrete Series* anticipates later serial poems like Berryman's *Dream Songs* or Lowell's *Notebook* (*Art of the Real* 204). Unlike these poets, however, Oppen does not shape his fragments by using a systematic organization and regular form, like Lowell's chronology and pseudosonnets, or by using the distinctive voice and consistent point of view of an "experiencing subject," like Berryman's "Henry." In fact, Oppen describes the series "Some San Francisco Poems" to Charles Amirkhanian and David Gitin as being "written in violation of my own speech," because "I don't want to be tied to the characteristics of voice" ("Conversation" 24).

The formal dilemma posed in *Discrete Series,* that of the relationship between particular fragment and overall series, functions as an allegory of an epistemological and social dilemma, that of the relationship between individual and community. "Party on Shipboard," the poem of *Discrete Series* that Oppen wrote last and which he says contains the seeds of "Of Being Numerous"

("Oppen on His Poems" 201), deals specifically with this latter relationship. By repetition Oppen connects an individual wave with an individual person: the poem begins, "Wave in the round of the port-hole / Springs, passing,—arm waved." Humanity as a whole, however, is "Like the sea incapable of contact / Save in incidents"; sea and humanity are "Homogeneously automatic" (*Collected Poems* 8). Oppen suggests that our daily experience is not of abstractions like "the sea" and "humanity" but of individual waves and humans. If that is true, Oppen wonders, is "humanity" even a meaningful concept?

When he returned to writing poetry after twenty-five years occupied with political activism, a variety of jobs, military service, and avoiding the attentions of HUAC, Oppen soon picked up this and other issues raised in *Discrete Series* where he had left off. *This In Which* includes the two series "A Language of New York" (an early, short version of "Of Being Numerous") and "A Narrative." Again Oppen uses serial form to give his mind free rein to explore questions of connection: here, between mind and world, inner and outer, word and referent. As in *Discrete Series,* he uses structural discontinuity in "A Narrative" to foreground these questions. One such discontinuity occurs between title and text. *Is* this a narrative poem? Whose narrative? A narrative about what? The title's oblique relationship to the text invites questions about language (is "narrative" a useful term?) and about literary mode (what are the boundaries and characteristics of the thing we call "narrative"?). The poem has none of the traditional features of narrative: no clear time or place setting, no characters, no plot, no narrative organization based on chronology or any of its accepted variations (like flashback). Narrative, Oppen has said, with its implications of an ordered universe apprehensible in a unified work of art, runs counter to his feeling that poetic form is local and temporary and that meaning is constructed disjunctively out of momentary insights: "Narrative has almost always been unfaceable for me. I have all sorts of doubts about it, and it violates . . . my sense of the poem, the 'moments of conviction' " (Oppen and Oppen, "Conversation" 35.) The late poem "Animula" suggests that, for Oppen, "narrative" means simply the ongoingness of the material world, what he calls in two poem titles "The Occurrences" (*Collected Poems* 126, 206) to which the poet must learn to attend: "In the starlight things the things continue / Narrative   their long instruction" (207). If "A Narrative" *is* a narrative, it is one of the mind grappling with epistemological and ontological problems, renewing its contact with the world and searching for an adequate language in which to talk about that world.

To pursue this project, "A Narrative" moves between the competing terms of binary opposition. A detailed reading of the poem is not to my purpose here; a few brief examples will suffice to illustrate my point. Within individual parts of the sequence, Oppen often adopts a binary stanza structure: two-line stanzas in section 1 and 2, and within section 2 itself, the word count reversed in the first two stanzas; an alternating two-two-one line pattern in section 3; two four-line stanzas split by a central isolated line in section 5; two four-line stanzas in section 6; and so on. Thematically, section 1 concerns itself with lying, section 2 with truth; the bulk of section 7 consists of two equal stanzas, one on the closed self imaged in the "Serpent, Ouroboros / Whose tail is in his mouth" and the other offering the counterstatement that "What breath there is / In the rib cage we must draw / From the dimensions // Surrounding" (137).[11] Implied in sections 1 and 2 is yet another dialectically organized theme, the relationship between words and experience, that becomes more explicit in section 9's mediation on "the fallacy / Of words" and section 11's contrary vision of "a substantial language / Of clarity, and of respect" (138, 140). Thus Oppen uses serial form to stretch the thematic and structural limitations of the lyric. As Norman Finkelstein puts it, "A Narrative" is "the thematic center of *This In Which*," structurally "not a unified whole, but a field in which themes may inform each other to a much greater extent than in any single lyric" ("Dialectic" 370).

The movement of "A Narrative" reflects Oppen's wrestling with what is for him the always problematic relationship between images, between general propositions, and between image and proposition. While he modifies the method of *Discrete Series* somewhat by linking the discrete parts of "A Narrative" through repetition and variation of theme and image, the links never become predictable. Rarely does Oppen use the same device to link more than two successive sections; in other words, he rarely uses the same device more than twice in a row. And while he may use a consistent stanza pattern within a section, only once (between sections 1 and 2) does he maintain a pattern *between* sections. Any sense of unity or continuity, then, remains local and provisional. Just as Oppen destabilizes almost every statement he makes by questioning it or proposing its opposite, so he destabilizes the possibility of any form that, simply by being maintained, excludes other formal possibilities.

When "A Narrative" was published in 1965, Oppen was already working on "Of Being Numerous." He seems to have had his purpose for this poem consciously in mind from the start: to see, as he says to Dembo, "whether or not we can deal with humanity as something which does actually exist . . . whether or not one will consider the concept of humanity to be valid, something that is, or else have to regard it as being simply a word" (Dembo and Pondrom 175). In pursuing this purpose Oppen shows an ambition that he measures, surprisingly, not by the achievement of those poets with whom he is most often associated—Zukofsky, Pound, and Williams—but by that of Eliot. He writes to

Andy Meyer, "I haven't, I'm afraid, written a Wasteland, haven't written a decisive expression of a period. I meant not to try in [*This In Which*]. I meant to try in [*Of Being Numerous*]" ("Letters to Andy Meyer" 106). Like Eliot, furthermore, Oppen does not equate this ambition with the need to produce a large-scale work. A significantly less allusive poet than Eliot, he seeks a compression similar to that which Eliot's allusiveness, as I. A. Richards famously remarked, affords *him:* "Allusion in Mr. Eliot's hands is a technical device for compression. 'The Waste Land' is equivalent in content to an epic. Without this device twelve books would have been needed" (290–91).[12] As Oppen's "decisive expression," "Of Being Numerous" makes explicit the question that *Discrete Series* left implicit: the relation of the individual to the group. It rests on the same methodological assumptions as *Discrete Series,* that one can construct meaning using imagist technique and that "the test of images can be a test of whether one's thought is valid" (Dembo and Pondrom 175). Despite the general resemblance between *Discrete Series* and "Of Being Numerous," however, Oppen modifies, as he does in "A Narrative," the purely serial organization of his first book. "Of Being Numerous" moves by reversal and contradiction.[13] Oppen uses this technique to make local transitions while resisting any overall systematic form. Thus he enacts in the poem's jagged form the dilemma of the relationship between the "singular" and the "numerous," between "me" and "them," between "the poet" and "the people." As before, the serial form allows Oppen to probe his subject in greater depth and complexity than would the lyric. After all, the lyric poem has room for only a limited number of reversals and contradictions, and even a book of lyrics may keep the issues of each poem tidily separate, by virtue of its very form and of the tendency toward closure in any single poem.

These reversals and contradictions occur both within and between the sections of "Of Being Numerous." To illustrate the principle briefly, I will review a few examples of the technique as Oppen uses it between sections. Sections 5–8 make up one thematically important cluster of poems that exhibits a pattern of alternating statements and counterstatements and that shows how "Of Being Numerous," like many of Stevens's longer poems, moves by responding to itself. Section 5 focuses on a stone set in the Brooklyn Bridge and dated "1875" as a metaphor for the isolated consciousness, "Frozen in the moonlight / In the frozen air over the footpath." Section 6 shifts the topic from isolated consciousness to the enforced community of life in New York: "We are pressed, pressed on each other" (*Collected Poems* 150). Section 7 turns from enforced to chosen community: "We have chosen the meaning / Of being numerous." But immediately section 8 reverses 7 and recalls 6. Section 8—which Oppen thought of as "the center of the poem, its meaning" (*Selected Letters* 111)—concerns "Amor fati / The love of fate," "destinies." Fate is the opposite of choice, and suddenly the possibility arises that the choice "of being numerous" is no choice but something as inevitable, as fated, as the passage of time itself, "day // Having only the force / Of days" (*Collected Poems* 151). As David McAleavey puts it, "the problem of 'numerosity' is *how* to be social since one *must* be" (388).

The pattern of reversals continues in sections 9–14. Section 9 raises the question, via a quotation from a Rachel Blau DuPlessis letter, of the poet's relationship to others: "Whether, as the intensity of seeing increases, one's distance from Them, the people, does not also increase." Perhaps it does, but of the "absolute singular" poet in section 10, Oppen says, "The isolated man is dead, his world around him exhausted // And he fails! He fails, that meditative man!" (*Collected Poems* 152–53). Section 12 offers a vision of a lost pastoral community, concluding that "This will never return, never, / Unless having reached their limits // They will begin over, that is, / Over and over" (155). Section 13 cuts from this country past to an urban present to confirm this skepticism and sense of loss: "unable to begin / At the beginning, the fortunate / Find everything already here. They are shoppers, / Choosers, judges; . . . And here the brutal / is without issue, a dead end." Oppen's disgust at these "ghosts that endanger // One's soul" has him ending section 13 with the lines "one may honorably keep // His distance / If he can" (156)—a chosen distance rather than one enforced by intensity of vision, just as community was first enforced, then chosen. With section 14, however, Oppen immediately qualifies this statement: "I cannot even now / Altogether disengage myself / From those men // With whom I stood in emplacements . . . // How talk / Distantly of 'The People'" (157).

This pattern of reversal, qualification, and self-interrogation continues throughout the poem. The pattern is discussed well in an early essay by Rachel Blau DuPlessis in which she describes the "structure of alternatives and the thematic concern for propositions and their negation" in Oppen's work: "[Oppen's] poetry constantly expresses dilemma—in the original sense of that word: di-lemma or two propositions. In the prototypical meditative drama of the poetry, Oppen will hold one position, weigh it, test it out, and then become compelled to consider an opposing proposition, equally true, which counters the first one" ("George Oppen" 63). This does not mean, however, that Oppen simply hops back and forth between A and not-A. He refuses such a predictable movement, and that refusal has a larger thematic point: that the relationship of one person to another and to the mass, of the "singular" to the "numerous," cannot finally be pinned down. While "Of Being Numerous" contains small clusters of related poems within the larger series in which the reversals and qualifications that I have touched on can be seen, the pattern cannot be used to impose any shape on the work as a whole. As with Oppen's other serial poems, structure in "Of Being Numerous" is temporary and provisional.[14] And along with this emphasis on local rather than overall structure, Oppen does not feel his sequence has to get anywhere. The end of "Of Being Numerous" circles verbally back to its beginning, the dilemma of self and society having been explored rather than resolved. (As Oppen once put it, his poem "simply shares the problem" ["Adequate Vision" 21].) Oppen begins and ends with awe before the world. Section 1 begins "There are things / We live among 'and to see them / Is to know ourselves.' // Occurrence, a part / Of an infinite series, // The sad marvels" (*Collected Poems* 147). In section 39 we find these lines: "Occurring 'neither for self / Nor for truth' // The sad marvels" (179). And as always, Oppen rejects the grand climax. He ends with a chunk of prose, a letter home by the great poet of numerousness, Whitman, the reader's attention left hanging on one word dangling in white space, "curious" (179).

Throughout his canon, then, both stylistically and thematically, Oppen foregrounds the problem of connection: of word to word, of word to phrase and sentence, of image to image, of singular to numerous, person to group—and of part to part and part to whole in his poetic series. Oppen's calculated discontinuity in his sequences, the writing of more or less discrete series whose individual pieces sometimes are themselves only part of a sentence, mirrors his breaking up of the sentence to attend to individual words. At both levels the technique creates enforced pauses, draws attention to parts, and throws into question the connection of those parts to each other and to the whole. But is this any different from the familiar modernist trope of suppressing transitions and using abrupt juxtapositions that force the reader to make his or her own connections? Does the use of a fragmented form to render a fragmented worldview take us beyond *The Waste Land?* I think so, if only because Oppen pushes the technique to such an extreme and because he uses a different *kind* of disjunctiveness, syntactic as well as narrative. Oppen's disjunctiveness is so ubiquitous, from the level of small phrase to the level of forty-page serial poem, that it becomes its own subject, far more so than it is in, say, Eliot, Pound, or Williams. Indeed, if a poet as complex as Oppen can be said to have one central subject, this may be it: exploring the limits of verbal, political, and human connection or relation. And one way Oppen conducts that exploration is through the form and structure of his serial poems.

As I suggested in my opening discussion of recent critical approaches to the serial poem or sequence, Oppen's work in this mode is often neglected because his work does not fit standard definitions of it. He is not alone on this point. Decades after Robert Creeley published one of the major postwar experiments in serial organization, *Pieces* (in 1969, the year after *Of Being Numerous*), one can still find poet-critics writing for influential journals and academic presses who do not know what to do with *his* work either. Witness Wyatt Prunty's New Formalist critique of Creeley's "Emaciated Poetry," an attack resting on an explicit and almost programmatic nostalgia for a traditional prosody, unproblematized syntax, and the New Critical virtues of wit, irony, ambiguity, and paradox. The Creeley of the serial poems, however, is one of the contemporary poets whom Oppen most clearly anticipates in *his* longer works. Creeley is usually, and rightly, associated with Zukofsky among the Objectivist poets. At the same time, he met Oppen, corresponded with him, and read his poetry enthusiastically. Oppen's apparent impact on Creeley's own work in and thinking about serial form—work that itself has powerfully affected many poets of the generation following Creeley's—is one measure of the importance of Oppen's serial poems.[15]

Oppen, in his longer poems, and Creeley, in *Pieces,* are confronting the same problem—how to write (or construct) a serial poem when one habitually tends toward a poetry of the lyric moment. Commenting on *Pieces* in a 1971 interview, Creeley starts by noting the appeal of Olson's and Duncan's longer works, which "gave them a range and a possible density of statement that was very attractive" in contrast to his own habit of "work in a small focus in a very intensive kind of address." The serial form of *Pieces* thus came out of Creeley's desire for an inclusiveness that he felt his own lyric practice did not allow: "I really had a hunger for something that would give me a far more various emotional state, that is, the ability to enter it. And also I wanted a mode that could include, say, what people understandably might feel are instances of trivia" (*Tales* 102). This shift in Creeley's work also represented a historically influential move in two related ways. First, Creeley offered the example of a liberatory shift in emphasis from the production of "poems" to that of "writing."[16] And second, he did so in a way that raised what became increasingly pressing issues of literary evaluation, and which in fact questioned the very necessity of evaluation—at a time, moreover, when definitions of the poem as well-wrought urn still dominated much mainstream assessment of poetry and when Creeley might reasonably have been concerned with bolstering the reputation derived from his first two books, *For Love* and *Words.* As he says of *Pieces,* "I wanted to trust writing, I was so damned tired of trusting my own opinion as to whether this was a good piece of poetry or a bad piece of poetry" (*Tales* 102–3). For Creeley, at this time, evaluation—that most basic of canonizing gestures, of inclusion and exclusion—sustained only "the most bleak, scared, spineless subservience . . . to the British core of taste." Hence his praiseful comment on an attitude close to the anti-canonizing stance of *Pieces:* "What I respect increasingly in students is the ability to stop encapsulating an attitude towards writing in the sentimental sense of evaluation: this is a good poem, this is a bad poem" (*Tales* 113). The craft-oriented "poet" in *Pieces* may still speak: "My plan is / these little boxes / make sequences." But the "writer" instantly, if wearily, responds: "Lift me / from such I / makes such declaration" (*Collected Poems* 440).

Like Oppen, then, Creeley in his middle books breaks down the traditional boundaries of the lyric while simultaneously refusing any overdetermined structure for his series. Creeley's boredom in the early 1960s "with the tidy containment of clusters of words on single pieces of paper called 'poems'" (*Real Poem* 103) led him to explore a new sense of what makes a poem. *Pieces* is a series of fragments, often only two or three words long. It is frequently impossible to separate individual poems; in fact, if we look for anything resembling the usual poem (with a title and a visible beginning and end), we'll be lost. The book's form "comes and goes / in a moment" (*Collected Poems* 382), a process continually completing itself but, at least in the sense of having formal poetic closure, never actually completed. Its principle of organization is to chart "the day's / particulars, one to one" (436), its effect cumulative rather than local. In *Pieces,* then, Creeley's interest shifted from the discrete poem-as-object to the formal possibilities of the series, of what he called "serialogy"—"the concept of poems as set instances of articulate statement yields to a sense of continuity." He says of *Pieces,* "I wondered what kind of modality would really give me something that could also in a sense continue as a situation of writing, that wouldn't each time contain itself in a singular statement" ("Interview with Ekbert Faas" 186).

From this account of *Pieces,* the areas of kinship with Oppen's serial poems should be clear. Oppen's poetry is always formally and intellectually exploratory, a poetry of open-endedness and process, and his serial poems are especially so. Not surprisingly, this quality has been noticed particularly by poets who have found in Oppen's work a valuable source for their own practice and in Creeley a kind of bridge between the older Objectivists and the present. John Taggart argues that Oppen's poetry "at every point radiates process, often in a jagged and hesitating manner, [and] frustrates expectations fed on 'finished' verse"; it is in "continual, if quiet, opposition to the whole conception of rhetorical completion" ("Anthologies" 256). DuPlessis notes how *Discrete Series* and "Of Being Numerous" have, because of the structure Oppen chooses for them, no means to achieve closure: "Both [series/poems] have no end sanctified by tradition or history; nor will a meaningful summary act show the ultimate purpose of each sequence. [Each] series is without an ultimate purpose beyond itself and the dilemmas to which it testifies" ("George Oppen" 72). If the parenthesis and the image of ongoing process ("Successive / Happenings / [the telephone]") with which *Discrete Series* ends were not evidence enough, a

1934 letter makes it clear that Oppen did not want a strong gesture of closure for the book; and "Of Being Numerous," he writes in another letter, "ends with retraction, question, fails, if that's failure, of a conclusion" (*Selected Letters* 372 n. 13; 160). DuPlessis puts the issue this way in a later description of "Of Being Numerous": "How amazing to have statements opening all over the poem like subatomic events happening. The accidents of perception not solidified to one form of matter but joined to each other by the force of occurring. To have that as structure without poems collapsing into drifts and fragments" ("On the Island" 114). This sense of structure overlaps with that evident in much of Creeley's work since the mid- to late 1960s. What Denise Levertov said of Oppen in 1963 has since become almost a cliché in Creeley criticism: "His poems are essentially of process, not tasteful art-objects" (27).[17]

Like Oppen also, Creeley puts a great deal of weight on the relational units or building blocks of language in his serial poems, on articles, prepositions, conjunctions. Key "little words" in *Pieces* are words like "here" and "there"—words that embody centuries of debate about the relationship between subject and object. Creeley uses the little words to meditate on this relationship: "Here I / am. There / you are" (*Collected Poems* 389). Creeley is drawn to attempt the poetry of presence that, at some point in their career, most Objectivists have aspired to: Charles Bernstein has explicitly linked Creeley and Oppen on this basis. As summarized by Burton Hatlen, an Objectivist poetics of presence assumes as its base the three famous imagist principles first laid out by Pound in the 1913 manifesto "A Few Don'ts." These principles assume in turn "that all the 'meanings' we need are already present in the things of this world"; "that language can render the immediacy of things accurately"; and that "language . . . can become translucent" ("Zukofsky" 66–67). These assumptions—or these hopes—show up in both Oppen and Creeley, though more so in the older poet. Oppen's emphasis on "moments of conviction" valorizes the present, the immediate. His most frequently quoted poem, "Psalm," celebrates the immediacy of the material world: "That they are there!" (*Collected Poems* 78). To conclude the fourth section of the sequence "Route," Oppen lays out this side of his poetics: "The purity of the materials, not theology, but to present the circumstances" (186). But to begin the section he has already asserted a conflicting pull: "Words cannot be wholly transparent" (186). Finally denying the transparency of even the most apparently straightforward statement, Oppen consistently draws attention to *how* he says something. "The simplest / Words say the grass blade / Hides the blaze / Of a sun / To throw a shadow / In which the bugs crawl / At the roots of the grass" (126)—those first four words mark the difference between a poetics of presence and a poetics concerned with the gap between the world and any statement made about it. Even Oppen's literalizing, superficially a trope of presence that promotes "direct treatment of the thing," paradoxically tends to highlight the circularity of language: "the present / Sun pours in the present" (54); "a child / Stands as a child" (63).

Similarly, Creeley, in his *Pieces* phase, wants to "present the circumstances," to write "Not from not / but in in," to show himself insistently "Here here / here. Here" (*Collected Poems* 388). "Inside / and out," he proposes in *Pieces*, are "impossible / locations" (380). As Charles Altieri puts it, Creeley "is trying in his use of terms like 'here' and 'the' to project the actual dynamic moment of apprehension, the field of energy exchange where self and world meet, before the encounter is translated into the irreconcilable terms of subject and object (the names of objects already imply the division of self and world)" ("Unsure Egoist" 184). This desire "to project the actual dynamic moment" by foregrounding the smallest units of language comes out in passages like the first stanza of " 'Follow the Drinking Gourd . . . ' "—"*Present again / present present / again present / present again*" (*Collected Poems* 392)—or in this passage:

> THE FIRST
> time is
> the first
> time. The
> second
> time think
> again. (433)

This projection of presence comes out in the smallest fragment, like "—it / it—" (391). Here the pronoun "it" is used to merge subject and object because grammatically it can function as either.

The Creeley of *Pieces* remains too self-reflexive a poet, however, to embrace a poetics of presence unambiguously. He knows that one is "never / only here" (391). And one site where both Creeley and Oppen play out issues of presence is the line. Oppen wrote in 1975 that "the purpose of prosody" is "the achievement of meaning and of *presence*"—following Duncan, "the feeling of presence, not concept" ("Statement" 27, 25). Yet his and Creeley's prosodies actually share a remarkable ability to enact both presence and the questioning of it. From one point of view, Creeley's non-lexical line breaks, the breaking of lines across words, and his minimalist line can all be seen to mark his moment-by-moment attentiveness to the act of writing. Similarly, Oppen's short (often one-word) lines, the gaps in his lines and page, his use of sentence fragments and lack of punctuation—techniques that pervade "Of Being Numerous," for instance, before the more radical fracturing of *Seascape: Needle's Eye* and *Primi-*

tive—draw attention to the care paid to the poem's, even the line's, construction. (Oppen, who produced his poems through a palimpsestic layering of alternative phrasings, employs much more of a constructivist aesthetic than Creeley, who claims to revise rarely.) In the context of discussing Williams, Burton Hatlen connects such a disjunctive prosody with claims to presence, arguing that "Williams's characteristic syntactic dislocations . . . force us to apprehend the poem phrase by phrase," that "through the line and stanza breaks and the (sometimes parallel, sometimes counterpointed) rhythmic and syntactic shifts, Williams holds our (and his) attention close to the sensory particulars" ("Zukofsky" 69).

Creeley's and Oppen's prosody, however, foregrounds or renders present the materiality of language as much as that of the world. In Zukofsky's well-known term, the Objectivist "particulars" that Creeley cares for are particulars of sound and syntax rather than of sight. Charles Bernstein similarly argues that Oppen's prosody—and here I would extend the point to Creeley—conflicts with, rather than reinforces, the ambition to write a poetry of presence. Thus Oppen's "use of the line break as *hinge*" (and "the typical Oppen hinge is made by starting a line break with a preposition, commonly 'Of' "), in its "insistence on the constructedness of syntax, the manipulation of words to create rather than describe," conflicts with his commitments to transparency and clarity ("Hinge" 240–41).[18] In Oppen, then, prosodic means for refusing fluency reinforce what I called earlier his calculated discontinuity. Meanwhile, in *Pieces,* the disjunctively broken short line that, like a poorly tuned car, "coughing moves with / a jerked energy forward" (*Collected Poems* 383) works against any unreflective immersion in poetic process. In one *Pieces* poem, Creeley writes

> Don't say it doesn't rhyme
> if you won't read it—nor break the
>
> line in pieces that goes
> and goes and goes. (*Collected Poems* 430)

Characteristically, in the moment that Creeley asks his reader to honor this book's seriality, not to "break the line" in *Pieces* "that goes / and goes," he disrupts his own injunction by separating article and noun across a line and stanza break. The poem's prosody contradicts its content; for Creeley, a commitment to process does not equate with any kind of organic seamlessness of effect.

Even what Ron Silliman calls "first phase Objectivism" ("Third Phase" 85)—represented by the early work of Oppen, Zukofsky, Reznikoff, Rakosi, and

Niedecker—contains the seeds of a slow growth away from a poetics of presence. This growth can be seen in Oppen's career in the shift from the more presentational *Discrete Series* to the more philosophically self-conscious later work. As many of his critics have noticed, if the typical Oppen poem contains vestiges of imagist principles, nevertheless it moves toward thought rather than toward things. The same is true of Creeley. Hence Laszlo Géfin links Oppen and Creeley on a different, although not contradictory, basis from Bernstein, as the two poets in the Objectivist tradition "for whom language itself posed enormous problems" (63). Creeley's worrying over particles of language, which often seizes vividly an instant of perception, just as often serves to highlight the artificiality of language. The inherent metaphoricity of words, their power to turn something into what it is not, the use of verb tenses to compartmentalize time—all these features of language work against the early Objectivist ideal of a poetics of presence. Creeley knows this; so did Oppen.

Pieces features this poem:

> The sun will set again on
> the edge of the sky or whatever
>
> you want to call it. *Out there,*
> not here, the sun 'will set,
>
> did set, is *now* setting.'
> Hear, goddamnit, hear. (*Collected Poems* 429)

The italics of "*out there*" and "*now,*" and the irritable "goddamnit, hear" show merely that the poet doth protest too much, aware that "hear" is "not here" and that he finds himself drawn not to the traditional visual account of sunset but to a grammatical account, the process of sunset as a conjugation of verb tenses. Equally revealing is the self-consciousness of "the edge of the sky or whatever // you want to call it," invoking the word "horizon" by pointing to its absence, a distancing trope akin to Oppen's "the simplest / Words say the grass blade / Hides the blaze / Of a sun." Such wrestling with the conflicting claims of presence and absence in Creeley constitutes perhaps his most important advance on Objectivist poetics, because it provides a bridge between the older Objectivists like Oppen and younger writers like the Language poets, for whom the workings of the language system are a central concern and who have often pursued this concern via experiments in longer or serial forms. Poets such as Charles Bernstein, Robert Grenier, Bruce Andrews, Ron Silliman, and Bob Perelman, as well as Taggart and DuPlessis, have written perceptively and sympathetically on both Creeley and the Objectivists, especially on Zukofsky and/or Oppen. I take my conclusion, however, from Oppen, commenting in a letter to his great-niece Eve Haight on the processual poetics that he and Creeley share: "I'm planning to show you Robert Creeley's remark: 'the possible is more important than the perfect'" (*Selected Letters* 201)—a remark that encapsulates the shift from a high modernist ("the perfect") to a postmodernist ("the possible") poetics.[19] One premise underlying the serial experiments of Oppen, Creeley, and those who have followed them is surely this: that the possible *is* more important than the perfect.

II
Politics, Class, and Ideology

5

Communists and Objectivists

Eric Homberger

Cultural and political changes are transforming the very terms within which we read the Objectivists. The fall of the Communist powers undoubtedly alters the way we think of the relationship between these writers and the Communist Party in the United States. Throughout much of their creative lives, the party was an unavoidable presence, a continuous reminder that there *were* political choices to be made. With a vestigial cultural Left in the 1990s struggling to redefine itself on the new terrains of race, gender, and sexuality, no such large choices are demanded of writers today. The politics of Objectivism is a minor issue at best in the concerns of those critics who have sponsored the revival of interest in their work since the 1960s. For readers in the 1930s, that the Objectivists were antifascists mattered a great deal; rather less so today. Their relationship to Jewishness, and to the Jewish worlds within which they were raised, were complicated and somewhat submerged issues in the 1930s. Paradoxically, the ethnicity and Jewishness of the Objectivists remain largely unexplored. What detached the Objectivists from their tribal Jewishness (Reznikoff is an exception) was also what kept them spectators on the margins of the Communist Party. That style of detachment, bitterly resented in the 1930s, has a wider currency today. Perhaps it is the ethnicity of the Objectivists, and not their politics, which will be the way we make them comprehensible in our climate.[1]

I

In his memoirs, Alfred Stieglitz recalled a meeting with Bill Haywood, the tall, burly leader of the Wobblies who had died in Russia in 1928, a revolutionary exile from the American class struggle. Haywood had known many New York writers and artists, but did not share their interests or regard them as serious allies. On his visit to Stieglitz's 291 Gallery in New York City, he asked the photographer why a big man like Stieglitz was wasting his time in such a "dinky little place." "I don't believe," he said, "the artist will ever win the fight for what we're after." Why not "leave this place and join the real fight"? Stieglitz's reply was carefully measured: "Mr. Heywood [*sic*], I don't believe you understand. You don't believe that my way is the way. You believe that your way is the only way. . . . When the day arrives and what you are doing proves to be true and what I am attempting to do proves to be equally true we'll be standing shoulder to shoulder wherever we meet" (137). Until then, however, there was nothing more to say. Haywood shook his head. "Too bad," he said, walking out of the gallery.

Margaret Anderson described an even more disastrous meeting in her autobiography. She had long looked forward to introducing her friend and assistant on the *Little Review*, Jane Heap, to the renowned anarchists Emma Goldman and Alexander Berkman in the hope that they would find Heap to be an incentive "toward their clearer thinking."[2] When they finally met, Heap teased Goldman and playfully appealed to Berkman for sympathy. This subsequently produced an indignant complaint by Goldman about Heap's aggressiveness. When they met a day later, they argued bitterly about art:

> They had tried to maintain that "The Ballad of Reading Gaol" was better art than "Salomé." When I used the black swan in Amy Lowell's "Malmaison" to illustrate a certain way of pointing emotion there was a general uprising. E. G. was a little beside herself.
>
> The working-man hasn't enough leisure to be interested in black swans she thundered. What's that got to do with revolution? . . . If only a few people understand the art you talk about that's proof that it's not for humanity, said Berkman. (*My Thirty Years' War* 119, 125–27)

Anderson and Heap were hardly to be persuaded by the earnest, ethical artistic ideas of the anarchists. As word of this meeting filtered into the pages of the *Little Review*, an unexpected consequence was a bitter exchange between Upton Sinclair and Margaret Anderson that succinctly captured the spirit of the uneasy relations between radicals and the avant-garde in the 1920s. Sinclair began by canceling an exchange of issues between the two periodicals: "I no longer understand anything in it, so it no longer interests me." Anderson brusquely replied: "Please cease sending me your socialist paper. I understand everything in it, therefore it no longer interests me" (*My Thirty Years' War* 128).

In the 1920s, relations between the Left and the artistic avant-garde were few and uneasy. The sole common ground was found in the American enthusiasm for the futurist poets, stage designers, filmmakers, and painters whose work stirred the imagination of left-wing visitors to the Soviet Union. Michael Gold came back from the Soviet Union in 1924 with news of the dazzling productions of the Workers' Art Theatre in Moscow. He argued that a similar theater was needed in New York, where revolutionary plays could be staged. Em Jo Basshe, John Howard Lawson, and John Dos Passos were drawn into the enterprise, eventually called the New Playwright's Theatre.[3] Gold also brought word to New York radicals of the Proletcult, and of the Soviet debate about proletarian art (Gold, 1921). For a brief period while the New Playwright's Theatre was staging the plays of Dos Passos, Gold, and Sinclair, and when the same group launched *New Masses* in 1926, there was hope that radical literary and theatrical practice and revolutionary politics were working together. But the moment of promise was stillborn. The visual style of left-wing magazines changed sharply in the late 1920s. Modernist styles were weeded out. The constructivist-inspired designs which appeared in early issues of *New Masses* were replaced by more representational images that were considered to be more accessible, less "arty." The spirit of antifascist art was clear, didactic, rough-hewn, and aggressively masculine—the very antithesis of the visually complex and nuanced radical modernist art of the 1920s (Whiting 25–29).

Within the notoriously humorless Communist Party, and on the American Left as a whole, bourgeois culture was viewed with contempt. The atmosphere within the party was frankly and aggressively philistine, and the prickly talents drawn to Communist parties in Europe (Toller, Piscator, Barbusse, Becher, Grosz, Mayakovski) had no American equivalents. The further one penetrated into the sectarian heart of the American Left, the more emphatic were the attitudes of Bill Haywood, dismissing literature as a waste of time, a pointless indulgence. In the aftermath of the executions of Sacco and Vanzetti and the 1926 textile strike in Passaic, New Jersey, younger radicals and intellectuals were drawing closer to the party. But they were faced with the awkward need to defend art among their party comrades, while simultaneously defending the need for a commitment to revolutionary politics among their literary acquaintances (Freeman, *American Testament* 392–95).

The most sensitive among party members to the dilemma of the poet in a worker's movement was Joseph Freeman. When Freeman—of bourgeois background and educated at Columbia University—gave lectures and readings on Eliot and Pound to workers at the Rand School[4] in New York, he found that they "fidgeted in their seats and looked out the windows." "The matter was as painful as it was simple," he wrote in *An American Testament.* "The creator of

Apeneck Sweeney was a barrier between the workers in my class and myself. The barrier must be destroyed" (240). Freeman believed that the man of letters should enter fully into the educational activities of the party. But the price he paid for commitment was a division in his sensibility. He published delicate, romantic verse in the *Liberator,* celebrating morning light, and the presence beside him of

> my love asleep
> Still a meditation; her dear head
> Lost in the dark releases of her hair ("Love at Dawn")

But when he tried to use certain kinds of political experience, the results were poetically deadening:

> Beat, drums of the world!
> let the workers storm from the factories,
> the peasants from the farms;
> sweep the earth clean of this nightmare,
> build new cities, a new world,
> ringing with the clear voices of new men! ("Four Poems" 46)

By the late 1920s Freeman grew increasingly unhappy with his earlier romantic and introspective poems. But the alternative, with its urgent gestural beating of drums and waving banners, embodying the dream of a proletarian uprising and revolution, did nothing to lower the barriers between workers and modern literature. His career as a poet, and the course of *New Masses,* which he edited for substantial periods from its founding in 1926, raises important questions about whether it was possible to be a "modern" poet and a Communist. This is not quite the same issue that Cary Nelson addresses in *Repression and Recovery,* about the rich diversity of poetic practices that have been forgotten under the pressure of the overriding view that radical poetry was "always formally conservative, thematically monochromatic, and rhetorically wooden" (102). The point is not that there are interesting poems written from a vaguely defined Left or radical perspective in American culture. Nelson makes that point quite strongly. But if we turn this argument on its head and look at the dilemmas faced by specific poets (Oppen) or groups (Objectivists) when confronted by the shifting and contradictory demands of the Communist Party and its cultural organs, the frustrating and destructive force of those demands is unmistakable.

The changes in political line, and rapid shifts in the mood of John Reed Club writers, dismayed people like Gold and Freeman who in the late 1920s had sought to radicalize *New Masses.* By 1931 Gold complained to Upton Sinclair of the youthful sectarians who were increasingly dominating the John Reed Clubs and who were trying to take over *New Masses* as well. They seemed to Gold nothing more than bourgeois college boys, who within months of turning Left began to patronize real revolutionaries and hunt heresies.[5] Freeman also felt that he was waging a lonely battle against "vulgar" Marxist literary criticism, and unsuccessfully tried to return *New Masses* to a more serious intellectual level in 1932 (Freeman, "Ivory Towers"). He encountered a range of opposition on the Left to "seriousness": from writers, who were hoping that the magazine would devote more space to creative work and less to polemics about proletarian literature (Jack Conroy, letter to V. J. Jerome, 2 August 1933), to leftists, who despaired of the compromises required of a revolutionary movement to bring bourgeois intellectuals into the party. Perhaps it was as much a problem with tone as of content. The division within the Communist Party between roughnecks and bureaucrats, theoreticians and organizers, remained a source of tension. Conflicts over the "correct line" were always more visible, but the inner life of the party was no less riven by considerations of style and carefully masked ethnic divisions. Jews in the party knew they were the constant object of ethnic and racial stereotyping. In 1932 Edmund Wilson attended a meeting of the League of Professional Groups, and noted rather nastily in his diary that there were only two Gentiles present, and that Jews seem to "love excluding people, asserting moral superiority (Communism, psychoanalysis)" (Wilson 339, cf. 379).

Against this climate, the publication of Jack Conroy's and Ralph Cheyney's *Rebel Poets* anthologies in 1929 and 1930 was frankly anachronistic. The dominant theme (and title) of both anthologies was "unrest": poems were included that satirized bourgeois manners, upper-class pretension, and hedonistic college life. There was nothing particularly Marxist about poems on strikes, racial discrimination, or unemployment; indeed, Upton Sinclair's *The Cry for Justice* (1915) contained 880 pages of similar material. But in the changing literary climate on the American Left, younger writers drawn to the John Reed Clubs were encouraged to write in a more overtly political manner. In the aftermath of the collapse of the stock market in 1929, Edmund Wilson articulated the need for writers to take sides. To earn their place within the Communist literary movement after the Kharkov conference of the International Union of Revolutionary Writers in 1930, a harder, more programmatic opposition to capitalism and imperialism was demanded, as was a more direct commitment to put literature at the service of the class struggle. Freeman's inner division between romantic poet and political activist was resolved; politics won. The John Reed Clubs were designed to ease the struggle and assure the outcome. "The poet who is making his beginnings now," wrote Isidor Schneider in 1934, "is to be envied. He does not have to remake himself as does the older poet" (42).

Schneider's assumption that the revolutionary poet was a "he" was near-universal in 1930s writing. The new Communist writer was much more aggressively masculine than the fun-loving, witty Greenwich Village radicals of the old *Masses.* While the subjection of women was universally scorned on the Left as a last vestige of capitalist and imperialist exploitation, women were without much premeditation ignored while men got on with the serious business of planning the literary revolution. After being excluded from a boozy meeting in the summer of 1931 between her husband (John Hermann), Malcolm Cowley, Edmund Wilson, and other writers, Josephine Herbst wrote to Katherine Anne Porter, "I told Mister [John] Herrmann that as long as the gents had bourgeois reactions to women they would probably never rise very high in their revolutionary conversations but said remarks rolled off like water" (Langer 120). The meetings in 1929 and 1930 between Oppen and Zukofsky, out of which Objectivism emerged, did not include Mary Oppen. Unlike Josie Herbst, she was not indignant at this exclusion.

The most interesting expression of the new mood was *We Gather Strength,* an anthology published in 1933 of poems by Herman Spector, Joseph Kalar, Edwin Rolfe, and Sol Funaroff. There is a hint here, though no more than a hint, of the Popular Front and the 1930s enthusiasm for Soviet industrial achievements (the collection drew its title from Funaroff's "Dneiprostroi"). Rolfe's "Homage to Karl Marx" identified a new cultural hero, as did Langston Hughes's "Ballad of Lenin," another act of cultural identification with Lenin and the Soviet Union, published in the *Daily Worker* on 20 January 1934.[6] There is a pastiche of Eliotian techniques and imagery in Funaroff's "What the Thunder Said: A Fire Sermon." Despite the presence of social protest clichés, of crimson banners "flying in the wind," none of the poems in *We Gather Strength* rhymes, and there are no sonnets; free verse and "modern" imagery are the order of the day:

> within these urban angularities
> and geometric patterns of despair
> the flowing lines of music trace
> emotions in sinuous, vague curves through garbage-air

> and a squat guy in a straw hat passing
> flips a stub of cigarette to the street . . . (Spector, "Saturday Eve, East Side" [16])

Within what is often a mechanical use of left-wing imagery, there is occasionally a despairing urgency:

> This is our land, we planted its first seed!
> These are our mines, our hands dig the coal!
> These roads are ours, the wires across the land
> are ours! THIS IS OUR EARTH! (Rolfe, "Kentucky—1932" [44])

More fastidious literary consciences might indeed be moved by the strike in Harlan County, Kentucky, and want to join Rolfe's cry. But there was a more persuasive master, William Carlos Williams, who urged a different tack in "Spring and All": "One by one objects are defined." The massive acts of appropriation in the Rolfe poem were more immediately satisfying than the modest suggestion of Williams that "so much depends" upon the seeing of a red wheelbarrow. But it would take a megaphone-art akin to Mayakovski's to make it work. As poetry, Rolfe is scarcely using the medium. Williams had much to teach the younger poets. His example and influence extended widely, his combination of powerful social criticism and a spare, disciplined technique strongly attracting the younger poets. The *We Gather Strength* poets were alive to the achievement of modern American poetry. Michael Gold was convinced that the book represented something new within the culture of the American Left: in the past, he wrote in its introduction, "in our revolutionary movement only doggerel has been esteemed" (7).

Many of the leading Objectivists were either sympathizers or actively engaged in left-wing politics. Yet their literary efforts were rebuffed by the Communist literary establishment, and contemptuously dismissed by roughnecks like Herman Spector, whose review of two volumes by Reznikoff in *Dynamo* in 1934 was essentially a political argument against Objectivism:

> Charles Reznikoff expresses in his poetry the limited world-view of a "detached" bystander: that is, of a person whose flashes of perception for the immediate esthetics of the contemporary scene are not so co-ordinated in any way with a dialectical comprehension of the life-process. . . . The fatal defect of the Objectivist theory is that it identifies life with capitalism, and so assumes that the world is merely a waste land. The logical

> consequence is a fruitless negativism. . . . Impartiality is a myth which defeatists take with them into oblivion. (Spector 104–5)

"Objectivism" was one of the many failings of which Henri Barbusse's journal, *Monde,* was accused at the Kharkov congress of the International Union of Revolutionary Writers in 1930: "*Monde* . . . should have regarded all the phenomena of the surrounding bourgeois life from the class point of view, this being the only attitude to take towards the objective world at the present historical stage; from the standpoint, that is, of the proletariat armed scientifically with dialectical materialism. Its objectivism should have been the 'objectivism of the class struggle' (Lenin)" ("Resolution" 105). On the Left the term "Objectivist" was a damaging confession of neutrality. Zukofsky was aware of this. He replied in the May 1933 issue of *Poetry* to Morris Schappes's cutting review (in March 1933) of *An "Objectivists" Anthology,* quoting a passage from Lenin's *Left-Wing Communism—An Infantile Disorder* on the need for a "strictly objective estimate of all the class forces and their inter-relation in every political action."[7] Zukofsky further stated that Lenin's perspective "is the concern of the editorial presentation and the poetry" of the anthology ("Objectivists Again" 117). Many of the poems are particularly "social" (especially Williams's "The pure products of America . . . "); or "historical" (Williams's "It is living coral . . . " and Reznikoff's "The English in Virginia"); Zukofsky's *"A"* contains a passage which, in the Poundian mode, undoubtedly registers a range of urgent contemporary concerns: strikes, unemployment, trade with the Soviet Union, social conflict:

> A country of state roads and automobiles,
> the great numbers idle, shiftless, disguised on streets—
> The excuse of the experts
> 'Production exceeds demand so we curtail employment';
> And the Wobblies hollering reply,
> Yeh, but why don't you give us more than a meal to increase the
> consumption! (*"A"* 5)

Schappes noted Zukofsky's content, but complained that "there is no coherence, no organization, *no direction* in this long but still incomplete poem" (342), which he likened to a nihilistic protest against the poet's isolation in a capitalistic and materialistic society. "The intelligent alternative . . . is completely to stride beyond these premises of the bourgeoisie: that is, to ally oneself with the revolutionary proletariat" (343).

As voters and citizens, as people deeply concerned about the casualties of the depression, the Objectivists desired to ally themselves with the people. That well-known poet "Louis Zukonski" [*sic*] was reported in the *Daily Worker* of 2 July 1937 to have been elected by the Middle Atlantic Division of the League of American Writers to an official committee to organize support for striking steelworkers. Reznikoff published a poem dedicated to the martyred socialists of Vienna in *Separate Way* (1936). Zukofsky and Carl Rakosi appear in *Writers Take Sides* (League of American Writers, 1938) favoring the Loyalist cause in Spain. But as poets, such is the paradox of their dilemma, they had far more to learn from writers like Pound, whose anti-Semitism and admiration for Italian fascism deepened in the 1930s, and "nationalist" liberal democrats like Williams, than from the Aragon of "The Red Front," the model suggested by Schappes (343) and often cited as a model for left-wing writing.

When Williams reviewed *An "Objectivists" Anthology* in the *Symposium* in 1933, he saw the absence of a connecting link between the "flashes of perception" and the meaning of such perceptions as "the presentation, simply, of certain new objects without obvious connection with the classics and which he [the Objectivist poet] entitles 'poems'" (114). Williams goes on to suggest that paradoxically the perception of the newness of the new affirms the "continued existence of the old" (115). At the end of the review he suggests another definition of the term "Objectivist": "they are successfully displayed to hold an objective view of poetry which, in a certain way, clarifies it, showing it to be not a seductive arrangement of scenes, sounds and colors so much as a construction each part of which has a direct bearing on its meaning as a whole, an objectification of significant particulars" (117). The "political" meaning of Objectivism kept the poets and the Communist Party at arm's length.

Spector's criticism of the "detached bystander" aspect of Reznikoff's poetry is well judged, though for Reznikoff detachment was a complex aesthetic and psychological statement of the man himself. Reznikoff's *Testimony*, in the prose version that appeared in *An "Objectivists" Anthology* and which Spector reviewed, was not a politically committed work in any obvious sense. It embodied a conception of art as the expression of a subtle and intense humanism; an art, in other words, for which the megaphone and crimson banner were less than useless. It is true that, for a variety of reasons, Reznikoff shied away from the crude assertion of "meaning" in his poems. Spector and other left-wing critics of the 1930s were asking whether, in a world threatened by fascism and in which millions were unemployed, it was enough merely to see (however clearly) what Oppen called the "Round / Shiny fixed / Alternatives" (*Collected Poems* 3), as one would see a red wheelbarrow, or "the senseless / unarrangement of wild things" (Williams in Zukofsky, *An "Objectivists" Anthology* 103), but not feel called upon to take a stand on larger public issues of the day. Critics on the Left were asking important questions about Objectivism; but they scarcely waited for an answer.

II

George Oppen's first book of poems, *Discrete Series,* was published in 1934 by the Objectivist Press, a cooperative that emerged out of the commercial failure of his To Publishers. As Oppen explained in a letter to Charles Tomlinson, the problems they faced in printing in France and importing the titles into the United States were legion: "Paper-backs were new to the US, and encountered trouble with the US Customs and . . . the men on the pier, and the men in the book stores. Both of whom said they were not books. The book stores simply would not stock them, or most would not" (*Selected Letters* 83). Without salesmen or editors, it was more a form of highbrow vanity publishing: "Each man," Oppen wrote to L. S. Dembo, "simply emerged with his own book—No sales machinery if I remember—If there was, Rezi [Reznikoff] must have handled it" (*Selected Letters* 202). Each volume carried on the dust jacket the statement that "The Objectivist Press is an organization of poets publishing their own work and that of others which they think ought to be read." Objectivist Press titles did not much distract American readers from their usual interests. Nonetheless, the voice of the Objectivists belongs to the cultural moment of the mid-1930s, when the proletarian literary scene was in high gear. There were novels in 1934 by Cantwell, Dahlberg, Farrell, Frank, Halper, and Herbst. It was the year of Kenneth Burke's "My Approach to Communism" and Philip Rahv's modest declaration that he hoped to become "an intellectual assistant of the proletariat."[8] John Strachey's *Literature and Dialectical Materialism* and Stanley Burnshaw's "Notes on Revolutionary Poetry" were published, and the *Partisan Review* was founded. The "Call" went out for the League of American Writers. Henry Roth's *Call It Sleep* was published in December 1934—and was favorably reviewed in *New Masses.*

Oppen's slender book did not make much of an impression on bourgeois critics. William Rose Benet thought that Oppen's writing was like "listening to a man with an impediment in his speech." Williams took the occasion of his review of *Discrete Series* in 1934 to make an important statement about art and revolution:

> An imaginable new social order would require a skeleton of severe discipline for its realization and maintenance. Thus by a sharp restriction to essentials, the seriousness of a new order is brought to realization. Poetry might turn this condition to its own ends. Only by being an object

> sharply defined and without redundancy will its form project whatever meaning is required of it. It could well be, at the same time, first and last a poem facing as it must the dialectic necessities of its day. Oppen has carried this social necessity, so far as poetry may be concerned, to an extreme. ("New Poetical Economy" 223–24)

In seeking to use the language of the party, and its preferred self-image ("severe discipline," "essentials," "seriousness," "dialectic necessities"), Williams sought to open a space for what *he* regards as "serious" poetry. The argument is striking, for it is one of the high-water marks of Williams's modest rapprochement with the Left (Weaver).[9] To look at Edwin Rolfe's "Kentucky—1932" through Williams's eyes is to see how little it achieves sharp definition, form without redundancy. Its effects are achieved at the cost of a blurring of perception, for only thus would we miss the way it is caught up in a web of clichés and unrealized social emotion. *Discrete Series* represents precisely the "sharp restriction to essentials" which Williams indicates. If anything, those essentials, those images through which Oppen works, are too spare. He describes people in a theater removing their coats and sitting down as a "semaphoring chorus." In another poem, a social portrait (reminiscent of things in Pound's *Lustra*) turns upon a single word, "Pertain," and its elusive connotation: "Your breasts / Pertain to lingerie." *Discrete Series* omits the explanations that we have come to expect from poetry. A point that Williams made in his review of *An "Objectivists" Anthology* provides us with an essential term: "These pieces, these lines, these words, neither are they fragments but their power is cumulative[,] rather in tension than in story." By *story* Williams identified what Spector felt was missing from Objectivism: the connections and explanations that would have clarified and asserted the meanings of the things seen. Oppen, who knew the imagist poets, has never felt the need to thicken the outline of the sharply defined object. The hunger for narrative has seldom seemed among Oppen's strongest passions. What unites the fragments in the end, and what is so truly humane about Oppen, is a tone of voice, an achieved person speaking to others clearly and honestly. "Perhaps what I would like is a truly democratic culture," he wrote to friends in 1962: "Not a polemic nor a moralistic culture in the arts but a culture which permits one man to speak to another honestly and modestly and in freedom and to say what he thinks and what he feels, to express his doubts and his fears, his immoral as well as his moral impulses, to say what he thinks is true and what he thinks is false, and what he likes and what he does not like. What I am against is that we should all engage in the most vigorous and most polemic lying for each other's benefit" (*Selected Letters* 64).

Oppen is a poet of estrangement, and his language is rich with layers of allusion to the historical experience of the Jews, of his own relations to Jewishness, and of his own alienation from that world and his family. "O rage / Of the exile," he wrote in "Of Hours" (*Seascape* 16).

> We cannot reconcile ourselves.
> No one is reconciled, tho we spring
> From the ground together— (*Materials* 10)

We know too little of his life to fully address the personal and spiritual meaning of estrangement as he experienced it. We may fall back upon a secondary meaning, his sense of writing in a society in which the connections, explanations, and stories had been corrupted, distorted, mystified, inevitably turned into the crude, masked force of ideology. The only escape available to a writer, the only sanity, lay in the struggle

> to redeem
> Fragments and fragmentary
> Histories in the towns and the temperate streets (*Seascape* 34)

The language of Kabbalah and of Jewish mysticism is similarly filled with the world as a place of fragments and redemption. Meaning in *Discrete Series,* the links between "fragments," can no longer be confidently asserted (as Spector thought) as a matter of "dialectical comprehension." In the face of a comprehensive and radical epistemological uncertainty, Oppen sought an art free from the smothering cloud of anecdote and story which envelops our culture.

He found no place in the left-wing literary movement of the 1930s, which was an ironic blessing. He had nothing to repent when repentance was in season. Mary Oppen describes the fate of *Discrete Series* in two sentences: "The Gotham Book Mart bought some of the books; very few were sold, and the rest were stored. Politics were dominant and danger was imminent" (146).

III

The Objectivists had been summoned into existence by Louis Zukofsky, who, for a brief, fertile moment in the early 1930s brought together Charles Reznikoff, George Oppen, and Carl Rakosi. Although in later years there was precious little agreement about what they had collectively sought to do, it is possible to return to contemporary documentation to trace the evolution of the group, and to suggest the place of the Objectivists in American letters.

Reznikoff, the oldest of the four, was born in New York in 1894. His parents were recent immigrants from the Jewish Pale of Settlement in Russia. By 1918 he was a published poet. Rakosi grew up in Kenosha, Wisconsin. His poems began to appear in *New Masses* in 1926, and in other little magazines at the end of the decade. Rakosi worked in the Midwest as a psychotherapist, and was the outsider of the group. Zukofsky was born in New York in 1904 of recent immigrant stock. Oppen, born in New Rochelle, New York, in 1908, came from a prosperous, long-established German Jewish family. His was "a childhood [which was] nurse-maided, butlered, chauffered." He knew no Yiddish, and possessed only a minimum of German: these linguistic disadvantages were signs of a successful, assimilated German-Jewish family in America before the 1930s (Oppen, *Selected Letters* 127–28, 276).

The Objectivists, then, were urban Jews, but not necessarily the same kind of Jews. The milieu of Oppen's early years resembled that of Howard Nemerov and his sister, Diane Arbus, whose father presided over Russeks, a leading Manhattan store, and whose domestic establishment was one of butlers, nannies, limousines, and vacations in Palm Beach (Bosworth 1–64). The parents of Budd Schulberg belonged to that same New York, Jewish world of wealth and assimilation. Before moving to Hollywood in the early 1920s, B. P. Schulberg was a leading figure in Adolph Zukor's Famous Players Film Company (Schulberg). Jewishness for such families was increasingly little more than a background to the large, glittering promise of wealth in America.

Nonetheless, the Jewish passion for education was a great unifying force in the lives of the Objectivists. As Reznikoff describes in *Family Chronicle,* his parents were uneducated, but they sent their eldest son to Cornell Medical School. Charles studied journalism at the University of Missouri, and took a law degree. Zukofsky's parents lived on Chrystie Street in the Lower East Side. (Mike Gold's family lived on the same street, though the two did not meet until they were adults.) He studied at Columbia University, and taught briefly at the University of Wisconsin at Madison. Oppen attended Oregon State University in Corvallis, but did not take a degree. Rakosi studied English, psychology, and social work at a string of universities in Chicago, Wisconsin, Pennsylvania, and Texas.[10] With the exception of Rakosi, who had professional training, they remained in social terms marginal men: Reznikoff did not practice law; Zukofsky had various irregular teaching appointments; Oppen became a political organizer among the unemployed in Brooklyn, and then a cabinetmaker; Reznikoff worked for many years in Zionist journalism. The Objectivists learned that they could not sustain themselves as writers. Poetry had to be squeezed in between other calls upon their nervous energy. The public response to their work was one of indifference or hostility, and it is hardly surprising that their literary careers were deformed or broken. For most of his life Reznikoff was forced to print and publish his verse on a small press that he stored in his sister's home in Brooklyn. Zukofsky "published" a mimeographed edition (fifty-five copies) of *First Half of "A"-9* in 1940. He had not exhausted that modest edition by 1958 (Quartermain, *Disjunctive Poetics* 70). Rakosi did not publish a volume until he was thirty-seven, the slight *Selected Poems* of 1941. It was followed by another small book, and then silence until *Amulet* in 1967. He had ceased to write, and was believed by his publishers to have died. Oppen, too, ceased to write when he became more directly involved in politics. "I did not write 'Marxist' poetry. I made a choice. Stopped for the crisis, writing" (*Selected Letters* 277). After *Discrete Series* in 1934, his next book, *The Materials,* did not appear until 1962: this was long enough to have been forgotten twice over. Zukofsky was the least fortunate in the publication of his work. His poems appeared infrequently in little magazines from the late 1920s, but he was not published in a trade edition until the 1960s. That was rectified in a great burst between 1965 and 1970, but reference books and critical studies of the period can take up to a decade to notice such a rediscovery. Sometimes they never do take notice. The Objectivists appear, individually or collectively, in few of the numerous books on American poetry.[11] They remain marginal as writers.

The Objectivists had their heroes, godfathers, patrons, and masters in Rutherford, New Jersey (William Carlos Williams), and in Rapallo, Italy (Ezra Pound). Never slow to encourage potential protégés, Pound printed a long poem by Zukofsky in the third number of *Exile* in 1928 and alerted Williams to the existence of a promising young poet in New York. Williams invited Zukofsky to visit him in Rutherford, and a fruitful relationship followed (Williams, *Selected Letters* 93). They exchanged manuscripts and commented upon each other's work. Zukofsky became, in the words of Williams's biographer, a "significant force" in the older poet's life (Whittemore 239–40).

Zukofsky's relations with Pound were more troubled.[12] Pound set his protégé Emanuel Carnevali to translate Zukofsky's review of *The Cantos* for *L'Indice* (April–May 1931); he also encouraged Eliot to publish the same essay in the *Criterion;* and urged Basil Bunting, who was then living in Italy as Pound's amanuensis, to make contact with Zukofsky. Bunting sent his manuscript poems to Zukofsky: "Zukofsky . . . went through poems I sent him very meticulously, word by word, making suggestions here, fierce strictures there and sometimes recommending the wastepaper basket. (He would also sometimes express enthusiasm for particular lines or passages.) This he did when, as in the early thirties, I think his admiration for my work was very tepid indeed" (Bunting, "Pound and 'Zuk'" 373). In addition, in 1930 Pound suggested Zukofsky to Harriet Monroe, the editor of *Poetry,* as a suitable guest editor of an issue devoted to the younger poets: "Waal, waal, my deah Harriet, I sho iz glad to let these young scrubs have the show to their selves, an ah does hope they dust out your office, My only fear is that Mr. Zukofsky will be just too Goddam prewdent" (*Letters* 307). As Pound's support became more unmistakable, other potential protégés sought to undermine Zukofsky's position. The rivalry for Pound's favor in the 1930s made sensible poets bitchy. The prize seemed so remote, so valuable (Pound and Laughlin 3). Who else could hand to an unknown poet control of an issue of *Poetry?*

The Objectivists assumed a public identity with the February 1931 issue of *Poetry,* but we need to complete the story of the formation of the group. Zukofsky met George and Mary Oppen at a party in New York in the winter of 1928–29, not long after they had returned from France (Mary Oppen 85; Oppen, *Selected Letters* 82). They lived in Columbia Heights; Zukofsky lived nearby, on Willow Street. "I would usually get sleepy and go to bed," Mary Oppen recalled, "and George and Louis would go on talking, and then Louis would have to go teach the next morning so they'd go home and George would walk him over and they would have coffee, and then Louis would walk George back home and they would go on and on and on" (Hatlen, *George Oppen* 43). Zukofsky was writing an essay on Pound and looking for American material for Pound's magazine, the *Exile.* He wrote to Pound on 6 March 1930 about Oppen's poems; he also showed the typescript, which was published in 1934 as *Discrete Series,* to Charles Reznikoff, and took Oppen to meet Reznikoff near the latter's law office in Brooklyn. "We met in the neighborhood of the office at a cafeteria," Reznikoff wrote, "and talked about verse and our respect for what Ezra Pound had written about writing verse" (Reznikoff, "A Memoir" 29). By January 1930 Oppen and Zukofsky were planning some sort of publishing venture. Zukofsky would assume editorial responsibility, from Madison, where he went to teach; the Oppens, who planned to return to France, would find a good cheap printer and superintend the actual production of the books. Other possibilities were also emerging. Zukofsky informed Pound in 1930 that Reznikoff had a small press. "In any kuntry but Murka," Pound wrote to Williams, "this wd. solve a lot of problems" (*Letters* 305). The Oppens traveled to Rapallo to meet Pound, but relations were uneasy; here, too, Mary Oppen was unwelcome. In the court of Pound, other men's wives, rival centers of attraction, were unwelcome.

Carl Rakosi, who had also been published by Pound in *Exile,* met Zukofsky at the University of Wisconsin in 1930–31. Pound was behind their first meeting, writing to Zukofsky on 25 October 1930: "I am glad you asked about Rakosi. The chap was feelin blue as a sambohillbo in his last letter, I wudnt be sprised if he shot himself. If he is still at Kenosha, you cd. establish personal vivavoce" (*Pound/Zukofsky* 53). Thus the basic connections were formed. Pound was the patron and instigator; Zukofsky the fulcrum and *animateur;* Oppen had a little money; Rakosi contributed poems; and Reznikoff had a small press, a little money, and some practical business experience.

Williams provided the Objectivists with a name and a theory of the poem. With Oppen and Reznikoff at Zukofsky's apartment in Brooklyn Heights, Williams elaborated the basic notion of what the Objectivists were seeking:

> But, we argued, the poem, like every other form of art, is an object, an object that in itself formally presents its case and its meaning by the form it assumes. Therefore, being an object, it should be so treated and controlled—but not as in the past. For past objects have about them past necessities—like the sonnet—which have conditioned them and from which, as a form itself, they cannot be freed.
>
> The poem being an object (like a symphony or cubist painting) it must be the purpose of the poet to make of his words a new form: to invent, that is, an object consonant with his day. This was what we wished to imply by Objectivism, an antidote, in a sense, to the bare image haphazardly presented in loose verse. (Williams, *Autobiography* 264–65)

The inadequacy of the "bare image" and the structural dilemmas of the imagist verse of the latter phase, described by Pound as "Amygism," stand for the Objectivists as the point of departure. In a letter to Zukofsky in 1928 we see Williams already using the term: "Poems are inventions richer in thought as image. Your early poems, even when the thought has enough force or freshness, have not been *objectivized* in new or fresh observations" (*Selected Letters* 101, emphasis added).

Recognizing that across the artistic world in 1930 there was a clamor for causes, positions, and movements, Harriet Monroe insisted that Zukofsky give his collection of poems a name, in effect urging him to transform the poems into an *ism.* Zukofsky obliged, and spent a lifetime explaining that he had not really meant what the name ("Objectivism") seemed to mean. In an accompanying essay he explained the Objectivists' program in *Poetry* in 1931, calling for a subtler totality of effect. He proposed a poetry that went beyond sincerity to a "perfect rest, complete appreciation": "This rested totality may be called objectification—the apprehension satisfied completely as to the appearance of the art form as an object . . . its character may be simply described as the arrangement, into one apprehended unit, of minor units of sincerity" ("Sincerity" 274). This sounds alarmingly like Pater's understanding of the beautiful, and places Zukofsky firmly within the symbolist perception of the work of art as a reconciliation of tensions, an achieved, atemporal stasis. The description of

Objectivism offered by Zukofsky intimates that form and arrangement would be the natural by-product of the authenticity of the "minor units of sincerity." Cary Nelson uses a similar phrase about Zukofsky's "A" as occupying a "field of powerful local effects." In Pound, he suggests, there was a "totalizing paranoia." In Zukofsky, we encounter "a series of specifically linguistic historical and political interventions" (Nelson 176). It is hard not to feel that the use of "political" in the criticism of Zukofsky is an honorific rather than a descriptive term. Perhaps it is *we* who need to see Zukofsky as making "political interventions." He seems in any meaningful sense not to have been a "political" writer at all.

Other Objectivists, we can now see, had a rather more modest understanding of the concept; or none at all. Zukofsky did not trouble to circulate drafts of his tortured essays to his fellow contributors. Reznikoff, who had throughout the 1920s remained faithful to the ideals of imagism circa 1915, regarded the term as describing a writer whose principal concerns were to register what was seen or heard, and who regarded himself as being constrained by the legal limitations of testimony delivered in court. Rakosi, who disliked Zukofsky's "aloof tone, the distant hauteur, the reasoning and language icily severe and rebuffing" (*Collected Prose* 105), seems to have been far closer to Reznikoff in temperament. The distance separating their work, with its bitter ironies and compassion, from the spare exactitudes of Oppen and the cerebral Zukofsky suggests how limited the group was from the start: it was smaller than contemporary observers noted, and grew smaller still in the intervening years. Rakosi went to Texas, and as "Callman Rawley" began training in social work; he wrote little for decades.[13] Objectivism *was* Zukofsky, and, to a lesser extent, Oppen; the others had different ambitions and cannot with justice be judged by their congruence with or divergence from Zukofsky's program.

This is not to say that there was no such a thing as an Objectivist poem. What Williams described in his autobiography of the meeting with Zukofsky, Oppen, and Reznikoff was essentially clear. They agreed in principle that the poem was not to be the vehicle for the expression of subjective or "personal" emotions; they were all anti-romantic. The insistence on form, on the poem as fully realized object, was perhaps too generalized to serve as an adequate definition of a school. But it left them with a clear distinction between the kind of poem they wanted to write, which would be spare, definite, minimal, imagistic, and the increasingly subjective and sprawling verse of the 1920s.

There was another consideration, however, which was to play an important role in all of their lives: the depression. The literary consequences of the collapse of the stock market in the autumn of 1929 was felt in various ways. Book sales fell off sharply; commissions from magazines were competed for more fiercely; little magazines like *Pagany,* which had printed many of the Objectivists, found it virtually impossible to pay printers' bills. The Objectivists, like so many other writers of their generation, and of their religion, were moved by the specter of mass unemployment, and feared the likely consequences of fascism at home and abroad. They drifted, or edged, or leaped into the orbit of the Communist Party.

The process of Stalinizing the literary Left demanded that proletarian and revolutionary writing be sharply separated from the bourgeois and liberal literary values that dominated American culture. Among the first criteria to be accepted was an explicit commitment to socialism and the class struggle. There was a developing expectation that writers on the Left should *write* as Marxists. Not only were poems to be about the class struggle, but poets should seek to incorporate the class struggle in the act of writing itself, a process both dialectical and materialist. Literature that suggested a neutral stance before the great issues of the day or was tainted by bourgeois aestheticism was harshly condemned.

The modernist aesthetic presumed the *absence* of such obligation. Between the poet and "society" there was, if anything, a trackless landscape of mutual indifference or hostility. The gap between the verse in *New Masses, Anvil,* and *Dynamo* (and in the little mimeographed John Reed Club magazines) and that which Zukofsky collected in *An "Objectivists" Anthology* was too great to be meaningfully crossed. The Objectivists knew that there were no readers in the 1930s for the kind of poems they wanted to write. Within the party, Objectivism was accused of a lack of explicit political commitment; their work was rejected. In later years the Objectivists tended to describe the idea behind the movement in formal terms. Oppen wrote that the term "Objectivist" was not a statement of objectionable objectivity, but rather had been meant "to objectify the poem, to make the poem an object. Meant form" (Weaver 55).

The choice facing them was clear enough: either to write the sort of poems that would be acceptable to the editors of the radical journals, or to write for the diminishing number of avant-garde little magazines. Or they could stop writing altogether. Oppen and Rakosi chose silence. They did not meet each other until 1971. Zukofsky wrote for his desk drawer. "Time fucks it," he wrote to Pound in 1935, "and if I keep my MSS. in my drawer or my drawers, I might as well shut up altogether" (*Pound/Zukofsky* 160). "I haven't heard from Zuk[ofsky] in years," wrote James Laughlin in 1945. "He seems to have burrowed down into his own private little world" (Pound and Laughlin 138). Which is precisely what happened for several decades. After a period in the mid-1930s during which Reznikoff published several political poems (especially "Jerusalem the Golden," in which he contrasted the remote God of Spinoza with the humane, secularized Judaism of Karl Marx), he turned to write about biblical history and Zionism. Politics, indeed the "noise of history," scattered the movement, interrupted their careers, and heightened the differences between them.

6

Irrelevant Objects: Basil Bunting's Poetry of the 1930s

John Seed

> A work of art is something constructed, something made in the same way that a potter makes a bowl. A bowl may be useful but it may be there only because the potter liked that shape—and it's a beautiful thing. The attempt to find any meaning in it would be manifestly absurd.
>
> —Basil Bunting, quoted in Davie, *Imaginary Museum* 288

This was a point Bunting repeated again and again, though poetry was generally compared to music rather than pottery. Poetry is nonreferential, an autonomous object. Its impact is through its music, its pattern of sounds and rhythms, and not through its meaning. For Bunting, literary criticism was a waste of time. There is, he once said, not much about literature worth reading since Dante's *De vulgari eloquentia!* His repeated message was clear and, voiced so forcibly by that shrewd old Northumbrian Gandalf, downright intimidating. Most of the early writings on Bunting's poetry during the 1960s and 1970s obediently conformed to his strictures. It was the music, the form, the rhythms, the prosody of his writing that were attended to.

It was, of course, this dimension of his work that marked it off as special, as in many ways unique, in England in the 1960s. The crispness, the taut energies and clarities of *Briggflatts* were so splendidly different from the dreary storytelling and slack attitudinizing of what usually passed for poetry in postwar England that it is not surprising that a new generation of readers (and listeners) was dazzled. *Briggflatts* was an astonishing and unexpected late flowering of some of the innovations of literary "modernism" of half a century before—Eliot's *The Waste Land,* Williams's *Spring and All,* and Pound's *Cantos* in particular. Though it was inflected in all sorts of ways by its specifically English contexts, it opened up a path back to a radically different poetic practice, one that had been all but obliterated in Britain (if not in the United States). In 1959 Donald Davie had protested about "the silent conspiracy which now unites all the English poets from Robert Graves down to Philip Larkin, and all the critics, editors and publishers too, the conspiracy to pretend that Eliot and Pound never happened" (67). A few years later *Briggflatts* helped to reconnect British poetry to this submerged tradition and to its North American development in the work of Williams, Zukofsky, Oppen, Rakosi, Niedecker, the Black Mountain poets, and others.

But the very disconnection of *Briggflatts* from its literary environment raises questions other than those to do with prosody. Before its publication in 1966, little or nothing of his poetry was in circulation and Bunting, a man in his mid-sixties, was almost entirely unknown. After *Briggflatts* Bunting found his poetry being reviewed and discussed, for the first time, in the national press in England. Within twelve months of its publication he was reading *Briggflatts* on the BBC Third Programme, and over the next few years he was to read and lecture on radio and television, at arts festivals, and at many universities in Britain, the United States, and Canada. His *Collected Poems* was published by Fulcrum in 1968, and his writing began to appear in a number of widely distributed anthologies, even in the *Sunday Times.*[1] He was Poetry Fellow at the Universities of Durham and Newcastle and Honorary Life Professor of the latter, President of Northern Arts, and President of the Poetry Society. Bunting's writing received some kind of official imprimatur with his appearance in Philip Larkin's 1973 *Oxford Book of Twentieth-Century Verse* and the publication of his *Collected Poems* by Oxford University Press in 1978—"a recognition," as G. S. Fraser put it, "that he belongs to the canon" (496).

Basil Bunting's exact stature as an English poet remains disputed. His work is still not securely part of the official canon. Nor is it part of the English curriculum in secondary and higher education. Nevertheless, Bunting is now widely acknowledged to be an important twentieth-century English poet—an acknowledgment based primarily on a single twenty-one-page poem, *Briggflatts.* Two sets of questions arise: (1) Why was Bunting so marginal to the dominant literary culture of England until he was approaching seventy years of age? Why did he write so little from the mid-1930s until the early 1960s? (2) What are we to make of his earlier poetry—most of it written between 1925 and 1935? Is it possible to begin to reinsert this work into a wider history of British poetry? In other words, what are the implications—for our understanding of Bunting's whole oeuvre, for our understanding of the situation of British poetry—of his writing *prior* to *Briggflatts?*

These are at one level distinct questions. The first involves some investigation of Bunting's biography, of his relations with contemporaries and with English literary culture, especially in the interwar period. The second involves close reading of his earlier poetry. And yet these two dimensions converge significantly in the case of Bunting, whose critical reputation continues to be a highly charged and politicized affair. They converge not just in the reception of the poetry and in various commentaries and ex cathedra statements that Bunting himself subsequently provided, but also in the poems themselves. *Briggflatts*—subtitled "An Autobiography"—tells a story about a poet's isolation, marginality, and failure.

Poet appointed dare not decline
to walk among the bogus, nothing to authenticate
the mission imposed, despised
by toadies, confidence men, kept boys,
shopped and jailed, cleaned out by whores
touching acquaintance for food and tobacco.
Secret, solitary, a spy, . . . (*Complete Poems* 47)

Bunting's earliest collection, *Redimiculum Matellarum*, was privately printed in 1930 in Milan and, hardly surprisingly, did not reach a wide readership. But in the early thirties his work was published in a number of important anthologies and periodicals—in, for instance, *An "Objectivists" Anthology* (1932), Pound's *Active Anthology* (1933), *Poetry* (Chicago) (each year from 1931 to 1934), and Eliot's *Criterion* (1936). And after that—apart from another appearance in *Poetry* (Chicago) in 1941—his access to publication seemed to cease. A 1935 collection of his poems, entitled *Caveat Emptor,* found no publisher in England or North America. His work was not included in major anthologies of the mid-thirties such as Yeats's *Oxford Book of Modern Verse* or Michael Roberts's *The Faber Book of Modern Verse,* both published in 1936. At the same time, his creativity seemed to fade. Of the Odes that survive in the 1968 *Collected Poems,* thirteen were written between 1924 and 1929, another sixteen were written between 1930 and 1935, and a mere four in the second half of the thirties. The last of his four prewar "Sonatas" is dated 1935.

Pound's dedication of *Guide to Kulchur* in 1938—"To LOUIS ZUKOFSKY and BASIL BUNTING strugglers in the desert"—was truer than he knew. These were years of restless wandering—from the Canaries to London, a period on the Devon Coast, back to Newcastle upon Tyne, then spells in various parts of the United States. Part of this was clearly personal and had to do with the final breakup of his first marriage in 1936. "I have written nothing (except official reports, 'appreciations,' & such) since Marian walked out on me," he told Dorothy Pound ten years later, exaggerating only slightly (quoted in Makin 102). World War II had also intervened, and Bunting was to remain in the

Middle East until 1952, far from what Auden once called "the tiny jungle" of the English literary world.

There was a brief flurry of activity with three Odes written in 1947, 1948, and 1949 and the long poem *The Spoils* published in *Poetry* (Chicago) in 1951. *Poems 1950* was published in Galveston, Texas, by Dallam Flynn, largely through the influence of Pound. And during the 1950s and early 1960s there were a few other reprints of Bunting's poetry in anthologies and collections in the United States, such as Hugh Kenner's *The Art of Poetry* and a New Directions anthology that Pound co-edited with Marcella Spann in 1964. Much of this, however, was prewar writing. After 1951 Bunting stopped writing for at least twelve years. In England in the first half of the 1960s his name was almost completely unknown, except to a few aficionados of the obscurer byways of modern poetry. Leavis pronounced in 1951: "If we ask what other poets Pound backed"—other, that is, than Frost and Eliot—"the answer is that it is hard to remember, because on the whole they matter so little" (quoted in Sullivan 218).

The *Times* obituary of Bunting commented on "his taste for out-of-the-way American publishers." Chicago is, of course, a dreadfully out-of-the-way place—even further away than Bunting's native Tyneside ("Exotic Northumbria" was the title of the anonymous 1966 review of *Briggflatts* in the *Times Literary Supplement*). The real intent of the *Times* obituarist was to ascribe Bunting's lifelong marginality and his embarrassing late success to his own self-willed perversity. It was, in fact, only the commitment to his work of a small English publisher, Stuart Montgomery's Fulcrum Press, founded in 1965, that finally made his work more accessible in the late 1960s. Nevertheless, a poet who produces one longish poem and a handful of brief lyrics in nearly thirty years can hardly be said to be the victim of systematic exclusion by English publishers—at least not in any straightforward way.

There were other forces in play in Bunting's case; for instance, the fading of his relations with an older generation of writers. The "men of 1914" to whom Bunting had hitched his wagon had broken up during the thirties. Their project—"to get away from romantic art into classical art, away from political propaganda back into the detachment of true literature"—had failed, in England at least, as Wyndham Lewis acknowledged in *Blasting and Bombardiering* in 1937. "We are not," he said, "'the last men of an epoch' . . . we are more than that, or we are that in a different way to what is most often asserted. *We are the first men of a Future that has not materialized.* We belong to a 'great age' that has not come off" (250, 256). Yeats—Bunting had been his "secretary" for a while—was to die in 1939, Joyce in 1941. The "literary modernists" as a coherent and influential formation had disintegrated.

The organizations of cultural production and distribution in England—the London literary scene, the publishing and reviewing networks, the university system—remained, as Frank Lentricchia has suggested (in "Lyric in the Culture of Capital"), predominantly hostile to the literary innovations of Pound, Eliot, Joyce, and others. Eliot, of course, had some success in redrawing the historical map of English poetry, downgrading the romantic and the Victorian canon as a strategy to undermine the legitimacy of the Georgians and other mainstream poetries in England after 1918. Yet F. R. Leavis recalled that the publication of his *New Bearings in English Poetry* in 1932—with its affirmation of a poetic revolution in the writing of Hopkins, Pound, and Eliot—was met with considerable hostility in Cambridge. And he added: "it continued to be regarded with the strongest disfavour by those who in the academic and literary worlds determine where credit is to be given and what books should sell" ("Retrospect 1950" 177).[2]

Eliot had already identified himself with Anglo-Catholicism, royalism, and conservatism by the late twenties and was becoming uneasily absorbed into the English Establishment. Bunting had risked burning his boats there in the early thirties. Much as he admired *The Waste Land,* he commented uncompromisingly in 1932: "Mr Eliot's *Criterion* is an international disaster, since he began to love his gloom, and regretfully, resignedly, to set about perpetuating the causes of it—kings, religion and formalism." The *Criterion* has, Bunting said, "gone about the business of blunting the English intelligence as systematically as the quarterlies of a century ago" ("English Poetry Today" 264, 266). Seven months later he went further in the *New English Weekly,* attacking the compromises of Eliot's new "devotional poetry": "He writes as though from conditions that have vanished, as a contemporary of George Herbert. He has his reward. What is antique enough is notoriously harmless, is supine, and the ruling powers can encourage its circulation without uneasiness" ("Mr T. S. Eliot" 500). The radical skepticism here about organized religion and a poetry acceptable to "the ruling powers" is explicit. One of Bunting's translations from Firdusi did appear in the *Criterion* in 1936, but Eliot thought little of Pound's *Active Anthology,* in which Bunting was generously represented. He rejected approaches for the publication of a Faber edition of Bunting's poetry in 1935 and again in 1950.

Association with Pound was not helpful to any young poet. Already in the 1920s he was outside the circles of influence in English literary culture. Richard Aldington commented to Amy Lowell in 1925: "I don't know if he has retained any reputation in America, but here he is almost forgotten, and as the rest of us go up, he goes down." It was, he said a few months later, "hopeless to try to get people to take him seriously" (Doyle 87–88). Pound's increasingly strident fascism during the 1930s marginalized him further as an extremist and a crank. "When I was at the 'Ezuversity' in 1934–35 the anti-Semitism only showed in jokes," according to James Laughlin. "But when Pound came to the United States in 1939, it was increasing" ("Pound's Economics" 79).[3] When "anti-semite bile" spilled over into Pound's correspondence with Zukofsky at the end of 1938, Bunting's response was uncompromising. He lectured Pound: "Every anti-semitism, anti-niggerism, anti-moorism, that I can recall in history was base, had its foundation in the meanest kind of envy and in greed. It makes me sick to see you covering yourself with that filth. It is not an arguable question, has not been arguable for at least nineteen centuries . . . it is hard to see how you are going to stop the rot of your mind and heart without a pretty thorough-going repudiation of what you have spent a lot of work on" (quoted in Makin 79). His relations with Pound were strained by the late thirties. Bunting maintained contact—often in letters addressed to Dorothy Pound rather than Ezra—but there was clearly continuing tension and distance between them in the postwar years. In 1946 Pound was protesting: "What the . . . hell CAN you say for a pen Empire that lets best poet of the generation Bunting (B. Bunting) disappear sans trace, and no breath of curiosity even among the ten alleged literates still on the dung heap" (quoted in Heymann 222–23). Confined to a mental hospital in Washington, D.C., he continued to give Bunting what little support he could in getting work published and circulated. And in public Bunting remained loyal to Pound as the master craftsman of modern verse, maintaining a discrete silence about their profound political differences.[4] However, in 1965, on its republication, Bunting commented privately, with some stiffness, that *The Spoils* "has, I believe, Pound's approval so far as an anti-semite can approve of a poem Jews find sympathetic."[5]

Bunting was deeply opposed to the rightward political turn—the emphasis on authority, hierarchy, and tradition—that "the men of 1914" had taken from the 1920s. As he commented many years later: "Hierarchy and order, the virtues of the neo-Platonic quasi-religion, were the prime virtues also to Yeats, Pound and Eliot. They are not virtues to me, only expedients that chafe almost as vilely as the crimes they try to restrain" ("Note on Briggflatts" 3). And this clearly contributed to Bunting's sense of isolation and of profound uncertainty in his efforts at critically disentangling the political ambiguities of the modernist aesthetic in the 1930s.

However, Bunting was no more comfortable with the new group of young leftist poets who were to be so conspicuous in England during the thirties. In *Poetry* in 1932 Bunting caustically surveyed contemporary English poetry—

"the frivolous imbecilities of cat poetry, bird poetry, flower poetry; country-house Jorrocks-cum-clippership poetry (as Mr Masefield does it); country-family cleverness (the Sitwells)." It was, he said, with few and severely qualified exceptions (Edgell Rickword and W. H. Auden among them), "a long and dreary list of highly advertised failures, beginning with the Sitwells" ("English Poetry Today" 264, 271). Bunting was only a few years older than the new thirties poets—Auden, Spender, MacNeice, Day Lewis, and others. Auden sent a copy of his first collection of poems to Rapallo in 1930. Pound saw nothing in them, but Bunting did and a brief correspondence ensued. However, though he did have a couple of poems alongside Auden in *Whips and Scorpions: Specimens of Modern Satiric Verse*, edited by Sherard Vines and published in 1932 by Wishart, the left-wing publisher, Bunting was never connected to the literary world of this particular generation in England. He did not mix in their circles or figure in their anthologies and periodicals. Any reading of their memoirs and correspondence reveals a remarkably tight social network. They came from similar sorts of upper-middle-class professional families and had generally been to one of the elite public schools and Oxford within a few years of each other. Their predominant homosexuality provided another common loyalty and form of exclusion of outsiders. They moved into the London literary world as writers, editors, reviewers, and publishers and proceeded to lever each other up. Another facet of the sociology of this literary grouping is crystallized in unwitting testimony from Stephen Spender's postwar autobiography: "When my book of poems was published I began to lead a literary-social life of luncheons, teas and weekends at country houses" (142).[6]

Bunting was never part of this fashionable literary world during the various spells he was resident in London in the twenties and thirties. He was hostile to "the sleek, slick lads" and despised the social elitism of the literary circles of Bloomsbury and Hampstead. In a 1933 review, originally in Italian, he described the artistic circles of Bloomsbury as "a dung-heap believed to be a bed of lilies" and the source of "the sweet, drippy, unbearable smell of decadence" that pervaded English art. Bloomsbury was "the stubborn rear-guard of a dying golden age in which the servants were servile and even the well-off tradesmen prudently bowed to Birth and Education" (Reagan 249). Or as *The Well of Lycopolis* had it:

> Squalid acquiescence in the cast-offs
> of reputed poetry. Here, Bellerophon,
> is a livery hack, a gelding,
> easy pace, easy to hire,
> all mansuetude and indifference. (*Complete Poems* 25)

Yet Bunting's social background was similar to that of many of his literary contemporaries, whether in London or Oxford and Cambridge. He had been brought up in a comfortable and cultured upper-middle-class household with a housemaid and a governess, had been educated at private boarding schools, and narrowly missed a scholarship to Cambridge University.[7] Nor was he politically opposed to the predominant leftism of young English writers during the 1930s. His family background placed him firmly on the radical wing of the political spectrum. He was born and educated among the Quakers, a dissident religious minority with a long and honorable tradition of pacifism and hostility to the British state. As a conscientious objector he was brutally treated in several prisons during 1918 and 1919, going on hunger strike at one stage. On his release from Winchester prison in 1919 he immediately went, so he told Edward Lucie-Smith, "on a wild tour of Scandinavia. I was going to convert Lenin and Trotsky to more peaceable means of producing heaven on earth. But they wouldn't let me in" (Lucie-Smith 33). He settled for a spell as a Fabian socialist, secretary to a Labour MP, and then a student at the Fabian intellectual headquarters, the London School of Economics.

Soon, however, Bunting had fallen among poets. First in London, then in Paris, he lived as a hard-drinking, womanizing Bohemian, scraping a frugal living where he could. In 1923 he shared a flat for a while with Ford Madox Ford while working as his assistant on the *Transatlantic Review.* Bunting recalled Ford as "the most friendly and tolerant boss you could have": "if I turned up at breakfast in the morning with an unannounced and unintroduced young lady Ford would never turn a hair" (quoted in Judd 350–51). It does not sound like an infrequent event. At one point he was rescued from prison by Pound. "I was put inside for kicking a cop when drunk" (Lucie-Smith 33; and see Kenner, *Pound Era* 527). Photographs show him tall and slim, in elegant poses complete with cane and extravagant goatee—the very archetype of the antagonist of bourgeois respectability. This is the Bunting of *Villon* (1925). The two poets had, after all, shared the same Paris prison, and Bunting felt some identity with the fifteenth-century scholar-poet who also fell foul of the authorities, loved women and wine, and lived in poverty on the edge of the Parisian underworld.[8]

Bunting's formation was, then, remarkably complex: Bohemian and rigorously avant-gardist poet, but also Quaker pacifist with leftist sympathies. He was also a fierce Northerner, born into the mining community of Tyneside. His father was a pit doctor on Tyneside, but both his grandfathers had worked in mining and his sympathy with miners and their unions was strong and active during the 1926 miners' strike. As he told Pound in a letter of 1934: "I know the solidity of those people, and I watched it break up in 26, when I was all the time in a mining village, took the chair at one of Cook's meetings, stuck a knife in the tyres of a government strikebreaking lorry and tried unsuccessfully nearly every paper in the country to get the scandalous faked benches of magistrates who condemned the strikers to years of hard labour shown up" (quoted in Quartermain, *Basil Bunting* 12).[9] "They Say Etna," published in 1933, has one crisp, restrained, and mournful passage suggesting the continuing imaginative pressure on Bunting of the coal-mining environment of Tyneside, even while he was living on the shores of the Mediterranean in Rapallo:

> We carry lighted Davy lamps,
> stoop along narrow track.
> Trucks scold tunnel.
> In a squat cavern a
> naked man on his
> knees with a
> pickaxe rips a nugget from the coalface.
>
> Four lads
>   led the pownies
> a mile and a half through rising water,
> lampless because the stife
> asphyxiates lamps,
> by old galleries to the North Shaft.
> The water rose.
>   The others
> came five months later when it was pumped out
> and were buried by public subscription.
> (The widows were provided for). (*Complete Poems* 166)

The widows and their children, as Bunting's laconic parenthesis signals here, were never adequately provided for. The massive defeat of the miners in 1926, the imprisonments and blacklistings that followed, the low wages, and brutal and sometimes fatal working conditions in the Northern coalfield obviously continued to haunt him.

Bunting remained remarkably clear-eyed and skeptical about political options in the 1930s. Despite his affinities with the English Left—or even *because* of them—he was not carried away with the contemporary leftist intellectual's enthusiasm for the Soviet Union. In a book review of 1927 he remarked that the philosophy of Bolshevism, far from being new and exciting and revolutionary, reminded him of nothing so much as "the youthful follies of our grandfathers who swaggered into scientific materialism and out again, expected salvation to come from machinery, and spoke of the People as an entity, forgetting that its name is Legion; Hegel, Ricardo, Samuel Smiles and the heroes of the Rationalist Press mixed in equal proportions, make a fair approximation to Bolshevik philosophy" ("Marvellous Moscow" 283). This is astute. The Webbs, Beatrice and Sydney, those chill eminences of Fabian socialism and the L.S.E. (London School of Economics), had no such problems with Bolshevism as a philosophical amalgam of political economy, Samuel Smiles, and the Rationalist Press—this was almost precisely Beatrice Webb's intellectual formation among the Unitarian middle class of Victorian England.

A 1936 letter to Pound made clear Bunting's leftism, his radical skepticism about the direction Bolshevism was taking, his sense of political frustration in England, and (since "someone else" is obviously Mussolini) his distance from Pound: "I'd rather have a revolution, blood and skulls, but since Stalin has reduced himself to a larger Hitler and pretty good imitation of someone else, I doubt whether I could work with communists except for exceedingly strictly limited objects and there's no other revolutionary party in sight" (Reagan 274). Bunting was not distracted by events in Spain. He spent 1933 to 1936 in the Canaries and had, apparently, played chess with the local military governor, one Francisco Franco. His account of the origins of the Spanish Civil War, published only nine days after the revolt of the Spanish generals in July 1936, was not cast in dramatic stereotypes of white and black, good and evil. He observed the electoral corruption and political violence on all parts of the political spectrum in Spain. Franco, he speculated, was not a "fascist" but "a moderate republican"—though events might push him into the arms of the monarchists or drive him "to disguise a purely military dictatorship as Fascism." The Left was incompetent and divided but, he concluded, still capable of winning in the end. His sympathies were cautiously expressed (not least perhaps because he was writing for the *Spectator* and, with a wife, two children, and no job, desperately needed the money): "If the Popular Front triumphs, it must fall wholly into the hands of the professed Marxists. The Right cannot be kept from arming in a country as chaotic as Spain since the Republic. The Civil War will be renewed many times. In my opinion the Left has the better chance in the long run, for it has, in Spain, the better cause. You cannot starve a nation forever. But the long run may be a Marathon of blood" ("Roots of the Spanish Revolt" 138). His final prediction, at least, was proved right. Around three-quarters of a million people were killed in three years of civil war. Bunting wrote no more about Spain.

In fact, Bunting was profoundly skeptical about the political rhetorics of the 1930s. He told Louis Zukofsky in 1934: "half the evils in the world come from verbalism, i.e. imagining that abstract words have anything more than a grammatical meaning or function. Adjectives, numbers, symbols like the word God, eat away all sense of reality and land us in every kind of social and economic mess, when people begin to think they correspond to anything genuine" (quoted in Quartermain, *Basil Bunting* 14–15).[10] This has extra force when we recall that Zukofsky, isolated in New York, was year after year perhaps Bunting's most loyal supporter at the outer Arctic margins of the literary world—and a Communist. In 1935 he sent Bunting the draft outline of *A Worker's Anthology*, which was never published.[11] Bunting would have had few quarrels with the selection of texts—it included Ovid, Chaucer, Villon, Shakespeare, Donne, Burns, and Blake among others, though only Apollinaire among twentieth-century poets. But its project to combine poetry and revolutionary politics, citing Lenin and talking about "the class conscious artist," was alien to Bunting. In May 1931 he wrote a grumpy letter to Harriet Monroe about a recent "repulsive" letter in *Poetry* (Chicago): "Will people never learn that the business of poetry is poetry and not social reform" (quoted in Forde, "Odes" 131 n). In "Observations on Left-Wing Papers" (1935), he denied the propaganda value of literature: "Its function is not propaganda, any more than the function of an analytical chemist is propaganda" (46). And he told Pound in the same year: "we don't do any appreciable good by turning aside to propagate the worthiest causes in economics or politics or patent medicines or quack religions or other subjects we've only a secondary interest in" (Reagan, 233).

This remained Bunting's position. In a letter of 1980 to Barry Redfern, after some acerbic comments on the poetry of E. E. Cummings, he wrote: "In the thirties, very many American writers liked to think of themselves as workingmen and wrote for left wing magazines, and I would not be surprised to hear that EEC had been one such writer; but that was eyewash for the most part. These magazines were neither written nor read by workingmen. Of course, Mr Auden's friends were acting the same farce in England, we can't complain about the Yankees. Leftish magazines that really try to do something about social and economic conditions don't usually attract people who are pleased with themselves."[12] Note that Cummings's affectation of lowercase for his initials is here peremptorily reversed. To imagine that writing political poetry makes much contribution to improving the real conditions of people is a form of casuistry. It is insufficiently political. In this skepticism about the political efficacy of poetry Bunting was close to his fellow Objectivist George Oppen, though the latter was an active member of the Communist Party of the United States in the later 1930s.[13]

This is not to say that Bunting's poetry is devoid of political edge or social content in the 1920s and 1930s. A 1928 Ode displays some political skepticism about British parliamentary democracy, ending perhaps ruefully:

> and never *rei novae*
> *inter rudes artium homines.*
> never a spark of sedition
> amongst the uneducated workingmen. (*Complete Poems* 85)

A certain inevitability in working-class indifference, from Livy to the 1920s, seems to be implied. (In "Attis: Or, Something Missing" in 1931 buses are described as "thundering like cabinet ministers / over a lethargic populace.") One or two of the Odes from 1930—"Gin the Goodwife Stint" and "The Complaint of the Morpethshire Farmer"—reflect the impact of economic depression on rural Northumberland. Both express a deep political pessimism, concluding that immigration to North America was the only solution for Northumberland's poor—as it had been for generations. "They Say Etna," published in Pound's 1933 *Active Anthology*, is more directly political, with its bitter comments on armament manufacturers, financiers, landowners, and coalowners.[14]

Much of his poetry during the late twenties and throughout the thirties was, however, not political in any straightforward sense and begins to illuminate his predicament as an impoverished and increasingly embattled poet, writing little and publishing less. Ode 11 from 1929 is a defense of the abandonment of his "fragments and false starts" to the dustbin—preferable to "one review-rid month's printed ignominy, / the public detection of your decay, that reeks" (*Complete Poems* 89). Ode 12 is a fairly jaunty sketch of the penniless poet, taunting bourgeois respectability:

> The Lady asked the Poet:
> Why do you wear your raincoat in the drawing-room?
> He answered: Not to show
> my arse sticking out of my trousers. (*Complete Poems* 90)

Some of the Odes celebrate the joys of beautiful women and sexual delight (see especially Ode 9), but a number are self-lacerating meditations on failure—both in love and in art. The recurrent figure of the failed writer sunk in hopeless boredom, impotence, and failure is reminiscent of no one so much as Bunting's Irish contemporary Samuel Beckett. Both shared a similar family background and refused to follow the obvious path to a respectable professional career, preferring an impoverished Bohemian exile. Each became the chosen disciple of one of the great masters of literary modernism—Pound and Joyce, respectively. And both were paralyzed by an inability to find a métier, a vein of creativity, in the interwar years. The parallels between their interwar writings are sometimes quite striking.

He lies with one to long for another,
sick, self-maimed, self-hating,
obstinate, mating
beauty with squalor to beget lines still-born. (*Complete Poems* 47)

This persona, from *Briggflatts*, is increasingly present in poems of the inter-war years. The longer 1931 poem "Attis: Or, Something Missing" and several of the Odes are suffused with violence and self-disgust, with references to shame and castration, with images of women as objects of hatred and fear. It is tempting to trace the tension between sensual delight and self-disgust and this overwhelming sense of guilt and failure to deep inner conflicts between Bunting's hereditary Quaker puritanism and his wild Bohemian lifestyle, between the civic responsibilities of the liberal-radical professional of his family background and the idleness and narcissism in the conventional picture of the artist. There may be something in this—and something which he had only worked through to a kind of equilibrium by the time of *Briggflatts*.

But the tensions within Bunting's poetry in these years were also a response to wider historical pressures. John Lucas, discussing the work of Edgell Rickword—who wrote little poetry after his 1931 collection *Twittingpan*—notes the prevalent "accidie" of the 1920s: "It is easy to forget how that decade was marked by deep-rooted cynicism, a feeling (and perhaps no more than a feeling, since the best lacked all conviction) that life had become a kind of posthumous existence without purpose or value" (149). Bunting said something similar in a personal letter, recalling the damage done to a generation by the disturbing effects of world war. That damage, he says, involved a loss of faith in "man's essential virtue" and being "left trying helplessly to believe in that because their fathers did, but with a lack of conviction."[15] The reference to the optimistic faith of the fathers has a personal resonance here. His was a doctor, a scientist, and a Fabian socialist, providing real material benefits to working people who needed it—not a faithless, workless, disreputable artist. But the situation was more widely shared by this generation. It was what made Eliot's *The Waste Land* and *The Hollow Men* so widely influential in the 1920s.

Bunting's *The Well of Lycopolis*, a Sonata from 1935, deserves inclusion in any anthology of thirties poetry in Britain. Its lines are suffused with despair, bitterness, and a general sense of social failure in a Britain still haunted by World War I. Venus has become an old whore, "ageing, bedraggled, a / half-quartern of gin under her shawl" (*Complete Poems* 21). The comforts of quietism, of aesthetic detachment, of utopian idealism are all impossible. Poetry and love equally have become corrupted and prostituted, "infamous" and "abject." Modernist strategies of discontinuity are fused with rhythms of popular speech and a harsh social realism. Where a straightforward moral conviction or commitment might be, or even a single voice providing some kind of meaningful coherence, there is fragmentation, the ambiguous and the discrepant. The final section combines images from Cantos VIII and IX of Dante's *Inferno* with images of the damaged lives of the "involuntary volunteers," survivors of the Great War.

> Surrendered in March. Or maybe
> ulcers of mustard gas, a rivet in the lung
> from scrappy shrapnel,
> frostbite, trench-fever, shell-shock,
> self-inflicted wound,
> tetanus, malaria, influenza.
> Swapped your spare boots for a packet of gaspers.
> Overstayed leave.
> Debauched the neighbor's little girl
> to save two shillings . . . (27)

And the poet is there in hopeless solidarity with them in their angry silence, defeat, and obscurity—a community of the separate and divided, joined only by their distinct alienations from a rotten world and a rotten self. The final lines are as magnificent as anything in *Briggflatts:*

> muttering inaudibly beneath the quagmire,
> irresolute, barren, dependant, this page
> ripped from Love's ledger and Poetry's:
> and besides I want you to know for certain
> there are people under the water. They are sighing.
> The surface bubbles and boils with their sighs.
> Look where you will see it.
> The surface sparkles and dances with their sighs
> as though Styx were silvered by a wind from Heaven. (27)

Chomei at Toyama (1932) is Bunting's adaptation of an unfinished prose work by Kamo no Chomei, a twelfth-century Japanese writer, and is also about internal exile and political despair. An old man, Chomei abandons the capital, Kyoto, and a reality of fire and earthquake, starvation, crime, violence, and public corruption. He prefers a life of solitude in the mountains, with a few books, a mandolin, and a lute. If Bunting clearly appreciated what he termed the "urbane, sceptical and ironical temper" of Chomei, the poem does not ultimately underwrite his withdrawal from the city and public life as either virtuous or comfortable. His is no safe and attractive rural retreat on the side of Hino mountain but "a hovel": "Two barrowloads of junk." And he lives in poverty:

There's a Lent of commandments kept
where there's no way to break them. (*Complete Poems* 72)

Chomei is, in the end, unreconciled, his anger and bitterness barely concealed.

I do not enjoy being poor,
I've a passionate nature.
My tongue
clacked a few prayers. (76)

Chomei at Toyama and *The Well of Lycopolis* are poems about defeat, failure, and exile. Neither offers hopeful messages or promising political remedies. In fact, both are profoundly pessimistic. Thus for Chomei social disaster is represented as a force of nature. History offers no redemption:

To appreciate present conditions
Collate them with antiquity. (69)

That is the political charge of Bunting's poetry in the 1930s—its refusal to compromise with a rotten present, whatever the temptations and pressures to point a message, to join a cause, to support a faith. And yet the critical force of some of Bunting's thirties poetry comes precisely from its refusal of the comforts of a communal faith of any kind. He preferred an unillusioned use of his own senses. Several Odes—see for instance 30 and 31—demonstrate the moral capacity to *see* the pain and damage inflicted by the established reality. Here Ode 35, written immediately after the war, is eloquent:

Search under every veil
for the pale eyes, pale
lips of a sick child,
in each doorway glimpse
her reluctant limbs
for whom no kindness is,
to whom caress and kiss
come nightly more amiss,

whose hand no gentle hand
touches, whose eyes withstand
compassion. . . . (*Complete Poems* 112)

The concluding lines rehearse various justifications or alibis, but they do not blunt the pain of knowing that things should be different: "every vein cries out."

This is perhaps where we can begin to think about Bunting's aesthetic intransigence. The technical and formal demands of the writing itself override all other considerations in a bitter utopianism which Pound voiced precisely: "that one man should have a vision of perfection and that he should be sick to death and disconsolate because he cannot attain it" (quoted in Lewis 276). Bunting's poetry of the 1930s is haunted by this sense of its own inadequacy ("mating / beauty with squalor to beget lines still-born"), its inability to integrate the pressures of external reality and subjective feeling, its failure either to achieve the formal perfection of art or to serve urgent human needs in a period of acute social crisis. In the words of Hölderlin, "wozu Dichter in durftiger Zeit?" What are poets for in a time of need?

Bunting's predicament from the later 1930s—and the ways in which some of his poetry negotiated it—is not only a matter of individual biography. It is part of a wider generational history. Two of his American fellow Objectivists—Oppen and Rakosi—published no poetry from the late 1930s until the early 1960s. Zukofsky was retreating into the increasingly private and arcane textualities of *"A"*, writing poetry that seemed unlikely to find a publisher, much less a readership. And even *"A"* was interrupted: "A"-10 was finished in 1940, "A"-11 not until 1950. Kenner points to a crisis in the literary economy in the United States at the beginning of the 1940s, "compounded of the war and the aftermath of the Depression." Every book of Faulkner's and Marianne Moore's, for instance, was out of print. William Carlos Williams was almost unknown, and Pound was forgotten (*Homemade World* 162–63). In this kind of context it was hardly surprising that a group of young poets like the Objectivists failed to find a public in the United States and disappeared without trace.

In Britain the environment for new and innovative poetry was hardly less hostile. Already in 1932 Bunting had commented: "There is no poetry in England, none with any relation to the country, or of any considerable section of it." Whatever the causes of this situation—he mentioned the high price of poetry books and the projection of the likes of Rupert Brooke, Humbert Wolfe, and J. C. Squire as *the* poetry of postwar England—the effects on poetry were damaging: "Poetry withdraws into itself. It can reach but a small audience, small enough to have special learning and, as it were, passwords; too small to hope to influence even a corner of the national culture, so that, proposing no end but the exercise of its special knowledge, it delights more and more in approximations to the acrostic, less and less in true concision, which implies force and clarity as well as paucity of words. The cure?—I can see nothing for it but patience" ("English Poetry Today" 265). By the late 1930s patience was running out.

"It is difficult to sustain the weight of an opinion singly for any length of way," Hazlitt wrote, and he too was an expert on the defeat and isolation of a particular generation of young radical writers. "The intellect languishes without cordial encouragement and support. It exhausts both strength and patience to be always striving against the stream" (35). Oppen spoke from the same experience in "Of Being Numerous":

> How shall one know a generation, a new generation?
> Not by the dew on them! Where the earth is most torn
> And the wounds untended and the voices confused,
> There is the head of the moving column
>
> Who if they cannot find
> Their generation
> Wither in the infirmaries
>
> And the supply depots, supplying
> Irrelevant objects. (*Collected Poems* 166)

Bunting's predicament was much more than a matter of his own perversity or his isolation from the networks of the English literary establishment. It was more complex than that, involving the intersection of multiple histories—an individual biography of immense complexity, literary modernism's English demise and its contamination by the political values of the extreme Right, a sense of the futility of poetry in a time of crisis, the deep elitism and savage torpor of powerful literary institutions in England, the disruptive impact of the depression and World War II on a particular generation. Bunting's poems of this period provide some insight into this complicated historical experience. Perhaps his silences are more eloquent, and the starting place for beginning to understand *Briggflatts*—in many ways a poem delayed for thirty years.

For too long the history of poetry in twentieth-century Britain has been written as a sequence of largely Oxbridge groupings who have been taken as somehow representative of their generation. Auden, Spender, Day Lewis, and MacNeice *are* "thirties" poetry in a whole series of critical studies. The Movement poets *are* the poetry of the 1950s. Blake Morrison, Craig Raine, Andrew Motion, and others in the 1982 *Penguin Book of Contemporary British Poetry* attempted to become the self-selected representatives of the late twentieth century. Though this self-privileging on the part of a series of little coteries has never gone uncontested, it has succeeded in marginalizing and obscuring the significance of a number of important British poets—Bunting, of course, but also Hugh McDiarmid, David Jones, Edgell Rickword, Sorley MacLean, perhaps Dylan Thomas, among others.[16] Bunting is not even mentioned in a whole series of books dealing with British poetry in the 1930s.[17]

I am certainly not arguing here that Bunting's interwar poetry is of such major significance as to radically revise the literary history of the period. "Basil wrote a small amount of extremely good poetry," Pound commented privately in 1954 (quoted in Makin 324). That is about right, and the significance of that small amount—*The Spoils, The Well of Lycopolis, Chomei at Toyama,* and a number of the Odes—should at least be registered. Alongside such writing, the often quite appalling verse of Spender, Day Lewis, and a number of other much-anthologized figures—discussed with po-faced seriousness by a number of critics as *the* poetry of "the thirties"—shrinks into its due insignificance.

7

Objectivists in the Thirties: Utopocalyptic Moments

Michael Heller

The 1930s began with any number of utopian ideas in place, whether it was communism's classless society, an American rural pastoralism, Douglas's Social Credit, or the fascist goal of an orderly society led by benevolent dictators or wise oligarchies who would save the state. The decade ended in apocalyptic fears and horrors, whether it was the rise of Nazism or the Moscow show trials or the advent of a world war encompassing most of mankind. "Utopocalyptic," then, is my made-up name for a sense of uncertainty, for that odd sociopolitical or cultural product, both fever and exacerbation, in which an individual is torn between idealized hopes and gnawing dread. The utopocalyptic might, then, consume a poet in the thirties faced with the warring forces of Left and Right, with peace and conflict, with the sense that every utopian vision is predicated on an apocalyptic vision of what would occur if it were not realized. Terms like "utopian" or "apocalyptic" are considerably larger and more grandiose than "Left" or "Right" or even such parallel pairings as socialism and fascism. But it is in their very largeness that these terms are most useful, for poetry embodies, even if only by implication, a powerful backward and forward dynamic, an admixture of hope and fear, of prophecy and foreboding, that is lacking in the more narrowly political terminology. In the thirties, such a passionate dynamic and its constructions constituted a virtual subgenre of poetic activity.

The role and function of poetry, as well as other literary forms, is a central problem for the writers of the thirties who viewed past and future with almost visionary intensity and desire and in anguish over human (social) possibilities. Was the poem to be seen as something personal and in some sense private, or was it to be useful, enlisted in the public good? If the poem was to have some sort of effect on the social order, what sort of poem would it be? Writers uncomfortable with current literary modes, unwilling to adopt unreflectively their inheritance of conventional literary forms, often correlated questions of craft with the larger sociopolitical or cultural conditions about which they felt concerned.

Even poets who rejected the categories of public and private spheres were, without exception, categorized on political grounds by the swirling currents and movements that surrounded them. In this double bind, a writer floated along on a stream of acceptance or rejection beyond his or her control. When a poet found an audience by whom to be published and read, it was often in accordance with the dictates of someone else's political and cultural interests. Being accepted or rejected by this or that group or faction might be solely based on the political consideration of the work in hand and/or its placement in one literary journal or another. On so categorizing poets, on demanding visions of them, there was much agreement. Archibald MacLeish may have best expressed this outlook when, in *Poetry* in 1931, he wrote: "poetry, which owes no man anything, owes nevertheless one debt—an image of the world in which men can again believe" (216).

The extent to which these notions reduce terms such as "avant-garde" or "traditionalist" to mere political qualifiers is one index of the degree to which writers felt they were caught up as writers in political and social circumstances, and therefore in writing circumstances, as a rule beyond their control. This political situation had, therefore, its effects upon craft as well, and the negotiation of a utopocalyptic moment manifested not so much in the poet's ambivalence toward his or her times, but in the poet's investigation of his or her own ambivalence.

Not all poets, of course, nurtured or honored this ambivalence, but the most successful or interesting negotiations of a utopocalyptic moment suggest that the poet, even while affirming something, has some capacity or dimension that allows him or her to see into the darknesses, into the ambiguities and difficulties of affirmation. In the most complex cases, we sense that such a poet has become aware of the psychology of judgment, aware that the imposing of a heavy closure on human affairs has the negative power to generate its own anxiety.

I

Left or Right. One poetical/political vector of the thirties was aimed at modern life, viewing left-wing politics as its worst excrescence. In many ways, the Fugitives embodied some of the most regressive aspects of this tendency.

Southern-aristocratic in orientation, antebellum in their view of the ordering of society and economics, the Fugitives were formalist in their poetics and anti-technological with respect to modern life. "Religion can hardly expect to flourish in an industrial society" (xiv), wrote the unnamed author of the introduction to *I'll Take My Stand* (1930), a title taken from the song "Dixie" and expressing the pugnacious character of the group. Allen Tate had already suggested that "only a return to the provinces, to the small self-contained centers of life, will put all-destroying America, to rest" (Spiller 1346). This was regionalism with a vengeance. Yet such a return did not mean becoming a provincial poet, for among the Fugitives an internal conflict expressed itself in the disparity between the poet's physical geography and his or her poetic machinery, heavily identified as it was with Eliot and his writings on the metaphysical poets. Tate, especially, raised Eliotic or metaphysical wit and irony to an almost parodistic degree because they afforded distance, which after all is a decidedly "cosmopolitan" consciousness, one enabling these poets to be "at home" in the cultural backwaters of the agrarian South. Like the Roman poets Juvenal and Horace, who were also models for the Fugitive group, a rueful acceptance of the status quo led to shrewd appraisals of the irony of the poet's situation rather than to visionary or utopocalyptic notes in the work. This expedient mystification was a subtle way of blocking out any disturbing truth. Thus John Crowe Ransom could write in 1938 that "the true poetry has no great interest in improving or idealizing the world, which does well enough. It only wants to see it better." The emphases on traditionalist craft and on the English tradition and canon in this "true poetry" were reflected as well in New Critical attitudes on the appropriate relation of life to art. They served to insulate the patrician Fugitive poet from the contingencies of history, in particular from the noise of those under one's foot clamoring for social change. Robert Penn Warren's early poems, full of windy abstract phrases such as "the leaves of the land / freshening the arbor / recall our honor," are typical examples of rhetoric used to avoid concrete reference to any ugly or offensive facts of southern history. Likewise, Tate's "Ode to the Confederate Dead" (written in 1928 and revised in 1937) manages never to allude to slaves or states' rights. Tate claimed that it was about "contemporary solipsism" (Spiller 1347). Both poems are, in fact, constructed of what Jonathan Morse, in his remarkable book *Word by Word*, refers to as "virtual history," history freed from the troubling burdens and "entrainments" of its own vocabulary. The idea that Confederate "honor" can be isolated from what that honor defended is one of the principal examples of the shielding effect of Fugitive self-reflexive irony.

Fugitive irony, however, is not the only means of dealing with the ambivalence I mentioned above, the knotted entanglements of hope and fear. In my category of utopocalyptic poet I would also place Hart Crane. Crane's poem *The Bridge,* begun in the late twenties before the cataclysm of the 1929 crash, was meant, as Crane says in his essay "Modern Poetry," "to absorb the machine, *i.e., acclimatize* it as naturally and casually as trees, galleons, castles and all other human associations of the past" (Crane 261). Behind the poem, "what has principally spurred them" (that is, the thoughts and conceptions concerning *The Bridge*), he told Waldo Frank, was "the Spengler thesis," not so much *The Decline of the West* but Spengler's morphology, that theory of transformative and metamorphic inherencies of destiny itself to which the poet could become attuned and so write out the myth of the age (Crane 230). The new hero of such an age would not be the warrior or poet but the engineer or technician.

Crane writes in "Cape Hatteras," section IV of *The Bridge:* "The nasal whine of power whips a new universe . . . / Where spouting pillars spoor the evening sky / under the looming stacks of the gigantic powerhouse / Stars prick the eyes with sharp ammoniac proverbs. . . . New verities, new inklings" (Crane 90). Here, Henry Adams's virgin and dynamo are replaced by technology cast in biblical dimension, one that constantly infers spiritual transcendence, as when the poet looks at the bridge and proclaims: "How could mere toil align thy choiring strings!" (Crane 46). The language of the poem wars between desperation and celebration, between the recalcitrant materialism of the subject matter and the attempt to place that matter on a mythic plane. What Yeats spoke of as rhetoric, as "the will attempting to do the work of the imagination," appears to permeate nearly all of its passages.

The real drama of the poem, the clotted language, the piled-on orisons all try to force connections. The rhythms in the lines, the jazz-inflected syncopations strive for a kind of expressive naming, as though Crane's ultimate American word would exhibit the torsions of a construction gantry or the interior of a power plant. The diction, loaded with its "thou's" and "thy's," is often at war with itself. So Crane's exhibition occurs in a language darkly qualified by the "nasal whine of power," by "looming" and "sharp ammoniac," phrases that suggest a writer caught in the half-conscious ambivalence of his project. For *The Bridge* roots *geist* in (of all things) the unyielding attributes of material objects. It is a bit of American animism or transcendentalism gone somewhat berserk, an animism partly alleviated by Crane's depiction of American "nomad raillery," its down-and-outers, those least capable of being caught up in the technological transformations that govern the mythic status of the work.

Crane sensed his own ambivalence, I think, when he wrote in "Modern Poetry" (1930) that "the mere romantic speculation on the power and beauty of machinery keeps it at a continual remove; it cannot act creatively in our lives until, like the unconscious nervous responses of our bodies, its connotations emanate from within" (Crane 262). In fact, one way to read *The Bridge* is to see it as continually trying to subsume within the psychic economy of a reader the material fact of the Brooklyn Bridge and the technological advances it represented.

Critics were divided over Crane's poem. Clearly, Crane's desire to make the physical object of the bridge into a spiritual fact could not be attempted head-on. R. P. Blackmur, writing in *The Double Agent* in 1935, explained Crane's ambivalence this way: "Crane labored to perfect both the strategy and the tactics of language so as to animate and maneuver his perceptions—and then fought the wrong war and against an enemy that displayed, to his weapons, no vulnerable target" (273).

Crane's later poems, such as "The Broken Tower," with its "visionary company of love," appear to deconstruct thoroughly the Spenglerian trope of *The Bridge*. "The Broken Tower" can be read as a minuscule reflector of Crane's epic, one suffused with an air of reflexive poignancy as it forsakes linguistic structural engineering and "builds within a tower that is not stone." Here Crane's poetry is no longer concerned with marvels of wire and steel (which he had claimed "lend a myth to God") but with something beyond the material, "the matrix of the heart" (Crane 194).

In his essay "American Poetry, 1920–1930," Louis Zukofsky attacks the "indefinite language and prolong[ed] verbal indecision past the useful necessity of meaning" of Crane's poetry. "Crane errs on the side of mysticism," Zukofsky writes, placing this "unfortunate" problem on Crane's "pseudo-substratum of idea contrasting with the [the poem's] feeling tone" (*Prepositions* 140). Rejecting Crane's "spirals of conceits" and, by inference, the near-mechanical application of Crane's idealism, Zukofsky's critique can be seen as part of a larger, career-long movement in his own work to find, as he later said of *Bottom: On Shakespeare*, a means of putting "all philosophy to rest"—in other words, of claiming, as the possibility of poetry, a way of seeing or being in the world that is superior to any allegiance to system or philosophy. If *Bottom* and *"A"* represent culminations of this intention, then the poem "Mantis" and its supplement, "Mantis, An Interpretation," a work of the thirties, constitute an important way station toward that goal.

We know that Zukofsky was deeply influenced by Marx at the time of writing "Mantis." His relationship to Marx's thought, however, was marked by a dialectical dilemma of the very sort that Marx himself invokes in his famous aphorism concerning the philosopher whose job is no longer to describe the world but to change it. The dilemma, as it arises in Zukofsky, concerns, of course, the question of the poet's role as either reflector of the world or as instrument of change. Written during a period when most Marxist-oriented poets were following the mandate of a "socialist realist" poetry for the masses, "Mantis," far from being a piece of propaganda or a purely Marxist "proof," is an example of Zukofsky's poetics at work—especially as given in statements like "An Objective."[1] That is, the poem itself appears to be governed by a poetics of open and unfinished composition, one that cannot be tamed to a philosophical conception. Such a poetics is clearly enjoined in Zukofsky's epigraph from the Latin to "Mantis, An Interpretation," that "names are sequent to the things named," and in Zukofsky's use, almost as a litany of Dante's and Cavalcanti's sense of poetry, of "*la battalgia degli diversi pensieri,*" "the battle of diverse thoughts," "thought's torsion" (*Complete Short Poetry* 68).

Like Crane's *The Bridge,* Zukofsky's poem, too, is a drama of the struggle of myth over and against the word. The utopocalyptic "moment" of the poem, the pressures brought to bear on poetic composition, here concerns not only the political status of the poem or poet, but the nature of words in relation to art and reality, especially as a totalized worldview, one form of which is Marxism's attempts to subordinate all human activity to its categories and analyses.

In a sense, Zukofsky's poem reminds us of the antagonism between high modernist art and the impulse to provide meaningful social commentary. "The growing oppression of the poor," Zukofsky writes in the "Interpretation," "is the situation most pertinent to us" (*Complete Short Poetry* 69). If this is so, then, for poets of the thirties, as I have described above, the condition of this oppression is bound up, not only in external political relations about which one could propagandize via one's poetry, but in the very nature of poetic activity. The poem tries, on one level, to resolve these tensions. It is part formal plaint for the poor, as in the sestina's last lines, unmistakably hortatory, which read: "Fly Mantis, on the poor, arise like leaves / The armies of the poor, strength: stone on stone / And build the new world in your eyes. Save it!" (*Complete Short Poetry* 66). At the same time, much of its modernist tendencies and idiosyncracies, its obeisance to "making it new," are contained in the "Interpretation," the "open-form explanation" that partly explicates the sestina while reminding us that "our world will not stand it, / the implications of a too-regular form" (*Complete Short Poetry* 70).

Now you will recall that Zukofsky elsewhere has stated that the poem has a function—is a "job," as he puts it. In this case, the job of the poem is not only a call to alleviate the condition of the poor, but, as I believe the "Interpretation" makes clear, to resist the strictures which a purely sociopolitical view would impose on the poem. To do this, Zukofsky must honor and be faithful to the starting point of the incident that, in effect, generated the poem, the gratuitous occasion of the mantis in the subway, an occasion that sets into motion ("movement") a series of thoughts and associations creating an order of relations faithful to the initial experience and contrary to the expected usages of the incident as symbolical ("no human being wishes to become / An insect for the sake of a symbol" [*Complete Short Poetry* 70]) of the poor's oppression or of the demonization of capital. In other words, the poem's turn is to be toward "an incident, *compelling any writing*" rather than the typical politicized use of language as propaganda or "message." By staying with "thought's torsions" wherever they will lead, Zukofsky places his trust, not in political rhetoric, but in something having "enough worth if the emotions can equate it," in this case, from "Provencal myth" to "airships" or comments by the "British Admiralty." "Mantis," in effect, offers its own felt series of interrelationships, a counter-continuity, one not made up of Marxist analyses but of intuitive connections established by having been faithful, as Zukofsky insists, to the "original shock still persisting." This is not so much a new making as a constant desiring, beyond a political schema, to be in touch with a social world. "So that," Zukofsky writes

> the invoked collective
> Does not subdue the senses' awareness,
> The longing for touch to an idea, or
> To a use function of the material:
> The original emotion remaining,
> like the collective,
> Unprompted, real, as propaganda. (*Complete Short Poetry* 72)

In effect, Zukofsky is trying here to find a way of refusing the hard conceptualizations of ideology and theory, so that he may return the act of poem-making to something that is simultaneously open-ended and analytical—not so much to deny his own Marxist insights as to prevent any "philosophy" from having a hegemonic hold over existence. Because the world in its entirety is beyond a single conception, so the poem must find its own unified form. The complexity of that form demands that the poem strive, as Zukofsky says in the brilliant final strophe of "Mantis," to hold "the simultaneous, / the diaphanous, historical / in one head" (*Complete Short Poetry* 73).

Now where such Zukofskian dexterity was absent, another powerful and fateful dynamic took over. I am thinking here of Oppen in the thirties. Reflecting back on the early days of the "Objectivist" project, Oppen said that its aim was to replace the dreariness of "right thinking by an act of perception." Like Zukofsky, Oppen had tried to reopen the poem to experiences and perceptions that political theory or "right thinking" would deny or obscure. "Perhaps," he wrote retrospectively in a letter to Martin Rosenblum, "the word *revelatory* does define a common intention or effort—all experience is valid—the revelatory experience of one's own life—it is this that was uppermost in my mind (age 20 or thereabouts)" (*Selected Letters* 285).

As I reread Oppen's *Discrete Series* (*Collected Poems* 3–14), looking for the "drama" of the poems, I now find that the work, more than anything else, embodies a troubled vocabulary and structure of absences which clearly embeds the creation of the poem in the utopocalyptic moment of the thirties and perhaps gives us, as well, a few hints about Oppen's abandonment of poetry. Lacking archival proof, my remarks here are necessarily speculative.

Oppen's poem, written at the tail end of the imagist movement and yet pushing against the boundary of language as it interacts with sensory and visual information, suggests an interrogation of imagism's limits. (We must recall that Williams's own questioning of imagism was occurring at this time.) But this interrogation seems only part of a yet deeper undercurrent running through much of the work.

Let us speculate: the first section of *Discrete Series,* unlike the remaining ones, is composed in a straightforward, even classical syntax. Its language is literary and allusive, as in such phrases as "rain falling, in the distance more slowly" and "the world, weather-swept" (*Collected Poems* 3), in the Jamesian referencing itself. These are the cadences of a language dying—dying, mind you, not because it has been deauthenticated but because the mechanical, scientistic, and machinelike world that began to emerge in both the economic and artistic spheres will no longer speak in or listen to such a language. It is, in fact, a language on the verge of abandonment because there is no longer any community to hear it except as museum piece or anodyne (such as in the popular fiction of the period). Still, Oppen's intention, as can be seen from this first and the remaining sections, is to see "what [is] really going on." Only now, whatever language is to be used must be the language of "perception"; that is, *what is* can only be registered by a perceptual act become language. If the poetic language of the nineteenth century was rhetorical (made rhetorical by circumstance) and is now unhearable, that of the twentieth must be sensible and tangible, that is, the strictest sort of imagism. But that consideration in itself creates a problem.

When Williams remarked that imagism failed because it lost all "structural necessity," he may very well have been referring to the kind of difficulty which Oppen confronted. Pure imagism, a poetry of the strictly visible, cannot establish a set of relations between its parts. It can render a datum; indeed, that is its forte. But it cannot articulate the discursive (communal, social, philosophical) order in which data are held (realism) or in which they ought to be held (prophecy).

At this time, Oppen, like Zukofsky, was deeply influenced by Marxist thought and by the desire to be a socially useful individual in the face of the massive poverty of the depression. So the question, as it came to him, was whether there was any social utility in poetry. If one thing having utility would be the poetic "truth" of the sociopolitical situation, then, in effect, the one poetic tool or technique Oppen can allow himself is imagism. This is because perception, imagism's basis, being undeniable, is always "true." But what if that one tool, a severe and rigorous imagism claiming to be free of ideological rhetoric, appears to be inadequate to the "job" poetry must accomplish for Oppen to remain a poet?

Clearly, such an inadequacy is continually signaled in the poems that make up *Discrete Series,* both in their syntactical and denominative porosity and in their constant reference to what is hidden or cannot be realized. For instance, reading *Discrete Series* (a short work), one finds that in addition to the numerous syntactical gaps that make up Oppen's poetic signature, as it were, there are, scattered throughout, no less than five question marks, at least four "if's" and over a dozen questions or implications of questions by way of negative troping. Here are some of his phrases that indicate what I think constitutes the tenor of the work (I have added a few words of my own to bring out my point): "Thus / Hides the // Parts" (*Collected Poems* 4); "Over what has the air frozen?" (4); the question of what is "Not evident at 'The Sailor's Rest'" (5); what is left unstated in "He has chosen a place / With the usual considerations, / Without stating them" (6)?; why is "the closed car" "less strange" (6)? How are we to resolve the passage which reads: "Tho the face, still within it, / Between glasses—place over which / time passes—a false light" (6)? What of that falsity? And what of the mystery of: "Is it you who truly / Excel the vegetable / . . . / Incognito as summer / Among mechanics" (12)? Why the questioning poignancy of: "O what O what will / Bring us back to / Shore" (13)? I find that these passages make a very interesting litany, one which suggests that at almost every turn the language of these poems is on the edge of disappearing, of curling under itself, into absence. And such absence leaves us with an unbridgeable distance between the poem and the reality it meant to see when the narrator in the first passage wondered "what really was going on" on the other side of the "windowglass." Here, the demand on the poet to invoke "right thinking" by perception—particularly placed on a poet who later expresses a strong belief in the small nouns, in the substantives of language—leads only to an abyss, a field of gaps and craters in meaning and even visualization.

Please understand me: the porosity of *Discrete Series* is not a failure of poetic will or integrity; it is the reverse. Indeed, as one reads the poem, one thinks of

Pound's line in Canto XIII about historians who were willing to leave blanks for what they did not know. In my reading, *Discrete Series* is less a poem about avant-garde technique or even about "making it new" than it is a desperate cry in the poetic-political wilderness over insufficient means and, given Oppen's politics, the ultimate insufficiencies of his own poetry to enact social change or offer hope. In other words, as I have written elsewhere ("Oppen and Stevens" 15–17), *Discrete Series* is a poem written "under duress" of Poundian imagist principles and yet, at the same time, it was written when Oppen felt most strongly, as he wrote in retrospect, "a tremendous difficulty of honesty, the whole weight of sincerity [seeming] to rest on one's shoulders" (*Selected Letters* 82). The "cry" of the poem, its resolving trope, is the voicing of its own inability to conform to the hegemonies of the Marxist thinking of the thirties.

A further inference here is that, in Oppen, the porosity of the poem signaled the failure of a purely descriptive/referential poetics. Imagist techniques alone had become insufficient to articulate the poet's personal internal struggle or torment between poetry and politics. A reading of his later poetry, and his letters after his return to poetry in the late fifties, would in my judgment confirm this inference. Thinking back over his experience of the thirties, Oppen returned again to his abandonment of poetry in this way: "Maybe I admire myself more however, for knowing what is one thing and what is the other and what are the levels of truth—that is to say, for simply not attempting to write communist verse. That is, to any statement already determined before the verse. Poetry has to be protean; the meaning must begin there. With the perception" (*Selected Letters* 22). When the means at hand failed him, when he could no longer reach to the level of truth he required of the poem, he dropped poetry for other tools.

I would add one more note on this subject. Someone assaying to write on the comparative poetics of Oppen and Zukofsky might begin with this thesis: the very rigor of a poetics of pure perception or of, at least, its attenuated version in imagism was to be Oppen's undoing, while for Zukofsky, "perception"—we remember the mantis as starting point—had been mainly a transformative beginning. Utopocalyptics at work.

II

Zukofsky's way was one way out of the dilemma that Oppen had posed to himself. Williams, that most difficult of writers to pin down, was involved in another. He was dealing with the political situation on a number of levels. On the one hand, perhaps with some irony, Williams in the 1930s was collaborating with Nathanael West on an issue of *Contact II* that was to feature the "good writing [even] among Communists." At the same time, in his well-known 1932 letter to Kay Boyle, a letter that is nearly a textbook of his poetics, Williams writes: "Bosh! All I want to do is to state that poetry in its sources, body, spirit, in its form in short, is related to poetry and not to socialism, communism or anything else that tries to swallow it" (*Selected Letters* 131). "Good writing" and "poetry" were, for Williams, not opposed to politics but were—on the level of thought—categories larger than sociopolitical systems. Poetry, he wrote in *The Embodiment of Knowledge*, is "the apex of knowledge." It is "the one purely articulate form, more so than action which involves the mind so scantily, or to know" (66).

Williams's views on this matter are most compelling stated in *The Embodiment of Knowledge*, a collection of miscellaneous writings from the years 1928 to 1930, but it may be useful here to see briefly how, in his letters and poetry of the thirties, Williams's poetics were already establishing the idea of the poetic word or language as a mode of realization which had priority to any systematized belief.

In a 1932 letter to Pound, Williams discussed the "inexplicitness of modern verse as compared with, let us say, the *Iliad*." He continues, "Whereas formerly the music which accompanied the words amplified, certified and released them, today, the words we write, failing a patent music, have become the music itself, and the understanding of the individual (presumed) is now that which used to be the words" (*Selected Letters* 125, 126). Here we sense an attempt by Williams to clear the ground for poetry—not that poetry does not always bear some ideological trace or burden, but that for the poet, the attempt to signify can precede or take into account or even nudge aside the ideological atmosphere in which the poem is written.

Zukofskian Objectivist poetics were, for Williams, the way for this ground-clearing to be achieved. In a 1932 letter to Marianne Moore, he remarked of this method, or honor code, as he saw it in her work: "The meaning of the objective, the realization of its releasing quality, instead of its walling effect when badly comprehended, has been nowhere so well forced to the light. It is the underlying reality as well as the supreme difficulty of an art" (*Selected Letters* 123). He pronounced this realization in her own poetry to be "a sense of triumph."

Such an intention, to show the "releasing quality" of the objective, strikes me as self-evident in much of Williams's most powerful poems of the period. "Perpetuum Mobile: The City," for example, a work which, formally, already prefigures the "variable foot" of the later poetry, is something of a demonstration. In the poem, the narrator is speaking to a woman about the city:

—a dream
we dreamed
each
separately
we two

of love
and of
desire— (*Collected Poems* 1: 430)

This is the dream "toward which / we love," a dream "a little / false," yet of such power that

There is no end
to desire—

let us break
through
and go there—

in
vain! (432)

The counterpoint of these lines—the force of desire and the hopelessness of attaining its object—becomes the repeated motif of the poem. A litany of brutal factuality, of meaningless work, crime, and gluttony is punctuated throughout the poem by the choral refrain of "for love." The poem is constructed, as Williams once defined his poetics, out of "inimitable particles of dissimilarity," a means by which the traces of a thing can imply what is left out as well as what is included. This is similar in effect to Williams's "obsolete" image of the rose in the earlier *Spring and All,* where the visual datum "becomes a geometry" which "penetrates / the Milky Way" (*Collected Poems* 1: 195).

The spatiality of "Perpetuum Mobile," its disjunctive deployment of images, rather than simply giving us a picture of the city, presents us with the ganglia of emotions that the modern city might induce. The poem, bent on embracing the harsh contraries of modern life, thus pits a utopian vision of the city—"for love" is its repeated refrain—against the human results, the way people actually live in the city. The poem's "dream," the city, is "a little false," its contradicting images and evidence, as in "For love / his eyes are blown out" or in the passage where the city's inhabitants are "Guzzling / the creamy foods /

while out of sight / in the sub-cellar" in "the foulest sink / in the world." The poem juxtaposes its images in such a way as to create a network of relations that palpably render the ambivalent texture of city life,

> —a dream
> of lights
> hiding
> the iron reason
> and stone
> a settled
> cloud—
>
> City
>
> whose stars
> of matchless
> splendor— (*Collected Poems* 1: 434–35)

As with nearly all of Williams's later work, the appeal of the concrete imagery, sensuous and visual, accounts, beyond rhetoric or conceptualization, for an actual historical matrix, an authentic datum, authentic because, in its unity, it has refused an easy surrender to a one-dimensional treatment of its subject. As with other objects in the world, the poem can be approached again and again for a variety of reasons from knowledge to pleasure. The poem as name, or as Zukofsky had it in his epigraph, "names are sequent to the things named." Which is what the English poet Charles Tomlinson wrote concerning the intention of Williams's work: "to name what possesses no name."

In yet another transposition of a utopocalyptic moment, Wallace Stevens's "The Poems of Our Climate" of the late thirties dramatizes the problematics of the poets such as the Objectivists above, who were torn between the heaven or utopian world of the beautiful image, and the restlessness of the mind faced with a very earthly apocalypse. For Stevens, a poetry of contemplative moments is insufficient and leaves a hunger to be fulfilled, not by a poetic dictum but by the uncertainties of existence, where "the imperfect is our paradise" and where "delight" lies in "flawed words and stubborn sounds" (Stevens, *Poems* 93, 94). The poem, if Stevens's counsel is to be observed, cannot escape reality and lead us into the sheltered precincts of an art. At the same time, Stevens wants to save the poem from a purely political usage. Having seen both the political and poetic waste of the thirties, he remarks in his 1942 address "The Noble Rider and the Sound of Words": "The truth is that the social obligation so closely urged is a phase of the pressure of reality which a poet (in the absence of dramatic poets) is bound to resist or evade." Echoing an earlier Williams, Stevens asks, "What is his [the poet's] function? Certainly it is not to lead people out of the confusion in which they find themselves. Nor is it, I think, to comfort them while they follow their readers to and fro. His function is to make his imagination theirs and that he fulfills himself only as he sees his imagination become the light in the minds of others" (*Necessary Angel* 28, 29).

Each in his own way, both Williams and Stevens were committed not to a narrow politics but to a certain idea concerning the word which did not so much exclude politics as look at it from another direction. What we need to ask ourselves is what was the nature of the word as both Stevens and Williams understood it.

I have in mind a complex political/poetics schema (which, thankfully, I cannot elaborate here) suggesting that the poet tries to make the words of the poem function in three ways: the representational word, the nonreferential or musical word, and the verdictive or naming word. These types of words all bear certain kinds of tests of their efficacy. With respect to the politics of poetry, representation belongs to confirmation and certainty, the nonreferential to trance or music or fantasy. Under the utopocalyptics of hope and fear, the naming word becomes the one most closely related to the truth function of poetry because it invokes a poetics of receptivity, of sensing those burdens which the world has placed on the poem rather than asserting a prior theoretical, vatic, or prophetic privilege. This concept of the word, alluded to in both Williams and Stevens, is a matter for further scholarly consideration.

As for Pound, to whom we are indebted for so much, in the "as if" of poetry—let us take *The Cantos* as a clear example—a particular world is projected. Not so much a world under Pound's hand, but the world as it might or ought to be and, indeed, by definition what it ought not to be. Pound was already seeing the arena of the poem as a sociopolitical field in his famous statement in a letter to Felix Schelling in 1922 that "All values ultimately come from our judicial sentences" (*Letters* 181). This was the same somewhat infamous paragraph in which Pound had said that "Humanity is malleable mud, and the arts set the moulds it is later cast into." And then curiously—especially in the light of later developments—Pound, by 1928 in the second issue of *Exile,* had already sensed something of a danger in the conflating of the personal and the political. Taking the Confucian tack, he argued against the loss of distinction between the public and the private and the tendency to "mess in other people's affairs before establishing order in one's own." Today, while I leave the ironies of these insights to others, one thing seems clear, that Pound, as I am suggesting, surely strayed from his own earlier *dicta,* present in the earlier poetry and in the first

Cantos. This, at least, is suggested by Geoffrey Hill in *The Lords of Limit* (155), where he penetratingly remarks that Pound's use of "judicial" in the sentence I quoted above may have already been an allusion to an attempt to employ the word, and by implication, the poem, in its post-Shelleyan legislative or executive sense as opposed to its "verdictive" or judging sense. "Verdictives," and I think this term comes to Hill from Austin, attempt to describe a state of affairs—that is, a verdictive word or poem is close to the idea of the name. If we think about it, politics tends to obscure the power of the name, for naming is almost always about singularities and one-of-a-kind individuations, while politics is about an agreed-upon collectivity (a subject requiring more space than I have here). But I will say this much, rightly or wrongly, that naming belongs to poetry, whose products remain in the realm of the mind, rather than to politics, whose products are in the realm of action.

Zukofsky's and Williams's words "sincerity," "objectification," and "rested totality," or Reznikoff's "witnessing," these are terms weighted heavily on the naming or verdictive dimension of poetry—a dimension which, like judgment in law, must invoke history and precedent. If we find that we value the Objectivists and their poetry, it strikes me that it is because they understood the history of the word and could so place it in a poem so as to account for the historical uses it had undergone. Or, if they could not place it, if they could find no place to place it, as in Oppen's *Discrete Series,* they left those syntactic and semantic blanks which, phenomenologically, suggest the meaning of what is actually presented. Oppen's absence to poetry for twenty years may be intuited as a similar lacuna.

I return to a variant on my original point. Poetry, by its nature, is always concerned with the utopocalyptic, which is not to say that it is essentialistic, but that the mind's impulse is, as Wittgenstein remarked, to make a world out of an utterance. The more complex and full that utterance is, the more valuable the poetry. The Objectivists' function was to create tools to accomplish this very goal, to create a language, as Kenner points out in *The Pound Era,* of "no myths," but also one that maintained a "sincere" relationship to the sociopolitics of the times. Inevitably, maintaining that balance meant keeping faith with ambivalence rather than with utopia. Where the Objectivists could not find within themselves such a language, where it did not square with the political spirit they had placed themselves under, as with Oppen and Rakosi, they left the field honorably to find it again on another day.

In a sense, among poets like Zukofsky and Williams, there was submission to neither myth nor politics, and while the poetry of these Objectivists may have had its drynesses, its intellections and long silences, it nevertheless left a baseline from which American poetry was able to proceed. In poets like Zukofsky, Reznikoff, and Lorine Niedecker, in Oppen's and Rakosi's return to poetry and in Duncan's and Creeley's use of them, the Objectivist procession has continued until our time. A poetry that has remained resolutely opposed to the ahistorical, it cannot be said to lead inevitably to what we term "postmodernism," at least in the forms in which postmodernism usually is discussed today. So I would conclude, if my speculations or *fictions* of composition are at all correct, that what the Objectivist poets of the thirties have to tell us is something very different from what much current criticism seems to say about them. This Objectivist "something" is as yet unlabeled and may very well be unlabelable.

Williams, inspirer of and participant in these early phases of Objectivist poetics, writes in *Spring and All* that "intelligence . . . stands still with time and forces change about itself—sifting the world for permanence" (*Collected Poems* 1: 220). The Objectivist poets, in their identification and testing of the century's specters of promise or doom, maintained a kind of honorable steadfastness of perception and vision. Their powerful resistance to the expediencies of history endures as a remarkable and moving "permanence" and makes of their work a continual tutelary presence.

8

Lorine Niedecker's "Folk Base" and Her Challenge to the American Avant-Garde

Peter Middleton

What is the effect of placing speech in a poem? What is the effect of placing a poem in a collection of poems by other poets? These ordinary cultural acts of displacement are taken for granted by most writers and readers, but for the Objectivist poet Lorine Niedecker they represented highly conscious acts alien to her everyday world. Although her fellow Objectivists were marginalized by the literary world for much of their careers, they mostly lived and worked within the metropolitan cultures where their avant-garde poetry was read. She spent almost all her life in rural Wisconsin in relative poverty, keeping her writing life quite separate from her various working-class jobs and the local community. This essay will read her poetry in terms of its relations with the poetic avant-garde and the acts of displacement required by these connections. Doing so helps make tangible the complexity of a poetic style that can appear to dissolve meaning into a limpid clarity leaving nothing to interpret, especially from the standpoint of the poetic avant-garde that promulgated her work and which had during her lifetime a tendency to make largely unquestioned assumptions about the universal transmissibility of its forms of poetry.

Lorine Niedecker was born in 1903 in Fort Atkinson, Wisconsin, and lived in this rural area dominated by lakes and rivers until her death in 1970, with only a few spells away, mainly in Madison. She began writing poetry in the thirties, visited New York, where she met the young Objectivist poet Louis Zukofsky, and began a lifelong correspondence with him which formed the basis of her relationship with the avant-garde network of poets who became the publishers and readers of her poetry. After a brief relationship with Zukofsky she returned to Wisconsin and lived a relatively solitary life devoted to an intensive poetic practice. Unlike the jobs she took to support herself, there was "no layoff / from this / condensery" (*Condensery* 141). After early experiments with surrealism and other modernist strategies, her poetry took as its theme the rural culture and landscape, until toward the end of her career she began to write about historical figures like Jefferson and Darwin. Throughout her career she showed an extraordinary precision in her use of sound in poetry. Only a few books of her poetry were published in her lifetime, and those by small presses, so her reputation depended on the continuing support of a few people, notably the editor and poet Cid Corman, who published her in *Origin* and maintained a correspondence with her in the latter part of her life. Even after her death her poetry remained hard to obtain, and there is still no reliable complete edition of her poetry available. Almost any brief account of the isolation and poverty of Niedecker's life is likely to give a false impression, however, because as Rachel Blau DuPlessis and Jenny Penberthy have both persuasively argued, Niedecker's life should not be read in terms of failure or exclusion.[1] Her isolation was a deliberate and creative choice that fostered her poetry, whatever its other costs and deprivations.

As a lifelong resident writer of Black Hawk Island, Niedecker lived a long way from any metropolitan or avant-garde culture, yet she was very aware of how her world might look from outside. During the thirties she was employed by the WPA as a research editor on the guide to Wisconsin, for which she would have had to learn some of the skills of the folklorist to record local idioms and anecdotes that could typify a regional culture, and so became that uneasy figure the participant-observer. Her relation to advanced literary culture was oddly similar, although in this case she was more observer than participant. The art world was familiar, and yet apart, because contact with it depended largely on one man, Zukofsky, of whose metropolitan art world she had little firsthand experience. Publishing a poem meant alienating it even further from the place where she lived and from the people around her, few of whom even knew she wrote, and placing it within the network of avant-garde publishing. Her poetry's continuance depended upon a small, discerning network of editors who recognized the value of her poetry, and would publish it, mostly in magazines, and only rarely in books or anthologies. Her work is still closely identified with certain small presses. The social and subjective distance that her poems traveled would have made her aware of the way this network could take control not only of the general significance of her poetry, but of the very meanings of poems themselves. Her emphasis on "local reality, a fusion of past and personal" (Caddel in Penberthy, *Lorine Niedecker* 282), is in part a poetic strategy for revealing the implications of such necessary appropriation.

What happens when these seemingly fundamental practices—making speech into poems, and placing poems among the work of other poets—become self-conscious, awkward, and distancing rather than taken for granted? The clarities, themes, address, and intertextualities of Niedecker's poetry insinuate surprising local critiques of such apparently unquestionable practices, and so what might have been merely a phenomenologically astute poetry of place becomes something much more unusual. The tensions between localism and internationalism in much twentieth-century American poetry are put to work in Niedecker's poetry to create a new poetics of cultural transmission.

She could have seen a pointed, instructive example of these tensions when, soon after the publication of her first book, *New Goose,* in 1946, Louis Zukofsky chose one of her very short poems, "There's a Better Shine," for his didactic anthology *A Test of Poetry* (1948), which places a wide range of old and new English poetry into short sets for the purposes of contrast and comparison. In its entirety her poem reads:

> There's a better shine
> on the pendulum
> than is on my hair
> and many times
> * * * *
> I've seen it there. (*Test of Poetry* 41)

The diacritical stars are an integral part of the poem at several levels, indicating a pause for breath and a break in thought, representing a measure of elapsed time, and forming an iconic image of the beats of a pendulum. This poem's elegant concision, musical control, innovative use of punctuation, and apparent simplicity of theme typify much of Niedecker's later work. A discussion of the wider significance of its unobtrusive meditation (one wants to say "reflection" until one realizes that this is a pun which the poem itself implies) on the relationship between self-image, time, and perceptual acts of mediation between subject and object could review the history of aesthetic argument since romanticism. Zukofsky pointed the poem in a different direction. He placed this poem in his anthology in such a context that its meaning could be bent into quite another shape too, and in doing so he was acting in accordance with his own acute sense of the need to recognize the genealogical, ideological, and formalist challenges to the value of one's own poetry. In an essay for *Poetry* written in 1946, he explains that to be a poet means that every poem or potential poem of one's own is placed alongside all the other poems of the past: "The poet may visibly stop writing, but secretly measures himself against each word of poetry ever written. Furthermore . . . he thinks of others who have lived, live, and will live to say the things he cannot say for the time being" (*Prepositions* 3). This anxious belief that the poet is engaged in some transhistoric poetry competition depends on the unexplored assumption that poetry is a transferable utterance. A poem begins as a wordless urgency to which the poet is trying to give voice, possibly helped by the utterances of earlier poems, and sometimes hindered by incapacity, while anxious that other poets will develop this capacity first, and so be able to say what the poet had hoped to claim originality for. The material of the poem can move freely from one location or moment to another, and does not inhere in one intersubjective network from where it could only be wrenched away at the risk of an attenuation of significance. His anthology offered a tangible demonstration of this belief in the transferability of poetry across a transhistoric and international network of poetic value.

Recontextualization is the strategic device chosen to make readers see the poems and extracts afresh, but its effect on Niedecker's poem is much more than an act of editorial defamiliarization. It transforms a poem that reflects upon self-consciousness and time into a poem that seems to confirm, from the mouth of a woman poet, that women are rightly depicted as dangerously seductive creatures of passion by the male poetic tradition. This is a reading with special resonance given Zukofsky's own history of relations with Niedecker.

"There's a better shine" is displayed at the end of a column containing poems by Keats, Lord Herbert of Cherbury, and Shakespeare, an exalted company of men. This balance of past and present is typical of *A Test of Poetry*, which is predominantly made up of seventeenth-century verse, with some nineteenth-century and a few contemporary poets such as Charles Reznikoff, Williams Carlos Williams, and Zukofsky himself. Contemporary poems are therefore placed in a particular literary history that derives particularly from modernist preoccupations. The poems in Niedecker's group appear anonymously with a series of labels, 23a–23d, that refer to a key at the back, from which we also learn that this group appears under the rubric "recurrence." Recurrence is unlikely to be a reader's first association, given the obviousness of two other themes, women and clarity, whose salience is encouraged by the interpretative license of anonymity and the lack of immediately discernible categorization. The delayed effect of the knowledge of authorship, especially awareness that the last poem is by a woman, then actually plays into the expectations the group generates poem by poem.

The set begins with a tantalizingly brief phrase. Keats's "Ode to Autumn" is represented in minimalist fashion by just three words, "hedge-crickets sing," an allusion to the final celebrations of nature before the death of the year. In the poem, autumn is a "close bosom-friend of the maturing sun," a personified figure whose gender is not identified, but closely associated with many feminine qualities, such as plumpness and ripeness, and is also a pastoral figure, the personification of a landscape about to be transformed into the wintry absence of feminizing presence. The hedge-crickets could be minor poets singing the imminent demise of mature sensuality. In the next extract, Lord Herbert of Cherbury asks Love to divide the properties of glass between himself and the woman he loves so that there will be "clearness for me, frailty for her" (the poem is called "In a Glass-Window for Inconstancy"). The request is full of delightful ironies, since the apparent impossibility of separating these qualities of glass could lead to the inference that the man's clarity of thought may itself fracture, or alternatively suggest that love will always be a mix of rationality and passion, for men as well as women. Whatever its ironies, however, the poem's ground is a strongly gendered division of the faculties into reason and emotion. This stereotypical rift is picked up even more strongly in the next extract, from Shakespeare's *Pericles:*

> Fair glass of light, I love you, and could still,
> Were not this glorious casket stored with ill:
> But I must tell you, now my thoughts revolt;
> For he's no man on whom perfections wait
> That, knowing sin within, will touch the gate.
> You are a fair viol and your sense the strings,
> Who, finger'd to make man his lawful music,
> Would draw heaven down and all the gods, to hearken,
> But being play'd upon before your time,
> Hell only danceth at so harsh a chime. (*Test of Poetry* 41)

Pericles makes this aside when he realizes that Antiochus and Antiochus's daughter are lovers and the king has no intention of letting Pericles or anyone else marry her. By juxtaposing these allusions to perverse love with Niedecker's poem, Zukofsky makes the passage say things he perhaps cannot, both of the more general kind his essay endorsed, and the most intimate. He himself had had an affair with Niedecker that was premature and not "lawful," at least in the religious sense. Whether consciously or, more likely, unconsciously, he has chosen a passage that would say what he feels about what had happened, and in doing so also takes over its gender assumptions as if to justify his attitude. Women are instruments upon which men make music, not makers of music themselves. With the reinforcement of the two previous extracts, this becomes a powerful coded statement in sharp tension with the evidence of a woman making music in the final extract.

The *Pericles* passage ends on the word "chime," which is then echoed both by the sound of the word "shine" and the image of the pendulum in Niedecker's lyric. The clever use in the last line of a pronoun whose antecedent is ambiguous, and the visual pun on the movement of the pendulum that represents time passing, reframe the appealing self-deprecating admission of the poet's lack of beauty. Instead of simply an amusing, idiomatic exaggeration of drabness, the poem becomes a meditation on the reflexivity of identity over time. By placing Niedecker's poem at the end of this set of poems, Zukofsky overshadows such interpretations, first by creating a private historical relevance projected as the motivation for his selection, which makes her poem into an admission of complicity with perverse desire, and then, through its placement as a late example of a topos with a long history, into an avowal of female narcissism that endorses the poetic tradition. For the few readers who knew of Zukofsky's relations with Niedecker, this sequence, far from universalizing their poetic relevance, would have actually demonstrated that the metropolitan art world could be a highly local place.

The sequence also produces another, potentially misogynistic, semantic drama about poetic vocation. The derogatory idea of woman as a mere instrument for the generation of music by a skilled male creator is reinforced by this thematization of male clarity, since clarity was a guiding preoccupation of the Objectivist nexus, and a concern of Niedecker herself, although less explicitly so. To understand how this drama is constructed, it is necessary to consider the importance of the concept of clarity for Objectivist poetics.

George Oppen wrote:

> Clarity, clarity, surely clarity is the most beautiful thing in the
> world,
> A limited, limiting clarity
>
> I have not and never did have any motive of poetry
> But to achieve clarity (*Collected Poems* 185)

The vehemence of this assertion is a tacit recognition of the difficulties of attaining clarity, both according to his theories of the relation between language and the world, and in his poetry, which often presents manifest difficulties, conceptual and syntactic, to the reader. Zukofsky, too, aspired to clarity as an ideal that his poetry might only gesture at. The belief that rationality depends as much upon visualization and sound as it does upon words, which he attributes to Wittgenstein, C. S. Pierce, and of course Spinoza leads him to an even stronger celebration of clarity: "the eye cannot look so that it cannot look. The wholeness it sees in looking is its inexpressible ethics" (*Bottom* 89). To lack the "clearness" of glass, or to be a "fair glass of light" that is corrupted within, is to lack an ethics entirely. Perhaps it is an act of ethical weakness even to admit that the "wholeness" one sees when looking at oneself in a simultaneous act of visual and cognitive self-reflection is also dependent on a concern with the success of one's feminine appearance. By placing Niedecker's poem in such company, the anthology makes possible a reading of her poem that questions whether a woman can ever be a poet, particularly a poet striving for the highest ideals of claritas, like the Objectivists.

Tempting as it is to imagine Niedecker decoding these meanings and taking them to heart, this is not the conclusion we can draw from the existing evidence. We do not know that Niedecker ever consciously made any of these connections, nor whether she registered the fact that she and Marianne Moore were the only women poets in the collection. She went on liking "There's a better shine," and referred to it as one of her five best poems (along with "Old man who seined," "Paul," "I rose from marsh mud," and "The clothesline post is set") in a letter to Cid Corman in 1960 (Faranda 24), so Zukofsky's use of it does not appear to have dimmed her attachment to it, and there is no evidence that the anthology itself affected her in any way. We cannot treat it as a trauma that generated a subsequent reaction formation in her poetics. What we can say is that throughout her career she was presented with plenty of evidence of the way in which the Objectivist version of avant-garde ideals could make poems speak in new ways, even running counter to one's aims, by treating poems as part of an international, transtemporal language of poets, regardless of their initial "webbing of relations" (DuPlessis in Penberthy, *Lorine Niedecker* 109) to a locality of readers and history. *A Test of Poetry* is simply an example that particularly rewards a critical archeology looking for enduring traces of such transformations. The question then is whether her poetry offers any challenge to, and investigation of, such appropriation.

Niedecker was certainly chary of the distortions produced by the contextualization of poetry by school or group. Near the end of her career there are distinct signs in the letters that she wanted to distance herself from Objectivism, notably concerning the Objectivist issue of *Contemporary Literature* because it seemed to encourage a superficial set of relationships between poets: "there is the talking about each other's poetry that bothers me a little. . . . [I]t's literary criticism but all the same a little also like gossip!" (Faranda 193). In a letter to Gail Roub, one of the few people outside the avant-garde network with whom she could discuss poetry, she says she is "much taken up with how to define a way of writing poetry which is not Imagist nor Objectivist fundamentally nor Surrealism alone" (Faranda 9). This negative poetics leads her to a redefinition that has a phenomenological ring to it as it tries to separate itself from simple clarity. "The basis is direct and clear—what has been seen or heard etc.... — but something gets in, overlays all that to make a state of consciousness.... I used to feel that I was goofing off unless I held only to the hard, clear image, the thing you could put your hand on but now I dare do this reflection" (9–10). Instead of a choice between clarity and frailty, the choice is between mere perceptual clarity and the complexities of reflective consciousness. Looking in the pendulum is an act of daring.

Although she lacked the range of opportunity available to even a poet as marginalized as Zukofsky, Niedecker was quite capable of intervening in the politics of recontextualization herself, within the limited fields offered to her, as a discussion of Oppen in one of her letters reveals. In this letter she seems surprisingly rude about Oppen, describing him as a latter-day grasshopper, as if obliquely recalling those "hedge-cricket" poets from Keats, and thereby acknowledging Zukofsky's other acts of poetic displacement. It is also an example of just how the nexus could represent itself through the transfer of images and phrases. "George Oppen—yes, there's something intriguing there. However, there are times I've felt he's down in the grass as an insect (singing from his knees), all angular, a kind of constipated grasshopper" (Letter to Corman, 30 January 1968, in Faranda 149). Almost certainly she would have had in mind his most recent book *This In Which,* and perhaps was conflating images from the poems "Seated Man" and "The Occurrences." In the first he imagines a man alienated from the everyday world by his experience of war—

> The man is old and—
> Out of scale
>
> Sitting in the rank grass. (*Collected Poems* 108)

—an experience which the poem goes on to equate in Whitmanic fashion with the world. Grass in "The Occurrences" is a trope that makes a romantic appeal to the vitality of living things in the shadow of the sun "In which the bugs crawl / At the roots of the grass" (126). It is a place that might teach even God—and certainly any father conscious of his minimal role in the creation of human beings—about the more fundamental male act of creation, "the creating / *Now*   that tremendous / plunge" (126) which makes temporality about as phallic as possible, and then projects it as an implicit poetic ideal. This is a polar opposite to the restrained, openly gendered awareness of temporality in Niedecker's pendulum poem.

Both Oppen and Niedecker write with an awareness of one of the best-known Objectivist poems, Zukofsky's "Mantis" (*All* 73), in which the praying mantis lost in the hostile urban landscape of the subway stone evokes the plight of the poor. The highly formal version of the sestina Zukofsky used provoked in turn a companion poem, "Mantis, An Interpretation" (74), a defense of the poetical language of the first. The quotation marks in which the insect's name is set are explained in this second poem as a reminder that to turn a human being into a symbolic insect may violate his humanity (78). Niedecker's remark about Oppen could be taken to mean that alongside Zukofsky's mantis, Oppen is merely a grasshopper, and more significantly, to imply that what she does to Oppen, turn a human being into a symbolic insect, he does to his urban denizens. But even Zukofsky comes close to admitting that he is doing this, saying at the end of the poem that the poor are a more constant memory than the poetic tradition, represented by the phrase "com' huom pietra sott' erba" (80). "Mantis" imagines the flourishing mantis hiding on a stone in the grass in its proper habitat, and still finding a base in the inhospitable stone architecture of the subway, where it preys symbolically on human life. (74). Pity, disgust, and economic cannibalism are so hopelessly entwined in the world depicted in the formal sestina that the following "interpretation" becomes a near-admission of failure in the conviction that it is nothing but a chaos within attempted order (79).

The poem succeeding "Seated Man" in Oppen's *Collected Poems,* "Street," also considers poverty, but in a manner that contrasts with both Zukofsky and especially Niedecker. Indeed, it makes one aware that even the idea that there is an underclass of people who could be designated the "poor" rarely surfaces in her poetry despite the evident poverty of her community. Oppen steps away from the people whose impoverished lives are easily visible on the street with an apodictic gesture, "Ah these are the poor," whose exclamatory particle expresses the moment of inarticulate sympathetic recognition when attention registers their existence and his own distance from them. Furthermore, the emphatic interjection somewhat showily demonstrates a deep feeling that resists language, for which reason modern poets have been wary of its possibly presumptuous romantic claim to such inner depths (Prynne). The poem stumbles, with an engaging honesty, through a series of responses that might well have irritated someone like Niedecker. By saying "I want // An end of poverty / As much as anyone," he risks dismissing the culture of the dispossessed along with their economic condition, and when he arrives at a climactic image of the human cost of poverty, the effect is compromised by his readiness to sentimentalize ethical violation as a fallen woman:

> It is terrible to see the children,
>
> The righteous little girls;
> So good, they expect to be so good . . . [ellipses in original]
> (*Collected Poems* 109)

The avant-garde poet is out of place, reduced for a moment to the semantic void of a phatic interjection, when he finds himself with the people Niedecker called the "folk." She herself was poor, and frequently referred to the folk as both spring and swamp for her ambitions, but she would never have been so willing to speculate whether these anonymous girls could grow up into some kind of goodness, nor would she have allowed herself such a distancing emphatical sigh, understanding from the inside as she did that ethics might vary according to one's class perspective. Sympathy like Oppen's might be more conservative than its apparent concern for the children's future would suggest.

Could Oppen's poetry also be acting as a screen memory for Zukofsky's poem from the thirties? At the beginning of the letter that morphs Oppen into an insect, Niedecker refers to a poem about a dragonfly she had recently sent to Corman:

> Smile
>   to see the lake
>   lay
>   the still sky
> And
>   out for an easy
>   make
>   the dragonfly (*Granite Pail* 65)

This subtle poem offers the sexualized metaphor of the landscape in an ironic frame that invites the reader to both enjoy the slight absurdity of this naughty trope and to see its explanatory power before teasing the reader with a change of scale from lake to dragonfly. It too is out for conquest, although whether as mate or hunter is deliberately ambiguous, as if to confirm the universality of sex. Mantis, grasshopper, and dragonfly—the subtle permutations on these almost heraldic insects signify another distinction. The dragonfly is described in terms that derive from "folk speech," a local humor about the landscape and its fauna that reveals the preoccupations of the indigenous people as much as the character of the place.

Placing everyday folk speech in poetry was something else that divided Niedecker from Oppen. Her momentary impatience with Oppen may also have had roots in her awareness of his criticism of poets who attempted to "reproduce common speech" in poetry. Such practices smacked of a suspect "populism" to Oppen. Asked by an interviewer what he meant by populism, he referred to the poem "The red wheelbarrow," saying that Williams appeared to believe in "the greater reality of certain kinds of objects than of others" (Dembo, "The 'Objectivist' Poet" 167), citing the wheelbarrow and chickens as an example. In the wider context of such differences between the Objectivists, it is as if Niedecker is saying that Oppen approaches American numerousness, the grass, with a predatory outsider's objectivity that results in a droning poetry's automatism of sound (the singing grasshopper that recalls Keats's hedge-crickets perhaps). His willingness to see the American masses as grass resembles the transformation of the dragonfly into a philandering male by the initial playful trope in its attempt to grasp the beauty and interpenetration of sky and water. Local playfulness redeems the imposition, whereas the greening of the people in Oppen's tropes appears to confirm a metropolitan aesthetic superiority. It turns out therefore that Niedecker herself is adept at this business of intertextuality and recontextualization, making arguments with layers of allusions to the work of the poets she knew and read. She can triangulate precisely her shared preoccupations about the poet's relation to society, the use of people and the natural world as symbols, and the pragmatics of their discourse, and in doing so measure her differences from her Objectivist associates Zukofsky and Oppen.

In no area did they differ as much as on the question of folk speech and its place in poetry. Niedecker's commitment to the "folk" led to a different sense of career, a curious resistance to publicly reading her poetry, and an active interest in folklore that creates a radically innovative form of poetry. Despite her unofficial membership in the Objectivist nexus, Niedecker's own position in relation to the avant-garde is unusual. Although she was published by some of the most prestigious avant-garde poetry presses, she lived more outside the urban centers of radical literary practice than almost any other poet one can think of. She never became a professional writer or teacher, as almost all of her contemporaries did, and this refusal to professionalize her poetry was both an economic and an aesthetic decision, for since the late nineteenth century aestheticism has helped provide an ideology for the emergence of professionalism in America, with its claims to special expertise. By rejecting professionalism she was also rejecting the long-standing claim that the work of literary practitioners could evince a special kind of expertise or "cultural knowledge" and its accompanying role of teacher to initiates (Freedman 55), which is so evident in a text like *A Test of Poetry.* Her own employments were not career jobs, and her everyday life put her entirely outside even the romantic models of the outsider who is able to use the position as a cultural position ahead of the more conformist artists who lag behind the scouts of the avant-garde. She simply was not outside in the sense that other poets and novelists who lived on the margins have been. She was inside the life-world where she was born despite her own differences and distances from it, which made her relations to the locality sometimes uncomfortable.

Her refusal to tour and give public readings of her poetry even extended to her resistance to the idea of recording herself on tape. Cid Corman tried to record her, but the result was a failure because she would not project her verse in the impersonal manner required ("I fell over one of the stanzas and nearly squashed it"), as she explained in this letter to Kenneth Cox written 23 November 1970:

> I got to thinking as I read how one can write for print and it means one thing and let it out of the mouth and into a listener to become something else e.g.: my Darwin commences:
>
> His holy
>   slowly
>   mulled over
>   matter
>
> from the mouth is it holy or wholly or holey???? And in the Thomas Jefferson I have:
>
> Martha (Patsy) stay
>
> so aloud it calls for a bit of explanation perhaps—e.g. "Patsy, that is" (not spoiling anything really). . . . For me poetry is a matter of planting it in deep, a filled silence, each person reading it a silence to be filled—he'll have to come to the poems—both writer and reader—with an ear for all the poems can give and he'll hear that as Beethoven heard tho deaf. (quoted in Dent, *Full Note* 41)

She wants an aural reception but does not want an oral means of creating it. As she explained to her friends the Roubs afterwards, in what was probably her last letter, "a person conscious of a listening audience would write just a tiny bit differently" (Faranda 241). Her reference to Beethoven betrays her awareness of the apparent contradiction of what she is saying. A composer denied the opportunity to hear his own music except in the auditory imagination is in a sorry state, and seems a poor parallel for what she wants. Her examples are perhaps at first sight unconvincing, because the written text is also ambiguous, but in both examples what she highlights is the problem of what philosophers call "implicature" (Grice), the necessity for the auditor to decide what is the probable shape and meaning of the word. In the second case she imagines being able to interject an aside—in other words, to create a momentary intersubjective relation in which its relevance will be made apparent. In the first she is imagining the lack of such an intersubjective world for the utterance, so that its significance goes begging. She describes it as a problem created by the translation of poem from text to speech, but it is really a problem created by her loss of control over the intersubjectivities within which her poetry is located. Niedecker's idea of the silence of the reader waiting to be filled is evocative because it underlines the importance of sound to her poetry, and her lack of the recognition onto which poets can project relations between poem and reader from within the poem itself. In a letter she wrote to Cid Corman three years earlier, on 3 May 1967, she described the audience at a reading as "mixed and nerve-crossed . . . somewhat inattentive," and said she would only be able to manage if she could find a way that "the silence could be governed among the people" (Faranda 121). The silence is an absence of dialogue, of conversation, owing to the distance between poet and reader. Her poem begins there, with this silence, this absence of intersubjectivity, rather than immediately appealing to the universalizing languages and frameworks of modern art and the avant-garde. This is why in the letter to Corman she is explicit about the intimate scale of the intersubjectivity with which her poetry aims to work: "Poems are for one person to another, spoken thus, or read silently." This is poetry conceived within a network of local relationships with a known history, a poetry that refuses the blandishments that promise it can be placed anywhere in public culture without loss, and does not believe that it can always put other people's thoughts into words without attenuation.

Niedecker's willingness to describe the foundation of her poetry as a "folk base" stems from this resistance to the idea that poetry should be an infinitely transmissible utterance, and helps explain why she might think of herself as located within a literary tradition quite different from that of Objectivism, and even come to believe that this was what made her work distinctive. "I probably show a folk base and even LZ knew it many years ago, and that so far as I see it might actually be my only claim to any difference between most poets and meself," she wrote to Jonathan Williams in August 1970 (Penberthy, *Niedecker Correspondence* 4). "Most poets" are presumably the poets she read in magazines like *Origin.* The self-conscious emphasis on her folksiness created by the idiomatic spelling of the last word of this sentence gives some ground for Jenny Penberthy's interpretation of this and other similar statements as typical of a deceptive self-deprecation that has helped maintain the image of Lorine Niedecker as someone to be remembered largely for "her folk poetry and her poems of place" (Penberthy, *Niedecker Correspondence* 4). Occasional references to the folk in her letters and poems suggest that she was conscious of this element long before she wrote to Jonathan Williams. She calls Group III of the poems in "For Paul" "the folk group, the American group," acknowledging the way she uses a deliberate mix of folk humor and avant-garde technique. The result is a mixture of poetic styles which includes "What horror to wake at night" with its painful refrain "I've spent my life on nothing," the mock ballad "Jesse James and his brother Frank," and the short poem about the other James brothers, "May you have lumps in your mashed potatoes." This latter poem juxtaposes an anecdote from the childhood of Henry and William James with Henry's consoling letter to Grace Norton (of 28 July 1883), in which he extols the "illimitable" power of consciousness and counsels her not to "melt too much into the universe but be solid and dense and fixed" as she is able—in other words, to be a lump in the mashed potato of the universe. The humor of the absurd parallel between the two sets of James brothers created by juxtaposing these two poems brings the great writers back from the thin air of transcendental concerns to an everyday domestic world of cooked vegetables. The opening line is actually a mock curse uttered by the brothers "to those who stood up to them in argu- / ment" (*Condensery* 61). Niedecker's poem could be asking what happens when a reader stands up to the argument made by Henry James in the letter to Norton, or to the similar themes to be found elsewhere in his writing.

Penberthy also cites another, more complex reference to the folk element in Niedecker's poems in the sequence "For Paul" which Niedecker made when a selection was published in the *New Mexico Quarterly Review.* Good poetry, she says, is the "outcome of experimentation with subconscious and with folk—all good poetry must contain elements of both or stems from them—plus the rational, organizational force," and Penberthy comments: "Her use of 'folk' refers, I suspect, to folk *speech,* the common currency of routine interactions" (*Niedecker Correspondence* 60). This could make Niedecker sound very like William Carlos Williams, who also valued ordinary speech highly as a source for his work. In the preface to *The Wedge* (1944) he said that a poem is made individual by the specificity of "the character of the speech from which it arises" (*Collected Poems* 2: 54). This meant letting the syntax and vocabulary alone during the process of arranging them into a composition: "When a man makes a poem, makes it, mind you, he takes words as he finds them interrelated about him and composes them—without distortion which would mar their exact significances—into an intense expression of his perceptions and ardors that they may constitute a revelation in the speech that he uses." Although Williams stresses that found speech or folk idioms must not be tampered with as they are carefully placed within the structure of the poem, he is perfectly willing to impose a new framing syntax around them, so that now they become a revelation of the poet's own perceptions and desires, just as Zukofsky did in *A Test of Poetry.* Williams, one might say, developing Penberthy's metaphor further, takes the currency of speech out of circulation and celebrates its value independently of the exchange represented by its "interrelations." Its revelation is a result of putting it on display in the poem. Niedecker's practice is oriented in a reverse direction. Instead of producing a revelation from this withdrawal from circulation, she actually intensifies the poem's immersion in those same "routine interactions."

Many of Williams's poems certainly acknowledge their source in such ordinary relations. His poem "This Is Just to Say" holds up for scrutiny an extremely familiar act of communication, the written note to an absent intimate (*Collected Poems* 1: 372). The poem uses the metalinguistic title knowingly, for this apparent kitchen note is *not* just an occasion to say something about plums; this is now also a poem, which will have what Niedecker described in Zukofsky's poetry in a letter from 1951 as "a supersense, not meaning in the ordinary sense" (Penberthy, *Niedecker Correspondence* 175). It works very similarly to some of Niedecker's, except that the disingenuous title disavowal signals to the knowing reader in a way that withdraws the poem from its immediate intersubjective drama and diverts attention away from its traces, through a mutual recognition of an aesthetic value that overrides any unsubsumable particularities. Niedecker's appeal to the "folk base" as the element that makes her poetry most innovative takes her poems in a different direction. Her poetry challenges the way avant-garde poetry is ordinarily read by demanding an alteration in the stance taken in the process of reception.

Is it sufficient to locate this folk element of her poetry in her interest in reproducing everyday idioms? The contrast with Williams suggests that more is involved. One way of clarifying its significance for her work would be to trace the vicissitudes of this now largely defunct term, which earlier in the twentieth century enjoyed widespread credibility, both in academic studies and in politics. I can only sketch this history here. For the many immigrants from Germany to the northern states, the idea of the "volk" was a powerful, evocative image of immemorial tradition in proximity with the land which had been at best disrupted, and for many simply lost, by immigration. Back in Germany it came to have a more sinister appeal as part of the new code of Aryan nationalism under National Socialism. Because of this taint, the term was dropped by socialists in the thirties in favor of other terms like "the masses," itself a concept that socialists after the war came to mistrust. Niedecker's adoption of the term "folk" needs to be understood within this political history. When she refers to working-class people like those at the print shop where she worked as "the folk from whom all poetry flows / and dreadfully much else" (*Granite Pail* 21), she does not utter a sigh like Oppen, nor does she give way to romantic populism. As the ambivalence of these lines indicates, she oscillated between immersion and alienation from the local community, and the term "folk" itself is a measure of this instability.

From her reading, politics, possibly her college studies, and certainly her WPA work, she must have been aware of other, more anthropological uses of the term "folk" which register the doubleness of participant observation among a people that are also "one's own." Academic study of folk culture—especially dance, song, and poetry which had apparently survived over long periods of time by oral transmission among ordinary people—was a long-established field by the time she became a poet herself, and it was usually considered then to be the field most appropriate for those interested in features of rural or premodern Western culture. A better-known writer of the twenties and thirties turned to folklore studies for reasons similar to Niedecker's. Zora Neale Hurston studied anthropology with Franz Boas in order to be able to research her own African-American culture, and in doing so encountered many contradictions similar to those found by Niedecker. Hurston collected folktales and other examples of black American speech in the Florida where she was born, and used the material for both documentary and fiction. She said that "folklore is the arts of the people before they find out that there is such a thing as art . . . folklore does not belong to any special area, time, nor people. . . . It is the boiled down juice of human living" (quoted in Johnson 161). Hence culture is a form of knowledge: "culture is a forced march on the near and the obvious. . . . The intelligent mind uses up a great part of its lifespan trying to awaken its consciousness sufficiently to comprehend that which is plainly there before it" (161). Barbara Johnson, who cites these comments on folklore, concludes that Hurston's aim in her novel *Their Eyes Were Watching God* was to use her knowledge of folklore to challenge the "seduction of a universal language through a progressive de-universalization that ends in the exclusion of the very protagonist herself" (172).

Niedecker also used such ideas about folklore to challenge the universalization implicit in the internationalized languages of modernity, by positioning herself as much as a folklorist as one of the folk, even though she had only a limited academic training compared to Hurston. Her main experience of folklore studies would have been as part of the WPA project to write the guide for Wisconsin. *Wisconsin: A Guide to the Badger State* is typical in the way it plays the folklorist with a sometimes sentimental or humorous twist. It tries to epitomize the culture of the town of Pepin with this example of folk speech: "Their speech draws many images from the great river. Seeing a drunken man staggering up the street in early spring, an idler remarks, 'He's sure goin' up the river' and his crony replies, 'Yep, he's gonna burn all the ice out of Lake Pepin'" (WPA 436). These WPA guides had ethnographic pretensions beyond mere description of architecture, topography, and history, although in the eyes of professionals the result was a "relative failure" because the amateurs had "little idea as to what they were seeking" (Thompson 256). Although the results of such a survey of the states might disappoint professionals, for a poet like Niedecker this undertheorized research into the way people might draw images from their locality as a means of creating local knowledge was an invaluable training for the writing of poetry, and the WPA project could be called her department of anthropology.

When Niedecker refers to the source of a poem as "folk speech," she is saying more than that the words are those of a local person. She could have said the speech was working class, or idiomatic, or even old-fashioned and quaint. Instead, she invokes a way of considering communities and their history that has considerable implications for what she is trying to achieve in her poems. Consider this poem:

> The museum man!
> I wish he'd take Pa's spitbox!
> I'm going to take that spitbox out
> and bury it in the ground
> and put a stone on top.
> Because without that stone on top
> it would come back. (*Granite Pail* 8)

This is a record of her mother's voice, and could be read simply as a memorial to her, a poetic stone with her mother's words inscribed on it, set firmly in the ground of modernist poetry. It could be read as the kind of populist appeal to the value and wisdom of ordinary, found speech made in the Wisconsin guide in its treatment of examples of local idiom like that collected in Pepin, which Oppen criticized in poetry. It could also be read as an amusing instance of the spirit shown by women who use their verbal dexterity to maintain their dignity in the midst of an impoverished life, manifested most immediately by the disgusting habits of their working men, who too readily give way to tobacco and drink in the face of the pressures of poverty. Doing so makes the spitbox metonymically represent a whole way of life. Or it could be taken to symbolize the father, and more generally patriarchy, a revenant that will not stay buried whatever the women do, because the dead father remains pivotal to the entire signifying system. At this point in our interpretations the anachronism of a Lacanian reading begins to gleam in the box, yet I do not want to simply dismiss this more psychoanalytic direction as a seduction that the poem never intended, nor to treat the other possible interpretations as too biographical to be persuasive engagements with its textuality. The poem deliberately offers multiple possibilities of interpretation, but they are embedded within a more complex relation to the reader that depends upon what is understood by folk poetry, and the intersubjective relations within which it works. To ignore this is to become a museum man, to put the spitbox too readily alongside the other exhumed memorials of different cultures on display in the museological culture of metropolitan modernity, which exhibits objects, including poems, as if their meaning resided in a discrete objectivity open to interpretative strategies which presuppose a generality of motivation and affect. The poem can sit on the desk all ready to be understood. Yet local cultures do not necessarily think of objects in this way at all. Their artifacts may be entirely embedded in relational networks that would never make possible the anonymous hermeneutic perspective on a distinct object, and by being so immanent within the culture would never have those necessary boundaries presupposed by these modernist methods of interpretation.

The spitbox poem could be read as a demonstration of museological skills, because it takes the folk speech and puts it on display. It also offers something more. "The museum man!" is an expostulation whose value is hard to assess, since it could be placed almost anywhere on a spectrum between a curse and a cry of delighted realization at the answer to a problem. Its speaker imagines the act of conferring value on the spitbox as one in which the box is taken out of its local context and placed in a museum where it would become an object that helped create an image of the material past. The only alternative appears to be burial, as if burial were somehow the cheap equivalent. This could be read as a parable of the problem faced by the poem itself, either burial in the locality of

Niedecker's world, or the museum of international poetry publishing. The poem knows that the poet will have to become "the museum man" and put the spitbox on show, but doing so will not solve the problem, because the object will be untouched and still disgusting. Some of this disgust is not directly communicable, so it excludes the stranger's reading the poem because the speaker hopes to create common cause against the father with those who have witnessed the intrusive habits and presence, especially the way he uses his mouth, the physiological site of the oral, folk speech in the poem, for spitting. The spitbox is therefore an image of a degraded source of poetry, an image of the repressed that will insist on returning, because the unconscious, Yeats's "foul rag and bone shop of the heart" (392), is the only source of poetry. This folk speech knows something of psychoanalytic truths, and it also knows that its knowledge is going to be put on display. What it can do is anticipate such recontextualization, and it does so by using folk speech as both medium and theme. Niedecker's language for ways of avoiding the ideology of the museum man was folklore studies.

Seven years after the publication of Niedecker's principal collection of what she called "folk" poems in *New Goose* (1946), a short essay appeared in the journal *Western Folklore* entitled "What Is a Folk Poet?" by T. M. Pearce. This essay is a useful indicator of what was meant by folk poetry at the time when Niedecker was composing her own folk poems. The most striking feature of the discussion is that despite the currency of the name "folk poetry," and despite the wealth of studies of folk poetry, there is, according to the author, no agreement about what the role and definition of a folk poet is. This indeterminacy probably helped make the term attractive to Niedecker. One reason for the uncertainty was the relative neglect of poetry in favor of other genres like songs, tales, and drama, and another was the methodological difficulty of dealing with printed material in a field that took as axiomatic that folk culture was orally transmitted. Writing in 1952, Stith Thompson, author of a multivolume tabulation of the structures of folktales, is emphatic that "folklore is transmitted by oral tradition" (266), but as Pearce and others recognized, oral poetry is almost always found alongside written counterparts in Western cultures. Eric Havelock has more recently argued that we still do not fully understand the relation of written texts to their oral counterparts, whether they are texts gathered in the field or those formed from oral materials, like Homer or the New Testament. Folk poetry highlights these problems.

Given these dilemmas, Pearce avoids abstract debate and offers a specific case study of a Spanish-American folk poet living in a small town near Albuquerque who has been writing poems for both sacred and secular occasions for many years, without publishing them in the ordinary sense. Lack of publication does not matter, because these poems do circulate in the local public sphere. They are regularly sung and read in public in the town, where he is very well known, and he keeps a written record of them in a ledger. Some poems celebrate the visit of important people, others murders and fatal accidents, and a few his own personal experiences, but the common element is the degree of specific relation to the community, "the sense of solidarity belonging to a homogeneous group dwelling in one community neighborhood, of one religious faith, united in a common activity, speaking the same language about it, in both literal and figurative senses" (245). The poet entirely lacks the alienation that is often taken as the starting point of modern art, and already implicit in the very term "avant-garde": "the poet is one of them: his words are their words and their thoughts are his" (246). This description sounds idealized (an idealization often heard in earlier folklore studies), because its measure of such continuity derives from an unexamined contrast with a modernity in which such pure intersubjectivity is no longer possible.

Some twenty-five years after Pearce's essay, Roger de V. Renwick, in his study *English Folk Poetry*, echoes most of Pearce's definitions. Renwick emphasizes that folk poetry is intended to have immediate local effects among the people known directly to the poet, so each poem is designed to "inform, to persuade, to manipulate," and more generally to help sustain community ties (3). Folk poetry nurtures active local intersubjectivities.

Pearce sums up his findings in a manner that unconsciously assumes a modernist role for the true poet, saying that for this Spanish-American writer, "identity as an author is not suppressed, but his individuality as a poet is submerged in the stream of group or community feeling which animates all his compositions" (248). Thompson also relies on this distinction between individuality, which is the mark of literary authorship, and the anonymity of the folk artist, whose work is authored by a "common milieu" (254). This opposition of author and poet assumes that poets are literary figures whose standpoint is not only necessarily distinct from the community but conforms to an aesthetic that transcends local historical circumstances, rather than emerging from them. Authors live in the stream of feeling that makes the more alienated role of the poet impossible.

This "stream of feeling" demands comparison with another image of collective sentiment, Raymond Williams's concept of the structure of feeling, which he first articulated at about the same time and went on using throughout his career in a series of changing theories. Individual literary achievement emerges from the social experience of new literary movements that take shape first as "structures of feeling," or common ways of thought that are still at "the very edge of semantic availability" (*Marxism* 134) as qualitative changes in a general form of life encourage artists to register "*changes of presence*" in "meanings and values as they are actively lived and felt" (132). The resulting art is therefore not wholly determined by existing traditions, forms, and institutions. It is to some extent entirely new, and so the field of cultural practice only gradually reaches conceptual, cognitive, and linguistic realization. One of the best-known forms of such structures of feeling in modernity is the sequence of avant-gardes, which come into being as a metropolitan network of individuals who are commonly immigrants to the metropolis, and therefore "share no common language but that of the metropolis and whose other (including visual) received sign-systems have become distanced or irrelevant" (*Culture* 84). This makes their work especially relevant to the developing urban culture itself, which in the modern period shows a marked tendency to agglomeration in a few metropolises, to an internationalization of its horizons, and "a correspondingly high cultural mobility" (84). Williams's account of the phenomenon of the avant-garde is only partially accurate, as the case of the rural avant-gardist, Lorine Niedecker, shows. Too many poets and artists have lived outside the metropolis for this generalization to stand, and other groupings that fulfill all of these criteria have not been avant-garde. What makes this formulation useful is the way it adopts the standpoint of the metropolitan avant-garde and then identifies problems of communication, circulation, and locality as central to its self-identity in terms that mirror the distinction between such a network and the situation of the folk poet as described by the folklorists.

These two images of the poet's social relations as either the emergence from a stream of feeling or a structure of feeling (climbing out of the river or leaving a building, perhaps) are apparently antithetical. In one case the stream of feeling suppresses the alienating development of artistic self-consciousness and avant-garde ambitions, and in the other it actually fosters such development in the absence of ordinary community. But the supposed difference between them does not bear close examination. Both images are dependent upon similar idealizations of a social life that is more heterogenous and more conflicted than either image suggests. Pearce's poet actually sounds more detached from his community than Pearce wants to recognize, and artists of the avant-garde often have more powerful local ties and ethnic connections than Williams acknowledges. Pearce and Williams, despite their different fields of inquiry, both assume that alienation and immersion in a community are mutually exclusive, and that the former is the necessary predisposition for innovative art. Niedecker's work can be read as an attempt to show that this assumption is wrong. Her interest in folk culture can be interpreted as an attempt to give the stream of feeling a structure, and to make the structure of feeling more fluid, as she becomes both the avant-garde poet who has undergone reverse immigration from the metropolis, and the small-town folk poet whose audience is an emergent cultural group in the metropolis.

And yet Niedecker is not a folk poet by the definitions of the folklorists. She kept her poetry secret from the local community, she avoided the clichés and the stereotyped forms that folk poets tend to use, and she was published in the most prestigious avant-garde journals. She is closer to Pearce and Renwick than to the poets on whom they report. It is as if Niedecker is both folk poet and folklorist in one. She believed her poetry was best transmitted "from one person to another, spoken thus, or (perish the thought, I suppose?!) read silently" (Faranda 15), a conception of the circulation of poetry that seems close to the folk tradition as the folklorists describe it, but in making this demand she was proposing a new set of relations between poet, poem, and reader to the sophisticates of the avant-garde in order to draw attention to ways in which words and forms of literary address operate within actual modern social structures. She takes the simplest structures and shows that they have a whole other dimension of meaning that the avant-garde sometimes misses because of the way its constitutive social structures necessarily form its reading practice as well.

Consider her poem "Remember my little granite pail" (which Corman singled out for the title of his selection *The Granite Pail* as if this object could be metonymic of an entire body of work) within a contextualization that Niedecker herself might have approved of, a comparison with William Carlos Williams's untitled poem known as "The red wheelbarrow." In a letter to Corman of 11 February 1965 she speculatively discussed a possible anthology of short poems, and named names: Mother Goose rhymes, haiku, Keats, Herrick, Dickinson, Blake, Donne, Dante, Hopkins, Burns, Shakespeare (her joking comment "We might let Shakespeare in!" could be read as a resistance to the kind of bardolatry that Zukofsky indulged in), and among contemporaries she mentioned Corman himself, poems from *Origin*, poems by Reznikoff and Zukofsky, and William Carlos Williams's notoriously sibylline poem about "a red wheelbarrow" (Faranda 51).

Niedecker's poem is a series of short end-stopped sentences which appear very simple:

> Remember my little granite pail?
> The handle of it was blue.
> Think what's got away in my life—
> Was enough to carry me thru. (*Granite Pail* 7)

Williams's poem is more gnomic:

so much depends
upon

a red wheel
barrow

glazed with rain
water

beside the white
chickens (*Collected Poems* 1: 224)

Williams's poem, although brief and articulated in a simple vocabulary, will probably strike most readers as more complex because of the way it moves in a column down the page without punctuation, isolating words and phrases with what appears to be portentous emphasis whose significance is not initially evident. Oppen, as we saw, singled out this poem as the symptom of a populist sentimentality afflicting modern poets. Both poems evoke an ordinary utilitarian object and then by a sudden twist of conceptual perspective invite the reader to speculate on much larger issues. Both use colloquial speech ("so much depends upon"; "was enough to carry me thru"). We have confirmation that folk idiom was uppermost in Niedecker's mind from a letter in which she told Zukofsky that she would have written "Was enough to have carried me thru" instead, "but folk don't say that, they slur it over into simply what I did say" (Penberthy, *Niedecker Correspondence* 290). Folk speech is the final court of appeal, so that what she says in the poem can be taken as a reliable guide to the actual phrasing used by "folk."

Williams's poem knowingly invokes the romantic tradition that would invest a landscape with emotional and spiritual meaning, and then challenges a reader to repeat the process with this nugatory scene. Niedecker's poem initially refuses such intertextual challenges to the literary tradition. Instead it insists upon its specific reference to her situation by its opening and excluding line, which invites its reader to do the impossible. Only she (and perhaps a few intimates) can perform this act of recollection. The poem's address effectively delineates a reader too precisely, so that readers who are not from this locale cannot make the initial imaginative act that will enable them to fulfill the demands of the poem. The pail remains out of reach of the reader's effort to fully realize its significance. Contrast this with Williams's poem, which actually affirms a common relation between writer and reader to the literary tradition, and so universalizes this relation in the process. The specificity of the red wheelbarrow remains only as a symbol of sensuous particularity that cannot be subsumed into conceptual thought, because the distinctiveness of this singular wheelbarrow disappears in the process of exemplification.

Charles Taylor argues that this kind of procedure is evidence of a persistent romantic strategy for creating something that cannot be simply subsumed into a large conceptual framework. He traces the avant-garde back to the romantic ideal of epiphanic art: "the aim is not just to portray but to transfigure through the representation, to render the object 'translucent'" (419). Modernist art has shifted focus from the representation of external objects to the making of the work of art itself but remains expectant of the same form of response. Even for romantic art, however, "we can't understand what it is qua epiphany by pointing to some independently available object described or referent. What the work reveals has to be read in it" (420). An epiphany is defined by Taylor in a way that reveals the degree to which its registration of an otherwise inarticulable experience is both paradigmatically "local" and yet paradoxically also a moment when the significance of the experience becomes transferable into other terms. An epiphany is "the locus of a manifestation which brings us into the presence of something which is otherwise inaccessible, and which is of the highest moral and spiritual significance" (419). Williams's poem about the red wheelbarrow registers a moment which the reader is invited to interpret as an epiphany without any supporting discourse. Not just anyone can testify to such moments. To be sensitive enough to recognize these moments the avant-garde artist has to be an exceptional being, experience exceptional suffering, and live an isolated life—one that is somehow ahead of bourgeois society (423). This claim to be exceptional—implicit, for example, in Zukofsky's desire to measure himself against all other poets—was rejected by Niedecker.

"Remember my little granite pail" insists that the sensuous particularity of experience depends upon the specific social relations in which it occurs. Niedecker's poem also implies that art should avoid the universal if universality means the complete fungibility of value exemplified by commodities. Her literary art insists on the absolute difference made to the meaning of the poem by the relations in which the work is received. The reader's inevitable failure to recall the granite pail is a reminder that this poem has or had readers for whom the intimate local reference gave it other significances unavailable to the outside, abstract audience. What the poem does is to insist that what it means depends upon the relations between writer, poem, and reader. The meaning of the pail will differ according to one's intersubjective relation to the history from which this poem emerges (as relative, neighbor, someone brought up with similar utensils, or a reader remote in time and space who might not even know that a granite pail is a pail or bucket that has a characteristic granite-gray finish). This tacit insistence that the reader's specific relation affects the poem directly, rather than through some free act of interpretative choice, is the poetic at work here, which therefore does finally make a countervailing move away from the utterly personal and local history of the relation to the pail, to this more general aesthetic point. In making a general move it is recognizable to the reader of the Williams poem, but only by inviting the reader to reflect on the kinds of assumptions that enable "The red wheelbarrow" to be at once red and read.

Niedecker's strategy can be described in another way. The answer to the question of what happens to an utterance when it is placed in a poem will depend upon what theory of the aesthetic we have. Her poetry questions fundamental assumptions about what constitutes the aesthetic, and can be placed within a quite different set of debates from those of the avant-garde poets. For poets, aesthetics is largely a matter of practice and pragmatic discourses on method, value, and insight, but philosophers trace their arguments directly back to a founding synthesis of Enlightenment thought in Kant's *Critique of Judgment.* Kant effectively argued that knowledge, morality, and art were independent realms of experience, and a work of art therefore could not be judged for its truth in the way a scientific theory about the boiling point of liquids could. Once the folk speech is in a poem, its significance changes utterly. This categorial separation of spheres has been the element in which the avant-garde flourished and fought to claim its importance, but is art really independent in the way that modern culture largely assumes (even if some poets struggle against this enfeebling autonomy)?

The philosopher J. M. Bernstein argues that modern post-Enlightenment philosophy separated off the arts from cognitive truth and ethics because it believed that the concepts that organized rational thought were independent of the context in which they were used. They were believed to be what he calls "topic-neutral," unaffected by the context in which they were placed, just as logical operators are not altered by the elements on which they work. He argues that most concepts are not like this: "Actual inferences, and hence patterns of inference, are dependent upon the practices in which concepts are employed" (168). The statement "all bachelors are married" is supposed to be logically contradictory, yet it is actually falsified not by the law of noncontradiction but by social practices. It might be possible for bachelors to be married if our social habits changed, and it is certainly the case that unmarried men are not necessarily bachelors. In Niedecker's poem, it is not just the pail that is specific to her world, but also phrases like "what's got away" and the concept of something being able to "carry" one through. Put these concepts into another context, another mouth, another poem, another collection of poems, and their meaning may alter. They are not "topic-neutral." Neither Niedecker nor the dictionary creates the meanings of these terms. "Intersubjective practice," as Bernstein calls it, is what does the work. This intersubjective practice may be a metropolitan network "who share no common language but that of the metropolis," in Raymond Williams's words cited earlier, or it may be an epistolary friendship like that between Niedecker and Zukofsky, or it may be the everyday world of Blackhawk Island. If it were only a matter of setting up a network or locating oneself within a strongly established geographically defined one, the problem would be largely a matter of choice, but unfortunately the entire process of modernization is moving against this. The economic doctrine of the "marketplace," for example, treats objects as all equivalent according to the one scale of monetary value. Many modern discursive and procedural frameworks turn fields of our life-worlds into systems, "rendering various objects and practices effectively intersubjectively meaningless" (169). Even something as benign as a didactic poetry anthology actually works by setting up a procedural structure of comparisons that is supposedly independent of the poems it organizes. Bernstein has a particularly useful linguistic metaphor for representing this process whereby a syntax seems to overwhelm the individual sensuousness of words. He says that frameworks like power and money "trump" the intersubjective world by placing their objects and concepts within a syntax that dominates them: "with the notion of . . . syntactical trumping, empirical predicates are subsumed within a structure that detaches their potential for meaning from both intersubjective practices and their referential objects" (169). Another way of saying this is that modernization, the rationalization of everyday life, works by replacing the kind of judgment associated with art in Kant's system—the "reflective judgment" that tries to respond to what is unique in an experience—with another form of judgment that instead subsumes the experience under an abstract category that then makes it recognizable to the methods of science or other kinds of formal knowledge that investigate general and invariant conditions. Such rationalization has brought enormous benefits. The problem lies in its undiscriminating sweep.

Poets have had to negotiate their own relation to these developments, and the avant-garde poets have tended to accept the seeming benefits of such rationalization as a means of placing their work alongside the other great intellectual developments of modernity, and therefore resisting the modern tendency to sideline it in an aesthetic museum, away from all possibility of active intervention in affairs. Zukofsky assumes that poems speak for all poets and demonstrate an ability to use the framework of the anthology as a syntax for transforming the local meanings of poems into units that then speak in both a universal and more surprisingly, a personal voice (making *Pericles* a comment on an old affair). Oppen believes that the use of folk speech depends upon the assumption that the reader will interpret its very use, not the content of the speech itself, as a general claim about the virtues of populism. Both poets imagine that a reader will make these metadiscursive moves as part of the practice of art. By contrast, Niedecker's poetry resists such incursions at a level that recognizes some of the implicit assumptions made necessary by the move to "supersenses" or aesthetic metadiscourses that affect the avant-garde practices of all these poets. According to Bernstein, the history of modern art is a story of increasingly hectic strategies aimed at keeping art local by using ever-changing methods (like resisting the reader's rush to interpretation by making the surface of the poem opaque in some way) so that the work cannot easily be assimilated by being subsumed into some exemplary narrative or universalizing commentary that would trump the art and neutralize its specificity. Niedecker's poetry suggests that the avant-garde has been too ready to accept the conditions of modernity, and that reexamining the relations in which poems circulate may be as radical as other, more striking forms of linguistic innovation. Her poetry shows that she was extremely aware of a problem that Bernstein's history does not go on to explore, the countervailing need for art to find networks of readers who probably do not share the local life-worlds that might provide ordinary contexts of intersubjective meaning. It is within this space of conflicting demands that Niedecker's poetry operates, and this is why she seems oddly suspended between the apparently incompatible worlds of the avant-garde and folk poetry. The complexities of her work arise from the way it challenges these features of the avant-garde which usually operate below the horizon of awareness to constitute its reception and institutionalization.

The consequences of Niedecker's resistances to appropriation are especially evident when she is seemingly engaged in just the same practice that Zukofsky promulgated in *A Test of Poetry.* Her poem "I rose from marsh mud" (*Granite Pail* 24) has a close textual relation with Emily Dickinson's poem "She rose to his requirement," which was originally published with the title "The Wife" (*Selected Poems* 47). Niedecker would only have known this heavily edited version at the time she wrote her poem, because the later version, with dashes as punctuation, had not yet appeared at the time she wrote.[2] In Dickinson's poem the woman's marriage is narrated in a remarkably double voice, which seems to endorse entirely the conventional standpoint on marriage, yet gradually allows an ironic distance from it:

She rose to his requirement, dropped
The playthings of her life
To take the honorable work
Of woman and of wife.

Only by becoming a wife does she become a woman according to the discourse reproduced here. The first line puns on the "rose" that the woman is often likened to, and also plays with the idea of rising and falling. In the following stanzas the wife's virtues are imagined as pearl and weed at the bottom of a sea of her husband's enveloping patriarchal presence, through a concealed pun on "sea," which emphasizes the degree to which the ocean represents concealment, not being able to see anything except the husband. Not only is he all that can be seen, but his honorable words have largely taken over the poem as well.

The poem's feminist irony seems at odds with a troubling passivity in the wife, and it is this that Niedecker considers in her poem. Dickinson's poem is written from outside the marriage by someone who admits not knowing what the wife misses or possesses in herself anymore because all that this observer can witness is the veiling sea. Niedecker displaces the verb "rose" to a first-person narrator who reports firsthand observation of the marriage of a "little white slave-girl" in church. This narrator actually emerges out of the mud where pearls and weeds might hide, but her element is marsh, not sea, a careful, precise "de-universalization" that relocates the scene to the exact place where she lives:

I rose from marsh mud,
algae, equisetum, willows,
sweet green, noisy
birds and frogs

By listing the fauna and flora, the narrator almost becomes one of them—a willow, or a bird, or perhaps a "marsh rose." The word "mud" clogs the rhythm, emphasizing dirtiness and fertility at once. But the most striking shift is the move into the first person, as if Dickinson's poem had been written about Niedecker (or more precisely the narrator of the poem). This is a strong act of appropriation. The drowned spirit of the married woman in Dickinson's poem has returned in Niedecker, who rises out of the weeds into the world of poetry.

"I rose from marsh mud" makes itself a daughter, or at least claims kinship with the earlier poet, so that its correction is not an overthrow in a fit of anxiety of influence, nor a homage to an enduring cultural monument, but something else. It wants to "inform, to persuade, to manipulate" Dickinson's poem, as if she were part of the poet's community, because it recognizes that the poem is, in Hurston's words, part of the "boiled down juice of human living" that needs to be recirculated to readers. By inhabiting Dickinson's opening phrase "she rose," Niedecker demonstrates an extension of the folk relations that her poetry inscribes within its practices of meaning. The apparent lucidity of Niedecker's poetry is like the sea in Dickinson's poem. Its significances, its virtues and its limitations, can easily remain unacknowledged, a poetics of weed and pearls within the sea of a largely masculine modernism, unless readers learn to recognize that this poetry is also capable of arising from the marsh mud to provide a disturbing witness at the marriage of false unities, the bride and groom "United for life to serve / silver" in the high temples of culture. Then the poetry's remarkable exploration of the poetics of cultural transmission, and what happens when a poem is placed alongside the poems of other poets, or when speech is placed inside a poem, will be able to play its part in the shaping of new understanding of the cultural dynamics of literary modernism.

III
Ethics and Religious Culture

9

Tradition and Modernity, Judaism and Objectivism: The Poetry of Charles Reznikoff

Norman Finkelstein

What does it mean to be a Jewish-American poet? Posed as baldly as that, the question is impossible to answer. And yet it must be posed, if only to point out that whenever critics have attempted an answer, they have found in the work of one particular poet—Charles Reznikoff—the lodestar of their speculation. Reznikoff has become the exemplary Jewish-American poet; his work is crucial to our understanding of the field, whether it is constituted from the perspective of religion, history, ethnology, psychology, or any combination thereof. Despite his professed modesty ("not for a seat upon the dais / but at the common table" [*Complete Poems* 1: 75]), Reznikoff is, as his friend Louis Zukofsky might say, the test of (Jewish-American) poetry.

There is no clearer proof of this than Reznikoff's portrayal in Harold Bloom's "The Sorrows of American-Jewish Poetry" (1972), an essay which may be said to inaugurate such poetry as a distinct field of critical inquiry. Based on what was then his emerging theory of influence, Bloom's argument at first appears as an attempt to foreclose on the possibility of "strong" Jewish-American poets, since poetic strength is narrowly defined according to Bloom's peculiar set of psychohistorical dynamics:

> Strong poets tend to achieve an individualized voice by first all-but-merging with a precursor and then but pulling away from him, usually by way of a complex process of fault-finding and actual mis-interpretation of the precursor. All post-Enlightenment poetry in English tends to be a displaced Protestantism anyway, so that the faith in a Person easily enough is displaced into an initial devotion to a god-like

> precursor poet. This, to understate it, is hardly a very Jewish process, and yet something like it seems necessary if are poets are to continue to be incarnated. However far from Jewish tradition they may be, something recalcitrant in the spirit of young Jewish poets prevents them from so initially wholehearted a surrender to a Gentile precursor, and indeed makes them nervous about the process itself. Displaced Judaism tends to become one or another kind of a moralism, but not the pragmatic religion-of-poetry that young poets, for a time, must accept. (253)

If Jewish poets are to write in English, they must initially "surrender to a Gentile precursor," a process they supposedly resist, consequently becoming moralists rather than devotees of "the pragmatic religion-of-poetry." This they cannot do, presumably, because even as secular Jews they intuit that the religion of poetry demands too radical a departure from *halakah,* "the Way," obedience to a singular, demanding moral idea which in traditional Judaism is represented by the one true God of Israel.

This thesis raises a number of questions which Bloom never answers: Why do Jewish poets resist giving themselves wholeheartedly to gentile precursors, when so much else in the cultural life of modern Jews involves integration with gentile forms and ideas? Is wholehearted surrender to the precursor really the necessary first step for Jewish—or, for that matter, gentile—poets? And once Jews do attain some sort of poetic status, is their purported moralism really at odds with a genuine poetic vocation, however that may be defined? Obviously, Bloom would as soon avoid these questions, for they raise serious doubts regarding the general applicability of his influence theory and reveal his morose view of secular Jewish culture in America.

The purpose of Bloom's dubious theorizing about gentile precursors and Jewish moralism becomes clearer when we consider his comments on individual figures. Bloom is tough on nearly all the poets he discusses, but he saves some of his harshest remarks for those Jewish-Americans who "accommodate [their] vision to the metric and rhetoric of Eliot, Pound, Williams and their followers" (251). Bloom's prejudice against these modernists is a cornerstone of his criticism; it is the converse of his predilection for the British and American romantics and their twentieth-century heirs, most notably Wallace Stevens. Marjorie Perloff, one of our best seismologists in the study of the modernist earthquake, has persuasively argued that Bloom's denial of modernism, especially Poundian modernism, indicates his preference for a post-romantic lyric poetry that maintains a sense of organic form and an isolated speaking subject seeking a latter-day version of sacred wisdom. What Bloom calls "The Internalization of Quest Romance" becomes, for Perloff, everything that Pound and his followers sought to overthrow by creating a poetry of generic instability: dialogic, collagist, exteriorized, and self-consciously constructivist (*Dance* 21–23).

A major tenet of "The Sorrows of American-Jewish Poetry" is that the modernist aesthetic derived from Pound and Williams is somehow inappropriate to the "desired stance" of their Jewish "followers," including Objectivists such as Charles Reznikoff. "Why attempt to translate Yehudah Halevi into the idiom of Pound and William Carlos Williams? Is the form of this in any way appropriate to its burden?" (251–52). Bloom asks this of Reznikoff, quoting the following lines:

> My heart is in the East
> and I at the farthest West:
> how can I taste what I eat or find it sweet
> while Zion
> is in the cords of Edom and I
> bound by the Arab?
> Beside the dust of Zion
> all the good of Spain is light;
> and a light thing to leave it. (*Complete Poems* 2: 69)

This passage does indeed come from Reznikoff's translation of Yehudah Halevi, but just what is the "burden" of the poem to which Bloom refers? The term "burden" could be regarded as a synonym for "content" or for "theme." In music, and by extension, in poetry, the word can refer to a recurring idea or motif carried by the melody or form. But Bloom's use of the term in the context of Jewish history and culture implies another meaning as well: to be a Jew, especially an assimilating, first-generation Jew like Reznikoff, is to carry a contradictory weight of culture and literary tradition that may be too hard to bear.

But does a closer look at the poem confirm this? If "burden" refers to the exilic longing of Halevi, and by extension, of diasporic Jewry up until the modern period, then Reznikoff's lines succeed admirably. His free verse form in this stanza is handled with great skill, as he moves from the two phrasally complete opening lines, to the troubled enjambment of the four following lines, back to the phrasally complete sigh of the last three. Bloom implies that Reznikoff's poem is flawed because of a dichotomy of content ("burden") and form, a dichotomy produced by his allegiance to what we now call an Objectivist aesthetic derived partly from Williams and Pound. Yet this is a red herring: as Michael Heller says of Reznikoff's poetry, its "shorn-down language simultaneously inhabits a number of linguistic realms at once; the datum and its meaning for the poet are so inextricably linked that the usual suspension of belief or accounting for poetic license no longer applies" (*Conviction's Net* 61).

In a footnote to his Halevi poem, Reznikoff argues against Franz Rosenzweig's insistence on translating Halevi by maintaining the rhyme and rhythm of the original. Reznikoff asserts that "the reproduction of a metre in another language does not necessarily have the same effect it had in the original: rhyme and rhythm stirring in the Hebrew may be cloying and merely tiresome in English; it may be light instead of grave and so clever as to be nothing else. And it is of interest to note that Jehuda Halevi himself said: 'It is but proper that mere beauty of sound should yield to lucidity of speech.'" Bloom overlooks this sensitivity to Halevi's aesthetic and simply dismisses Reznikoff's version as inappropriate because of what he deems its Poundian idiom. Actually, Reznikoff is faithful to both Halevi and Pound. For as Perloff observes, one of Pound's greatest contributions to modern poetry is "the use of translation as the invention of a desired other" (*Poetic License* 122). That desired other, for Reznikoff, is a historically derived vision of Jewish longing and Jewish endurance—that is, an other found in Jewish history, such as Halevi, which reflects Reznikoff's modern cultural ambivalence. In the Halevi translation, as well as in hundreds of his other poems derived from the Jewish past, Reznikoff finds a way to express in contemporary terms what Gershom Scholem describes as the problem produced by the messianic idea in Judaism: "in Judaism, the Messianic idea has compelled *a life lived in deferment,* in which nothing can be done, nothing can be irrevocably accomplished" (35).

The historical irony here (which Bloom fails to appreciate) is that in Reznikoff, and to some extent in the other Jewish Objectivists, the poetic vehicle for this sensibility becomes the modernism of such figures as Pound, Eliot, and Williams. As in the case of the mostly Jewish New York intellectuals (consider Eliot's immense influence on the verse of Delmore Schwartz), modernist poetry makes sense to the original Objectivists: the children or grandchildren of immigrants, on intimate terms with historical upheaval, they see in it a literature which acknowledges that history is accelerating to the breaking point. This modernist vision of apocalyptic history (in English, the locus classicus of this vision is the end of *The Waste Land*) resonates strongly for Jews in the late nineteenth and early twentieth centuries, for it accords with their own drastic experiences of assimilation, geographic displacement, and extreme changes in political and economic climates. In Europe—and, as we shall see, in America too—the Jewish attraction and contributions to modernism reach down to the deep pools of Jewish messianism. As Anson Rabinbach explains, "Apocalyptic, catastrophic, utopian and pessimistic, Messianism captured a generation of Jewish intellectuals before the First World War. The Messianic impulse appears in many forms in the Jewish generation of 1914 . . . secular *and* theological, as a tradition that stands opposed to both secular rationalism and what has been called 'normative Judaism'" (81).

But it is not only a modernist vision of history that appeals to first-generation Jewish-American writers; it is also the modernist attitude toward language. Modernism's antagonism to elaborate rhetoric and the concomitant emphasis on the direct, unadorned image promised writers like the Objectivists a linguistic newness that was, strange as it may seem, still in keeping with certain Jewish principles. Many of the formulations that have been used to define Objectivism—Oppen's "test of truth," Zukofsky's "thinking with the things as they exist," Reznikoff's own emphasis on "the testimony of a witness in a court of law"—correspond not only to Halevi's insistence on "lucidity of speech" but also to the even older and more centrally Jewish notion: personal responsibility in the determination and judgment of truth. Objectivist attitudes toward judgment and truth may be compared to the attitude expressed in the *Pirke Aboth* (literally *Chapters* but usually translated as *Ethics of the Fathers*), the best-known tractate of the Talmud, read for centuries as a touchstone of traditional Jewish wisdom: "By three things is the world preserved: by truth, by judgment, and by peace; as it is said, Judge ye the truth and the judgment of peace in your gates" (Aboth 1:18). Through their emphasis on truth and judgment, cast in a direct language that tests the epistemological and ethical grounds of its utterance, the Objectivists remain in touch with a persistent Jewish stance.

In this light, Bloom's objection to Jewish "moralism" in poetry makes little sense, especially when he declares at the end of his essay that Jewish-American poets can recover their covenant (and their voices) "only by somehow again walking His Way." But while Bloom admits that "persistence in seeking to recover what once our ancestors had" (262) may take many forms, Objectivism apparently is not one of them. Clearly, this is not because the Objectivists lack a Jewish "stance" or the means of recovering some sense of Jewish tradition. Yet Bloom's critique of Reznikoff and the aesthetic he represents, however inchoate it may be, still points to an unresolved problem close to the heart of Reznikoff's poetry and his identity as a Jew.

A number of readers have detected what appears to be a dichotomy in Reznikoff's poetry. Sometimes, as in the case of Bloom, this dichotomy is perceived to be a split between Jewish content and an incompatible (because rhetorically ineffectual) Objectivist style: a split that can be traced to a supposedly inevitable loss of poetic or cultural authority when literary assimilation takes its toll. By contrast, two other important critics find Reznikoff's Objectivist procedures relatively successful when applied to an urban American content, but more problematic when used for Jewish material, a circumstance arising out of the poet's attempt to reconcile his Jewish and American identities. "No one," says Robert Alter of Reznikoff, "has gone farther than he in the explicit effort to be both a conscious Jewish writer and an emphatically American one" (120). Alter tends to see the work most readily identifiable as "Objectivist" (and most comparable to Williams's) as the most American, and the most successful. But Alter regards the poet's treatment of Jewish material as "a radically contradictory enterprise: to 'objectify' in poetry the impelling spirit of a body of historical experience from which he himself, standing on the other side of the chasm of modernity, is alienated" (127). The result "is no more than a rehearsal of ritual gestures, literal and stylistic, a piece of willed piety, the intervention of a kind of poetic superego rather than the expression of an integrated poetic self" (128).

Setting aside the canard of "an integrated poetic self" (more New Critical than psychoanalytic, despite Alter's "poetic superego"), we can acknowledge the presumptive split in Reznikoff between a poet of urban American immediacy and prophetic Jewish historicity without accepting Alter's view that the Jewish poetry is "a rehearsal of ritual gestures" or "a piece of willed piety." L. S. Dembo, perhaps more sympathetic to Reznikoff's project than Alter, puts it almost in terms of a Jewish joke: "Being himself, however, really meant not just a Jew or just an American but both and neither. When he wrote Objectivist poems, he was an Objectivist; when he wrote of 'his people' he was, in a manner of speaking, a psalmist. . . . An exile, he sits down by the waters of Manhattan to weep; a wry smile comes over his face, for he realizes that he is home. And then he really weeps" (*Monological Jew* 129). Compared to those of Bloom and Alter, this is a more balanced attitude, for Dembo at least intuits the *necessity* for dialectical tension in Reznikoff's work. Dembo implies that the contradictions that arise out of being a Jew in America are sadly inevitable but must be taken in stride. Indeed, as I read Reznikoff's poetry, such contradictions are central to the work; they are textually productive, not only in Reznikoff's poetry, but whenever Jewish Americans work in an Objectivist mode. As a crucial discourse for Jewish-American poetry, Objectivism is, as Derrida would say, "contradictorily coherent. And, as always, coherence in contradiction expresses the force of a desire" ("Structure" 279).

This contradictory coherence is created by and expressive of the desire to be both a Jewish poet and an American poet. Reznikoff is a first-generation American already somewhat distant from traditional Jewish religious and cultural practices; he is also a second-generation modernist who wants a poetry that is more than "fake flowers / in the streets in which I walked" and is thus attracted to "the brand-new verse some Americans were beginning to write" (*Complete Poems* 2: 171). The contradictory task of the Jewish-American poet is to produce work that maintains both a remembrance of history and a sensitivity to the immediacies of mundane experience. The situation is further complicated by an equally powerful contradiction in the modern Jewish attitude toward the past. As Yosef Hayim Yerushalmi demonstrates in his magisterial *Zakhor*, memory and history are actually in opposition in modern Jewish culture. Collective memory is a function of the Jewish people "transmitting and recreating its past through an entire complex of interlocking social and religious institutions" (94)—in other words, the tradition that more or less assimilated Jewish writers and intellectuals experience as having lost. The same forces of secularization that lead to "the unravelling of that common network of belief and praxis" (94) give rise to the Jewish consciousness of history, the attempt to understand the collective past as a problematic object of study distinct from any notion of divine providence or biblical covenant. As Yerushalmi explains, "The modern effort to reconstruct the Jewish past begins at a time that witnesses a sharp break in the continuity of Jewish living and hence also an ever-growing decay of Jewish group memory. In this sense, if for no other, history becomes what it had never been before—the faith of fallen Jews. For the first time history, not a sacred text, becomes the arbiter of Judaism" (86).

When we think of Reznikoff's work and its relation to his cultural heritage in terms of this passage, we can better comprehend the poet's obsession with Jewish history, particularly the suffering of the Jewish people. Reznikoff's is not altogether a secular sensibility, for a strong messianic current runs through his work. But in Yerushalmi's terms, there is no question that Reznikoff could be understood as one of those "fallen" Jews for whom history, not Torah, is the arbiter of Judaism. Jewish history, not Jewish belief or tradition, is what Reznikoff draws upon to maintain himself as a Jew. The treatment of Jewish history in Reznikoff's poetry is itself a product of Jewish history, and being a Jew in this historical sense is crucial to him as a poet. For Reznikoff, poetry gives meaning to history: just as history becomes the arbiter of Judaism, so poetry becomes the arbiter of history. The secular awareness of Jewish history and the secular activity of writing poetry compensate for the loss of tradition, though they may come into being despairing of that loss.

How is this the case? On the one hand, it could be said that for Reznikoff, out of touch with the reality of the tradition, poetry rescues historical phenomena from mere facticity: it charges them with a vitality and existential meaning they would otherwise lack. On the other hand, poetry—particularly a modernist poetry of seriality and fragmentation—interrogates historical phenomena, rescuing them from their dangerous transformation into a reified "heritage" that becomes all too ideologically pliable. Charles Bernstein observes that

"There is no poet more dedicated to foregrounding the detail and the particular than Reznikoff and no poet more averse to blending these details into a consuming or totalizing form" ("Reznikoff's Nearness" 13). Against which we may juxtapose this passage from Walter Benjamin: "From what are phenomena rescued? Not just or not so much from the ill-repute and contempt in which they've fallen, but from the catastrophe when a certain form of transmission often presents them in terms of their 'value as heritage.'—They are rescued by exhibiting the discontinuities that exist within them. There is a kind of transmission that is a catastrophe" ("N" 63). The rescue of phenomena through the demonstration of their discontinuities, the transmission of phenomena not as an artificially constructed heritage but as catastrophe: this production of knowledge by fragmentation and constellation is perhaps the most important strategy of messianic Jewish modernism. For such a sensibility—opposed, as we have observed, to both secular rationalism and normative Jewish belief—the inherently fragmented nature of phenomena is the sine qua non of a world always awaiting redemption.

Messianism, then, is one of the most important keys to an understanding of the instability of Reznikoff's Jewish identity and to the contradictory coherence of his poetry. In his essay "Voices around the Text," Jonathan Boyarin defines "identity" as "a sense of collective belonging without loss of individual consciousness. Perhaps in Judaism, the lack and the desire, along with the conviction that there is or can be a center, motivate the diverse phenomenon scholars call messianism. Perhaps as well it is this lack and desire by which the past exercises its claim on 'our *weak* Messianic power' and which ensure that the 'secret agreement between past generations and the present one' [Benjamin, "Theses" 254] is fulfilled in study" (222–23). Boyarin's reference here to Benjamin's notion of our *weak* messianic power, which resides in the link or agreement between generations, indicates that there is hope of transmission and continuity, but that such continuity must be continually redefined. Boyarin's article is concerned with the ethnography of reading in a contemporary talmudic study group on New York's Lower East Side, the very existence of which is a sign of that *weak* messianic power. For Boyarin, the power connecting us to the past comes into play when Jews gather around the text and form a community of readers; it is an expression of "the lack and the desire, along with the conviction that there is or can be a center"—a existential center, that is, of Jewishness. I would expand Boyarin's formulation to include modern Jewish writing as well as Jewish reading, for it is the production of new Jewish texts as well as the study of traditional ones that encode this lack, this desire, this conviction. As I have argued elsewhere, modern Jewish writing constitutes a "ritual of new creation," one in which devotion to the text—even the profane text of history rather than the sacred text of the Law—honors tradition through the very event of rupture (Finkelstein, *Ritual* 2–3 and passim). Reznikoff is one of the best examples of this paradigm.

According to Boyarin, communal Jewish reading represents a need "to find our common ground without losing ourselves" (223). Reznikoff's contradictorily coherent poetry likewise represents this need, a need felt most acutely during periods of rapid social transformation. As much as any recent Jewish author, Reznikoff confirms Boyarin's intuition that the tense duality which we name Jewish identity constitutes a weak messianic power. But how does a Jew in increasingly assimilated circumstances such as Reznikoff's settle the messianic claims of the past? What claims does collective messianic history have upon a modern, self-consciously secular Jew? And if a poetry written in American English is to be the means through which this claim is settled, what procedures will best maintain the messianic possibility in a writing that seems to bear little resemblance to traditional textual practices?

Given such questions, Reznikoff's "Messianic," from *Separate Way* (published by the Objectivist Press in 1936), is an appropriate poem to consider. The poem is part of a sequence that includes "Depression" (drawn from contemporary anecdotes and observations of urban poverty), "The Socialists of Vienna" (based on an article in *New Masses* reporting on the 1934 Socialist revolt), and "New Land" (a montage of promise and struggle taken from early American history). Jewish messianism is therefore set in a broader international and historical context. But the sequence also focuses on the Jews as the special bearers of hope, given the account of their travail in "Palestine under the Romans" and the last poem, the magnificent "Kaddish," in which Reznikoff interpolates the traditional blessings in the prayer of mourning with images of those victimized by modern injustice.

The first stanza of "Messianic" presents an urban pastoral of the sort that Reznikoff, like Williams, had already perfected: by night "the river is brimming over / with the light / of street lights and electric signs"; by day "the sparrows will wheel about the shining twigs" (*Complete Poems* 1: 173–74). But the theme of urban modernity is radically changed in the second stanza:

> How far and wide
> about the upper and lower bay,
> along the rivers and beside the sea,
> how close and evenly
> the street lamps shine:
> you shall know the forests of your fathers
> among these posts,

and you their deserts
upon these miles of pavement
whose mica
glistens in the sunlight and the lamplight
in the heat of summer or the frost of winter,
wet with rain or white with snow.
Though your tribe is the smallest and you are the least,
you shall speak, you shall drill, you shall war;
and, dying,
wheeled away so swiftly
you see the sun
no larger than the evening star,
their boots shall carry your blood—
its corpuscles
seeds
that will grow in sandy lots,
between the cobblestones of alleys and on the pavement of avenues.
(*Complete Poems* 1: 174)

These lines quiver with the Objectivist sense of sincerity, of testimony. They are charged with intense yearning, but for the most part that yearning is expressed indirectly. As is often the case in his poetry, Reznikoff here relies on a rhetoric of ironic conflation. Traditional Jewish identity is both renewed and undermined as ancestral forests and deserts become streetlamps and pavement; the people's history is telescoped as conquerors' boots carry the "seeds" of Jewish blood to the "sandy lots," the "alleys" and "avenues" of New York. The sincere testimony in these lines is less that of a witness in a modern law court than that of a biblical prophet or psalmist who must speak an inspired truth to his people. Parallelism ("in the heat of summer or the frost of winter, / wet with rain or white with snow") and second-person repetitions ("you shall speak, you shall drill, you shall war") underscore this biblical voice.

The promise of renewal and redemption carried throughout Jewish history, as well as the emphasis on the bitter knowledge of suffering and endurance, make this poem, of course, "Messianic." The military training and violent death in the text indicate that Reznikoff may be thinking of the Jewish revolts against the Romans, especially the Bar Kochba revolt (132–35 C.E.), which was charged with messianic fervor and had the support of the religious establishment. Declared the Messiah by Rabbi Akiva, Bar Kochba ("son of a star" in Aramaic) became, in his defeat, the "evening star" of his people. In Reznikoff's presentation of the messianic scenario, apocalyptic violence gives way to a patient waiting amidst the diminished but sincerely admired details of the modern urban milieu.

In Reznikoff's treatment of this milieu, he revises what we think of as Objectivist methods, bringing Jewish historical (often biblical) material to bear on contemporary life through various metaphoric or allusive procedures. A two-line poem, #40 from *Jerusalem the Golden* (1934), is a good example of such negotiations:

> Rooted among roofs, their smoke among the clouds,
> factory chimneys—our cedars of Lebanon. (*Complete Poems* 1: 115)

It could almost be a poem from Pound's imagist period, except that Pound (and, for that matter, almost all of the other Imagists and Objectivists) rarely turns toward the Bible, while Reznikoff is continually attracted to it. As a rueful response to modernity, drawing on the same restrained irony found throughout the early work of Pound, Williams, Zukofsky, and Oppen, the poem could be giving voice to a thoughtful, relatively cultured urban community adjusting itself to the realities of an industrial landscape. The first-person plural appears in this context throughout the volume, as in #26 ("The twigs of our neighbor's bush . . . ") and #38 ("Of our visitors . . . "). As Oppen will later say in "Of Being Numerous," "This is a language, therefore, of New York" (*Collected Poems* 149); thus "our" can be read as inclusive of all urban Americans. The motivating tension in Oppen's great poem is "the shipwreck / Of the singular" (151)—that is, the conflict between the "meditative man" (153) in his urban isolation and the overwhelming power of mass urban life, which continually threatens to overwhelm individual thought and expression, even among artists and intellectuals who are sympathetic to "Them, the people" (152). But in *Jerusalem the Golden*, a book with a title recalling the biblical glory of David and Solomon, "our" may mean "Jews in the American diaspora" as much as "all New Yorkers" or "all urban Americans": when factory chimneys are our cedars of Lebanon, it is specifically Jewish loss as well as the dilemma of mass American modernity that speaks. Yet discovering that factory chimneys are our cedars of Lebanon also indicates not only loss, but also the survival, even the renewal, of Jewish sensibility in the New World. It is just this sense of both loss and recovery that constitutes what I have called Reznikoff's contradictorily coherent procedure.

Jerusalem the Golden draws a great deal of its verbal energy from this conflicted sense of identity: however much the poet seems at home in New York, on intimate terms with its most common sights and unassuming details, he still claims to feel the accumulated weight of centuries of Jewish exile. The poems continually rehearse themes of linguistic difference, geographic displacement, and historical rupture. A lyric about autumn in the city, for instance, is titled "Lament of the Jewish Women for Tammuz" and given a prophetic sense of disaster:

> Now the white roses, wilted and yellowing fast,
> hang in the leaves and briers.
> Now the maple trees squander their yellow leaves;
> and the brown leaves of the oak have left Ur and become wanderers.
>
> Now they are scattered over the pavements—
> the delicate skeletons of the leaves. (*Complete Poems* 1: 115–16)

This poem is a revealing example of the way in which Reznikoff complicates imagist/Objectivist strategies through an infusion of biblical material. As Reznikoff notes, the title refers to Ezekiel 7:14: "Then he brought me to the door of the gate of the Lord's house which was toward the north; and, behold, there sat women weeping for Tammuz." The Book of Ezekiel uses its prophetic mode to deal with the historical disaster of the Babylonian Captivity, the first Jewish experience of diaspora. Ezekiel speaks his prophecies in exile, "in the land of the Chaldeans by the river Chebar" (1:3). As Joel Rosenberg observes, "So many of Ezekiel's discourses in the first half of the book—before the destruction of Jerusalem—are retrospective visions: Israel's whole pre-Exilic history is repeatedly reviewed, as if in a kind of premature postmortem" (198). This includes the verse on which Reznikoff bases his poem: it is one of many abominations taking place in the Temple, which will be destroyed in just a few short years. The women weeping for Tammuz are participating in a pagan ritual, for Tammuz is the Near Eastern version of the Greek Adonis, a slain fertility god.

Autumn is the season for lamenting a dead fertility god, though one would hardly expect to hear such lamentation in New York City in the 1930s. (By contrast, Pound, working in Rapallo just a few years later, will draw on Frazer's accounts of rituals commemorating the death of Tammuz/Adonis to produce Canto XLVII, one of his most overt endorsements of the pagan mysteries.) Reznikoff is struck by the beauty of his hometown in the fall, but at the same time, he wishes to remind himself and his readers that as a Jew, he is also in exile, and to become too comfortable with the charms of a gentile nation is to court disaster. Like the women lamenting Tammuz, he may be forsaking his Jewish identity. On the other hand, he cannot help declaring that "the brown leaves of the oak have left Ur and become wanderers." Switching from Ezekiel to Genesis, the poet sees the leaves as similar to that original Jewish wanderer, Abraham. Hence the lovely melancholy of the fall in this poem becomes originally Jewish, however mindful of historic rupture.

That Reznikoff's own Hebrew name was Ezekiel, a fact of which he was strongly conscious, makes the play of identity in this poem all the more poignant. As he notes years later,

> Because, the first-born, I was not redeemed,
> I belong to my Lord, not to myself or you:
> by my name, in English, I am of His house,
> one of the carles—a Charles, a churl;
> and by my name in Hebrew which is Ezekiel
> (whom God strengthened)
> my strength, such as it is, is His. (*Complete Poems* 2: 80–81)

In his remarkable meditation on Reznikoff's names, Stephen Fredman calls this poem "an elegant attempt at synthesis, evincing a subtle midrashic interpretive ability, but the braiding of traditions the poet engages in unravels because he does not address the incommensurability of the social worlds of feudal England and Orthodox Judaism" (57). By playing upon his Hebrew and English name(s), Reznikoff projects this acute sense of social incommensurability back upon both the Jewish and the Anglo-Saxon past. This sense likewise afflicts him in "Lament of the Jewish Women for Tammuz," where his double awareness of himself as a prophet who keeps the faith and as a Jew who worships strange gods charges even the most common objects and scenes in the city around him.

This ambiguity may also be observed in "God and Messenger," from the sequence "Autobiography: New York":

> This pavement barren
> as the mountain
> on which God spoke to Moses—
> suddenly in the street
> shining against my legs
> the bumper of a motor car. (*Complete Poems* 2: 30)

The same irony as in the cedars of Lebanon piece deflates the poet as urban Moses. God will not speak to him though the New York pavement is as barren as Sinai: the motor car as messenger bears God's silence in the modern world and not his voice. Or is the poet the messenger? In that case, his prophetic desire is thwarted, and his only message (to his fellow New Yorkers? to American Jews?) consists of his rueful observations of secular life.

But is this life entirely secular? Although, as I have argued, Reznikoff's Jewish identity is based in history rather than belief, that history is ineluctably charged with an awareness of Presence, a numinous quality that may be felt not by ascending Sinai but by crossing a Manhattan street. For Reznikoff, so drawn to biblical analogies, the car bumper paradoxically creates an experience of Presence: by being so resolutely secular, it dialectically creates a space for the sacred. As Walter Benjamin proposes in his uncanny "Theologico-Political Fragment": "just as a force can, though acting, increase another that is acting in the opposite direction, so the order of the profane assists, through being profane, the coming of the Messianic Kingdom. The profane, therefore, although not itself a category of this Kingdom, is a decisive category of its quietist approach" (312).

In his seminal essay on Reznikoff, Paul Auster cites "God and Messenger" just before insisting that "Reznikoff the Jew and Reznikoff the American cannot be separated from one another. Each aspect of his work must be read in relation to the *oeuvre* as a whole, for in the end each point of view inhabits all the others" ("Decisive Moment" 158). In Reznikoff's work, Judaism and Objectivism both sustain and counteract each other; as in Benjamin's formulation, they are dialectical counterforces of the sacred and the profane, and the one is continually exposed in the other. As Auster notes, "the eye is not adequate. Not even the seen can be truly seen. The human perspective, which continually thrusts us into a place where 'only the narrow present is alive,' is an exile from eternity, an exclusion from the fullness of human possibility" (158). Thus Judaism, which insists on the ongoing possibility of messianic redemption posed against temporality, continually asserts itself in Reznikoff's poetry. The city's pavement is never sufficient in itself; informing the poet's temporal sight is the vision of the eternal in human affairs, which for the Jew is represented by God's giving of the Law to Moses on Sinai. But conversely, the eternal vista of Presence may shrink as the car bumper looms close. Neither an ancient Hebrew nomad nor a talmudic scholar in the enclosed study house, Reznikoff is a walker in the modern city, with a sustained awareness of the present moment, the vagaries of crossing not the biblical desert nor the textual ocean but the crowded streets of New York.

In Reznikoff's work, the urban milieu becomes the site of rescue from what Benjamin would consider the "catastrophe" of modern history. We see this in the two-line poem, #69 from *Jerusalem the Golden*, so admired (though still misquoted) by George Oppen: "Among the heaps of brick and plaster lies / a girder, still itself among the rubbish" (*Complete Poems* 1: 121). The poem acknowledges—indeed, it is almost a blessing upon—the integrity of the girder, when all the other materials of the world have been reduced to heaps of rubbish. The girder is a made thing, a whole that was part of a larger whole now no longer intact. In this respect, it is like the poem itself, which maintains its integrity despite its fragmentary status as part of a series of more or less fragmentary texts that make up *Jerusalem the Golden*—an ironic title indeed when considered in messianic terms. Reznikoff's vision of Jerusalem, his transmission of a Jewish worldview, is not a heritage but a catastrophe. Like Benjamin's angel of history, blown backward into the future by a storm from paradise, Reznikoff's "face is turned toward the past. Where we perceive a chain of events, he sees one single catastrophe which keeps piling wreckage upon wreckage and hurls it in front of his feet" ("Theses" 257).

That Reznikoff's world is one of endless wreckage becomes all too clear in his long poems, *Testimony* and *Holocaust*. In both, "wreckage upon wreckage" are hurled at our feet. The poems, particularly *Holocaust*, could be regarded as the endpoint of Objectivism's testimonial strain, as the subjectivity and presence of the poet virtually disappears, replaced by the dispassionate court records from which the texts are drawn. Like the angel of history, we can only stare, aghast at the sight of human violence and depravity as we are blown into an ever-worsening future. Yet this is not to say, as does Robert Alter, that "this is an extended exercise in masochism conducted under the cover of an act of testimony." According to Alter, "History, it would seem, had become a hypnotic vision of unrestrained murderous impulse for the poet: the ultimate breakdown of his whole problematic relation to the past is starkly evident in the flattened landscapes of disaster that take the place of round imagined worlds in these two long poems of his old age" (132). Granted, Reznikoff's relation to the past is problematic, but *Holocaust* does not constitute a "breakdown." It is, I believe, a *confrontation* with history set at the limit of Reznikoff's art:

> The bodies were thrown out quickly
> for other transports were coming:
> bodies blue, wet with sweat and urine, legs covered with excrement,
> and everywhere the bodies of babies and children.
> Two dozen workers were busy
> opening the mouths of the dead with iron hooks
> and with chisels taking out teeth with golden caps;
> and elsewhere other workers were tearing open the dead
> and looking for money or jewels that might have been swallowed.

And all the bodies were then thrown into the large pits dug near the
gas chambers
to be covered with sand. (*Holocaust* 46)

Holocaust offers so radical a challenge to the conventional category of poetry (or, perhaps, of the aesthetic) that in reading it we must put aside most of our assumptions about literary texts and historical representation. Drawn entirely from records of the Nuremberg and Eichmann trials, Reznikoff's poem demands a sort of religious silence from its readers, in much the same way that witnessing the event of the Shoah itself demands silence of those in the presence of such testimony. As George Steiner says in "Postscript" (1967), his essay on witnessing and representing the Holocaust, "The best *now,* after so much has been set forth, is, perhaps, to be silent; not to add the trivia of literary, sociological debate, to the unspeakable" (163). By contrast, Steiner is critical of the dramatized, but still largely accurate, account of events in the French study *Treblinka:*

> But because that evidence is mastered by the literary talent of the writer, because a narrative persona full of distinct rage and stylistic force interposes between the insane fact and the profoundly exciting economy, hence order, of the book, a certain unreality obtrudes. Where it is represented with such skill, intricate modulations affect the hideous truth. It becomes more graphic, more terribly defined, but also has more acceptable, conventional lodging in the imagination. We believe; yet do not believe intolerably, for we draw breath at the recognition of a literary device, of a stylistic stroke not finally dissimilar from what we have met in a novel. The aesthetic makes endurable. (166)

In composing *Holocaust,* Reznikoff seems to intuit that "The aesthetic makes endurable," and yet given his understanding of the testimonial role of poetry, he is still obliged to produce a text in which what Steiner would call "a narrative persona"—that is, the voice of the poetic subject—faintly lingers. The order of the sections of *Holocaust* moves in a loosely chronological fashion, from "Deportation" and "Invasion," through "Massacres," "Gas Chambers and Gas Trucks," and "Children," to the last sections, "Marches" and "Escapes." The poem ends with an account of the Warsaw ghetto uprising and the escape of six thousand Danish Jews to Sweden with the help of their gentile fellow citizens. In other words, Reznikoff proceeds from the beginning of this *saison d'enfer,* to its darkest moments, to the new beginning of a period of struggle, hope, and recovery. Furthermore, a horrible irony can sometimes be heard just below the surface of the narration, as in this last stanza from the section called "Entertainment":

> On Sundays there was no work and Jews would be placed in a row:
> each had a bottle on his head
> and the S. S. men amused themselves by shooting at the bottles.
> If a bottle was hit,
> the man lived;
> but if the bottle landed below,
> well, the man had it. (75)

The ironic resignation of that "well" in the final line can only belong to a narrative voice that cannot lose itself entirely in the *univers concentrationnaire.*

Reading *Holocaust* throws us back on the rest of Reznikoff's poetry with a renewed sense of his cultural predicament. As we have seen, identifying with Jewish *history* means suffering the loss of Jewish *tradition.* Compelled to bear the historical burden of Jewish identity without the inner strength provided by the continuity of Jewish faith, secular Jews like Reznikoff experience the intertwined processes of secularization and assimilation as a full-blown crisis of transmission. This is certainly true for Reznikoff in comparison to his fellow Objectivists George Oppen and Louis Zukofsky. Younger, wealthier, and much more assimilated to begin with, Oppen, after one book, embraces Marxism, itself a displacement of traditional Judaism. According to Mark Shechner, Marxism served Jewish intellectuals of this generation "as a substitute Judaism, endowed with all the powers once possessed by halakhic or Orthodox Judaism for interpreting the world, dictating principles, forming character, and regulating conduct" (8). Yet Oppen probably turns to Marxism less because of ethnicity than because of class. He emerges years later as one of our greatest political poets, one for whom Jewish identity means "Burying my dogtag with H / For Hebrew in the rubble of Alsace" (*Collected Poems* 211): a powerful but relatively isolated reference to his Jewishness in the late poem "Of Hours," addressed to his erstwhile mentor, Ezra Pound. In her study of Oppen and Pound, Rachel Blau DuPlessis writes of that moment of danger in Alsace, and of "the metal tag which characterizes oneself as anathema, torturable . . . one fears one's identity because it is one's otherness" ("Objectivist Poetics" 137). For Oppen, being Jewish means claiming a kind of cultural otherness; Pound fails miserably to imaginatively identify with that otherness, despite his general sympathy with the exile and the outcast. Zukofsky, a less orthodox Marxist than Oppen but an even closer disciple of Pound, may write nostalgically of his father, Reb Pinchos, or eccentrically "translate" the opening of Job in "A", but most tellingly inscribes his own ironic relation to Judaism in the early work which Pound published in *Exile,* "Poem beginning 'The'": "Assimilation is not hard, / And once the Faith's askew / I might as well look Shagetz just as much as Jew" (*Complete Short Poetry* 17).

These are lines that Reznikoff could not have written, for even with the Faith askew, he could never regard himself as a shagetz, a gentile male. (Nor did Pound ever reach out to Reznikoff as he did to Oppen and Zukofsky; as Charles Bernstein pointedly notes, "Pound's disinterest in Reznikoff is foundational" ["Reznikoff's Nearness" 13]). Instead, consider this fairly late poem from *Inscriptions 1944–1956* (1959):

> My parents were of a great company
> that went together, hand in hand;
> but I must make my way alone
> over waves and barren land.
>
> My grandfathers were living streams
> in the channel of a broad river;
> but I am a stream that must find its way
> among blocking rock
> and through sands and sand. (*Complete Poems* 2: 80)

Reznikoff's subject here is the weakening of Jewish tradition and community over generations. Transmission is catastrophe, as the broad river of ancestral culture and learning dwindles to the figure of the poet, a stream blocked by rock and sand. It is interesting to note that when Reznikoff's anxiety over this situation is most acute, he resorts to a more traditional *English* verse form, as if finding in rhyme and comparatively regular meters a sense of connection to the *Jewish* (linguistically, the Hebrew) culture which he is otherwise losing.

Yet the images of the river and the stream have a peculiarly Jewish resonance: in rabbinic literature, the Torah (and hence those who enter into its study) is a great river or fountain that nourishes the soul. Reznikoff's failure to master Hebrew and become a traditional scholar weighs heavily upon him all his life. As early as *Five Groups of Verses* (1927), he writes, "How difficult for me is Hebrew: / even the Hebrew for *mother,* for *bread,* for *sun* / is foreign. How far have I been exiled, Zion" (*Complete Poems* 2: 72). And in his "Early History of a Writer," from *By the Well of Living and Seeing* (1969), he recalls how, as a sixteen-year-old going to the University of Missouri, he said farewell to his grandfather, who blessed him in a Hebrew that the young Charles could not understand. The old man, who died before Reznikoff could see him again, then began to weep:

> Perhaps my grandfather was in tears for other reasons:
> perhaps, because, in spite of all the learning I had acquired in high school,
> I knew not a word of the sacred text of the Torah
> and was going out into the world
> with none of the accumulated wisdom of my people to guide me
> (*Complete Poems* 2: 167)

From the beginning to the end of his career, Reznikoff never ceases to brood upon the rupture that constitutes Jewish modernity, and how he himself is a typical product of that rupture.

10

Reznikoff's Nearness

Charles Bernstein

I

1. Charles Reznikoff was born in Brooklyn in 1894. The date is interesting because Reznikoff is somewhat older than the poets of the "second wave" of radical modernism, with whom he is often associated. Zukofsky, for example, was born in 1904, Oppen in 1908, Bunting in 1900, Riding in 1901, Hughes in 1902, while Toomer was born in the same year as Reznikoff. Sterling Brown, with whom Reznikoff shared the great project of using the American historical record of injustice and social barbarism as a primary subject, was born seven years after him.

2. Reznikoff is a bridge figure between Williams, the poet he most resembles, and a decade older than he, and the poets born at the turn of the century, a decade after him. Like Williams, he came from a family in which English was not a native tongue. His parents (like my own grandparents) came from Russia, sometime after 1881; his paternal grandparents joined the family somewhat later.

His mother's father, Ezekiel, never made it to the New World, having died before Reznikoff was born. Ezekiel, a cattle and wheat broker, had written Hebrew verse on his travels. Just after he died his wife destroyed all trace of his writings, fearing his manuscripts might contain material that would create trouble for the family if discovered by the czarist authorities. The destruction of his grandfather's poetry is an emblematic story for Reznikoff, and he comes back to it in two poems, the first opening *By the Well of Living and Seeing:*

My grandfather, dead long before I was born,
died among strangers; and all the verse he wrote
was lost
except for what
still speaks through me
as mine.[1]

The poetic or psychic economy suggested here helps to explain Reznikoff's resolve to continue with his work in the face of intense waves of indifference—indeed, his resolve to ensure that his own verse would not disappear entirely: "I would leave no writing of mine, / if I could help it, / to the mercy of those who loved me" (*CP* 2: 176). Reznikoff's work echoes this subtext in a number of ways: the poems are an act of recovery, where recovery becomes a project of immense proportion far beyond this initial point of focus. A few times, the poems register the difficulty of this recovery in terms of the poet's loss, or exile from, Hebrew, a language he does not really know (Reznikoff's parents would have spoken Yiddish and increasingly English) but which seems part of his identity.

Reznikoff tells the tale of his parent's life in Russia and of their painfully difficult work in the New York rag trade in scrupulous and informative detail in two remarkable autobiographical works, "Early History of a Seamstress" and "Early History of Sewing Machine Operator," as well as in his own continuation of their story in "Needle Trade."[2]

3. Reznikoff attended Boys High School in Brooklyn and from 1910 to 1911 went to the School of Journalism at the University of Missouri. During the following year he worked as a salesman for his parents' millinery business. But in 1912, remembering that Heine (the reference may at first seem peculiar but begins to make sense) had gone to law school, he enrolled at NYU. Reznikoff graduated law school in 1916 and was admitted to the bar the same year.

4. Legal studies provided Reznikoff a sharp contrast to the poetics of metaphysical and symbolic overtone, of fashionable literary conceits and static ornamentation. Indeed, legal argument provided an analogue for the poetic principles he did find interesting, such as the "brand new verse" of Pound and H.D., which he read in *Poetry* when he was twenty-one and studying law ("Talk with Dembo" 98.) It was at this time that he first formulated a poetics that emphasized "the pithy, the necessary, the clear, and plain" (*CP* 2: 172), principles that, like most of his statements of poetics, stressed what he was breaking away from (the influence of Pound is unmistakable) more than the new poetic space he was inventing.

Remembering his years at law school, Reznikoff writes:

I found it delightful
to climb those green heights,
to bathe in the clear waters of reason,
to use words for their daylight meaning
and not as prisms
playing with the rainbows of connotation:
. . . .
I had been bothered by a secret weariness
with meter and regular stanzas
grown a little stale. The smooth lines and rhymes
seemed to me affected, a false stress on words and syllables
fake flowers
in the streets which I walked.
. . . .
The brand new verse some Americans were beginning to write
after the French "free verse" perhaps
. . . .
seemed to me, when I first read it,
right:
not cut to patterns, however cleverly,
nor poured into ready molds. (*CP* 2: 168–71)

5. After a very brief attempt to start a law practice, Reznikoff returned to millinery sales, saying his "mind was free" as he waited for hours to see the buyers at Macy's.

Reznikoff claims to have been very good at selling ladies' hats, although his wife, Marie Syrkin, in her marvelous memoir, demurs on this point (Syrkin 38–39).

In 1918, *Rhythms*, Reznikoff's first book, was privately printed and distributed just one year after Pound's first *Cantos*. Reznikoff kept in mind the fate of his grandfather's poetry in choosing to arrange for the printing on his own. He also showed an independence from literary fashion and career that would mark his entire life.

Two years later, in 1920, Samuel Roth published his *Poems* in an edition of 250.

6. In 1927, Reznikoff bought his own press, setting the type and printing *Five*

Groups of Verse in an edition of 375 copies, and later *Nine Plays* in an edition of 400 copies. During this time he was able to stop working entirely, living on a very modest income of $25 per week from his parents.

7. Reznikoff seemed to accept the fact that there was, and would be, little interest in his poetry. But by the late 1920s he had met Zukofsky and George and Mary Oppen; they formed not a school but a small circle of support and mutual interest in each other's work. There was, for a while, a pool of light in a world of poetic darkness: "against the darkness: / a quadrangle of light" (*CP* 2: 136).

8. In 1927 and 1928, Ezra Pound had included in his magazine *Exile* poems by Williams and Zukofsky, McAlmon and Rakosi, as well as Reznikoff. In 1928, Pound wrote Zukofsky that he ought to bring together a group of younger poets (Sharp 21).

In February 1931, Harriet Monroe's *Poetry* published a special issue edited by Zukofsky that began with a short statement under the heading "Program: 'Objectivists' 1931," immediately followed by an essay entitled "Sincerity and Objectification with Special Reference to the Work of Charles Reznikoff." As compared to the far longer manuscript version, the published essay cut references to Reznikoff's neglect and to his plays, altogether eliminating about half the original citations to his work; this process of elimination was radically accelerated in the intervening years so that in Zukofsky's collected essays, *Prepositions* (1977), all references to Reznikoff are removed for the final citationless distillation of Zukofsky's thought, now titled simply "An Objective."[3] Reznikoff was not alone in his obsession to cut and keep cutting.

From 1931 to 1932 the Oppens published three books (Pound, Williams, and Zukofsky's *An "Objectivists" Anthology*) under the imprint To Publishers, with Zukofsky as the press editor.

In 1934, Zukofsky, Reznikoff, and the Oppens founded the Objectivist Press, with the advice of Williams and Pound. That first year they published Williams's *Collected Poems*, edited by Zukofsky with an introduction by Stevens, in an edition of 500 copies. Williams put up $250, of which $150 was refunded (Sharp 505). Reznikoff was much surprised to find their first book reviewed by the *New York Times;* it sold better than expected. In 1934 the Objectivist Press also published Oppen's *Discrete Series;* after that, Oppen stopped writing for twenty years. Finally, in the same year, the press published the initial installment of Reznikoff's *Testimony,* with an introduction by Kenneth Burke, in an edition of 200 copies.

Three years later, in 1937, New Directions was founded, and began publishing Pound, Williams, and others.

9. Reznikoff met Marie Syrkin in 1929, and they were married the next year.[4]

At around this time (Hindus says 1928, but Syrkin says 1930), Reznikoff's parents' businesses went bad and, like many other small businesses during the depression, went into debt. Not only had he lost his meager income, but also Reznikoff was now obliged to help out his family. Reluctantly, he took a job at *Corpus Juris,* a legal encyclopedia, as a copywriter. Eventually, he was fired from *Corpus Juris.* Syrkin recalls the editor telling him, "When I hire a carpenter I don't want a cabinetmaker" (Syrkin 45; see also Hindus, "Introduction" to *Man and Poet*).

10. From 1938 to 1939 Reznikoff went to Hollywood for a $75-a-week job as a quite peripheral writer for a movie studio where an old friend worked. This period is described in his posthumously published novel *The Manner Music,* a book that includes prose adaptations—less musical, less shapely—of at least nine of his late poems. The novel ends with the protagonist—an unrecognized, perhaps unrecognizable, artist—burning all of his work, again bringing to mind the destruction by fire of Reznikoff's grandfather's verse: "He tore up everything, everything he has ever written and burnt it. They found the heap of ashes next to him when they took him to the hospital."[5]

When Reznikoff returned to New York, he worked at a number of odd editorial and research jobs, including writing a history of the Jewish community of Charleston and editing the papers of Louis Marshall.

11. Between 1941 and 1959 Reznikoff did not publish any books, although he continued to work on his poems and his anti-epic, *Testimony.*

12. In 1948, Reznikoff received a letter from Williams: "A confession and an acknowledgement! In all these years that I have owned a book of yours, nineteen years! a book you gave me in 1929 I never so much opened it except to look at it cursorily. And now, during an illness, I have read it and I am thrilled with it" (quoted in Hindus, "Introduction" to *Man and Poet* 31–32).

13. In the 1950s, while Syrkin was teaching at Brandeis, Reznikoff became managing editor, at $100 a week, of *Jewish Frontier,* a labor Zionist monthly with which Syrkin was involved. "With no aptitude for journalism," Syrkin recalls, "he despised the facile generalizations of the craft and the superficial edi-

torials . . . in response to a current crisis. . . . I had to contain his natural inclination to reduce pages to paragraphs and paragraphs to sentences" (53–54).

The printers, however, appreciated his incredible meticulousness. "That he was a poet, a designation privately equated with schlemiel, explained any failure to fit into a familiar mold" (54).

14. When Reznikoff turned sixty-eight, in 1962, New Directions published a selection of his poems, *By the Waters of Manhattan,* with an introduction by C. P. Snow, and subsequently published the first volume of *Testimony.* In 1968, however, the publisher turned down the second volume of *Testimony,* and Reznikoff arranged to have it printed privately in an edition of 200.

15. In 1975, Black Sparrow published *Holocaust,* based, like *Testimony,* not on firsthand reports but exclusively on court records, here from the Nuremberg and the Eichmann trials.

16. In 1976, with the first volume of his *Complete Poems* in press from Black Sparrow, Charles Reznikoff died.

II

The Abbaye de Royaumont, not far from Paris, was a center of Christendom in the thirteenth century, when it was built. During the Revolution it sustained heavy damages, and the abbey has never been fully reconstructed. In recent years Royaumont has been used as a literary, music, and business conference center.

In the fall of 1989, Royaumont was site for a conference on the American Objectivist poets, a group more prominent in the French map of American poetry than in many of our homemade maps. The library of Royaumont, with its forty-foot ceilings and walls lined with ancient books, was an extraordinary setting for an occasion honoring four relatively obscure American poets, whose parents had come from Europe from Jewish shtetels to settle into the New World. Even more extraordinary, the conference began at sunset on the Friday night upon which fell Rosh Hashanah, the Jewish New Year.

At the invitation of Emmanuel Hocquard, who has translated Reznikoff's The Manner Music *into French, Michael Palmer, Michael Davidson, Lyn Hejinian, David Bromige, and I had come from America to speak on one or another of the Objectivists, while Carl Rakosi gave a reading and commented on many of the talks presented.*

I had brought along a tape of Reznikoff reading in 1974 at the Poetry Center of

San Francisco State, along with a transcript of the forty-six poems, and fragments of poems, he had selected for that reading, which I had cut and pasted together, as he must have done in constructing this sequence, from almost every section and period of his poetry. The following remarks are based on that talk.

1. How does a poem, these poems, enter the world?

2. Measured and scaled, particular and necessary: that would be one answer. Reznikoff gives his own "platform as a writer of verse," as he wryly puts it in an introduction to the reading, given when he was eighty, at the Poetry Center of San Francisco State:

> Salmon and red wine
> and a cake fat with raisins and nuts:
> no diet for a writer of verse
> who must learn to fast
> and drink water by measure.[6]

Reznikoff's selection, at the Poetry Center reading, of work from over sixty years of writing is a masterful weave "mastermix" creating not "the intricate medallions the Persians know" (*CP* 2: 75) but a discrete series of poetic encounters that marks his work from beginning to end, without end or beginning.

3. *Rhythms,* in 1918, marks the invention of literary cubo-serialism. By "cubo-seriality" I mean to identify the more discrete development that characterizes Reznikoff's work from that point in 1918 on—the permutation of briefly etched, identifiable details that don't quite stand on their own and which separated by a gap, or interval, that requires a full stop. The prefix suggests rhetorically consonant permutations of angles of view on related (or linked) subjects.

4. From his 1927 collection *Five Groups of Verse* (which included *Rhythms*), Reznikoff numbered each of his often quite tiny poems and ran them together on the page, rather than isolating each poem on its own page (as he had up to this point) or separating the poems in some other way. This very explicit, even intrusive, numbering expresses Reznikoff's radical commitment to the poetic sequence, or series, as details open to reordering. In Reznikoff, the process of composition is as much a matter of the shaping of sequences as of the creation of particular elements of the sequence: the otherwise unrepresentable (and overlooked) space between poems has become the location of the work's poesis

of unfolding and refolding, separating and recongealing. In Reznikoff, the meaning of the poem is always twofold: both in the detail and in its sequence. That is, the detail works in counterpoint to its locus in a series to create the meaning of the poem.

Reading Reznikoff formally means attending to the relation of the part to the whole (and the whole to the part) in his work, along lines that also suggest the relation of the shot to the sequence (in film and photography), surface to depth (in painting but also in rhetoric), the fragment to the total (in philosophy but also in Kabbalah).

To create the text of his 1974 reading, Reznikoff stitched together forty-six individual bits and pieces. As with any work of disjunctive collage, each frame or unit recontexualizes the subsequent frame or unit. Reznikoff's "groups" (as he sometimes called them) are not governed by a principle external to the compositional process. His series are not ordered narratively, or chronologically, or historically; there is no necessarily logical or causal connection between the links of the chain. Rather, Reznikoff employs a variety of thematic and tonal shifts to create an overall "musical" arrangement, to use his own phrase for the process. What Reznikoff calls, right from the first book, *Rhythms:* "The ceaseless weaving of the uneven water."[7]

5. There is no poet more dedicated to foregrounding the detail and the particular than Reznikoff, and no poet more averse to blending these details into a consuming or totalizing form. The numbers that obtrude into the visual field of almost every page of Reznikoff's verse represent both this commitment and aversion. This is not to deny that the individual sections add up to a larger form, but to affirm that the particularity and integrity of each detail is not diminished by the newly forming whole. While this structural allegory of polis echoes through the work of several of his contemporaries, notably Williams, Oppen, and Zukofsky, it is Reznikoff's tenacity combined with an uncanny lack of didacticism that especially characterizes his approach.

Reznikoff rejected the "depth" of field simulated by various realist and mimetic self-centering procedures in which each detail is subordinated to an overall image or theme or meaning. By constantly intercutting, or jump cutting, between and among and within material, the poem's surface of local particularities gains primacy, in contrast to the rhetorical depth of narrative closure that is aimed for in such epic montage formats as *The Waste Land* and certain of the *Cantos* (not to mention more conventional poetry). Reznikoff's network of stoppages is anti-epic. It enacts an economy of perambulation and coincidence, of loss rather than accumulation (a general rather than a restricted economy, in Bataille's terms).

Scrap of paper
blown about the street,
you would like to be cherished, I suppose,
like a bank-note. (*CP* 2: 76)

Pound's disinterest in Reznikoff is foundational.

6. Parataxis is a manner of transition. Elements are threaded together like links on a chain, periodically rather than hierarchically ordered and without the subordination of part to whole. The *OED* defines "parataxis" as "the placing of propositions or clauses one after another, without indicating by connecting words the relation (of coordination or subordination) between them."

Parataxis is a grammatical state of adjacency, of being next to or side by side. Besideness. As the mind lies next to its object, or one finds oneself a neighbor in conversation, or in reflection one thought follows the next. A nonlinear network of interconnections.

7. As a term of art, adjacency is distinguished from adjoining or abutting, as land that is adjacent to a common square, but nowhere touches.

Reznikoff's is an art of adjacency, each frame carefully articulated and set beside the next.

8. Reznikoff's cubo-seriality is modular and multidirectional, marking a series of sites available to rearrangement in ever new constellations of occurrence. (Reznikoff's own refiguring of his lifework at the 1974 Poetry Center reading is a model for this potential for reconfiguration.) Resembling the long walks through the city he took every morning, Reznikoff's poems move from site to site without destination, each site inscribing an inhabitation, every dwelling temporary—contingent but sufficient.

Those of us without house and ground
who leave tomorrow
must keep our baggage light:
a psalm, perhaps a dialogue—[8]

So Reznikoff continues his "platform." "Without house and ground" hints of the wandering of exile and the absence of foundations, but this nomadic poetry refuses exile in its insistence that grounds are only and always where one sleeps, a view suggested by the poem's epigraph from the Mishnah (Aboth 6:4): "and on the ground shalt thou sleep and thou shalt live a life of trouble." Exile suggests expulsion from a native land, but in Reznikoff's verse the native is what lies at one's feet, ground for walking on: so no loss of prior foundations, no absent center, as in Edmond Jabès, but "finding as founding," to use Stanley Cavell's Emersonian phrase from *This New Yet Unapproachable America.*

Perhaps there are those who possess house and land, who can afford to live higher off the ground, imagining possession as a prophylactic for loss. Damage is given, not chosen. The nomad, neither uprooted or uprooting, roots around, reroutes. Reznikoff's new world is not one of absence, but neither is it one of plenty.

Like a tree in December
after the winds have stripped it
leaving only trunk and limbs
to ride and outlast
the winter's blast.

The "writer of verse," like the nomad, "must learn to fast / and drink water by measure." Reznikoff's baggage is, literally, the *light* that emanates from conversation and song (dialogue and psalm), exactly the measures of his verse. This is a poetry not of dislocation or banishment but of the "blinding" intensities of location as relocation, relocalization.

9. A typology of Reznikoff's parataxis would begin by distinguishing his nondevelopmental seriality from sequential seriality, to use Joseph Conte's terms in *Unending Design,* a distinction that is in some ways similar to that between analytic and synthetic cubism.

Certainly, the modulation of disjunctiveness between poems in a Reznikoff "group of verse" is one of the poetry's most distinctive features. As Burton Hatlen has argued, reading Reznikoff means reading each of his groups as a series, not as autonomous poems ("Objectivism in Context"). Such readings will need to take account of the fact that Reznikoff reordered the sequences of his groups in ways that underscore the modular, permutable status of each discrete poem.

Reznikoff's groups are composed by varying the degree of continuity and discontinuity among the sections. The most typical relation between sections is one of simultaneity of occurrences, as if each poem were preceded by an implied "meanwhile."[9] However, some of the modules of a series do share thematic interconnections, with subject clusters connected by family resemblances, commonly involving a permutation of tangentially related motifs, with shifts among themes varying from slight to abrupt. Reznikoff's "Similes" (*CP*

2: 103) demonstrates this principle within a single poem, presenting four images, each of which seems teasingly related to the others, but which share no single statable topic. Sometimes small thematic clusters are placed within larger nonthematic series. These may be given an overtitle—a sequence within a series, as "Winter Holidays" or "Early History of a Writer"—or the cluster may simply share the same subject, as the motifs of the subway, birds, rain, and the moon identified by Hatlen in his reading of *Jerusalem the Golden.* Moreover, some of Reznikoff's works are framed by a single theme or subject, such as the biblical studies of "Editing and Glosses" in *By the Waters of Manhattan: An Annual* (1929), or, most prominently, his books *Testimony* and *Holocaust,* which, while thematically linked, are nonetheless serial rather than sequential.

10. Seriality encompasses a vast array of modernist and contemporary poetry, much of it better known for its nonsequentiality than Reznikoff's verse. The usefulness of the term depends on the degree to which the different types of serialism are distinguished. The early modernist history of seriality could easily start with Stein's *Tender Buttons* (1912), the most original rethinking of poetic form in the period. One might also think of the serial ordering of long individual poems in Pound's *Cantos* or Zukofsky's *"A".* Conte identifies Williams's *Spring and All* (1923) as the prototype for serial form, noting the twenty-seven numbered, untitled poems that are interpreted with prose improvisations. But consider also Jean Toomer's *Cane* (1923), with its interspersing of loosely associated poems and prose.[10]

A pre-(modern) history of the serial poem would have much to account for, famously, Büchner's *Woyzeck,* but equally Dickinson's fascicles, the most radical serial poems of nineteenth-century America. (I return again to Dickinson's lines "This world is not conclusion. / A sequel stands beyond / Invisible as Music / But positive, as Sound," where *sequel* is a possible variant for *species* [poem #501; *Poems* 2: 384–85].) In *Emily Dickinson's Open Folios,* Marta Werner makes a convincing case that what we now know as Dickinson's letters or prose are, to a surprisingly large extent, better classified as serial fragments. The relation of fragments to seriality leads to a further deepening of both categories; Hölderlin's late fragments would be particularly relevant to consider in this regard.

During the period following World War II, the most influential conception of the serial poem came from Jack Spicer, who contrasted the "one-night stand" of the individual poems to a composition by book in which the order of the poems, like each individual poem, is determined by "dictation." Both Robert Duncan and Robin Blaser were comrades with Spicer in this project.

Zukofsky's great cut-up collage, "Poem beginning 'The'," composed of 330 numbered lines, prefaced by a list of several dozen sources for the work, was written in 1926. As in much of Zukofsky's poetry, the poem's lines flow from one to next, working in counterpoint to the disjunctive nature of the sources and the numerical framing. The process of running in such disparate material by the use of intricate syntactic, syllabic, and thematic patterning which characterizes much of Zukofsky's *"A"* is a formal practice quite distinct from Reznikoff's cubo-seriality.[11] Many of Zukofsky's shorter poems are, like Reznikoff's, presented in numbered sequences. But unlike Reznikoff's splinters, Zukofsky's individual poems in *All* are longer and stand up by themselves as autonomous works. Zukofsky's short poetry, less dependent on the series, makes less of it.

More directly akin to Reznikoff's cubo-seriality is George Oppen's *Discrete Series* (1932–34); the work of Lorine Niedecker, whose discrete seriality is explicitly shown only in the most comprehensive collection of her work, *From This Condensery*, edited by Robert Bertholf; the "Love Songs" (1915–17) of Mina Loy; and Langston Hughes's *Montage of a Dream Deferred* (1951).

More recent work that continues a poetics of adjacency, in which elements are discrete, incomplete, and recombinatory, would include, among *many* others, George Oppen's "Of Being Numerous"; Robert Creeley's *Words, Pieces* and "In London"; Ron Silliman's "new," that is, permutable, sentences; Lyn Hejinian's *The Cell;* Ted Pearson's *Evidence;* Tom Raworth's *A Serial Biography;* Ted Berrigan's "Tamborine Life"; and John Ashbery's "Europe."

One criterion that usefully differentiates paratactic forms is the degree to which the parts are mobile or recombinable. On one end of the spectrum is nonserial parataxis, bound to narrative or chronology, such as in the Homeric epics and the Bible. (There is another way of reading the Torah that suggests its nonsequential undertow: the Kabbalistic practice of gematria, as developed by Abraham Abulafia in the thirteenth century, which involves the recombination of numerically equivalent words and in some ways resembles anagrammatic and aleatoric methods of recombination.)

A second category, in which the arrangement of the elements is intrinsic to the meaning, covers most serial poems. Further recombination is, by definition, possible without compromising the prosodic structure of the work; nonetheless, the meaning of the series is dependent, to a greater or lesser extent, on the particular array or temporal ordering that had been made or the procedure that has been used. By "temporal ordering," I mean works that foreground the process of composition (elements are ordered as they were written); by "array," nontemporal and nonsystematic configurations of modular elements; by "procedure," external or explicit principles of design used to order elements of a series.

A third category consists of modular poems that have not yet been serialized: poems in which the arrangement of elements is extrinsic. In the strictest sense, few works fit into this category since the format of books binds an order onto even the most discontinuous set of leaves. In a broader sense, there are a number of serial works that are not intended to be read only or principally in the order in which they are printed. (Serial *reading* opens all works to recombination. My favorite image of readerly seriality is David Bowie, in Nicholas Roeg's *The Man Who Fell to Earth,* watching a bank of TVs all of which were rotating their channels.) Robert Grenier's *Sentences*—five hundred discrete articulations each on a separate index card and housed in a blue Chinese box—is the best example I know of extrinsic seriality, though two other boxes of cards also come to mind: Jerome Rothenberg and Harris Lenowitz's *Gematria 27* (twenty-seven recombinable numeric word equivalences) and Thomas McEvilley's cubo-serial *4* (forty-four four-line poems). In principle, hypertext is an ideal format for this mode of composition since it allows a completely nonlinear movement from link to link: no path need be specified, and each reading of the database creates an alternative series. What's remarkable is that this structure is already a potential in Reznikoff's first book in 1918.[12]

I have in mind two other criteria for differentiating serial poems (though what good all this classification will do I can't say; not likely much): the degree of congruity or incongruity among elements of the series (this might be called coefficient of weirdness, with cubo-seriality, for example, having a low coefficient) and the extent of found or preexisting material used in the poem.

11. In Reznikoff's cubo-seriality, it's a matter of the *cut:* as in the cut of a dress or of a fabric. Also a double cutting: the shapeliness of the lines as units inside each poem (the cut of each poem, Reznikoff as miniaturist), and the rhythm between the poems (the intercutting). The numbered poem as unit, but also the line as unit: isolating/emphasizing discrete words or word pairs, half-puns, and off-rhymes and echoes and repetitions; modulating, pushing against too easy a rhythm, too quick a reading: "Her work was to count linings / the day's seconds in dozens" (*Poems,* 1920; *CP* 1: 29).

12. Reznikoff is a "literary realist" only if one unit is considered in isolation, as has been the assumption of most readings of his work. Understood serially, in terms of their plasticity, the poems can no longer be read with the trivializing appreciation of being plain, descriptive, flat, simple, artless, and unassuming; or as being without rhetorical effect or "modernist discontinuity." Indeed, the early negative reviews of Reznikoff's works reveal a difficulty with his poetry that suggests his radical approach better than many of the more positive sub-

sequent assessments: "a fragmentary style that annoys and bewilders"; "cumulative effect . . . is promising shavings"; "He is unable to focus . . . apparent incoherence" [Malcolm Cowley]; "half-baked, [showing] a lack of development."[13]

13. Subject matter is literally *beside* the point of this formal innovation, which would be possible with different subject matter and even without explicit subject matter (as in Stein). As Reznikoff notes, "Half the meaning [of poetry] is the music" ("First, There Is the Need"). Milton Hindus, apparently reporting on a conversation with Reznikoff, remarks: "Literature was capable of making something out of nothing (indeed, it was Flaubert's dream to write a work about 'nothing at all'); it was capable of making interesting (by the quality of its style, by its emphasis, by the purity and freshness of its language, by the depth of its feeling or thought) the most commonplace and the least exciting or unusual occurrences."[14] The comparison between Reznikoff and Flaubert seems particularly apt on the question of style; it's incredible that the exquisite stylizations of Reznikoff's poems have been lost in the tendency to call him, virtually, styleless.

14. Reznikoff does speak of poetry as the communication of feeling, but he is explicit that this feeling, in an "objective" poem, is not expressed as the direct personal statement of the author.

Reznikoff's manner, or method, as he calls it: the feeling comes *indirectly* as a result of the *selection of objects* and the "music" that composes the object ("First, There Is the Need" [2]). It is a matter of the cut and the cutting.

15. Jewish forms (not just themes): the idea of Jewish holiness (blessedness): in the detail, the everyday: every activity, every moment, holy: "How brilliant a green the grass is, / how blinding white the snow."[15]

In Jewish thought, the holiness of the ordinary can be traced to the eighteenth-century founder of Hasidism, Israel Baal Shem, as well as further back to earlier Jewish mystics.[16] In orthodox Judaism, as in other orthodox religions, the holy is external; graspable, if at all, only through law and ritual; it is an "object of dogmatic knowledge," as Gershom Scholem puts it (*Major Trends* 10). In Jewish mysticism, holiness is present in everyday "low" activities and not separated out to particular sites, such as the synagogue, or to particular times, such as the High Holy Days—just as we might say, following Reznikoff (or Duchamp), that the aesthetic is not confined to the "beauty" of traditional forms, but is fully present in the quotidian. Kabbalism is anti-dualistic, seeking to break down the distinction between God in itself (God on high, set apart) and God in its appearance, in its immanence (in the low, a part). *There is no separation:* for holiness is found in the most common deeds and language, the most base and vulgar acts: the holiness of walking, the holiness of drinking, the holiness of sitting, the holiness of talking, the holiness of looking, the holiness of touching, the holiness of witness:

> Not because of victories
> I sing
> having none,
> but for the common sunshine,
> the breeze,
> the largess of the spring.
> . . . .
> not for a seat upon the dais
> but at the common table. ("Te Deum"; *CP* 2: 75)

Allen Ginsberg's litany of "holy's" in "Footnote to Howl" invokes the holiness of the common "The skin is holy! The nose is holy! The tongue and cock and hand and asshole holy! / Everything is holy! everybody's holy! everywhere is holy! everyday is in eternity . . . / The bum's as holy as the seraphim!" (134); indeed, I would suggest that Ginsberg's poetics derive equally from Blake, Whitman, and Reznikoff—an interesting trio (even if this extravagance conflates Williams with Reznikoff).

16. Gershom Scholem points out that a positive attitude toward language distinguishes Kabbalism from other mystical traditions: "Kabbalists who differ in almost everything else are at one in regarding language as something more precious than an inadequate instrument for contact between human beings. To them, Hebrew, the holy tongue, is not simply a means of expressing certain thoughts, born out of a certain convention and having a purely conventional character. . . . Language in its purest form, that is, Hebrew . . . reflects the fundamental spiritual nature of the world. . . . Man's common language . . . reflects the creative language of God" (*Major Trends* 17).

17. It comes to this question: what is the status of the detail, the particular, in this work? Why is it so important? For Reznikoff, as for Williams, the detail is not a "luminous particular" in Pound's sense—not extraordinary but exactly ordinary, even if indeed luminous. So, then, why this particular detail, and then that one?

Metonymy: the fragment as substitute for, hinting at, something else, something that only it can stand for, is an instance of a manifestation or emanation. The part for the (w)holy.

Witness of the detail understood as metonymic.

Scholem, again, is a useful guide. Kabbalism rejects the allegorical for the symbolic, where allegory—"the representation of an expressible something by another expressible something"—is akin to the literary conceits and symbolism that Reznikoff rejected. In contrast, "the mystical symbol is an expressible sensation of something which lies beyond the sphere of expression. . . . Every living thing is endlessly correlated with the whole of creation . . . everything mirrors everything else" (*Major Trends* 27).

Reznikoff, a secular poet refreshed by "the clear waters of reason," committed "to use words for their daylight meaning" is no mystic, if mysticism is understood as elevating his work above "the common table," as he puts it in "Te Deum." Reznikoff is not a poet of the ecstatic, directed to the beyond, but a poet of the near, the close at hand: of a returning to oneself as to the world.

18. Fragment as shard of a broken or cracked totality that cannot be represented in its totality (the taboo against graven images) but only as splinters (of light), details: "but the cracked glass held in the frame" (*CP* 2: 121).

19. The ordinary, the everyday, the common, the neglected, the disregarded/unacknowledged as the site of paradise (*there is no other—only recover*): *Arts de faire,* the art of doing, as in *The Practice of Everyday Life:*

> As I was wondering with my unhappy thoughts,
> I looked and saw
> that I had come into a sunny place
> familiar and yet strange.
> "Where am I?" I asked a stranger. "Paradise."
> "Can this be Paradise?" I asked surprised,
> for there were motor-cars and factories.
> "It is," he answered. "This is the sun that shone on Adam once;
> the very wind that blew upon him too."[17]

Looked and saw: it is this twofold action that the poems constantly replay; looking is never enough, for it shows only what can be seen by using light; in contrast, the world may be beheld, beholded—held, cradled, rocked. The very wind.

20. First-generation immigrant to America not as exile (as it was for Jabès coming to France: Europe already "inhabited") but as founder—one who finds/ inhabits and one who makes new a language (a new world). It is Reznikoff's mother who says, "We are a lost generation. . . . It is for our children to do what they can."[18] For Reznikoff, finding as founding means finding as foundering (to fall to the ground, to come to grief).

21. The recovery of the ordinary: then was it lost?

22. NOT flatness or absence of rhetoric but . . . a *nearness* to the world not seen as "nature" but as social (urban). Materials of the world at hand, as found: *words* as materials.

Not, that is, reports of things seen (narrow definition of the "Objectivist" as ocular or transparent imagism) but bearing witness to things not seen, overlooked. Entering into the word as a descent, not (idealized) ascent, to borrow Simone Weil's terms.

23. Hanukkah

> In a world where each man must be of use
> and each thing useful, the rebellious Jews
> light not one light but eight
> not to see by but to look at. (*CP* 2: 84)

Delight. Finding the light in. "Not to see by but to look at" in multiple, serial array. Not sight but display. A festival of lights.

24. "In *Testimony,*" Reznikoff tells an interviewer, "the speakers whose words I use are all giving testimony about what they actually lived through. The testimony is that of a witness in court—*not a statement of what he felt but of what he heard or saw*" ("Talk with Dembo" 107). In "First, There Is the Need," Reznikoff writes:

> With respect to the treatment of subject matter in verse and the use of the term "objectivist" and "objectivism," let me again refer to the rules with respect to testimony in a court of law. Evidence to be admissible in a trial cannot state conclusions of fact: it must state the facts themselves. For example, a witness in an action for negligence cannot say: the man injured was negligent crossing the street. He must limit himself to a description of

> how the man crossed. . . . The conclusions of fact are for the jury and let us add, in our case, for the reader. [8]

Philosophically, however, description is always an epistemological question: the *act* of describing constitutes what is described; this act is never neutral. Witnessing is less a matter of "sight" than of action, not static but dynamic. In Reznikoff, witnessing opposes the predrawn, preprocessed conclusion: it *unfolds.*

25. Witness versus distance versus assimilation versus exile.

26. Nearness as attitude of address: not isolated, deanimated "images" of distantiated ocular evidence. The *intimacy* of address, the fondling/comment/intrusion into the "material" is a nearing toward a dwelling, making a habitation:

> Rails in the subway,
> what did you know of happiness,
> when you were ore in the earth;
> now the electric lights shine upon you. (*CP* 1: 111)

In the talk with Dembo (110), Reznikoff reports that a Japanese listener had questioned the last line of one of his poems, presumably because it violated the ideal of Haiku—a violation that is just the point of his practice of comment on, or interference into, the scene:

> What are you doing in our street among the automobiles, horse?
> How are your cousins, the centaur and the unicorn? (*CP* 1: 115)

Just as the absence of the first-person pronoun in this poem marks its break from traditional expressive poetry, so the use of the second-person pronoun marks its break from an ocular imagism.

27. The poetics of adjacency are aversive of the detachment and irony associated with the "high" modernism of Eliot, or, more accurately, the tradition of Eliot. Are you apart from the language or a part of it? What we do is to take back language from symbolical allusions and metaphysical contraptions. Yet this swings back to the question of exile, as Reznikoff laments his exile from Hebrew in his most Jabèsian moment:

How difficult for me is Hebrew:
even the Hebrew for *mother,* for *bread,* for *sun*
is foreign. How far have I been exiled, Zion. (*CP* 1: 72)

To be exiled from one's language is to be lost as a son or daughter, to be a foreigner in one's own tongue, as Jabès says the writer, as Jew, is exiled even in his or her own language. Since the Jewish tradition imparts to the word a fundamental spiritual nature, this exile from a language that one has never learned suggests the deepest sense of spiritual disconnectedness. Yet the poem also touches on the idea, fundamental to anti-Semitism, that all Jews, even monolingual native speakers of English or German or French, have a "hidden language" to which they owe fundamental allegiance—a belief that, if internalized by the Jew, incites self-hatred, as Sander Gilman discusses in *Jewish Self-Hatred.*

Like many of his contemporaries, Reznikoff was a second-language speaker of English, and it was no doubt his newness to English that contributed to the newness of his approach to founding an American poetry broken off from Island English, forged by syntax and music previously unheard in the language. Reznikoff's poetics of location as relocalization is not a poetry of exile. Yet loss rips through this poetry, like hot water spurting from a frozen geyser.

The Hebrew of your poets, Zion,
is like oil upon a burn,
cool as oil;
after work,
the smell in the street at night
of the hedge in flower.
Like Solomon,
I have married and married the speech of strangers;
none are like you, Shulamite.[19]

28. The social engagement of the Jewish secular Left meant not assuming the "social" as an abstract, static entity but as something to be located, particularized.

In the poetics of nearness, others exist prior to oneself; you do not look out onto other people as if through a preexisting subjectivity, but find whomever you may be as person, as poet, in relation to them, by virtue of your acknowledgment of their suffering, which is to say their circumstance or bearing in the world. This is the grounding of Reznikoff's work.

29. Vividness not as design but texture:

I have neither the time nor the weaving skills, perhaps,
for the intricate medallions the Persians know;
my rugs are the barbaric fire-worshipper's:
how blue the waters flow,
how red the fiery sun
how brilliant a green the grass is,
how blinding white the snow.[20]

30. Witness as care / in-volved / as care-taken, caretaker, care in the language, for the world. Language is caretaker of the world.

31. Witness/testimony as "self-cancellation" so that the language/event speaks of/for itself (modernist autonomy), as Reznikoff remarks in "First, There Is the Need," quoting an article on Zen that discusses the "forgetfulness of self" [3]. Compare *Testimony: The structure of event:* constellation of particulars: picture is *produced* by this *method,* not presumed.[21]

32. Nearness/unfolding of event breaks down the subject-object split. Subject/object; observer/observed; the paranoia of the objective depersonalized gaze. "apart and alone, / beside an open window / and behind a closed door" ("Autobiography: New York"; *CP* 2: 27).

Here these dualities collapse onto one another, the distantiation/irony is collapsed, the observer enters into the observed through a process of participatory mourning: "The room is growing dark, / but the brass knob of the closed door shines / *ready for use*" ("Autobiography: Hollywood"; *CP* 2: 46; emphasis added).

I would be the rock
about which the water is
flowing; and I would be the water flowing
about the rock.
And am both and neither
being *flesh.*[22]

33. "The infinite shines through the finite and makes it more real" (Scholem, *Major Trends* 28). Dickinson's "finite infinity":

There is a solitude of space
A solitude of sea
A solitude of death, but these

Society shall be
Compared with that profounder site
That polar privacy
A soul admitted to itself
Finite Infinity. (Poem #1695; *Poems* 3: 1149)

34. It's a question of the poem's attitude toward its materials: condescension, sentimentality, impersonality, identification, misidentification, detachment, erasure, appropriation, approbation, deafness, blindness, scorn, ecstasy, depression, anxiety, hypocrisy, reflection, management, control, possession, flirtatious, annihilating.

35. Serial composition, one detail adjacent to the next, one perspective permuted with another, refuses the binary. Oppen:

There are things
We live among 'and to see them
Is to know ourselves'.

Occurrence, a part
Of an infinite series (*Collected Poems* 147)

36. My aim not to explain the poems but to make them more opaque.

37. The sensation of not understanding, comprehending (say in Zukofsky or Stein): poems charged with the intractability, the ineffability, of the world.

I like this secret walking
in the fog;
unseen, unheard,
among the bushes
thick with drops;
the solid path invisible
a rod away
and only the narrow present is alive.[23]

Reznikoff's very extreme attitude toward elision and condensation has the supplemental effect of producing density in exact proportion to its desire for clarity. This is not the clarity of conventional poetic or expository discourse because its poetic space has been transformed into a gravitational field in which every word matters in the sense of having matter, musical or notional weight.

In "Early History of a Writer," Reznikoff recounts how a friend had applied Kittredge's method of microanalysis to some of his early poems:

> he read my verse as I had never read verse before,
> scrutinizing it, phrase by phrase
> and word by word, thought and image, thought and sound;

Reznikoff immediately realizes that this method was similar to what he had at law school

> prying sentences open to look for the exact meaning;
> weighing words to choose only those that had meat for my purpose
> and throwing the rest away as empty shells.
> I, too, could scrutinize every word and phrase
> as if in a document or the opinion of a judge
> and listen, as well, for the tones and overtones,
> leaving only the pithy, the necessary, the clear and plain.[24]

Reznikoff asks that we pry his words open, listening for the tones and overtones—a way of reading that intensifies the conflict between "the clear and plain" and "the necessary," between the accessible and the ineffable: for when words are weighed and measured for their undertones as well as their piths, the empty shells that fall away, like scales falling from "unseeing eyes," leave only the "narrow present" of the fog.

38. "A poet's words can pierce us. And that is of course *causally* connected with the use that they have in our life. And it is also connected with the way in which, conformably to this use, we let our thoughts roam up and down in the familiar surroundings of the words" (Wittgenstein, *Zettel* #155; 28e).

39. William Carlos Williams and Gertrude Stein are the paradigmatic modernist poets of the ordinary. Just as Williams found the poetic in the back-lot "cinders // in which shine / the broken // pieces of a green / bottle," so Stein found the poetic in the materials of the poem, "actual word stuff, not thoughts for thoughts," to use Williams's formulation.[25]

For Reznikoff, a poetry of the everyday is a poetry of the city. As he remarks in his introduction to the Poetry Center reading, his pervasive urbanism marks a decisive break with the nature poetry of the verse tradition. Moreover, Reznikoff's is a poetry of the found, a disposition apparent in the found details of the everyday that people his poems, but never more evident than in the found material of *Testimony,* Reznikoff's testament to the foundering of America and to the possibility of its founding in fondling, call it care in, the everyday.

40. I've been told that Reznikoff disliked obscurity and would certainly not have wanted his work to be characterized as obscure. Yet from the beginning he seemed to expect that obscurity was the likely outcome for his poetic work and seemed to accept that with remarkable equanimity. Perhaps he understood the nature, the social structure, of obscurity better than his contemporaries. Neglect, disregard—the socially obscure, the forgotten and repressed, the overlooked—this was his subject.

Hiding in plain sight, you may never be found: if sight is not to "see by but to look at," not to use but behold.

41. Reznikoff's investigations have something of the sublimity that Wittgenstein assigns to logic, but which might be assigned equally to poetry:

> . . . it is rather of the essence of our investigation that we do not seek to learn anything *new* by it . . . as if by this end we had to hunt down new facts. . . . We want to *understand* something that is already in plain view. For *this is* what we seem in some sense not to understand. . . .
>
> Something we know when no one asks us, but no longer know when we are supposed to give an account of it, is something we need to *remind* ourselves of. (And it is obviously something of which for some reason is it difficult to remind oneself.) (Wittgenstein, *Philosophical Investigations* #89)

Reznikoff's poetry reminds of very general facts that we already knew are in plain view but which we have difficulty accounting for. Above all, we have difficulty accounting for the fact that the poetry is *difficult,* because it doesn't seem, at first, to be difficult at all, but patent; as if the difficulty of such patency isn't the first thing we might wish to deny (repress).

42. Reznikoff in an interview ten days before his death: "Whatever the difficulties, your business is to write what you think you should. You owe that much to yourself and to other humans, too" (Simon 428).

43. The perspective here is extreme only if it's extreme to read a poem's forms as an inextricable part of its content. Nor does it stretch the point to insist,

against all odds, that Reznikoff's formal innovations are essential for understanding what his work is "about" and that to neglect these features is to repress what he has labored to say.

I've often heard Reznikoff damned with the faint praise of his accessibility, as if he is a kind of Jewish, urban Frost, or the Norman Rockwell of poetry—ashcan snapshots of city life. Ironically, it is this very surface of accessibility that has tended to dissipate interest in his work. In the absence of recognition of the formal and phenomenological intensities, even opacities, of this work, it can, as his detractors charge, seem without literary interest, pointless.[26]

If Reznikoff is accessible, it is an accessibility so fragile as to make him, for many readers, more difficult to read seriously and thoroughly than his apparently less accessible, but more often accessed, contemporaries. The history of Reznikoff's reception suggests that his work could not, except for a few initiates, be understood in its own time; or if it was understood, beyond his few serious readers, it was understood in such a way as to allow it to be discounted as superficial.

The paradox is that the difficulty of his work, which is related to its understatement and subtlety, its iconoclasm and darkness, and the freshness and originality of his music, is of a different order than the more famous "obscurities" of Pound or Eliot or Joyce, difficulties that our present habits of reading tend to valorize more than they do the kind of difficulty the poems of Charles Reznikoff surely present.

The paradox is that Reznikoff's apparent accessibility stands in the way of a recognition of the significance of his poetic achievement: if he is liked for being "easy," then he is at the same time disregarded for being insignificant. But both these approaches seem not so much to read Reznikoff as to read through him.

44. In *Reading in Detail,* Naomi Schor argues that working in detail has a history of being stigmatized as feminine, which is to say, of peripheral value. Unlike the "heroic" sweep and "grandeur" of hypotactic order, detail is marginalized as ornament, blemish, weakness, deficiency, simplicity, *easy:* ultimately as disregardable as the "lost" women and men whom Reznikoff refuses to thematize or caricature or stereotype. Reznikoff never states his themes in generalized, abstract terms but leaves it for his particulars, so ordered, to speak for themselves.

45. To be sure, Reznikoff's stated intentions are for "clarity" of "communication" against the "cryptic," but his insistence is on—*above all else*—"intensity" produced by "compression" and "rhythm" (cut and shapeliness) that is "pas-

sionate" and "musical" and *not*—in *his* words—"flat."[27] Opacity, in this sense, is the refusal of the flatness of ocular or idealist imagism: is the opacity of the object, of objectification; just as opacity is also the antithesis of the cryptic, with its "cloying music / the hints of what the poets meant / and did not quite say" ("Early History of a Writer"; *CP* 2: 169), the symbolical assertion of a puzzle to be deciphered: words not ciphers but things of the world to be thickened, weighted, condensed, so that they may be heard and felt.

46. Then how to understand Reznikoff's choice of recurrent, dark subject matter in his work . . . or how to understand why so much violence, so much darkness in the world?

47. "When you least expect it the lights go out. & when you least expect it, too, the lights come back on again." Reznikoff, during the Poetry Center reading.

48. Yet flesh is opaque: when you catch it (comprehend it), it's dead.

49. *Testimony* is perhaps the darkest, and certainly most unrelenting, of modernist long poems. Reznikoff spent years in various libraries pouring over trial records from the 1890s and 1900s, selecting a few cases out of each hundred he surveyed and then styling them so as to allow the event itself to speak, as if without interference, without teller. A chronicle of industrial accidents, domestic violence, racism, *Testimony* tells the story of America's forgotten, those who suffer without redress, without name, without hope; yet the soul of these States is found in books like this; the acknowledgment of these peripheral stories turns a wasteland into holy ground.[28]

Reznikoff worked on *Testimony* through the 1930s and 1940s, at a time when both Oppen and Carl Rakosi had stopped writing, in part because of the conflict they felt between their leftist political commitments and their poetic commitments. Perhaps *Testimony* can be seen as a labor-intensive counterpart to the lacuna in these poets' work.

Reznikoff's work is preoccupied with those left out of society, people whose lives were destroyed by things (machines, circumstances, an economy) out of their control: again, the neglected, the overlooked. His one reference to Marx is placed strikingly as the last of four poems in a series about prophecy called "Jerusalem the Golden," which is itself the final series of his book of the same title, published, significantly, in 1934 (#79; *CP* 1: 127–29). "Jerusalem the Golden" begins with "The Lion of Judah," a poem in which the prophet Nathan denies the right to permanent foundation even, or already, to the Jews ("you shall not build the Lord's house / because your hands have shed much blood"). This poem, considered in the light of the first poem of *Jerusalem the Golden* ("The Hebrew of your poets, Zion / is like oil upon a burn / . . . I have married . . . the speech of strangers") suggests the intractability of the Jewish diaspora (understood, however, not as exile but a series of displacements/replacements). In the second poem, "The Shield of David," the prophets locate "all the lights of heaven" in "the darkness of the grave," abjuring the emptiness of ritual as shells for "unseeing eyes," eyes that look but do not see: *looked and saw* the Light in the Darkness:

> worship Me in righteousness;
> worship Me in kindness to the poor and weak,
> in justice to the orphan, the widow, the stranger among you,
> and in justice to him who takes hire in your hand

The third poem, a brief evocation of pantheism, is entitled "Spinoza," after the prototypical Jewish "excommunicate" or "non-Jewish Jew," in Isaac Deutcher's phrase, whose pantheism and determinism significantly prefigure historical materialism (both Marx and Spinoza are crucial sources for Zukofsky's "A"-9). In the last of the series, "Karl Marx," Reznikoff writes:

> We shall arise while the stars are still shining,
> . . . .
> to begin the work we delight in,
> and no one shall tell us, Go
> . . . .
> to the shop or office you work in
> to waste your life for a living
> . . . .
> there shall be bread and no one hunger for bread
> . . . .
> we shall call nothing mine—nothing for ourselves only

50. Darkness and light; or dusk, when dark and light can no longer be separated: "Suddenly we noticed that we were in darkness; / so we went into the house and lit the lamp."[29]

51. Thrown into the world through EVENT as TESTIMONY/TESTIMONY as EVENT, the poem merges the objective and subjective so that no polarizing can occur.

"Event" emerges as the world/word materializing process takes place.

52. *Testimony:* to found America means to find it, which means to acknowledge its roots in violence, to tell the lost stories because unless you find what is lost you can found nothing.

Against the indifference of the juridical gaze (paradigm of detachment), founding means giving witness to what is denied at the expense of the possibility of America. "In and about the house darkness lay, a black fog; / and each on his bed spoke to himself alone, making no sound" (*CP* 1: 35).

To speak out against the Dark is to make Light: this is the poetic alchemy, call it economy, that Reznikoff enacts over and again: to recover the lost, make sound in the presence of silence, behold the Light.

53. *Testimony* as memorial: an act of grief/grieving, of mourning. The cost of life, the cost of lives lost, is poetic/psychic economy, of which this an account/accounting. "No one to witness and adjust" 'cept *here.*

"Calling the lapsed Soul . . . / O Earth O Earth return."[30]

54. "Shipwreck of the singular" (Oppen, "Of Being Numerous"; *Collected Poems* 151): mourning/grief as part of the celebration of the New Year (Yom Kippur), as prerequisite for new world/new word. "America" not so much a "place" but an attitude toward language.

55. Ignored, like Stein, partly because he does not use symbological allusion or historical reference (Pound/Eliot) that requires you to look elsewhere than to what is happening, Reznikoff makes the reader (not himself) into the witness of language, where events are enacted in words and we don't so much judge them as come near to them.

56. The observer and the observed meet at dusk in the midst of shadows. How can we tell the seeing from the seen, the see-er from the seer?

57. Reznikoff's Rosh Hashanah poem ends this way:

> You have given us the strength
> to serve You,
> but we may serve or not
> as we please;
> not for peace nor for prosperity,
> not even for length of life, have we merited
> remembrance; remember us

as the servants
You have inherited. ("New Year's"; *CP* 2: 66)

Jewishness not as "chosen" but *inherited:* can't get rid of. Jewishness in the sense of an inhering possibility for poetry and its testimony as engaged witness that *changes*—intervenes in—what it witnesses by its care in and for the world/word.

III

January 1, 1990

Dear Jean-Paul Auxeméry,[31]

At a party last night, for the Christian New Year, a guest brought our host, a Czechoslovakian-Jewish emigrè, a piece of the Berlin Wall. A piece of rubble, to be sure, but packaged in a brightly designed box assuring, with a red stamp, that papers attesting to the "authenticity" of the contents had been enclosed by the importers, a New Jersey firm. A small label on the top indicated that the item had been purchased at Bloomingdale's. Here, indeed, was the essence of late, or multinational, capitalism: a commodity created, by the alchemy of packaging, from that which is intrinsically worthless. It's the sort of "symbolism" that is diametrically opposed by what you usefully call Charles Reznikoff's "ethics of style," which has as its method acknowledging the details of intrinsic value that this same culture has discarded, as by the reverse alchemy of turning things of substance into rubble by *disregard.*

I won't ever forget the first night, and first morning, of this year's Jewish New Year, where we celebrated the work of Reznikoff in a former Christian abbey at Royaumont, near Paris. I won't forget that our Reznikoff panel ended with your overwhelming reading of *Holocaust*—your French translation of a work barely known in its native land. My own intervention had focused not only on Reznikoff's *Testimony,* as you note, but also more particularly on his *Complete Poems.* What I remember thinking was that *Holocaust* had never sounded so necessary, so appropriate (in your sense that Reznikoff always found the most "apropos" words). Yes, I have had my difficulties with *Holocaust*—the most unrelentingly painful to read of Reznikoff's work, about the most unmitigated horror of our common, "modern" history. I think I must have said this work was about a problem *specifically* European; I could not have meant that it was "solely" European, however, since the destruction of the European Jews is of the most urgent relevance to all Americans, to all Jews, indeed to all humans. I think I must have suggested that *Holocaust* is necessarily Reznikoff's most problematic work at a technical—in the sense of aesthetic or formal—level, in the sense that no American work of poetry had found a form to adequately acknowledge that which is beyond adequate acknowledgment; so that *Holocaust* stands apart and beyond the achievement of Reznikoff's *Poems* and *Testimony.*

I say *specifically* European for a very practical, literal reason that you, with your remarkable involvement with Olson, would certainly appreciate the implications of: Reznikoff's work, apart from *Holocaust* and his biblical poems and talmudic "collages," has been a profound investigation of "American" materials: it is work immersed in the local and particular details of this place that he found himself in, first generation in his family, and also of a language, English, that was an intrinsic part of that emplacement. One of my favorite Reznikoff remarks is one he made to Marie Syrkin, his wife, in explaining why he would not go to Palestine with her in 1933; he told her that "he had not yet explored Central Park to the full." Indeed Reznikoff never left North America or English (an "American" English of course) in real life or in his poems, with the primary exception of *Holocaust,* which not only involved a European site or place (*lieu*) but also for the first time working with documentary materials not originally in English. For me, what was so striking about your reading of *Holocaust* in French was that one could imagine those incidents happening near the place, even Royaumont; we were *close by* the *scene.*

Reznikoff's *Complete Poems* and *Testimony* explore the tragedy and violence that is the grounding of this Republic, call it United States. It is not a story that Americans are familiar with or, even now, ready to acknowledge. Each poem of Reznikoff's, always placed in series, shocks by its recognition of something otherwise unstated or unsaid: say, unacknowledged or repressed or denied or suppressed. *Testimony,* while a litany of sorrows, finds new avenues to locate the transgression of dominance against the human spirit.

By contrast, the violence, the repulsiveness, of the incidents in *Holocaust* are always and already known, hence preclude the insinuating subtlety of *Testimony.* And, for Americans, always and already projected outward to the German, to the Nazi, to a European story. If it does not hit home, it is because the story of World War II has been the greatest source for American self-congratulation: we defeated the Nazi monsters. *NOT:* the Nazi monsters in us, which go on, largely on the loose. This is like saying, North America has not had a twentieth-century war on its soil. Reznikoff shows otherwise. The *Complete Poems* and *Testimony* testify to a system of domination and disregard that has *won; Holocaust* to a system of explicit violence that, at least on the face, *lost.*

Poetry is always technical, an order of words, at least in the first instance. If

I put aside, yes even disregard, the sentiment of "la raison d'un coeur noble" to reiterate these technical questions, it is not without an appreciation of the integrity of the whole of Reznikoff's oeuvre or of the noble gesture of your bringing into French, into France, Reznikoff's final testament, a testament that, to be sure, does go beyond his concern for any one nation or language, a work that we can only wish he had never *had* to write.

With all best wishes,

11

Of Being Ethical: Reflections on George Oppen

Peter Nicholls

The poems of George Oppen continue to occupy a marginal place in most literary histories, even though his work encapsulates some of the major shifts in American writing between high modernism and contemporary Language poetry. In part this marginalization is due to the habit of tying Oppen to Louis Zukofsky's short-lived "Objectivist" tendency of the thirties. Oppen did indeed publish his first collection, *Discrete Series,* in 1934, and with a strong endorsement from Ezra Pound ("I salute a serious craftsman, a sensibility which is not every man's sensibility and which has not been got out of any other man's books" ["Preface" 13]). Yet after this propitious start Oppen fell silent for twenty-five years, jettisoning poetry for politics. He and his wife, Mary, were members of the Communist Party between 1936 and 1941, their activities eventually attracting close scrutiny from the FBI.[1] In 1949, Oppen and his family opted for political exile in Mexico to avoid harassment. They would not return until 1958; only then did Oppen begin writing poetry again, initiating a sequence of major volumes, from *The Materials* (1962) to *Primitive* (1978).

The break in Oppen's literary career raises important questions about where we "place" his work historically, questions that are highlighted by the recent publication of two fat anthologies of twentieth-century American poetry. In Douglas Messerli's *From the Other Side of the Century,* for example, Oppen appears in the early pages in the company of fellow Objectivists like Louis Zukofsky, Lorine Niedecker, Carl Rakosi, and Charles Reznikoff. In Paul Hoover's *Postmodern American Poetry,* on the other hand, Objectivism is not represented at all, and the volume opens instead with works by Charles Olson and John

Cage. Clearly, Hoover sees writers like Oppen as contributors to an earlier modernism, whereas Messerli locates the original Objectivist group within the main line of innovation that runs from 1960 to 1990.

Of the two choices, Messerli's seems to me the better one. To begin with, there are the historical facts of publication: each of the poets I have named above was still bringing out collections in the seventies (Zukofsky, *80 Flowers*, 1978; Niedecker, *Blue Chicory*, 1976; Rakosi, *Ex Cranium, Night*, 1975; Reznikoff, *Holocaust*, 1975; Oppen, *Seascape: Needle's Eye*, 1972, and *Primitive*, 1978), and this continued productivity to some extent compels us to reckon with a sort of double chronology. On the one hand, there is Objectivism, a phase or tendency that is often (misleadingly) seen as merely an offshoot of Pound's imagism; this is writing that develops its particular texture and perspectives from the experience of the depression years. Then there is the later work that shows these writers offering an influential alternative to the so-called "personal" poetry of later decades.[2] The matter of designation—whether those in the Oppen-Zukofsky group were modernists or not—is not of special importance in itself, but what does interest me is the intermediary position they now seem to occupy: *between* modernism and postmodernism, perhaps; a betweenness, at any rate, that seems highly characteristic of much of this writing at the level of both its formal and social ambitions.

As was clear in Zukofsky's own manifesto essay, "Sincerity and Objectification" (1931), Objectivism was (somewhat paradoxically in view of its name) a practice of writing that was ultimately concerned less with objects than with the "shape" of the poem and "the resolving of words and their ideation into structure" (273, 274). What was objectified was the poem itself; as Zukofsky put it, "This rested totality may be called objectification—the apprehension satisfied completely as to the appearance of the art form as an object" (274).[3] The word Zukofsky had reluctantly chosen at editor Harriet Monroe's insistence would, however, continue to mislead; Oppen signaled the problem on several occasions: "Several dozen commentators and reviewers have by now written on the assumption that the word 'Objectivist' indicated the contributors' objective attitude to reality. It meant, of course, the poets' recognition of the necessity of form, the objectification of the poem" (Oppen, "Three Oppen Letters" 79).

At first sight, this version of "objectification" may sound like just another formalism, but it actually entails a significant departure from Poundian modernism. As Rachel Blau DuPlessis observes, "This poetics . . . had an ethical dimension, for it began with the person, not the word, that is, began with sincerity" ("Objectivist Poetics" 125). Pound's notion of "technique as a test of a man's sincerity" lay in the background (*Literary Essays* 9), though the absoluteness of that axiom would lead in *The Cantos* to the very different assumption that linguistic precision was *in itself* adequate proof of authorial honesty and sound judgment (see Nicholls, *Ezra Pound* 100). Oppen seems not to have been an avid reader of that poem, responding to its local felicities rather than to its grand ambition,[4] but as one of his own poems, "Of Hours," makes clear, the perceived failure of *The Cantos* and the tragedy of the life that sustained it came to represent one blind alley of a modernism disastrously wedded to a politics it hardly understood ("What is it you 'loved,'" asks Oppen of this finally "Unteachable" poet [*Collected Poems* 212]). What had begun as unplanned adventure, an Odyssean "sailing after knowledge," mutated across the thirties into a vision that Pound habitually defined as "totalitarian" (as, for example, in the 1938 volume *Guide to Kulchur*). Increasingly the poem concerned itself with definitions of just authority, even as the writing began to close down questions about its own judgmental legitimacy. Where the early Cantos had to some degree invited the reader's skepticism, now the poem began to demand a certain faith; and as Pound began to discover in Mussolini a stronger, more authoritative self-image, so the poem acquired an intransigent, often hectoring tone.

It is important to appreciate the difference between the forms of objectification increasingly at work within Pound's poem and the kind of writing that Oppen and Zukofsky define as "Objectivism." In the latter case, as I have said, it is the poem that is objectified, whereas in one major strand of the earlier modernism—the strand represented by Pound, Eliot, Lewis, and Hemingway—it is "the world outside, the other [that] is always object" (Jessica Benjamin, *Bonds* 190; Nicholls, *Modernisms*). In this aesthetic, the self's relation to the other is generally construed as one of domination and is characterized by discontinuity and separateness. Successful individuation entails the establishing of boundaries that divide the self from others. Psychic maturity is associated with a break from the feminine and maternal, which is now conceived as other and object. The modernist avant-garde we associate with the writers I have named thus has a strong agonistic component—aesthetic form is seen to be won from struggle, in the process of which a masterful and coherent self emerges over against the chaotic, purely appetitive forces of a decadent modernity.

The principal interest of Objectivism is arguably that it marked the point where a new generation of poets initiated a radical departure from these forms of objectification and from the politics they embodied. Pound's *Cantos* was thus, for this generation, a crucially ambiguous work, offering, on the one hand, an array of dazzlingly new formal devices while, on the other, exhibiting all the dangers of an increasingly pragmatic politics of mastery. As the poem moved into its late sequences—*Section: Rock-Drill* (1955) and *Thrones* (1959)—it must have seemed increasingly clear to those readers still in the dinghy astern that Pound was becoming more and more comfortable with an openly didactic mode. These late Cantos developed the mixed tones of the Pisan sequence, oscillating between the fragmentary and indeterminate, on the one hand, and the assertive, not to say imperative, habit on the other. In line with Pound's dependence on neo-Confucian texts like *The Sacred Edict of Kang H'si*, the rhetoric became increasingly paternalistic while the model of social order invoked was nakedly feudalistic. At this point, myth, politics, and ethics seemed to fold into one, a synthesis that could seem untroubling only insofar as it was projected back into an idyllic and remote past.

Almost from the first, Oppen was keen to dissociate the terms of Pound's synthesis of myth, politics, and ethics. The two poets' divergence in this respect is particularly striking given that both were drawn in different ways to a vision of social totality: Pound came to invest more and more heavily in a unitary model of social process—"The whole tribe is from one man's body," he declared in *Thrones* (*Cantos* 722)—while Oppen returned again and again to the formal and conceptual problems of collective identity. Yet the divergence in their thinking was a telling one—not simply because Oppen went Left rather than Right, but because he insisted on the rigorous separation of poetry from politics. Of twentieth-century American poets, Oppen was perhaps keenest to drive home that lesson in both his work and his life, as his long period of "silence" amply testifies.

For some critics, though, Oppen's political commitments cannot but be felt in the later work, and Burton Hatlen, among others, has made a strong case for the persistence of certain Marxist themes in these volumes.[5] Oppen himself, however, was adamant about the incompatibility of politics and poetry—not simply because the poetry of the Left had proved to be little more than sloganeering, but also because "the aesthetic will be defined outside of anybody's politics, or defined wrongly," and "the poet, speaking as a poet, declares his political non-availability" ("The Mind's Own Place" 137). In comments like these, Oppen seems to look to "writing" or "poetry" as a sort of defense against a totalizing vision. "I was right," he concluded in a retrospective look at the thirties, "not to write bad poetry—poetry tied to a moral or a political (same thing) judgment" (*Selected Letters* 66). And, in similar vein, he asserted that "art can no longer present a system, a belief" (68), a view that led him to emphasize "Not . . . that I take truthfulness to be a social virtue. I think very probably it is not. But I think it is poetic: I think really that nothing else is" (82). This "poetic" truth is hard to define, though we may take it that once again

Oppen is trying to dissociate his own work from any taint of (Poundian) instrumentalism. "There are situations," he declares, "which cannot honorably be met by art, and surely no one need fiddle precisely at the moment that the house next door is burning" ("The Mind's Own Place" 136).

Does this divorce between aesthetics and politics distinguish Oppen's work from high modernism, or does it actually tie him more closely to it? Andrew Ross thinks the latter: "Regardless of whether we might agree with Oppen that it is not a question of aesthetics, or 'bad fiddling,' his final opinion—that 'the question can only be whether one intends, at a given time, to write poetry or not'—would have to be regarded today as a superannuated one" (362). Oppen's dissociation is by this account a modernist one, and he is thus to be distinguished from postmodern writers like the Language poets, for whom poetry can become "politically sufficient in itself" (Ross 365). Ross is thinking of claims made by contemporary poets like Bruce Andrews for "writing *as* politics, not writing *about* politics. Asking: what is the *politics* inside the work, inside *its* work? Instead of instrumentalized or instrumentalizing, this is a poetic writing more actively *explanatory*" (Andrews 50). Yet Oppen is wary of this word "political" and its tendency to cohabit with "truth"; for him, poetry has a different role to play: "It is a part of the function of poetry to serve as *a test of truth.* It is possible to say anything in abstract prose, but a great many things one believes or would like to believe or thinks he believes will not substantiate themselves in the concrete materials of the poem. It is not to say that the poet is immune to the 'real' world to say that he is not likely to find the moment, the image, in which a political generalization . . . will prove its truth" ("The Mind's Own Place" 133–34; emphasis added). Oppen thus warns us that poetry is not a purveyor of "truth" but rather that it submits "truth" to a kind of "test." Exactly what this "testing" might be becomes clearer if we consider politics not just as social action but as also, in some sense, akin to Poundian myth in its aspiration to totality and "generalization."

The idea that poetic language may somehow refuse to "substantiate" such myths brings to mind Jean Luc Nancy's more recent account of writing as an "interruption" of myth. In *The Inoperative Community,* Nancy suggests that myth expresses a desire for communion—"fusion in a shared, immanent Being" (xxxiii), the community that becomes "*a single* thing (body, mind, fatherland, Leader)" (xxxxix); by way of contrast, Nancy proposes an idea of community based on "being *in* common" in which there is no single social identity, but rather an experience of "singularity" through which Being is understood as divided and shared (xxviii), what Nancy calls a "strange being-the-one-with-the-other to which we are exposed" (xxxix). It is literature which "puts into play nothing other than being *in* common," concludes Nancy, and, more specifically, it is writing which has the capacity to "interrupt" those fantasies of immanence and fusion that characterize the condition of myth: "once myth is interrupted, writing recounts our history to us again" (69).[6]

Nancy's account has several points of connection with Oppen's work. First, his notion of "being *in* common" stresses "the impossibility either of an individuality, in the precise sense of the term, or of a pure collective totality" (6).[7] This refusal of the conventional polarity of individual and society parallels Oppen's evasion of the agonistic structure of the modernist avant-garde, with its tensed subject-object relation. It was this dimension of Pound's poetics that most troubled Oppen: "Pound's ego system, Pound's organization of the world around a character, a kind of masculine energy, is extremely foreign to me" (Dembo, "The 'Objectivist' Poet" 170). So too was the related sense of what Oppen termed "the closed universe, the closed self" ("Letters to June Oppen Degnan" 223); he would base his own work on a deliberately alternative model of subjectivity as "encountered, not found" (Oppen, "Interview" with Schiffer 19). The encounter is somehow tentative because it is grasped as a movement or process, so when Oppen recalled in an interview that "The first question at the time [the early thirties] in poetry was simply the question of honesty, of sincerity,"[8] the point was that a poetics founded on the (philosophically) simple recognition of actuality—"That it is" ("Adequate Vision" 17)—would ultimately concern itself with an equally "simple" and non-agonistic perception of social relationships. Viewed in these terms, poetry might offer a way of acknowledging the world and others without seeking to reduce them to objects of knowledge.

Such a poetics would be quite different from Poundian modernism. In eschewing "knowledge," for example, it would deprive us of any sense of context or ground, yielding instead, as Marjorie Perloff has remarked, a peculiar sense of disconnectedness ("Shipwreck" 193). Take the first section of Oppen's major sequence, "Of Being Numerous":

> There are things
> we live among 'and to see them
> Is to know ourselves.'
>
> Occurrence, a part
> Of an infinite series,
>
> The sad marvels;

Of this was told
A tale of our wickedness.
It is not our wickedness.

'You remember that old town we went to, and we sat in the ruined window, and we tried to imagine that we belonged to those times—It is dead and it is not dead, and you cannot imagine either its life or its death; the earth speaks and the salamander speaks, the Spring comes and only obscures it—' (*Collected Poems* 147)

Disconnected, certainly: Perloff observes that "the number of prepositions and pronouns, taken together, is greater than that of nouns, adjectives, and verbs combined" ("Shipwreck" 193). This unexpected displacement of emphasis gives the lines a curious feeling of provisionality; the thought is, we might say, precisely pre-positional, postponing any resolution or closing formulation (see Naylor). The form of the writing thus enacts its main theme, which appears to be the inadequacy of narrative as explanation. So "occurrence," which here suggests a moment in which we grasp the connectedness of ourselves and the world, is placed over against the biblical "tale of our wickedness" which has tied humanity to a dogma of guilt and false humility (though "It is not our wickedness"). The past in fact escapes us—"you cannot imagine either its life or its death"—whereas the essentially non-narrative "series" offers us an opening into "presentness" rather than the dead weight of past experience.[9]

We may recall here that Oppen's first collection takes the title *Discrete Series* from mathematics as a way of deriving form from the praxis of perception rather than from any predetermined "rule": "A pure mathematical series would be one in which each term is derived from the preceding term by a rule. A discrete series is a series of terms each of which is empirically derived, each one of which is empirically true. And this is the reason for the fragmentary character of those poems. I was attempting to construct a meaning by empirical statements, by imagist statements" (Oppen in Dembo, "The 'Objectivist' Poet" 161). One of Oppen's favorite examples of such a series was the sequence of stations on the New York subway (14, 28, 32, 42), a sequence expressing contiguity but no extrapolable logic (see *Selected Letters* 122). Following this example, Oppen aimed to jettison narrative for what Derrida ("Living On" 130) has aptly termed a "seriality without paradigm."[10] This takes us closer to one of the major themes of "Of Being Numerous," which is that of the apparent unknowability of what is not the self: "the world, if it is matter, / Is impenetrable" (*Collected Poems* 148). Like the city, which implies the individual's tie to place while all the time actually expressing only pure "flow" (149), the poem moves forward, bringing one thing within the field of another, but (in contrast to *The Cantos*) hesitating to insist on the meaningful connection between them. Hence, perhaps, the ambiguity which plays around the idea of "being numerous": have we "chosen the meaning / Of being numerous" (151) simply because of our bewilderment over "the shipwreck / Of the singular"? Or is Oppen suggesting that we have chosen merely the *meaning* of being numerous and not its reality? Readers have, reasonably enough, been so pleased to find a poet confronting this theme that they have tended to wish away ambiguity in order to discover a powerful sense of social collectivity here. Almost alone, Marjorie Perloff has read the poem more skeptically, observing that "A good deal has been written about Oppen's relationship to the masses, but at least in 'Of Being Numerous,' the point is that there is no relationship" ("Shipwreck" 197). In fact, she continues, the sequence exemplifies the poet's "withdrawal from human contact" (200); we are closer to the world of Beckett than to any kind of populist vision.

One can sympathize with Perloff's skeptical reading—after all, this does seem a poem that is often as concerned with the distances between people as it is with images of collective experience. Yet we should acknowledge too that the poem itself is skeptical about the power of such images, and this testifies not to some ill-concealed "alienation" on Oppen's part, but rather to his sense (comparable to Nancy's) of social being as both divided and shared. We may get closer to Oppen's meditation on this theme if we see it as primarily philosophical rather than political, and informed in part by the poet's enduring interest in the work of Heidegger. For even in his first small volume of poems, *Discrete Series* (1934), where Oppen looking back discerned a clearly "Marxist" component,[11] the major question raised seems to relate to the attempt to see "humanity as a single thing," as Oppen later put it in relation to the poem called "Party on Shipboard" ("a statement, and a very clear one, of what I was going in search of when I quit writing" [*Selected Letters* 20]).

Rather obviously, that poem turns on the relation of the particular to the universal, of the waves to the ocean as a whole:

> The shallow surface of the sea, this,
> Numerously—the first drinks——
> The sea is a constant weight
> In its bed. (*Collected Poems* 8)

The transition between "this" and "numerously" (the old enigma of what is both one and many) pinpoints the principal dilemmas of Oppen's work. "I try to get again to humanity as a single thing," he observes in the same letter, "as something like a sea which is a constant weight in its bed" (*Selected Letters* 111). Yet that singleness and constancy is, like Pound's whole tribe sprung from one man's body, a mythic condition, and even in this early poem the vision of totality splinters before it can be fully grasped ("They pass, however, the sea / Freely tumultuous").

Reflecting on his early books, Oppen explained: "I had thought I could arrive at the concept of Being from an account of experience as it presents itself in its own terms" (*Selected Letters* 410 n. 29). He had chosen, with Heidegger, "the arduous path of appearance," a decision with which he deliberately closed the way to any conception of Being as Platonic essence.[12] Instead, Being is characterized by what Heidegger calls a movement of "withdrawal" (*Zurückziehung*) by which it constantly retreats into individual beings.[13] That sense of withdrawal colors Oppen's handling of the concept of "humanity"; as he puts it in a letter glossing "Of Being Numerous": "We *cannot* live without the concept of humanity . . . and yet we cannot escape this: that we *are* single. And face, therefore, shipwreck. And yet this, the tragic fact, is the brilliance of one's life" (*Selected Letters* 263).

Even as we think the condition of "humanity," then, the collective reveals itself as a collection of singularities, and our only way out of a static ambiguity is to map the constant oscillation between these two conditions, their constant fading into each other.[14] This may help to explain Oppen's skepticism about narrative at the beginning of "Of Being Numerous" and, indeed, the otherwise puzzling reduction of "history" to a date "Frozen in the moonlight" in the fifth poem of the sequence (*Collected Poems* 150). As Nancy puts it, when writing interrupts myth we may recover our history, "But it is no longer a narrative—neither grand nor small—but rather an offering: a history is offered to us. Which is to say that an event—and an advent—is proposed to us, without its unfolding being imposed upon us. What is offered to us is that community is coming about, or rather, that something is happening to us in common. Neither an origin nor an end: something *in* common. Only speech, a writing—shared, sharing us" (*Inoperative Community* 69).[15]

"Neither an origin nor an end"—Nancy's conception of the event (or advent) stresses the in-betweenness that is, for him, a condition of both authentic social relations and of the writing in which they are exemplified ("we would not write if our being were not shared," he observes [*Inoperative Community* 69]). The double condition of language, as both personal and collective, as opaque and transparent, embodies the interdependency of self and other: "But compearance is of a more originary order than that of the bond. It does not set itself up, it does not establish itself, it does not emerge among already given subjects (objects). It consists in the appearance of the *between* as such: you *and* I (between us)—a formula in which the *and* does not imply juxtaposition, but exposition" (29).[16] That idea of "exposition" by contiguity rather than juxtaposition-as-opposition (arguably the Poundian mode) seems very suggestive in view of Oppen's idea of "series" as a "cadence of disclosure." So too Nancy's sense that "something is happening to us in common" is close to Oppen's creation of an open syntax that constantly proposes relationships and shared experiences without formulating them absolutely. In place of Pound's increasingly didactic relation to the reader, we approach what Language poet Lyn Hejinian calls a "generative" as opposed to "directive" writing: "Reader and writer engage in a collaboration from which ideas and meanings are permitted to evolve" ("Rejection" 272). And as Hejinian has said of Gertrude Stein: "it was not truth but understanding that was of value—a shift of emphasis, from perceived to perceiving, and thus to writing, in which acts of observation, as complex perception, take place" ("Two Stein Talks" 129–30).

Many of these features can be seen together in "Occurrences," a poem from the late collection *Seascape: Needle's Eye* (1972):

> Limited air   drafts
> In the treasure house moving and the movements of the living
> Things fall   something balanced   Move
> With all one's force
> Into the commonplace that pierces or erodes
>
> The mind's structure but nothing
> Incredible happens
> It will have happened to that other
> The survivor   The survivor
> To him it happened
>
> Rooted in basalt
> Night hums like the telephone dial tone blue gauze
> Of the forge flames the pulse
> Of infant
> Sorrows at the crux
>
> Of the timbers
> When the middle Kingdom
> Warred with beasts Middle Things the elves the

Magic people in their world
Among the plant roots   hopes
Which are the hopes
Of small self interest called

Superstition chitinous
Toys of the children wings
Of the wasp (*Collected Poems* 206)

I am not sure that I completely understand this poem, but nor am I sure that I am meant to. The syntax seems broken, precarious, though to describe it as "fragmented" would misleadingly assume a reconstitutable logic of propositions.[17] As is often the case in Oppen's work, the poem might be said to enact the inadequacy of thought, or at least to propose poetic form as a desirable substitute for more conventional habits of thinking. The difficulty of the text—registered emphatically in the double spacing between words and in the characteristic ambiguity of line endings (see Bernstein, "Hinge" 240–42)—dramatizes a resistance to thought and to dialectic, a resistance which the lacunary syntax of the poem seems to signal as that of language itself.

But what are these "Occurrences"? Oppen glosses the word in a letter as follows: "Occurrences—events   the heavy events——and down or somewhere to the toys of everyday, small self-interest, the wings of the wasp" (*Selected Letters* 419 n. 52). The poem is caught between the large, catastrophic forces of "history," we might say, and the minute temporality of the "commonplace" and "everyday." Like many of Oppen's later poems, this one seems to be written in the shadow of the Holocaust, though we deduce that rather obliquely, through references to the survivor and through images of estranged communication (the telephone dial) and the forge flaming. There is no collective pronoun in this poem, no "we" to alleviate the narrow perspectives of "small self interest." The "incredible" has happened to someone else, the survivor, and all that is left to do in the present is to "move" into the commonplace, as Oppen puts it, a move which in "piercing" or "eroding" the mind's structure will somehow open the sensibility to a sense of community with the experience of that survivor. Yet perhaps the main point of the poem is that such a relationship cannot be formulated directly or rhetorically. Nor can the wasp provide a reassuring image of the natural world, as it could momentarily for Pound at Pisa.[18] Instead, the anticipation of relationship is articulated through the hesitancy of the syntax, through ambiguity and apposition, through the heavily stressed and repeated "Of"—all elements that evoke relationship without reducing it to two terms, to a subject-object dualism.

This deliberate lack of closure is for Oppen a primary instance of poetry's difference from politics, placing the poem within that intermediary space of which Nancy speaks. To speak politically of the Holocaust would be to move within the world of distinct positionalities and moral judgments, whereas these inchoate forms are meant to open up that space between "you *and* I," as Nancy puts it, in which the survivor's experience can be understood without being appropriated as part of "our" historical narrative. The lack of totalization here thus seems to suggest that poetry, in contrast to political discourse, can open relations that precede ideology and morality. As Oppen puts it in a prose section of the long poem "Route": "We are brothers, we are brothers?—these things are composed of a moral substance only if they are untrue. If these things are true they are perfectly simple, perfectly impenetrable, those primary elements which can only be named" (*Collected Poems* 189).[19] Naming, as Oppen makes clear in his interview with L. S. Dembo, entails "an act of faith" that testifies in turn to the "simplest" of theologies: "I do believe that consciousness exists and that it is consciousness of something, and that is a fairly complete but not very detailed theology, as a matter of fact" (Dembo, "The 'Objectivist' Poet" 163). This equation of "truth" with a nonmoral impenetrability implies that the sense of commonness Oppen has in mind is one that is primary because it exists prior to social codes and prescriptions.

We may recall at this point a definition of "ethics" that has been much discussed in recent years. I am thinking of the work of Emmanuel Levinas, for whom the Western tradition, and especially the thought of Hegel, has been characterized by a pursuit of knowledge that seeks the subordination of objects and other people to its own power. Philosophy has not, according to this line of argument, been primarily concerned with the claims of other people, but rather with the capacity of the self to elide difference, to make the other like itself. Levinas's antidote to this tradition is what he calls "ethics," a relation which presupposes that the self comes into being only by first recognizing its responsibility to others. "Ethics" in this usage, then, denotes the claims of others rather than a body of moral rules and values.[20] In the words of Jean-Francois Lyotard, it entails "obligation without conditions" (137).

I am not suggesting, of course, that Oppen knew of Levinas's work, but only that this way of understanding "ethics" may help to elucidate Oppen's evolving poetic. Levinas's sense of a relation to the other as the quintessential expression of the ethical may define something in Oppen's writing that has strong social motivation but which is not, in his terms, "political" as such. At least, once we think of the ethical in Levinas's sense at least two consequences follow, both at odds with Poundian modernism. First, a poetics of "encounter" will assume that the domain of the ethical is also the domain of the ordinary and the everyday, of relationships expressing proximity rather than contemplative or legislative distance ("Near is / Knowledge," says Oppen in "Of Being Numerous" [*Collected Poems* 176]). Second, the ethical subject is not only open, but vulnerable and in question. Levinas thus speaks of "the risky uncovering of oneself, in sincerity, the breaking up of inwardness and the abandon of all shelter, exposure to traumas, vulnerability" (quoted in Bruns 89, who comments that "the ethical subject according to Levinas is no longer a propositional agent but is dialogically situated, that is, *in question*").

This way of understanding "sincerity" not as a question of truth but rather as one of relation and exposure to the claims of others has more than a little in common with Oppen's work. For "sincerity" is not so much a true account of one's inner feelings (manifest, then, Pound would say, in precise verbal formulation) as an acceptance of what *exceeds* the self. In Levinas's sense, this self is always unbounded, open to a perception of radical heterogeneity. As Maurice Blanchot nicely puts it, "the other withdraws me from what would make me unique" (13), a view that accords with Oppen's own attempt to transcend what he calls in "Philai Te Kou Philai" "a ruined ethic // Bursting with ourselves" (*Collected Poems* 76). "The self," he warns us in "World, World—," "is no mystery" (143) but there is instead "a force of clarity, it is / Of what is not autonomous in us" (185). But what is "The act of being, the act of being / More than oneself" (143)? Language that hovers on the brink of intelligibility, handing over to the "materials" of poetry rather than producing clear self-expression—this is perhaps one means of "being / More than oneself." But the difficulty lies in saying what that "more" exactly is, for this transcendence of self is toward something ultimately "impenetrable," to use Oppen's favorite word again. The idea of collective social being is in this sense "impenetrable," which is why its strongest expression will always be in the intermediary forms of poetry rather than in any kind of political discourse. As Oppen puts it in his interview with Dembo: "we have a kind of feeling that the absolutely unitary is somehow absolute, that, at any rate, it really exists. It's been the feeling always that that which is absolutely single really does exist—the atom, for example. That particle of matter, when you get to it, is absolutely impenetrable, absolutely inexplicable" (Dembo, "The 'Objectivist' Poet" 163).

It is the idea of a related linguistic impenetrability or opacity that contemporary poets have discerned in this work. For many of the Language poets, it is in the recognition of language as a material and social medium that some sort of "ethical" frame for writing is to be found. Charles Bernstein, for example, assumes that "Language is commonness in being," arguing that "The move from purely descriptive, outward directive, writing toward writing centered on its wordness, its physicality, its haecceity (thisness) is, in its impulse, an investigation of human self-sameness, of the place of our connection: in the world, in the word, in ourselves" (*Content's Dream* 32). Oppen, as we have seen, certainly moves toward this perception of writing as a kind of intermediary space in which a certain "connection" might be felt. Yet the temptation remains to speak *about* that connection, and as Bernstein notes acutely, "Oppen's often claimed commitment to clarity, however qualified, annuls a number of possibilities inherent in his technique. . . . That is, he tends, at times, to fall back onto 'clarity' as a self-justifying means of achieving resolution through scenic motifs, statement, or parable in poems that might, given his compositional techniques, outstrip such controlling impulses" ("Hinge" 241). Bernstein's observation invites us to read Oppen's work as a sort of hinge between modernism and something we may choose (or not) to call postmodernism. At some point in that trajectory, ideas of a "commonness" in language underwent a drastic change; Oppen's poems are there to help us see how poets could begin to associate an "ethical" relation with a certain linguistic opacity.

IV
Affiliations

12

Reading Reznikoff: Zukofsky, Oppen, and Niedecker

Robert Franciosi

For George Oppen, no work displayed Charles Reznikoff's loyalty to "the small nouns" better than a two-line poem first printed in the 1931 Objectivist issue of *Poetry*, but slightly revised in *Jerusalem the Golden* (1934):

> Among the heaps of brick and plaster lies
> a girder, still itself among the rubbish. (*Complete Poems* 1: 121)

Despite his claim that Reznikoff's poem is perfect, beyond explication, Oppen nevertheless offered an intensely personal commentary by consistently misquoting the last line as "*the* girder, still itself among the *rubble*": "That line of Reznikoff's and the poem of which it is a part, and the line upon line of his perfect poems have been with me for forty-eight years since I first came upon them. If we had no other poetry I think we could nevertheless live by virtue of these poems, these lines, these small precise these overwhelming gentle iron lines and images of all that is and our love and pride and our small life which is immeasurable as these lines which are still themselves among the rubble" (Oppen, "Foreword"). What, in fact, does the girder poem reveal to us about each poet? Oppen's transformation of "rubbish" into "rubble" bespeaks the different lives these two men led, as well as their different fears. Whereas "rubbish" suggests a casting aside of objects as without value, "rubble" implies the breaking down by outside forces of something still useful. Reznikoff's line expresses a spirit of endurance, of persistence in the face of neglect, where Oppen's rewriting suggests a spirit of resistance, of holding to one's convictions in the midst of destructive forces. Yet Oppen fails to weigh the significance of "rubbish" to the poem and to Charles Reznikoff, so vulnerable to doubt and to a wistfulness that surfaces especially during the 1950s:

> Scrap of paper
> blown about the street,
> you would like to be cherished, I suppose,
> like a bank-note. (*Complete Poems* 2: 76)

Often expressing fears about his poems being lost, cast off as mere rubbish, Reznikoff told how his grandmother, after his grandfather's death, burned all his Hebrew poetry, his lifework, fearing it might include thoughts dangerous to a Jewish family living under the czar. In part to ensure against such a loss, Reznikoff printed his own work privately. Asserting that the girder remains "still itself" even "among the rubbish," he assigns its tenacity a significance equivalent to his persistence in a literary life.[1]

Although Oppen's eloquent response is certainly approbative, his rewriting of Reznikoff's poem tellingly registers his own personal and social ethos. "The girder, still itself among the rubble" betokens his and Mary's life together ("our love and pride and our small life which is immeasurable") and confirms the personal and political "way" they had chosen:

> George—Quoting Rezy, too, "We wanted to be ourselves among the rubble" which held us half in and half out of political things. And that line to me is one of the most powerful lines in poetry.
> Mary—"The girder . . . "
> George—"The girder still itself among the rubble" and we recite that line over and over to ourselves—and we meant to be ourselves among the rubble—and it was rubble or it was very close to rubble. It was very close to catastrophe. You know. Not only close but was catastrophe because a world war is catastrophe, after all. (Oppen, "Poetry and Politics" 29)

As we read this line now, in the light of both men's poetic careers, its power rests as much in Oppen's rewrite as in Reznikoff's original.

Supporting a social vision of small lives, of poetic subjects lost in Robert Lowell's age of confessional poetry and imperial selves, Reznikoff's "gentle iron lines" bear a formidable weight for Oppen. As Michael Davidson has pointed out, the poem's second line "could easily stand for the governing ethos in Oppen's poetics": "It defines those enduring products of human labor that exist despite and yet within the 'rubble' of modern history. In a metaphoric sense, the line describes those 'small words' upon which Oppen's aesthetic rests and for which Reznikoff's poetry so often became the model. It is not the Imagist's ideal of a transitory moment caught by the artist between juxtaposed images and removed from time. It is the poem in time, part of the rubble and yet 'still itself,' unchanged by the synthetic imagination" (Oppen, "Adequate Vision" 5). But however much Oppen loved these lines, the poem he remembers is more his own than it is Reznikoff's, the girder a powerful and recurrent image, a fixed point on his poetic compass which would both guide him and serve as a test of other work.

I

From their first visits to him in the late 1920s, George and Mary Oppen incorporated Charles Reznikoff into their personal mythos. Reznikoff would prepare for these guests fourteen years younger than himself by stocking bottles of cream soda. Oddly, some forty years later Mary Oppen still emphasized the age difference, declaring in an interview that Reznikoff, born in 1894, was not only much older than herself and George, but older even than William Carlos Williams, born in 1883 (Gruber 112). She pushes Reznikoff clearly into a "parental" generation, a role he seems to have played, too, for other Objectivists. That loose association of companions can be described rather easily in familial terms: Reznikoff's roles in the Objectivist family drama included favorite uncle to the Oppens; father *and* son to child-parent Louis Zukofsky; sympathetic brother to Lorine Niedecker.

Oppen's relationship with Reznikoff belies Harold Bloom's notion, outlined in *Poetics of Influence,* of poets contending with a growing sense of "belatedness," engaging in psychic struggles with "strong" precursor-fathers in order to secure linguistic breathing room. Although tensions and distortions can certainly be found within the Objectivist family, Bloom's schema, with its emphasis on conflict between poetic generations, is not a good fit. It has no place for a literary relationship in which the parent figure is insufficiently acknowledged, in need of celebration or rehabilitation; nor for an epigone secure in accomplishment, willing to claim a birthright; nor for *women* positioned at either place in the Oedipal drama. Bloom's insights on poetic influence, then, are suggestive but limited when applied to the Objectivists.[2] For Oppen's misreading seems to reflect not so much the anxiety that Bloom diagnoses as the desire to claim literary kinship in a time of neglect, to locate himself in a shared endeavor.

Yet the Objectivist poets could no more "place" themselves in poetic history than could their more honored contemporaries. "Poets may try to design their own memorials," Lawrence Lipking writes in *The Life of the Poet,* "but all they can be sure of is the body of their work; the monument, the way the work will be remembered, must be left to other hands"—hands that make the admired poet's texts sometimes unrecognizable. The literary means by which "posterity arrogates the poet to its own needs" Lipking terms the *tombeau* (139). Several poets have written *tombeaux* to Reznikoff since his death in 1976—most notably Allen Ginsberg as well as George Oppen—but we can adopt Lipking's concept even as we consider accolades written for Reznikoff during his lifetime.

Any tribute to a poet like Reznikoff, so little noticed in his own day, inevitably seems memorial in nature. When Zukofsky and Oppen celebrated the poet, living but positioned as essentially dead to his world, they implicitly challenged mainstream critical judgments that had conferred status on T. S. Eliot and Robert Lowell but had withheld it from Reznikoff—and from themselves. Even when explicitly acknowledging their debts to Reznikoff, Zukofsky, and Oppen expressed his poetic career in terms relevant to their own struggles within American literary and social history. They viewed "Reznikoff" through the scrim of their own interests, as did their female counterpart from rural Wisconsin. But Niedecker, despite the experiential distance between country and city, female and male, presents Reznikoff himself more clearly than either did Zukofsky or Oppen. Especially familiar with poetic isolation, Niedecker felt clear kinship with the vocational stance of another marginal figure.

When all three poets read Reznikoff during the most difficult stage in his career, the one sealed by the 1959 publication of *Inscriptions 1944–1956,* they mark a seemingly inauspicious close to that career. By necessity they resist a Bloomian struggle with this precursor by figuring him as a benevolent relative, a shiftless but nevertheless attractive alternative to Bloom's "father." Hence Zukofsky, Oppen, and Niedecker offer modifying *tombeaux,* tributes, to the living Reznikoff's endurance in the face of neglect.

II

Zukofsky once confided to Hugh Seidman, one of his students at Brooklyn Polytech and later a poet himself, that "'Rezzy' was one of the few poets that had ever taught him anything." What exactly did Zukofsky learn from Reznikoff? The fate of poets in America? Consider the impression young Seidman and his companions at Poly had of Zukofsky's poet-friends: Zukofsky "described Lorine Niedecker as the best American woman poet after Marianne Moore and broke our hearts with the tale of her scrubbing floors in a hospital in Wisconsin. Reznikoff became heroic composing poems as he walked the miles from Riverdale to his law work in lower Manhattan only to be eventually fired for lateness" (Seidman 98). The explanation of Reznikoff's dismissal is fanciful, as is the job location (which was in Brooklyn), but the heroic sentiments assigned to his solitary poetic labors correspond to those Zukofsky felt toward his friend.

Early on, in "Program: 'Objectivists' 1931," the introduction to a special number of *Poetry,* Zukofsky includes Reznikoff in a reading list "absolutely necessary to students of poetry." But his praise for these models is necessarily mingled with solicitude. He laments that many of the poetic fathers on his list, "Pound, Williams, McAlmon, Cummings, Reznikoff, etc., have had to publish a good deal of their own work in privately printed editions" (268). In the awkward position of asserting the value of a poet whose writing was largely unknown to readers of *Poetry,* Zukofsky struggles against the injustice of Reznikoff's neglect. He attempts to validate by both invoking and debunking literary lions.

"Sincerity and Objectification" enacts tensions defining American poetry in 1931 and begins with reference to twelve lines Reznikoff published in 1918. Zukofsky claims they contain "in their elements the atmosphere of Eliot's *Waste Land* and *Hollow Men.*" Quoting the line "Smooth and white with loss of leaves and bark," he asserts that "since Eliot's *Poems* were first published in America in 1920, there can hardly be a question of the influence of method in a discussion of the line's value" (272). Of course Zukofsky forgets that Reznikoff may well have read Eliot's pre-1918 work in *Poetry* itself. His suggestion that Reznikoff anticipated the mood of *The Waste Land*—undoubtedly the most prominent work included in his list of essential readings—is an attempt to establish in a single stroke the unknown poet's legitimacy. But the overreaching backfires, inviting negative comparison. Still, Zukofsky presses on: just as Harriet Monroe had vouched for his editorial judgment by citing the "high authority of Ezra Pound," Zukofsky invokes Pound's authority in praising Reznikoff: "Ezra Pound has expressed the opinion that Reznikoff's verse and prose are 'good'; also 'after reading Reznikoff's work, [he has] suspicions as to whether the next wave of literature will be Jewish; and whether the lack of prose in German is due to drainage of the idiomatic energy into Yiddish'" (285). Like Zukofsky's relationship with Pound during the 1930s, the sentiment expressed here is peculiarly complicated.

The rest of the essay follows a pattern in which Zukofsky asserts Reznikoff's qualities as a poet and then contrasts his neglect with the ill-deserved fame of more popular writers. He describes Reznikoff's narrative verse as "perhaps the most neglected contribution to writing in America in the last ten years" and adds that he has avoided "the subterfuge of those who have 'written narrative poems' with one eye on the glory that was Greece (Sophocles or the *Anthology*), or the glamour which was Arthurian romance, or the agility which was Chaucer" (280). Reznikoff's willingness "to infuse his care for significant detail and precision into the excellent verbalisms of others" Zukofsky views not only as a sign of his devotion to craft, but of his understanding that a poet's "objectifying of good writing wherever it is found" is "more important for the communal good . . . than that a plenum of authors should found their fame on all sorts of personal vagueness—often called 'sophistication'" (283–84).

Zukofsky's personal investment comes into focus by the essay's final paragraph. Noting Reznikoff's dissatisfaction with the ending of his "David and Michal," Zukofsky suggests that a "defense of his lapse may well be the continual strain of having to publish one's own writing for a 'literary market' not interested in sincerity as craft" (284). Only twenty-six when he wrote these words during the depression, he probably found little solace in Reznikoff's example as one who had largely *chosen* his privately-printed way. Younger poets seldom come to terms with the compromises made by admired older ones, and the more prominent examples of Pound and Eliot also lured Zukofsky. His attraction to the powerful mythos of early modernism—exile, little magazines, "movements," and manifestos—did not, however, lessen his resistance to Pound's urgings to create a "gang" or to Monroe's desire, through the Objectivist issue, to return *Poetry* to the glories of the imagist era.

William Carlos Williams had already endorsed Zukofsky's enthusiasm for Reznikoff, saying his work "gives me a feeling of great honesty, as you have said, and a sturdy resistance to cheap art." Reznikoff, Williams agrees, is "an important link in the chain we are all working at," and Zukofsky remained steadfast, helping to organize the Objectivist Press, although he could never afford to print a book of his own through this communal venture (Letter to Zukofsky, 7 May 1929). That Williams at age fifty had still to struggle for recognition, that he in fact needed the Objectivist Press to issue his *Collected Poems, 1921–1931*, must have disturbed Zukofsky, especially as he saw his own chances for a literary livelihood grow progressively worse during the decade's last years. But at the end of his *Poetry* essay Zukofsky declared bravely that "sincerity, even in isolation, persists"; the next thirty years would severely test the strength of Objectivist persistence.

Always cognizant of the difficulties Reznikoff faced as a writer, Zukofsky continued to offer encouragement. In 1949, when Reznikoff's "Meditations on the Fall and Winter Holidays" appeared in *Commentary*, for example, Zukofsky wrote a note to his friend elaborately praising the text. Yet he could not resist a slap at Eliot, 1948 Nobel laureate, internationally successful and culturally conservative, saying that Reznikoff's poem could offer Eliot instruction on both culture and religion (Letter to Reznikoff, 9 November 1949). The remark is reminiscent of his 1931 essay. But Reznikoff had affirmed the value both Eliot and Pound had for him, and without the traces of aggrievement and aggrandizement we hear in Zukofsky. "Other than Pound," Reznikoff wrote in 1933, "I know no one now except T. S. Eliot who is genuine." Reznikoff derived much excitement from his own poetic project, but he had few illusions about its tenuous place in the world: "there is much to be done, for both Eliot and Pound are in high-grade furnished rooms in good neighborhoods, but I think myself on the highway—with little done and very far to go" (Letter to Lewin, 17 September 1933). He seemed not to resent Eliot's place in the world of poetry, but he was uncompromising about the route he would take to a "high-grade" room.

We know that for Reznikoff the 1940s and 1950s were particularly difficult. Around 1950 he wrote a novel loosely based upon his brief work for Albert Lewin at Paramount Pictures, yet *The Manner Music* is more than just another Hollywood exposé; it is a bitter tale of artistic neglect and despair. Jude Dalsimer composes strange music which has no audience, enrages his wife, and befuddles his friends. Yet Jude refuses to abandon or even to compromise his work until at novel's end he burns it all in Central Park. He is committed to Bellevue and dies soon after. The fictional nightmare of a self-published poet who did not often yield to such fears, the book seems a product of the very strain that Zukofsky had noted earlier.

The Manner Music was discovered only after Reznikoff's death; not even his wife had known of the manuscript. But Zukofsky had read or heard the novel in part, for as Cid Corman has shown, in 1950 he adapted a section of it, recounting a brief narrative about trying to feed a stray dog (*"A"* 208–10). Immediately preceding this moment in "A"-12 is a long discussion of the political aspects of World War II and its aftermath. Abruptly another voice intrudes, sounding very much like Reznikoff in his narrative poems: "You remind me: / On one of my long walks . . . " Reznikoff rarely discussed either poetics or politics and would more often digress into amusing stories from his days as a salesman or from his most recent walk. Zukofsky's incorporation of this story in a major section of *"A"* is both a comment on Reznikoff's "use" of story and a loyal gesture. "What deeper homage finally can there be between friends," Cid Corman asks, "than this 'lifting' of a common language into an offering—presumably for us?" (453). Presumably for Reznikoff as well. But Zukofsky "lifts" beyond Reznikoff's own practice of infusing "care for significant detail and precision into the excellent verbalisms" of others by having an explicit commentary as coda at the end of the "A"-12 narrative:

—Reincarnated?
An old friend, maybe
Free to run off
In his other life
Refusing
Obligations
That come
From being fed?
Shall we have some coffee?
Dutch, if you insist. ("A" 210)

However, Reznikoff seldom offered commentary in or on his narrative poems: "I see something and it moves me," he said, "and I put it down as I see it. In the treatment of it, I abstain from comment" (Dembo, "The 'Objectivist' Poet" 193). At the same time, in his commentary Zukofsky offers a moving tribute to his "old friend" at perhaps the lowest point in Reznikoff's life as a writer. Reznikoff, who had indeed struggled against the daily "obligations" that hindered his writing, by 1950 seemed to have lost the battle. That year his wife accepted a professorship at Brandeis University, and they agreed to live apart; Reznikoff supported himself with freelance editorial tasks and had little time for writing that did not pay. Although Marie Syrkin suggests that Reznikoff's situation was hardly comparable to Jude Dalsimer's in *The Manner Music* (which she believed was written in the wake of her move to Brandeis), a single fact offers a poignant rejoinder—from 1918 to 1941 Reznikoff published twelve volumes of poetry; from 1942 to 1959 he issued only one.

But Zukofsky's coda reflects not only on Reznikoff. It illuminates his own recognition of the disparity between *his* situation and that of the dog in his echo of Reznikoff's narrative. Zukofsky had much consolation in the joys of family life so wonderfully celebrated in "A"-12, but his obligations to Celia and Paul were more demanding than any Reznikoff accepted. Teaching at Brooklyn Poly required much of him, and Zukofsky was not always "free to run off" to writing. But if Zukofsky was tempted to indulge in "what if's," any envy of Reznikoff's situation remained wry. Both he and Reznikoff struggled through the 1950s unaware that the succeeding decade would bring at last a measure of modest recognition. A short poem by Reznikoff from *Inscriptions* might serve as response to the coda Zukofsky composed for the dog story:

The dogs that walk with me are Now and Here
and a third dog I do not trust at all,
for he would lead me far into the past
and there I'd lose myself: his name is If. (*Complete Poems* 2: 80)

III

George Oppen was not one to be led into the past by "If." The nature of his and Mary Oppen's political activism, as well as their faith in a myth of escape, precluded any doubtful glances over traveled roads. Oppen did not describe his almost thirty-year abandonment of poetry, for example, in terms of regret, nor did he long for recognition as Zukofsky did. While Zukofsky could say of the largely imagined readers of their poems, "George, they don't care," Oppen resisted despair and defensiveness.

He remained relatively untroubled by neglect, but like Zukofsky he looked to Reznikoff's work for confirmation of his chosen stance: "Present the problem of 'neglect'—and how very slowly indeed the mills of the anthologists grind and the critics and the public grind. So many mills, and they move so slowly. Rezi's neglect has been largely I think due to the fact that he is of little use to those who would teach or explicate a poem. Rezi's poetry is merely perfect and profound and infinitely moving. The least of Rezi's one line poems say more—does more—than anything that anyone can say about it" ("Adequate Vision" 20). Neglect, Oppen speculates, may actually be "a blessing." There are, after all, "Some very lovely stories about men who carried such a light thru deserted places." In 1959, however, after the publication of *Inscriptions,* Oppen pens an atypical response to Reznikoff. He shows the same kind of competitive outrage as had Zukofsky earlier—and again, the whipping boy is T. S. Eliot: "The lines beginning 'penniless, penniless' render Eliot simply absurd," he writes, commenting that "critics would have made these things famous if they were Christian" (*Selected Letters* 34). By 1959 the dominant agenda of Eliot and the New Critics had at last provoked George Oppen.

As he helped initiate efforts in 1960 to print *By the Waters of Manhattan,* Oppen continued to focus on why the mills ground so slowly, on why Reznikoff's work had been ignored when that of lesser talents had been celebrated: "It occurs to me that the hardest to recognize is a major poet. Anyone can recognize a minor poet—it's more of the same. People looking at Charles' work the first time must ask themselves, where's the whatsit, where's the whosis, where's the assonance the dissonance the ambiguity the Eliot the etc. If they could approach it as major poetry they would find themselves at once considering whether it is better or less good than Eliot or than Yeats" (*Selected Letters* 377).

Contradicting ideas from "What Is Minor Poetry," where Eliot asserts that a minor poet is one known primarily in anthologies, whose full body of work is not essential reading, Oppen claims that encountering a "major" poet such as Reznikoff requires "a new effort of sensibility, in fact a revolution of sensibility" (377). However just his argument, Oppen had few illusions about the damage that isolation—or, in his own case, self-silencing—could inflict on a literary career. "People are injured by non-recognition perhaps—I think Van Gogh was, I am sure Joyce was," he tells his sister. "Maybe even Rezi, in limiting his experience and range" (37). Having only recently resumed his own writing, Oppen ponders in a therapeutic gesture "what Rezi would have been if the world had invited him in." Again, he reverses the usual values: "Possibly less than he is—because that has happened too. The faults of a man with only his own judgment to go by are certainly less suffusing—they leave what he has" (37). When in 1962 New Directions accepted Reznikoff's *By the Waters of Manhattan* (to a large extent because of the sponsorship of Oppen's sister June Oppen Degnan and her *San Francisco Review*), Oppen congratulated his friend, reiterating thoughts on poetic neglect: "The rewards for solid worth and beauty may be a study for geriatricians, but Alright. They grind slowly. But I think they grind just fine" (Letter ca. 1962).

Regardless of the slow grinding, Oppen's praise for Reznikoff's short poems never wavered, nor did his belief that such poetry was beyond explication. These poems fulfilled for him the "totality of perfect rest," called "objectification" by Zukofsky. "There are no poems more perfect," Oppen wrote in the same 1962 letter to Reznikoff, "no poems more precise or, in spite of the modesty of precision, more profound." The profundity these poems held for Oppen is most evidenced in his *tombeau*, "In Memoriam Charles Reznikoff":

    who wrote
in the great world

small for this is a way

to enter
the light on the kitchen

tables wide-

spread as the mountains'
light this is

heroic this is
the poem

to write

in the great
world small[3]

Oppen's *tombeau* alludes briefly to a 1921 poem evoking the urban world of Reznikoff's boyhood:

> As we walked back, the city stretched its rows of houses across the
> lots—
> light after light, as the lamplighter went his way and women lit the
> gas in kitchens to make supper. (*Complete Poems* 1: 45)

"We no longer clearly remember those significances of the city, the significances of those lives" ("Adequate Vision" 27)—in his tribute Oppen reasserts Reznikoff's allegiance to small lives and small nouns. His arrangement of monosyllabic words and meshed disparate nouns and adjectives (world/kitchen, tables/mountains, great/small) is masterful, as is his isolation of "heroic," the only trisyllabic word in the poem. While Oppen's disjointed syntax does not echo Reznikoff's voice, his wonderful pivoting of language on our very expectations—"the great world / small"—diffuses one phrase into another, expresses and enacts their mutual faith in the simple words and things which illumine the great world.[4]

These small words, Oppen says, capture a "knowledge which is hard to hold" and confirm Heidegger's statement that "in the mood of boredom the existence of what-is is disclosed." Unlike some of Pound's work, for example, which Oppen says is diminished by "Too much machinery" and "Too many reading lists," Reznikoff's short poems authorize themselves, prove themselves, prove that "it sometimes pays / to have a look / And to keep still till one has seen" ("Adequate Vision" 17). Based on what he had seen, Reznikoff created small poems that are more than "mere pretty bits." Oppen recognized and celebrated their blending of historic and contemporary particulars, their mixing of simplicity and depth, and—especially—their remaining comment-free. "Likely [Reznikoff] could mull along and tell you what he had in mind. But how other than with [an] image," Oppen asks, "could he put into your mind so clearly the miracle of existence—the existence of things?" (*Selected Letters* 24). "I think that poetry which is of any value is always revelatory," he concludes. "Not that it reveals or could reveal Everything, but it must reveal something" ("Adequate Vision" 14).

IV

Despite their admiration for Reznikoff's work, Oppen and Zukofsky filter their readings of him through the lenses of their particular concerns and attitudes, leaving Reznikoff elusive. But Lorine Niedecker identifies *with* him: "Hard to write and then get it printed. I try to along with scrubbing floors in a hospital. Every now and again, tho, there's a chink where a poem comes thru. Altogether life is not really too hard—I gather this is what you say too" (Letter to Reznikoff, 23 November 1959). These are spare but telling terms, identifying Niedecker with the heart of Reznikoff's life and work—a spiritual stoicism in the face of difficulty and neglect. As a woman poet, Niedecker would almost certainly have feared subsumption back into a more typical "woman's role," despite her domestic labors.[5] Reznikoff also lived his life on home ground and against the powerful expectations of an immigrant family and friends, his humble way in the world sharing aspects of what our culture calls "feminine." An independent life in poetry may always entail complication and cost, but for such writers as Niedecker and Reznikoff the greatest expense can be incurred simply by holding fast, continually honoring the choice. That they both shied away from activist literary politics, that they were uncommonly persistent in the face of significant neglect, and that they made similar choices in their poetry—all this suggests that Reznikoff and Niedecker could both have benefited from a literary comradeship even closer than the one they managed: "Reading *Inscriptions: 1944–1956* I often find a kinship between us in the short poem. And if you are my brother-in-poetry then we have Chinese and Japanese brothers. But I have a great deal of practicing to do—of quiet insight—before I can enter such a good family." In particular, Niedecker's favorite poems from *Inscriptions*—"One of my sentinels, a tree," "The Indian of Peru, I think," "Hardly a breath of wind"—as well as two she sent to Reznikoff on postcards—"Linnaeus in Lapland" and "Old man who seined"—reveal their similarities, especially the roles of place, self-effacement, and vocational stance in their short poems and obscure careers.

For both Niedecker and Reznikoff, locality is central. "Unless you've become so much a part of your natural surroundings that you can't imagine what it would be like to live elsewhere," she wrote to Zukofsky, "feel it as a living center and source—consciousness and memory awakening at the mere sight of it—you don't know what I mean" (Penberthy, *Niedecker Correspondence* 76). Similarly, when Mary Oppen recalls Reznikoff's directions to a passerby—"first you go down this street as far as where the statue used to be"—we register afresh the role of place and its historical temporalities for his poetry (86). Often choosing a haiku-like compression, each wrote poems on place, whether urban or rural, what Niedecker termed, in speaking of Cid Corman's work, "short poems on large subjects," expressing a dual sense of "Wonder" and "Contentment" (*Condensery* 308).

Their attention to details of place was yoked to that avoidance of self-absorption typical of the haiku-influenced modern short poem, with its "strictly reduced emotional vocabulary," as Jenny Penberthy notes, in which feeling is "allowed only an oblique presence" (*Niedecker Correspondence* 76). Penberthy restates Reznikoff's poetics, enacted in his girder poem and other haiku-like works, that poetry should be "precise about the thing and reticent about the feeling," and that it "presents the thing in order to convey the feeling" (Dembo, "The 'Objectivist' Poet" 193).

Modesty and precision characterize Niedecker and Reznikoff. Consider his wry comment on his "position":

> One of my sentinels, a tree,
> sent spinning after me
> this brief
> secret on a leaf:
> the summer is over—
> forever. (*Complete Poems* 2: 62)

Besides the consistent end-rhymes so familiar from her own verse, Niedecker would have enjoyed the ironic whimsy of tree as guardian and informant. The attitude is consistent with her book *My Friend Tree;* and she once claimed to have more trees for friends than people. Nor would she have missed the weight and finality of "forever." The youthful and acclaimed Shelley could emphasize spring on winter's heels, but poets never experiencing a bright summer of recognition might understandably anticipate a cold and uncertain winter. Harvey Shapiro recalls Reznikoff as "the only poet I've ever met who never uttered a complaint about the way life had treated him, no talk at all about more successful poets, no criticism of a culture that had given him almost nothing and had lavished gifts on meretricious entertainers" (86–87). Yet we should not underestimate the psychic toll exacted by a hostile literary world—even on poets who seldom complained. Neither their conscious self-effacement in poetry nor their conscious refusal of political self-promotion would have lessened the injury of disregard.

Indeed, in 1959 Niedecker measures some of the strain on Reznikoff, offering Zukofsky an apprehensive reading of his isolated literary situation and, by implication, of her own. After spending "a lovely day reading Rezzy's book [*Inscriptions 1944–1956*]," she confesses, "I always felt he was writing my poems for me only better," a remark of inscrutable humility, given the relationship of Zukofsky and Niedecker (Penberthy *Niedecker Correspondence* 257). She goes on to pose troubling questions about *Inscriptions* and its author: Who will review such a book? Why don't the little magazines recognize Reznikoff's achievements? Couldn't poets such as Zukofsky and Williams do something to relieve his neglect? Years back, in 1931, Zukofsky had noted the "continual strain" that private publication and little attention had exerted on Reznikoff's work, while in 1946 Niedecker had published in *New Goose* (1946) her own haunting meditation on literary despair:

What horror to awake at night
and in the dimness see the light.
        Time is white
        mosquitoes bite
I've spent my life on nothing. (*Condensery* 82)

By 1959 Reznikoff's muted pain is very palpable to Niedecker.[6] As she tells Zukofsky: "You get the idea he leads a lonelier life than I do but freer of trash? Years ago his poetry was of the same order but more whimsical while now there is something a bit harder there. I think 'Night-Piece' affects me more than any mebbe" (Penberthy *Niedecker Correspondence* 257). Writing to Reznikoff on the same day, Niedecker lists her favorite poems from *Inscriptions 1944–1956* but in a protective gesture declines to mention his own ghostly "Night-Piece":

I saw within the shadows of the yard the shed
and saw the snow upon its roof—
an oblong glowing in the moonlit night.

I could not rest or close my eyes,
although I knew that I must rise
early next morning and begin my work again,
and begin my work again.

That day was lost—that month as well;
and year and year for all that I can tell. (*Complete Poems* 2: 86)

Similar anxiety pervades many of Reznikoff's poems from the 1950s. Still, Reznikoff and Niedecker managed to bridge distances of age, geography, and experience to offer each other sustenance. In a 1946 letter to Zukofsky, Niedecker quotes Reznikoff's response to *New Goose:* "It is very kind of you to send me your book," he had written. "I picked it up when I was tired and dispirited and put it down quite refreshed by the words and music" (Penberthy, *Niedecker Correspondence* 138). Better than most, Niedecker understood the value of such refreshment, even, perhaps especially, in a book that also contains seeds of despair. It was, after all, during a celebratory moment for Reznikoff, his first publication of a book of poems in sixteen years, that she had noted the subtle "hardness" entering his voice, the bitterness, perhaps, of a life spent "on nothing."

By affirming their common situation, by embracing "the condition of anonymity as a gesture of career building," Niedecker offers encouragement to Reznikoff in a form most useful to him—and to herself (DuPlessis, "Niedecker: The Anonymous" 100). She had been pleased by his account of the Peruvians who by "chewing / the leaf of a shrub / could run all day"—consider the poem's concluding lines:

> I, too,
> with a few lines of verse, only two or three,
> may be able
> to see the day through. (*Complete Poems* 2: 62)

Similar gestures of bemused acceptance can be found throughout Reznikoff's work, but especially in the writing after 1962. A Chinese proverb in 1969's "Early History of a Writer" could serve as motto for both poets: "one who can work ten years without recognition / will be known everywhere" (*Complete Poems* 2: 176).

Both Niedecker and Reznikoff had intricate poetic attitudes about anonymity and fame. Niedecker's anonymity, as Rachel Blau DuPlessis proposes, was "a utopian gamble," her "pretended simplicity" a vocational choice, a wager that social and political changes would finally grant her a "name" ("Niedecker: The Anonymous" 114). The comments can be extended to Reznikoff. Both poets rejected "the feedback loop of impersonal publication, prize-winning poetry, and fame" (108) and adopted, along with the self-protection, the cost inseparable from what Lawrence Lipking has termed an "anti-career" (xiv).[7] Living in Wisconsin with fishermen in semipermanent vacation camps meant that Niedecker did not live with other poets. Is it possible that other poets would have overwhelmed her poetry?

Both poets remain clear-sighted, protecting their projects from their own aggrandizing desires and those of others. Even from a friend, Reznikoff found recognition embarrassing. He responds to Oppen's lavish commendation in December 1959: "It is very pleasant to be praised, but I still wince. I suppose the reason is that I compare my own work to other work I admire and I cannot help thinking of all that I want to do but am too busy with a lot of trivia to do" (Letter to Oppen, 15 December 1959). Niedecker's sisterly support, in contrast, was generous and direct. Unlike Zukofsky and Oppen, she neither dwells on Eliot and literary politics nor risks her poetic "situation" by immersion in career promotion. She does wonder, though, whether *Williams* and *Zukofsky* could not do more for Reznikoff.[8] But like him, she chooses to lead a life aside:

> If I were a bird
> . . . .
> I'd sit on a quiet fence
> and sing a quiet thing: sincere, sincere.
> And that would be Reznikoff. (*Condensery* 104)

Perhaps Niedecker's perceptive responses helped fuel Reznikoff's resurgence during the 1960s. Three years after the "hardness" of *Inscriptions,* when he, with Oppen, assembles selections from his life's work in *By the Waters of Manhattan* (1962), he leaves out "Night-Piece." Seven years later, for *By the Well of Living and Seeing* (1969), his last privately published volume, the seventy-five-year-old Reznikoff revises it. The poet thinks once again about the "vexations of the day" and ponders the same image—a garage in the yard, its roof covered with snow, reflecting the moonlight:

> From where I lay I could not see the moon
> nor the yard itself
> but the garage roof was shining like a quadrangle of light
> against the darkness:
> a quadrangle of light
> against the darkness.
> Looking at it I forgot myself
> and fell into a deep and untroubled sleep. (*Complete Poems* 2: 136)

When Niedecker died the following year, Reznikoff explicitly acknowledged his debt to her by contributing to the *tombeau* volume *Epitaphs for Lorine:*

You write
"I walked
beside the trees
my father planted.
Each spoke."
They still do
but we have lost the interpreter. (Jonathan Williams n.p.)

V

Poets in varieties of "the Pound Tradition"—Objectivist, Black Mountain, and Language—are particularly bound by their explicit acknowledgments of literary obligation. Often, as Christopher Beach explains, "they thematize the question of influence in their work in such a way as to foreground their relationship with or debt to their predecessors, rather than repressing or escaping [them]" (44). Zukofsky's, Oppen's, and Niedecker's creative "misreadings" of Reznikoff both relieve the stresses of his—and their—obscurity and acknowledge those qualities that enable or validate their own poetry. For all three poets, Reznikoff's work served as affirmation, inspiration, and, most importantly, justification for the writing of more poems. Zukofsky's particular absorption in literary history and Oppen's in social transformation deter them from Bloomian competition; Niedecker's poetics of exchange not only complicates Bloom's model but illustrates how influence can be both generative *and* gendered. In particular, Niedecker's felt kinship with Reznikoff and his work challenges the family schema Bloom posits for strong poets—the struggle between precursor-father and ephebe-son. Where "generosity is involved," Bloom has asserted, "the poets influenced are minor or weaker" (*Poetics of Influence* 83). It is a curious judgment. Reznikoff as read by his Objectivist colleagues offers data for a reexamination and modification of Bloom's model of influence.

For Niedecker, the poetry of Charles Reznikoff fostered not competition but a mutual sharing, an exchange where the pleasures of giving and receiving became indistinguishable. She saw and accepted a poetic exchange not as a site of struggle, but as a shared place "below the salt" at the common literary table. In a memoir of her husband, Marie Syrkin recalls evenings when they attended formal dinners to mark an anniversary of Israel or to raise funds for varied Jewish causes. A prominent American Zionist, Syrkin "generally sat at the dais, while Charles would be seated elsewhere" (60). This "distinction in the seating," she says, "had not gone unnoticed" by her husband, had in fact been put to a poetic end in "Te Deum":

Not because of victories
I sing,
having none,
but for the common sunshine,
the breeze,
the largess of the spring.

Not for victory
but for the day's work done
as well as I was able;
not for a seat upon the dais
but at the common table. (*Complete Poems* 2: 75)

Despite its apparent simplicity, this poem is many-faceted, as Milton Hindus has reminded us, expressing both "the pathos of that moment of acute self-awareness which comes when one has been placed by the world . . . 'below the salt' " and the proud irony reminiscent of Emily Dickinson's "I'm Nobody! Who are you?" (*A Critical Essay* 14). Never pushing his way onto the dais—indeed, resisting its lure—Reznikoff clearly savored his place at the common table, still himself among the poets.

13

Zukofsky's List

Andrew Crozier

I

There is surely no gainsaying the fact that the Objectivists are an enduring embarrassment to criticism and poetry alike for the sole reason that they disturb an ordinary understanding of history as chronology. They appear to flout the law of contradiction by their ability to occupy two positions at the same time in our cognitive map of poetry in the twentieth century, for they are equally of the 1930s and the 1960s. I state the problem of the Objectivists' historical standing in terms of its effect on us in order to draw attention to its obduracy, for it has been with us since their return to public view in the 1960s.[1] Since then it has been routine to see them as necessarily filling an abhorrent vacuum (not previously detected), the poetic lost generation or missing link between the modernism of Pound and Williams and the "New" American poetry of 1945–60. Quite where the gap is supposed to occur, of course, is altogether another matter, whether in the continuum of critical attention and esteem or in the sequence of poetic production. Certainly, in the sequence from Pound and Williams it is not necessary to postulate a gap before Olson and Duncan, but to acknowledge this to be the case is precisely to confront our embarrassment in its most acute form: our necessitarian version of what the Objectivists stand for historically, following their historic reemergence, restages contradiction by making them at once the problem and its solution. There would be no problem, needless to say, had their reemergence been a matter merely of critical rediscovery, or had they reemerged as revivalists of a period style; but, as we know, critical rediscovery followed their reemergence as poets of late maturity. And this is the key to the embarrassment they have induced ever since, for with this second flowering they reemerged discontinuously, it would appear, from a prior history that nevertheless—for it was there to be investigated—provided the only terms in which they could be thought. They were interviewed half to death as witnesses to their own pasts, so that it should not be wondered at if, resistantly, they drew attention to the integrity of their lives and careers. Inconvenient ancestral ghosts, their flesh-and-blood existence made them unaccountable.

I exaggerate, of course, but for a purpose. If we continue to be embarrassed it must be on our own account because we have been unable to describe for the Objectivists a position in history that accords them the status of agents. In the 1930s they were not around long enough to leave a lasting impression, yet in the 1960s, and attached to their prior history, they appear belated. The passage of time, with its telescoping effect, is not quickly going to improve matters on our behalf. If they will not fulfill the intermediary role invented for them because they have affronted us as a historic anomaly since the 1960s—and it is apparent that they need not—their situation remains that between their two epochs they are (what amounts to the same thing) either squeezed out of history or set in its margin as a special instance. The reason for this is not far to seek: historical and chronological belatedness are not the same thing ("confessional" poetry is a prime example of the former), and it is our sense of history as chronological incrementation that the Objectivists disturb. A history fully predicated of the Objectivists, however, is somewhat farther to seek, and would not consist of the bare chronicle of their self-manifestation in the 1930s, for it would need to account for the significance of their disappearance from the chronological record as more than a terminus of events, and it would need also to implicate them fully in the more familiar history that includes Pound, Williams, Olson, and Duncan. Such requirements, admittedly, imply considerable claims on the Objectivists' behalf, for they entail major adjustment of our received history (already undermined to disclose that explanatory gap), on behalf of which we feel the embarrassment we do in tacit acknowledgment of their claim on our attention. We should not continue to deal with them (aided and abetted by versions of the seamless unities of their separate bodies of work) by superimposing and conflating their different epochs, covering contradiction in the dust of history.

The argument required by the counter-history I propose, and the evidence to be gathered, fall outside the scope of this essay, which will nevertheless sketch the outline of such an argument in the course of an examination of a single item of evidence. Of immediate concern, therefore, is what the premises of such an argument might be, what view it takes of the historical context in which the Objectivists emerged. That context, of course, will be a construction, but given its proper context, it will be claimed, the term "Objectivists" might be understood to denote a much wider historical field than its recent use has documented, so that—speculatively at least—the identity "Objectivist" does not merely designate the four-man team (Rakosi, Reznikoff, Oppen, Zukofsky) that was defined in the 1960s. Such different denotation, feminist critics and historians might be pleased to note, would take off the pressure to bolt on Lorine Niedecker as an honorary fifth Objectivist, and avoid depriving her of her own idiosyncratic history. (Admirers of Basil Bunting, strangely enough, with the exception perhaps of Donald Davie, have not attempted to affiliate him in this way, probably because in the England of the 1960s, which bracketed him with Hugh MacDiarmid and David Jones, a myth of native ancestry and longevity answered to various local needs.)

The Objectivists' historical context brings us directly to the question of Objectivist theory, implicit in the classification of poets as Objectivists. Here we should not be concerned with the belated rationalizations of the term of the 1960s and after, overdetermined as they are by reminiscence and eager hindsight, but with the theory (insofar as it was such) indicated and transmitted by Zukofsky in his role as collective mediator, publicist, and specifically, in a word, as the Objectivists' *editor.* What needs to be registered about this, in addition to Zukofsky's reluctance to theorize—much advertised, but more important than it—is that the reluctance was theorized: the critic was secondary to the poet. What we read as theoretical statements by Zukofsky are promulgated as axioms and taxonomies, the specific terms of which are defined by illustration. The terms "sincerity" and "objectification," that is to say, do not remain in the conceptual domain, although they are concepts of particulars (poems and their elements), but are referenced in the work of Reznikoff. We may suppose that in these instances, in which he is not redeploying Poundian categories, Zukofsky's terms derive from his own poetic concerns, that they state his poetic aim and method, for of course they are not conceptual categories for analytical purposes. Were they so they would not require demonstrative illustration. But for analytical purposes Zukofsky catalogues the properties of poems in triads which indicate that his theory, at the formal level of composition and reading, is a development of Poundian axioms. Pound's phanopoeia, melopoeia, and logopoeia are rendered as image, cadence, and idea. (Or, in a later formulation, with the pleasures of reading in mind, as sight, sound, and intellection.) Zukofsky's development from Pound becomes clear if we correlate terms that are distinctively his own with those adapted from Pound, and place sincerity with image, objectification with cadence, for it is then necessary to suppose that "idea" has been in some way subsumed by both. It is important to emphasize at this point that Zukofsky is not merely applying or extending Pound's earlier theory; he retains Pound's theoretical axioms, which were a contribution to the study of poetry's formal properties, but subsumes them to a larger conceptual structure designed to accommodate questions of value as well. There is an ambition here to go beyond matters of craft, although Zukofsky's theory functions as well to preserve and consolidate modernist gains in technique, but to understand it we need to see it as an intervention within a specific historical situation. It is at once the counter-offensive and the rearguard defense of the younger modernists.

II

Situations are constantly being modified by agencies we also understand to be determined by them. With this in mind, we might see Zukofsky's Objectivist theoretical intervention as acting against the drift of events in order to assist the real direction of historical development, and indeed quite directly so by virtue of actions purportedly in a pragmatic mode. The attractions of such dissimulation are readily apparent, for theory can give an account of poems in terms of itself, it can instill preferences, but it cannot know poems directly or make judgments about them. The material contingencies of practice will always cause it to exceed theory; the most theory can then do is draw attention to those unpreconceived effects for criticism to judge of. Zukofsky's historical situation made dissimulation possible because it was so unlike Pound's: whereas Pound, pioneering his way out of the wilderness of Victorian culture, had recourse to *a priori* principles derived from an ahistorical notion of innovative practices, Zukofsky could cite the example of his contemporaries' achievements. This active Poundian legacy provided him with admirable cover as that discriminator of values, the editor. And there is no doubt that, in adopting this role, Zukofsky performed an important service, underwriting the canon of modernist poetry as we still, to a great extent, have it today. Nevertheless, modernist theory, as part of his inheritance from Pound, was inadequate to the task of justifying that canon, let alone enforcing it. Indeed, it had been deployed elsewhere to become a cultural program, in consequence of the tactical inflections it received from Eliot, or, recalled as Imagism, it received a token assent as a primitive hygienic regime. All very well to patronize its limitations if Glenn Hughes's revivalist *Imagist Anthology 1930* was taken for its up-to-the-minute embodiment.[2]

To speak of Zukofsky as having underwritten the present-day canon of modernist poets is not, needless to say, to claim that he instituted it. Far from it. What he proffered was a list, something far short of the canonical, but instead current, provisional, appropriate to the moment. And of course the perception of what such a reading list should essentially prescribe, the sense of what constituted the historical ensemble of contemporary relevance, was not peculiar to him. It comes to us with an air of familiarity not because we recognize names from the canon but because our scholarship enables us to reconstruct systems of mutual esteem. Canonicity and historiography are not, however, to the present point, and need to be set aside if we are to address the significance of Zukofsky's list in relation to the Objectivists—who, it needs to be recalled, are neither canonical nor the subjects of a sufficient history. We need to attend, instead, to what is idiosyncratic in Zukofsky's list in order to detect how poets who are for us canonical are positioned there in a quite other order of values. It is indeed the presence of certain canonical modernists on his list, there perhaps indeed as Objectivists, the argument here outlined proposes, that is basic to a historical understanding of the Objectivists.

If I have been slow to introduce the piece of evidence—Zukofsky's list—which I consider exemplary for the historical argument I have in mind, it is because, as will by now appear obvious, I do not suppose that its significance can be yielded inductively. Its significance lies not so much in what the poets cited have in common as in how they are grouped together. Prefatory remarks have not served to signify this setting aside of inductive method by tendentious deferral but were designed to indicate the range of problems this evidence can be applied to. What remains, before the evidence is finally produced for inspection, is to indicate its situation in relation to Zukofsky's dissimulated theoretical project.

In a letter to Pound dated 8 September 1930, Zukofsky indicates the connection as "aesthetic criticism" of four essays he has written: "Henry Adams: A Criticism in Autobiography," then being serialized in *Hound & Horn;* "Ezra Pound: His Cantos," published in French translation in *Echanges;* and "American Poetry 1920–1930" and "Sincerity and Objectification," published the following year in *Symposium* and *Poetry* respectively (Pound and Zukofsky 41). It is in this group of ostensibly disparate essays, rather more than in the editorial statements he contributed to the "'Objectivists' 1931" issue of *Poetry* and the 1932 *An "Objectivists" Anthology,* that we will more profitably look to delineate Zukofsky's theory.[3] Taken as a group they will be found to deal, respectively, with an exemplary poetic intellect, an exemplary poem, the current achievement of American poetry, and the work of a largely unknown poet (Charles Reznikoff) whose work exemplifies the qualities in poetry which need to be known for purposes of critical judgment. (It will be recalled that in defining these qualities Zukofsky was integrating, in terms of larger and smaller units, Pound's threefold distinction of poetic properties.) Zukofsky's method throughout these essays is to draw attention to particulars, and this is consistent with a recognizable theory of knowledge and communication as well as, by implication, a critique of dominant cultural practice. In keeping with this method is the device of the list.

Of immediate concern is "American Poetry 1920–1930," which was explicitly a sequel to René Taupin's *L'Influence du Symbolisme français sur la Poésie américaine (de 1910 à 1920)* (Paris, 1929).[4] We need to note both the method of Zukofsky's approach to his topic and the strategic possibilities it provided. Zukofsky's method implies that his sequel to Taupin's book is not simply its continuation, and this is not merely because the question of influence is consistently discounted, specifically, where he finds Taupin thinking in terms of poetic generations, and what he regards as "evolutionary implications" linking one generation to the next, Zukofsky prefers to "study the progress of individual work rather than its use in an 'evolution' of poetry" (61). Focus on individual poets, rather than poetry in general, allows room for critical censure without requiring Zukofsky to undertake a general survey of his period. The essay is not a critical balance sheet drawn up at the end of a poetic decade, and indeed its sense of timing is quite different. Accepting Taupin's notions of a "first generation" and a "younger generation," Zukofsky's strategic purpose is to combine them, and so he refuses to see the first generation (Pound, Williams, Eliot, Marianne Moore) as a "gang-plank for a younger generation to step onto" (61). Zukofsky's sequel to Taupin is thus the occasion to insist that poets of the first generation continued to develop or progress after 1920 (and thereby detach them from imagism; indeed, "they never started merely with the image") and hence that their relation to the younger generation is that of contemporaneity rather than influence (61). Citing Pound and Joyce, he suggests that the question of influence might more appropriately be explored in terms of the relations between contemporaries.

We can understand all this as "aesthetic criticism" because it is insistently evaluative, with Zukofsky's list as the outcome of a complex and wide-ranging act of judgment. The theory entailed by his criticism is evidenced by the axioms that direct and justify his observations and judgments, and by the different occasions this essay and the other three address. Theory provides both tactics and strategy in these essays, and the absence of systematic theoretical exposition should not be taken as evidence that Zukofsky's thinking is without either system or the capacity to explain itself.

III

In "American Poetry 1920–1930" Zukofsky's theoretical position is invested in the poets who provide his point of departure: "For bearings this essay returns to the several poets it started with" (72). They were those members of the first generation (but not, for example, H.D., "whose later work . . . suffers from an Anglicized dilution of metric and speech value") whose work had continued to progress, and certain members of the younger generation (61). His "portmanteau bibliography of poetry after 1920 is brief" (72). I now give it in the form in which it was reprinted in *Poetry* (there are minor differences) as the headnote to "Program: 'Objectivists' 1931" as the "list of works absolutely necessary to students of poetry" (268). This is Zukofsky's list:

> Ezra Pound—*XXX Cantos* (Paris, 1930); William Carlos Williams—*Spring and All* (Dijon, 1923); Marianne Moore's *Observations* (New York, 1924); T. S. Eliot's *The Waste Land* (New York, 1922) and *Marina* (London, 1930); E. E. Cummings' *Is 5* (New York, 1926); references to earlier volumes of Cummings; Wallace Stevens' *Harmonium;* Robert McAlmon's *North America;* Charles Reznikoff; and *The Exile Nos. 3 and 4,* edited by Ezra Pound (Chicago, 1928). (268)

However judiciously compiled, this is self-evidently a working list, for the contemporary student, and it requires some elucidation before we can either comment or interpret its historical significance. Today's student will not find copies of *Exile* readily at hand, but with this citation Zukofsky is directing readers to poets of the new generation without books to their credit; specifically, he is referring to himself ("Poem beginning 'The'" in issue no. 3) and to Carl Rakosi ("Extracts from a Private Life" in issue no. 4).[5] Their inclusion, together with that of McAlmon, and perhaps of Cummings, marks the positive deviation of Zukofsky's list from our own canon. Its negative deviations, both from the contemporary canon and our own, are possibly less obvious, in the former case at least. Zukofsky was swiftly rebuked by the proprietor of *Poetry* herself in the next issue. Harriet Monroe denounced the "theoretic scheme" that left so many "poets of the last two decades consigned to outer darkness": Robinson, Lindsay, Frost, Masters, Sandburg, Jeffers, Millay, Lowell, Wylie, and the "once-revolutionary imagists."

More significant exclusions from our point of view, once it is borne in mind that the list is of poetry published during the 1920s, include Crane, Tate perhaps, but also the Eliot of *The Hollow Men* and *Ash-Wednesday.* What caused Zukofsky particularly to approve "Marina," which he republished in *An "Objectivists" Anthology?* Can this question be rephrased to ask, instead, if it is feasible to categorize Eliot with other Objectivists? The line of reasoning behind such a question will be obvious, but it should be approached with the necessary caution that three of the poets in Zukofsky's list—Cummings, Moore, and Stevens—did not appear in either of Zukofsky's "Objectivists" compilations.

Additionally, it may be noted that Pound's contribution to "'Objectivists' 1931" was blank space: "Mr. Pound gave over to younger poets the space offered him" ([Monroe], "Notes" 295). This might suggest that Zukofsky's view of his editorial project, and that of Pound, who had sponsored it, were somewhat different.[6] We are, of course, concerned with Zukofsky's, since the term "Objectivists" was his, and will recognize that the term was used at one time or another to describe most of the poets on his list as well as a considerable number of others of the younger generation whose names have altogether lapsed from memory.

But more than this, for having cited his list of works Zukofsky adds that the poets named seem to him "to have written in accordance with the principles heading this note" (268). The derivation of that statement of principles, after Zukofsky's reading of the dictionary and Spinoza, indicates the close alliance of his theory and poetry. In "'Recencies' in Poetry," his "Preface" to the 1932 *Anthology*, Zukofsky felt it necessary to point out that the lexical definitions of the noun "objective," including his own "use of this term extended to poetry," which comprised the statement of principles in "Program: 'Objectivists' 1931," were transcribed ("slightly reworded") from his poem "A"-6 (9).[7] The optical and military senses of the noun—as an objective glass ("the lens bringing the rays from an object to a focus") and as "that which is aimed at"—correspond, surely, to those qualities sought in poems under the terms "sincerity" and "objectification" (10). They also correspond to those aspects of nature differentiated in the distinction between "natura naturata" and "natura naturans" encountered in the scholium to Proposition XXIX of the first part of Spinoza's *Ethics*.[8] In "A"-6 the military usage of the second sense of "objective" is not alluded to (as indeed it is not normally implied when we use the word in this way; only the dictionary gives the military prior claim on this sense), and in its extended use in relation to poetry, with Spinoza in the background, the term "objective" brings together things seen sharply and intention toward things in that mode in a synthesis which adjusts the creative powers of the poet and those of history. I quote Zukofsky's statement of principles as cited by him in "'Recencies' in Poetry," but note a significant variation of wording: the version of "A"-6 given elsewhere in the *Anthology* reads "naturans" rather than "nature as creator" (10).

> An objective—rays of the object brought to a focus,
> An objective—nature as creator—desire for what is objectively perfect,
> Inextricably the direction of historic and contemporary particulars (10)

"Nature as creator," Zukofsky's final form of words, glosses "natura naturans," which for Spinoza is synonymous with God as a free cause, as distinct from everything else which derives from God's nature or attributes. William Hale White annotated this passage in the *Ethics* by citing the Scholastic idea of the oneness of God and the world which was yet not their absolute identity.[9]

Spinoza knew all about lenses, but both Christians and Jews have tended to doubt whether he knew much about God.[10] He tends to attract those whose faith has failed, such as White and Zukofsky. But how do the principles stated by Zukofsky, derived (it would appear) from a version of natural theology, apply to the other poets on his list? How might they apply, for example, to the belief in revelation of the Anglican Eliot? How do they square, for that matter, with Zukofsky's Marxism? Only the first question needs an immediate answer, which we can approach if we consider that whereas Zukofsky has derived some form and substance of thought from Spinoza he has not retained its meaning. The desiring creative nature, or the desired perfection of creation, is not eternal but historic and contemporary, and exists independently as poetry.

IV

If we return to Zukofsky's statement of principles, in either of its forms, we can observe that it follows a returning curve from the object, to the perfect, back to particulars. In "Program: 'Objectivists' 1931" particulars are glossed as both things and events, Marianne Moore's "Egyptian pulled-glass bottle" and the Russian Revolution. This sequence instates the perceived object, as a particular thing or event, within the perfect. Quite how the sequence unfolds and folds back on itself is not without its ambiguities: "inextricably" lacks a verb to modify, so that by ellipsis it cannot be certain which of "desire" and "perfect" is relative to "direction"; nor is the sense of "direction" certain, even as we follow the trajectory of Zukofsky's thought. Just as we move and are moved by desire, so Zukofsky's particulars both have and receive direction. These ambiguities are intrinsic, just as is, within the complex mediation of Spinoza's thought, the double focus of "objective," which is both gathered to and projected from the subject. Now, while I am fairly sure that within the phrase "the direction of historic and contemporary particulars," the historic and contemporary themselves inextricably linked, we may detect the hope of the communist, our attention should remain on "particulars," and the modes of knowledge and communication associated with them.[11] It is in relation to this term that other poets on Zukofsky's list can be thought of as having "written in accordance with" his principles, or that those principles can be seen as not exclusively appropriate to his own writing.

In Spinoza's thought, as Zukofsky might render it, God is a particular from which other particulars derive their being and which exists in them. In the same way, sincerity and objectification are particulars distinguished by scale and position. To distinguish between things and events, historic and contemporary particulars, is not, it would appear, to distinguish between kinds of particulars but merely to emphasize one quality of particulars rather than others. We might recognize all four qualities in Marianne Moore's Egyptian bottle.

But it is a characteristic of particulars, as of God, to exist in the present, where—unlike God in the popular notion of him—they exhibit change. Contemporaneity stands in contrast to the past, not history, and the present is stuffed with husks of the past. When Zukofsky praises Henry Adams for remaining young, we are reminded, perhaps, of Cummings. So a poetry of particulars might be understood as a poetry of history's manifestation in the present. Such a complex understanding of contemporaneity might well yield a principle common to the poets on Zukofsky's list. Indeed, in "American Poetry 1920–1930," quoting from Marianne Moore's "New York," Zukofsky says of the first generation of his poets that they "did not stop with the monolinear image; they extended it to include 'a greater accessibility to experience' " (61). However, neither contemporaneity nor accessibility to experience, as far as poetry is concerned, is a matter of disposition; they require constructive achievement. In Pound the monolinear image gives way to "the poetic locus produced by the passage from one image to another. His *Cantos* are, in this sense, one extended image" (73). In analogous ways Williams and Moore are seen to have coordinated multiple images as complex structures.

Images, we may suppose, are the particulars that make up poems and from which the complex particular that is a poem is produced—or at least, that this is so in the case of the small body of work that comprises Zukofsky's list of American poetry in the 1920s. But how, we may well ask, is an image produced in language from the historic and contemporary particulars of the age? I think it is in relation to this question that Zukofsky's most stringent criticism of contemporary work is deployed, in precise relation to a sense of the specificity of meaning to particularized words. Words are particulars, as opposed to general lexical items, when spoken; they achieve a meaning specific to the particular occasion of their enunciation (though no doubt words may be spoken over and over again without losing their conventional generality and imprecision: this was, after all, one of T. E. Hulme's great themes) from performative features such as gesture and intonation. Zukofsky's criticism throughout "American Poetry 1920–1930" is focused on prosodies and graphic devices capable of providing the written word with performative equivalents to "clarify and render the meaning of the spoken word specific. The things these poets deal with are of their world and time, but they are 'modern' only because their words are energies which make for meaning" (79).[12] It is in this context of prosodic inventiveness that we can understand Zukofsky's coolness toward the later H. D., and Stevens and Eliot as well ("like Eliot, [Stevens] has purposely led his rather submerged intellectual excellencies . . . to a versification clambering the stiles of English influence"), on account of the metrical tug in their verse toward "anglicized" regularity (65).

It appears, then, that in "American Poetry 1920–1930" Zukofsky provided the articulate demonstration of Objectivist principles in action, and that they can sufficiently explain both the exclusions and inclusions based on them. On this showing the statement that the poets on his list write in accordance with common principles is fully justified in terms of the principles themselves, and those principles define the term "Objectivist." But two questions remain to be posed, the first of which is crucial to the historical argument alluded to previously, but one which requires the second if it is to be properly answered. Can the poets on Zukofsky's list usefully be considered as Objectivists? Do Zukofsky's Objectivist principles adequately encompass their work? Some readers may have registered as intransigent modernist backwardness the primacy allotted to speech values by Zukofsky, even though his principles, his criticism, and his theory are all concerned with writing. If so, Zukofsky nevertheless does appear, even while resisting some applications later made of it, to endorse de Saussure's primary distinction between *langue* and *parole.* His poetics of speech and music (the lower and higher levels of poetry in his later formulation of it) thus reveals a blind spot in his theory, which performs a disappearing trick with the dance of the intellect among words, as Pound defined *logopoeia*—that metonymic capacity of poetic language to mark words and phrases with contextual inflection as it shuttles between different registers and codes. It might be said that while Zukofsky had an ear for particular words, he had no time for particular jargons. (We might recall his reported rebuke to Pound in 1939, when he was seeking audience with sundry political crackpots in the United States, "Whatever you don't know, Ezra, you ought to know *voices*" ["Statement" 55].) But theoretical blind spots are prone to be negated by practice, and although we find little or no irony—of the sort encountered in Moore and Cummings, or in the earlier Pound and Eliot—in Zukofsky's writing, his method disposed him to be, like Pound and Moore, and McAlmon as well, a collector of quotations, of particulars of writing, and to build from them. Moreover, if Zukofsky is not disposed to dwell on the ironies of contemporary life, are they not a shared preoccupation of Rakosi and Oppen? If we would not withhold the term "Objectivists" from them on that account, why might we not apply it, in the light of Zukofsky's conception of their common principles, to the other poets on his list? I propose this as the question best suited to frame the early history of the Objectivist poets.

14

"And All Now Is War": George Oppen, Charles Olson, and the Problem of Literary Generations

Stephen Fredman

The convenient notion of literary generations has been an important part of the fictional structure of literary history, helping to separate it from history proper. In literary histories, we have used named generations as markers in the assembling of an orderly narrative of innovation, struggle, triumph, and succession. By means of this generational narrative, we have been able to tell ourselves stories about "literature," presenting it as a self-enclosed entity that constitutes its own world. Historical fact, though, can step in and disturb our recounting of these comforting tales of dynastic succession—as, for instance, when we notice that both Keats and Carlyle were born in 1795. We can take such a fact as a synecdoche for the plethora of historical facts that has troubled the generational narrative of romanticism and Victorianism and has caused a wholesale revision of views about nineteenth-century English poetry. "Romantic" and "Victorian" are not equivalent names, either, for "romantic," as a generational term, has been used traditionally to designate in English poetry the works of six men, while "Victorian" has been used in less generational and more historical senses to cover a larger period of time and a much greater diversity of writers.

For the poetry of the twentieth century, both poets and critics have been anxious to identify and promote literary movements and to give these movements generational characteristics. When poets invent a movement and ascribe certain qualities to it, critics often follow suit by grouping the poets together and by interpreting the poetry solely through the lens ground by the poets. In the cases of most of the poets of our century, we are just beginning to look at their writing from perspectives other than the generational ones they themselves supply. One way to resist enclosure in generational fictions is to explore the historical factors behind the invention by poets of specific generational narratives. For example, Lawrence Rainey has recently demonstrated two major personal and social exigencies behind Pound's promotion of imagism: the collapse of the means Pound had worked out to secure himself a livelihood, and his observation of Marinetti's spectacular success in commodifying futurism while in London in 1912–14. Discovering the efficacy of generational discourse for securing a hearing (and a living) for new writers, Pound then passed along this public-relations tip to other new poets. A full thirty pages of the Pound/Zukofsky correspondence are taken up with discussions in 1930 about how to position the "Objectivists" issue of *Poetry.* Charles Olson inaugurated another Poundian generation in 1950 with his platform essay for *Poetry New York,* whose composition occupies Olson and Robert Creeley for much of the first 220 pages of their correspondence. Generally, literary historians have been only too happy to follow the lead of these two aggressive forays into public relations (that is, Zukofsky's essays "Program: 'Objectivists' 1931" and "Sincerity and Objectification," and Olson's essay "Projective Verse") and have thereby presented Objectivism and Projectivism as two distinct and successive generations in American poetry. It is instructive to ponder how our received literary history might differ had L. S. Dembo not decided to make the reconstruction of Objectivism a central focus of his 1968 interviews with George Oppen, Carl Rakosi, Charles Reznikoff, and Louis Zukofsky, or had Donald Allen not featured Charles Olson, the Black Mountain poets, and "Projective Verse" as headliners for his 1960 anthology *The New American Poetry.* Such editorial contingencies often have everything to do with the creating of a literary history.

I would like to throw a wrench into the narrative of succession that posits an Objectivist generation, launched in 1931, followed by a Projectivist one, launched in 1950. The easiest way to do so is to introduce another historical fact: George Oppen and Charles Olson were born two years apart, in 1908 and 1910, respectively. Routinely, this potentially disturbing fact is glossed over by designating Oppen the youngest Objectivist and Olson the eldest Projectivist. This preserves the generational narrative, but at the cost of distorting the careers of these writers by framing them solely by the decades in which their generations came to light: we view Oppen as a man of the thirties, for whom the depression, populism, and communism are defining issues, and we view Olson as a man of the fifties, enmeshed in the cold war and the nascent counterculture. Such contexts demonstrably aid our understanding of these writers, but choosing to read their works exclusively through the concerns of one particular moment restricts our vision unnecessarily; in particular, such a way of reading blinds us to a number of similarities in the works of Oppen and Olson. To begin to rectify this situation, I would like to focus upon World War II as a defining influence upon both poets. World War II represents a moment between the thirties and the fifties, a moment whose impact has been remarkably poorly explored in our generation-bound history of American poetry.

In this century of horrors, World War II holds pride of place for Americans as the most devastating event, both for the numbers of Americans killed and for the difficulty of coping with the unthinkable destruction caused by the Holocaust and the Bomb. We must take this crucial era more fully into account in order to render an accurate history not just of the writing of that time but, in a larger sense, of the writing produced by those who lived through it. The two poets under consideration participated in the war in different but vitally consuming ways—George Oppen as a soldier, who was wounded fighting in France, and Charles Olson as a propagandist, working in Washington, D.C., for the Office of War Information. Right off the bat, thinking about Oppen in the context of the war allows him to escape from the tight little room we have designated as "Objectivism." In some measure, Hugh Kenner can be held responsible for constricting the dimensions of that room with his unfortunately memorable statement: "The Objectivists seem to have been born mature, not to say middle-aged" (*Homemade World* 169). This image of prematurely wizened poets—who felt, Kenner says, "that the arts ought not to exhilarate, save austerely, and moreover that in a gray time (1931) they had best be gray" (168)—contrasts vividly with Mary Oppen's portrait of George's energetic determination in 1944, when he entered the Army at age thirty-six: "he was overage for the draft, but he wanted to go. . . . He went in as a responsible Jew, who someone was trying to wipe out and he was not going to stand still" (Young 37). This hardly sounds like a man who, thirteen years before, had slipped into a premature middle age. Nor does the poetry Oppen wrote after the war—which includes all but his short, precocious first book—sit comfortably in the imagist tradition that Kenner has been so instrumental in delineating. In fact, the incredible pressure that Oppen exerts upon both language and thought brings him much closer to a younger European poet like Paul Celan (1920–70) than to Pound or Williams (both born in the 1880s). As a Jew whose military unit liberated a concentration camp, Oppen "certainly saw those horrors firsthand" (Young 37), so that the world of "that which happened" (Felstiner xvi), as Celan designates the Holocaust, was not at all distant from the threatened facticity of "this in which" (Oppen, *Collected Poems* 78) Oppen set his writing. Another crucially formative influence for both poets—one that the war complicated considerably for each of them—was the philosophy of Martin Heidegger. Both poets found decisive Heidegger's investigations of the relationship between language, thought, and being, yet each fought off the philosopher's dispassion in an effort to enunciate an ethic of caring appropriate to a devastated world.

Taking into account Oppen's experience of World War II and his connection to Heidegger, a strong case can be made for thinking of him as an existentialist rather than as an Objectivist—or else we must open our definition of Objectivism to include much more than the pallid epithet "second-generation imagism." One index of the difference it makes when we think of Oppen this way concerns his commitment to "the real" or "the actual." Is it enough to assume that these terms return to the imagist hygiene prescribing the accurate visual representation of things or that they draw upon the impressionist equation of visual data with emotional states? During an interview with the Oppens in which Kevin Power engages them in a discussion of Camus, Sartre, and Heidegger (Power 196–97), he asks George to "talk about 'actualness' and how that enters the poem." George replies, "Well there's that prose section of Pierre Adam in 'Route' when he tells me about his experience. I was conscious, when I wrote that, that any of the Existentialists could have written it. I wrote it, nevertheless, because it was actually what he said to me. Existential in the sense that you do what you do and that is the answer. . . . Simply that you are yourself" (197). The story Oppen alludes to was told to him in Alsace, where he was fighting in the Battle of the Bulge. Many Alsatian men, upon learning they had been drafted into the German army, dug themselves holes in the ground, in which they hid for as long as two or three years. When the Germans learned that men were in hiding, they made reprisals, killing family members and sending wives to the army brothels in Germany. Pierre fed and assisted the men in the holes. "Men would come to Pierre and they would say: I am thinking of making a hole. Pierre would say: yes. They would say then: but if I do they will kill my parents; or: they will take my wife and my children. Then Pierre would say, he told me: *if* you dig a hole, I will help you" (Oppen, *Collected Poems* 187–88).

For Oppen, this kind of terrifying existential choice defines the realm of "the actual." Such was the actuality French resistance fighters like Sartre and Camus faced, and it remained the (often unstated) background for their existential philosophies. In his essay "The Resistance," Charles Olson provides something like a gloss on Pierre Adam's story, asserting that the horrors of World War II have rendered the body as the only meaningful instrument of resistance: "When man is reduced to so much fat for soap, superphosphate for soil, fillings and shoes for sale, he has, to begin again, one answer. . . . It is his body that is his answer" (*Human Universe* 47). By bodily acts of resistance, such as those practiced by the Alsatians against the Nazis, Olson claims that human beings can learn to think concretely through the body rather than through the dangerous abstractions such as nation, race, and class. In "Causal Mythology" Olson avers, "I don't believe in cultures myself. I think that's a lot of hung up stuff like organized anything. I believe there is simply ourselves, and where we are has a particularity which we'd better use because that's about all we've got. . . . Put an end to nation, put an end to culture, put an end to divisions of all sorts" (*Muthologos* 94). This notion that large abstractions are dangerous and that what we think and do must be grounded instead in who we actually are jibes perfectly with Oppen's statement that his recounting of Pierre Adam's story was "Existential in the sense that you do what you do and that is the answer. . . . Simply that you are yourself."

Although Olson did not fight in the war, he read the daily dispatches in Washington, and they directed his thinking along lines that could also be called "existentialist." A pivotal example of such thinking occurs in the aphorism around which he organizes his "Causal Mythology" lecture: "That which exists through itself is what is called meaning" (*Muthologos* 72). This proposition can be read as a perfect synopsis of existentialist metaphysics and epistemology. When Olson delivered it at the Berkeley Poetry Conference in 1965, Oppen received a report from a friend. Writing back, Oppen comments: "Olson's [']that which seems to exist in itself we call meaning['] is a good statement of the thing— . . . That which exists of itself can not be explained   it cannot be analyzed, it is the object of contemplative thought, it is known by 'indwelling.' The Given. 'things explain each other / Not themselves'" (*Selected Letters* 115). The last phrase consists of two lines from Oppen's "A Narrative" (*Collected Poems* 134)—indicating that these two poets share a notion of resistance which extends from the political to the epistemological and is grounded in the inexplicable actuality of people and things. From this perspective, knowledge and action rest solely on individual responsibility, and yet they have ramifications for society at large. Both poets believe there is no substitute for the existential encounter; as Olson says in "Causal Mythology," "You're simply stuck with the original visionary experience of having been *you,* which is a hell of a thing" (*Muthologos* 72).

Prior to *The Maximus Poems,* Olson's poetry consistently weighs the effects upon thought and action of the devastation of World War II. For one thing, there is a recurrent preoccupation with the dead, as in the dreamworld of "As the Dead Prey Upon Us" or in the opening of "La Préface," an inaugural poem that portrays the concentration camps as the background to Olson's setting forth on a new poetry. No matter in what direction the poet sets out, the dead cannot be ignored:

The dead in via
                    in vita nuova
                                        in the way

Not only does the speaker find the way toward a new poetry (and a new life) blocked, but he must stop immediately to read what might be called "the writing on the wall":

"I will die about April 1st . . . " going off
"I weigh, I think, 80 lbs . . . " scratch
"My name is NO RACE" address
Buchenwald new Altamira cave
With a nail they drew the object of the hunt. (*Collected Poems* 46)

The walls of the camp at Buchenwald provide a palimpsest upon which the new poetry will be inscribed. Changing the image but remaining focused upon the dead of World War II, Olson finds "among the DPs—deathhead / at the apex / of the pyramid" (46). This poem implies that for a postwar culture to emerge from the ashes and become capable of creating works of the first order, such as the cave art of Altamira or the pyramids, these new works must be conceived of as a kind of projective funerary art, for "We are born not of the buried but these unburied dead" (47). Likewise, Olson's most famous poem, "The Kingfishers," bases its exploration of primitive mysteries in Greece and Mexico upon a Heraclitean acknowledgment of the universal condition of war. At one point, Olson turns from a depiction of "the priests / (in dark cotton robes, and dirty / their dishevelled hair matted with blood, and flowing wildly / over their shoulders)," urging the Mexicans to protect their gods against the invading Spaniards, to a general statement:

And all now is war
where so lately there was peace,
and the sweet brotherhood, the use
of tilled fields. (*Collected Poems* 89)

Out of a recognition that when "all now is war" everything has changed, and that what it means to be a human being is something new and newly terrifying, Oppen and Olson begin to write a new poetry. In locating a common ground for aspects of their poetry, I do not mean to suggest that the two worked in direct conjunction. Olson seems to have kept his distance from Oppen. In 1962 he wrote William Bronk: "I do know Oppen, and though some of my friends thought his review of *The Distances* and *Maximus from Dogtown* . . . was the old business of measuring me by Pound, and I thought myself he raced his motor on *Maximus from Dogtown,* I thought his picking 'The Satyrs' for a voice which was peculiarly my own, true enough. (I haven't yet seen his poems at all . . .)" (Butterick 495–96). In the review, Oppen states that "*Maximus from Dogtown* is obviously not part of Olson's best work," but he praises *The Distances:* "What is happening in these poems is that the poet is speaking: they are a discourse, always beautifully modeled and beautifully constructed" ("Three Poets" 330). Speaking to L. S. Dembo in 1968, Oppen says, "I've read a lot of Olson. I think 'In Cold Hell, In Thicket' is a very fine poem. I don't really like the *Maximus Poems* nor accept them at all" (Dembo and Pondrom 184). It is not at all surprising that two such ambitious poets would seek to circumscribe their points of contact.

Despite their uneasy accommodation to each other and the many differences in poetics and in personalities, some striking similarities in the work of Oppen and Olson appear when attention centers on the impact of World War II. For example, both poets engage extensively in practical politics, stretching back to the thirties, but after the war they leave political activism and begin to use poetry as a vehicle for a political thinking shot through with metaphysics and epistemology. This leads both poets to ponder deeply the relationship between the individual and the collectivity, between what Oppen calls "being singular" and "being numerous." In conjunction with the affirmation of resistant individuality noted earlier, both poets feel a newfound urgency to speak for the entirety of what Robert Duncan calls "the company of the living": Oppen's use of "we" throughout his central poem, "Of Being Numerous," testifies to this desire, as do Olson's attempts to place the present at the crosshairs of time and space in *The Maximus Poems.* Ultimately, both poets adopt what might be called a wary prophetic stance, addressing the most pressing concerns of contemporary life in terms that do not rely upon the old rallying points of religion or nation. I say "wary" to mark the way in which both poets disavow received concepts, as though it were necessary not only to save the world but to reinvent the terms by which it is known. Formally, this wary prophetic stance results in truncations of both line and syntax; such formal disruptions insist that readers, too, practice vigilance against falling into the easy grooves that both poets roundly condemn. And stylistically, both poets oscillate between lyric and didactic modes of address, in order to keep knowledge existential and yet to demonstrate the social constituents of the personal.

If the historical connections between the works of George Oppen and Charles Olson are this strong, does it follow that we should discard completely generational terms like "Objectivism" and "Projectivism"? I don't think so. I am arguing not for the abolition of literary-historical terminology but rather for a more nuanced historicizing of poetry. Inevitably, this would involve exploring the historical exigencies that contribute to coining and maintaining generational terms like "Objectivism" and "Projectivism," just as much as it would necessitate a more careful historical placement of the works of individual poets and more specific comparisons of poets based upon their responses to particular circumstances. On the practical level, we certainly can do more than repeat the shopworn clichés that Objectivism is concerned with the "object" and Projectivism is a poetry of "process." Instead of remaining fixated on these shibboleths, why not return to the practice Louis Zukofsky recommended in 1931 as "thinking with the things as they exist" ("Sincerity and Objectification" 273)?

15

Land's End

Yves di Manno

to Henri Deluy

For this roundtable, Michael Davidson had initially asked me to discuss what motivated me to translate George Oppen into French.[1] I could say a great deal on that subject, but instead I want to broaden the focus, passing up the temptation simply to be autobiographical or anecdotal so that I may focus my remarks on matters that concern everyone here. The implications of the issues that I will attempt to raise seem particularly relevant to the debate in which, for better or worse, we are all involved, given the opacity of current poetics and practices.

In the light of the variety of remarks and presentations that have already been made at this conference, and which have contained singularly compelling disclosures, not the least being their contradictions, I would like to grapple with a question that has not yet been publicly posed, despite the fact that it seems, especially here and now, to be a central one. That is: why have some of us French poets been attracted to American Objectivists—so compelled by them that we found it necessary to translate them, which is to say, to integrate them into our contemporary poetic scene and practice? And why have we taken to referring to them as "masters" whose equivalent we simply haven't found in France?

Moreover, these questions can be extended to include our fascination, in the last fifteen years, with a certain mode of American poetry, at least of the great precursors, as if we felt obliged to look elsewhere, to look to foreign literatures for resonance or for models which our own tradition could not offer, given the dead ends to which we have come and the bankruptcies we have declared.

I hasten to add, indeed to underscore, that the questions of our attraction to a certain poetic mode and to other literatures can't be limited to the "American" field; there are certainly plenty of other poetic worlds besides the anglophone. For efficiency's sake, however, I will only summarize and schematize this one. When all is said and done, our use of the United States seems to offer a particularly exemplary case of the kinds of issues in which we are all involved.

Challenged by the questions I've just sketched—what have we taken, or reappropriated, from American poetics—the most obvious answer, and the answer most frequently offered as a working hypothesis, is that we were seeking new formal "models," new prosodies: our own literary history prevented the necessary evolution of our verse forms *from the inside* (so to speak). In this narrative, surrealism is the culprit, because of its emphasis on love and romance, on metaphysics, and on dream. In contradistinction to what happened in other countries, surrealism in France cut off any concern for the issues opened by the abandonment of traditional metrics and prosodies. Certain works of the sixties put a lot of stress on the importance of a quick resolution to this problem, calling, in brief, for a return to what we may call "formalism." So we began to discover a range of possibilities which our rereading and translation of "foreign" materials opened up to us.

For a long time, I believed this account myself—or rather, I saw it as the only possible one. But now it seems a bit too simple to me. It's not without merit, but I rather think that this "theory" of our need for American poetry considers only one factor among a number. Better explanations would be more complex. Let me give you a few examples.

Taking as a basic principle the dissolution or effacement of the speaking subject, Emmanuel Hocquard, in *La Bibliothèque de Trieste* [The Library at Trieste], proposed the critical importance as an approach to writing of a procedure employed by Reznikoff in writing *Holocaust* and *Testimony*[2]—that is to say, the use of source materials fundamentally and totally "prosaic," upon which the author performs no operations but determining and selecting passages and reframing them *in terms of the verse line.* This documentary procedure thus excludes all personal expression; in other words, it gets rid of that suspect element—inspiration. Objectivism becomes, in this case, a synonym for "objectivity" rather than for "objectification."

It goes without saying that I agree, at least partially, with Hocquard. But I'd like to bring up a question that might be a little embarrassing. Why, in that case, invoke Reznikoff at all? If this is the procedure and praxis he wants us to follow or claim, let me remind you that the exact same kind of work was done in France from about 1924. I mean in the writing of Blaise Cendrars with his *Kodak,* which were renamed *Documentaries,* composed following the exact same method, from the reckless prose of Gustave Le Rouge.[3] Even less well known than this model, Paul Nougé used this technique in the 1940s, putting Maupassant into verse lines in his *Un miroir exemplaire de Maupassant* [Exemplary Mirror of Maupassant].[4] So given the fact that there is no lack of such cases at the very heart of our own literary tradition, it was probably not purely formal issues that led Hocquard to follow Reznikoff so faithfully.

Many more examples could be offered. Even conceding—what's true in a *partial* sense—that the surrealists compromised, stifled, and cut off the evolution of the verse line, still one must remember that before their taking of cultural power, a turbulent debate about formal issues took place in France during the years 1910–20.[5] I'm thinking of Apollinaire, whose influence on Zukofsky was just yesterday the subject of comment, and about the plurality and richness of Apollinaire's responses to the rupturing and breaking of traditional metrics, which he had, alas, barely time to sketch out. I'm thinking about the *Eloges* of Saint-John Perse, about Arthur Cravan's magazine *Maintenant,* about the *Stèles* of Victor Segalen.[6] I'm thinking about Pierre Reverdy, whose centenary we are at present rather tepidly celebrating, and how he was the first instinctively to invent a new verse line between 1915 and 1920.[7] I'm thinking of those first steps in Reverdy's journal *Nord-Sud,* in which the writers who would later become known as the surrealists began to publish, and of the poems written by Aragon, Breton, and Soupault around the end of World War I. I'm even thinking of *Champs Magnétiques* [*Magnetic Fields*] of Breton and Soupault where prose poems offered one way of moving beyond the dilemma of the free verse line. I'm thinking of Tristan Tzara, translating African oral poetry in Zurich during the first years of Dada, and of Max Jacob's *Laboratoire central,* of Robert Desnos, or even Albert-Birot or Picabia . . . [8]

This overlong catalogue has the function of affirming once again that, in the matter of prosodic and formalist revolutions, our own French heritage is by no means as worthless as we have been tempted to believe. I'm hardly suggesting that our own literary history is necessarily rich enough for us or that it offers sufficient material, nor do I want to propose that a simple rereading of key texts from the period of early modernism would have pulled us out of those ruts in which we have been, more or less, stuck. I'd just simply say that our own literary legacy has been somewhat disdainfully treated, even sidelined, because of an old cultural masochism which, in France, expresses itself by exaggerating all the virtues that can be seen in foreign materials and all the faults in our own. Don't mistake what I'm saying for some kind of "nationalist" agenda; I have always been strongly opposed to the *frontiers* against which and in which poetry must always contend—such frontiers, anyway, are linguistic, not national, and poetry tries to abolish them. This sort of self-denigration really isn't worth fussing over. Nevertheless, we are living with the reality of this phenomenon: it's clear that we've got a problem somewhere. To move French poetry forward, we think we have to look beyond it. And if we're not talking—at least not exclusively—about technique or about formal issues, then the question is: what is the problem really?

•

In fact, it's possible that the problem never was in the realm of form, but in the realm of fundamentals, of the foundational.

•

Having reached this point, we need to consider the deep gulf between our poetic tradition and what, at least since Whitman, developed in North America. Let's say (though it's a vast oversimplification) that historically, from its very inception in *Proensa* in the twelfth century, the most compelling aspects of our poetry were always in the realm of the *lyric.* Lyric—intimate, interior, subjective, the love poem, however you want to characterize it.[9] In contrast, in the United States for a number of literary generations, those who are *i migliori fabbri* [the better makers] have been committed, in a privileged though again not exclusive fashion, to the composition of *epic.* I am taking "epic" in the broadest and most capacious sense of that word. I don't just mean long poems, a work designated "epic" because of sheer bulk as a "poem of some length" [in English in original]. What I mean instead are those works grouped by their goal of reclaiming the possibility of a collective song, a social voice, putting the emphasis on the bonding of a poet to a community. This social voice comes in contradistinction to a strictly individual trajectory of development.

The list would be a long one, if one wrote it down, but anyway it's pretty familiar. Everyone can provide plenty of examples, from the *Cantos* of Ezra Pound to *Poland* by Jerome Rothenberg, including *Paterson* of William Carlos Williams, *The Bridge* by Hart Crane, *The Maximus Poems* of Charles Olson, and *"A"* by Louis Zukofsky. In this category, we should include *Testimony* by Charles Reznikoff, *Passages* of Robert Duncan, *The Tablets* of Armand Schwerner, *Americana* of Carl Rakosi—I'm just mentioning the most obvious.

All these works could be grouped under one critical rubric, given that the principle that animates them is the one elucidated by Pound in his *Guide to Kulchur:* "There is no mystery about the Cantos, they are the tale of the tribe" (194). Despite their diversity and the obvious contradictions of one with another, all these works express a collectivity through the poem (a task *completely unattempted in our own cultural context*), whether we look at songs and their individual registers or look at plural speech, what I'm tempted to call polyphonics, in which the collectivity as subject takes on strictly biographical material (such as emotions, feelings) as these are located in the specific poet. For all these reasons, these texts seem exemplary of the "modern," especially when we consider that the French poem has been drawing on entirely opposite impulses. Over the past two hundred years, the French poem has depicted the enclosed universe of the isolated poet, exiled from the company of his peers—the "maudit," as we used to say.

On the other hand, this New World poetic practice does not take shape by "neutralizing" or erasing individual consciousness behind some "mask" of the collectivity. A reader has only to consider these texts to be convinced otherwise. Each of the universes created inside these long poems is rich with, forged from, the profound circumstantiality of the author's life, and is distinctive to its particular author. There is a great disparity, for example, among the uses of archival sources in Pound, Williams, and Reznikoff; between the conceptions of the city in Oppen and Olson; between the irruption of war in Zukofsky and in Duncan. . . . But in reference to the critical position traditionally taken here in France, New World works postulate a considerable distinction between the poem's subjectivity and its author. That distinction can be made manifest in how an author belongs to a specific site, and how authors embed and root the poem in the history of the specific society in which they find themselves, in that process even interrogating those very connections, problematizing them over time. Indeed, the analytic proclamations offered by Pound suggest that the link between the artist and/or citizen and the nation was already problematic from the middle of the nineteenth century on.

In other words, if indeed there is collective song, it is because the poem weaves, knots, and unravels the fibers connecting the artist to a particular place and time. As a result the whole function of the poem is regrounded, returning to the ritual or epic origins of song, and seeking to reformulate these origins and functions, bound to the fate of the society from which it has emerged. That, at any rate, is the ideal. One does know (I'll come back to this point) that the failures and the compromises are hardly in keeping with the richness of the project as ideally conceived. . . . Nonetheless, it's in the assumption of a necessarily open-ended song, renewing the dialogue between a person and his or her society and peers, that the works I've mentioned have made their most significant and elegant mark.

Well, I believe that this is the poetics we have yearned for, or at least grappled with, consciously or not, from American practice. We look to America because such an approach has been denigrated here; or because it has been erased, or rendered unreadable. I myself hope that the necessity and the terms for such a poetic project will nevertheless begin to be manifested here, in France. Such a return to the roots of song will be avowedly impossible if we remain prisoners of those metaphysical or stylistic rhetorics in which our own most useful precursors have gotten entangled—Mallarmé first and foremost. For we are, in our crisis-laden era (and whether at the crest of the wave or at its ebb), placed before the compelling dilemma concerning both the source and the ultimate goal of the poem, from its origin to its return into a *public* consciousness. And further, in this situation the poem must refuse to be pure exercise or pure game—whether of the laboratory or of the salon.

It's at this juncture that the projects of the Objectivists have assumed, for us, the most crucial importance.

The other night Carl Rakosi said some moving things to recall to us how much his friends and he himself had been engaged in the materiality of life—"the real world, the real real world," to echo his words—while regretting, it seemed to me, that such a sense of engagement had little by little deserted contemporary poetry in his country. And these were not empty sentiments, as we all know, because that sense of necessity had led him, much like Oppen, to a quarter century of silence. A painful irony, doubtless linked to the project itself, implies in fact that the reinscription of the poem into a collective history underlines once again the immense and insurmountable gap which has opened between the values (and forms) defended by the artist and those which are puffed and consumed by the majority of an artist's peers. In fact, how to reconcile the ambition and rigor of such a conception of the poem with the indifference greeting its appearance is a perpetual problem, just there, at the very site at which one wants to rediscover, that is, to reinvent, from the voice of the isolated figure, a plural song, a song engaging and questioning, with all possible means, any sense of shared community values.

The paradox is indeed that this work goes on despite both the general indifference to it and the solitude of each creator, isolated, morally vulnerable, and in need, all of this constituting our shared condition and our secret inheritance.

If it is nonetheless necessary (as I think it is) to pursue this difficult and silent struggle which is ours—*all of ours*—no matter our differences or our divergences, it is because we learned this respect for and this necessity *to connect with the real* from the Objectivists (along with Pound, Williams, and a few others). They grasped how to defend and to maintain the connection with the real at the same time that they gave us the formal means (a sense of measure, jump cut, line break) to get that sense of the real on the page in new terms. They brought to a close the first chapter of modern poetry in English.

However, the long reverberations of their practices and their careers have had many consequences for us—indeed, precisely those on which we are reflecting.

I want to underscore, in conclusion, the fact that the motives that have compelled us to study these foreign oeuvres are hardly "entomological," taxonomic, encyclopedic, or even pleasantly altruistic. It's not fascination with the exotic, nor partisanship either. Rather, such study has made possible—and continues to provoke—a recentering and revitalizing of French poetry, a poetry that has wandered in strangely abstract realms for rather a long time. Even if one can barely see it, some of us here have begun to meet this necessity to reclaim, concretely, the soul and the roots of song—the link *in the verse* between the language and its era, its materials, its dilemmas.

It is important to continue this struggle. Despite being rich and suggestive, the large-scale task of translation in which we have been active during the past ten or fifteen years is beginning to reach the end of its usefulness. First because translation opens unsoundable perspectives—even virtually infinite ones—and because it gives everyone epigones. But especially because it was never a process that was going to end here, with translation alone. And still less was it going to lead to the imitation of works, in a kind of obeisance to the logic of other languages, of other customs, of other places. Nonetheless, in part because of these openings, the future of the French poem seems rather more redeemed today than it was before. It remains for each of us to welcome the "blank pages / of the unwritten volume of the new," in all its diverse potential.[10] The work of tomorrow begins to inscribe, beyond literary history, the promise of a new song.

16

The Transformations of Objectivism: An Afterword

Charles Altieri

I wrote the essay called "The Objectivist Tradition" in 1978, a time when poets like Robert Creeley had convinced me that the objectivist tradition could provide substantial contemporary alternatives helping writers resist the scenic lyrics and narcissistic self-projections dominating mainstream contemporary American poetry. Literary history now shows that I was right only about there having to be fresh alternatives to that dominant writing. There has been very little significant new writing that we could accurately label "Objectivist." So it is tempting to claim that current work on Objectivism has to concern itself with why this became a road not taken. And then two basic questions have to be confronted: what major changes have occurred since the seventies in the ways poets develop alternatives to the romantic lyricism that is still preferred by the most prestigious American literary institutions, and what languages about values afforded by Objectivism might still prove significant because they establish powerful contrasts helping us characterize the strengths and limitations of this new writing?

As a precondition for undertaking such tasks, however, we have to qualify the claims just made about the contemporary status of objectivist writing. While objectivist styles per se are no longer generative, there are, I think, substantial continuities linking objectivist poetics to the theories inspiring some of the most highly regarded recent efforts to develop alternative poetic modes. Therefore, emboldened by the license afforded by the genre of the afterword, I will try to sketch briefly the case for considering the three objectivist styles I deal with as constituting one of the two basic imaginative frameworks out of which experimental contemporary writing has emerged—the other being the

New York school. Rather than ask how contemporaries repeat objectivist strategies, I will try to show how the original practices have inspired different but parallel alternatives to the indulgent lyricism that remains the common enemy. This project should help us appreciate the values driving these more radical experiments, and it can establish contrasts with those experiments helping us to speculate on alternative paths and so to locate pressures within or limitations of the roads that were taken since the seventies. And that should help us appreciate some of the basic challenges now facing younger writers as they wonder how to transform the prevailing transformations.

The dominant contemporary transformations of Objectivism can be mapped in quite broad strokes. Objectivist ideals of sincerity still drive work extending from Creeley and Duncan to Lyn Hejinian, Leslie Scalapino, and Nathaniel Mackey, while the Objectivist insistence on the poem as material object, most influentially summarized in Olson's claims about the intelligence manifest in the vitality of the poem's play among syllables, carries over into the ways Language writers like Charles Bernstein, Bruce Andrews, and Ron Silliman foreground the centrality of the medium. But the large picture is not very helpful unless we develop a more finely grained analysis of just how each of these objectivist principles takes new form.

Let us begin this analysis by returning to my first essay's characterization of the values at stake in Objectivist ideals of sincerity and in the corollary insistence that poems can take on the force of independent, impersonal objects living distinctive material lives within culture, since these two principles establish the basic lines of continuity. Objectivist sincerity can be understood as a commitment to resist two different kinds of closure—one rhetorical and the other formal. As a rhetorical principle, this sincerity demands pursuing what I call an eloquence based on the resistance to eloquence: lyric speech becomes personal and resonant to the degree that it manages actively to counter the temptations to lyrical self-staging basic to romantic ideals of the poet. Then, if we imagine formal closure as another kind of narcissism, we can appreciate how such rhetorical ideals have direct structural consequences. Objectivism could make "measure" so central a value because the contrast to interpretation thereby established also makes it clear why imposed formal structures are so severely limiting. Poetry as measure must have a sense of formal order emerge not from some imposed framework but from the specific ways that the poem brings into an internal balance the range of perceptions, desires, and contradictory impulses with which it has to deal.

One could trace this emphasis back to romantic organicism, but one would have to be careful to distinguish that genealogy from the far more thematic and allegorical versions of unity championed differently by humanists and by New

Critics. Objectivism's emphasis on measure as concrete balancing enabled it to insist that poems were not simply ideal objects. Objectification was a psychological discipline, a way of understanding how mind and emotions could take on a concentrative force whose life was inseparable from the internal dynamics provided by the various textures within the poem. Consequently the Objectivists could envision their poems' struggles against allegory as a force giving them the status of vital material objects literally manifesting organizations of mental energy that culture could make available to subsequent generations.

For a brief example of how these principles work in practice I turn to George Oppen's "Eclogue," the first poem of *The Materials* (1962):

> The men talking
> Near the room's center. They have said
> More than they had intended.
>
> Pinpointing in the uproar
> Of the living room
>
> An assault
> On the quiet continent.
>
> Beyond the window
> Flesh and rock and hunger
>
> Loose in the night sky
> Hardened into soil
>
> Tilting of itself to the sun once more, small
> Vegetative leaves
> And stems taking place
>
> Outside—O small ones,
> To be born! (*Collected Poems* 17)

Thematically and performatively this poem faces the challenge of attributing significant power to the smallness with which it concludes. So from the start Oppen establishes a fundamental opposition between the boasting talk that the poem describes and the specific process of measuring enacted by the efforts at concentration that it embodies. Confronting this arrogant male imagination, the poem has to define values available for a consciousness marginalized to an "outside," where flesh and rock are placed on the same ontological plane as a generalized and pervasive hunger.

Accomplishing that requires considerable abstraction. The poem frames the pressures imposed within the scene by also examining the very idea of scene as an enclosing and centering structural principle. The space "beyond the window" must provide an alternative to the talk, but directly thematizing that alternative runs the risk of turning beyondness into a version of the vague transcendental ontologizing that Hegel calls the "bad infinite." Oppen finesses this problem by substantially modifying the relations to size and scope that traditional idealization would be likely to propose. His focus seems far too narrow to satisfy the expansive speaker within the poem, yet it is only in this narrow concentration that there can emerge the full intricacy of what has to be borne in order for any new actual birth to take place for consciousness. Rather than assault the "quiet continent," the poem intensifies that quietness until it can realize all three registers invoked by the final "to be born"—as a future indicative, as an exclamation, and as a participial phrase indicating the pain inseparable from this kind of birth.

Perhaps I thematize too much. But only by doing that do we see how the specific material features of the poem give it a form of objective existence capable of resisting the kind of place near the center of the room sought by thematic criticism. Here the structural relations establish a material texture for the poem's concentrative energies that leads us beyond the spaces talk has to occupy. One set of formal relations is organized around the force of the unwobbling pivot provided by the fourth stanza, which at the very center establishes the poem's basic transition from the room to what lies beyond the window. We need not underplay the evocative qualities of this thematic transition in order to realize how for Oppen the material transitioning itself, the power of transfer that also holds the parts in place, is at least as important as the idea developed. But were Oppen to rely only on this structural principle, it would be tempting simply to align the poem's materiality to its thematizing energies. So he also establishes another set of overt relational principles establishing a very different material economy. The first and sixth stanzas are three-line units; the other stanzas have only two lines. Semantically this pattern allows the two stanzas presenting different modes of expansiveness to echo one another. But its more important effects take place simply as distributions of energies within the verbal object. The central stanza cannot quite dominate the structure, and hence establish an impermeable frame. Instead, the partial closure afforded by the sixth stanza seems to guarantee the final stanza its own place beyond the frames. Perhaps because it provides the fullest explicit reference to the psychological burdens that the poem has been dealing with, this last stanza also has to work the hardest not to transform the space of pain and potential of the "to be born" into any confident self-satisfaction.

When we turn to contemporary writing we find each of these governing principles given far more radical recastings, so that sincerity's resistance to closure requires a much greater degree of internal imbalance and indeterminacy, and the insistence the semantic force of material properties becomes a full-scale anti-representational constructivism. Where Oppen sets the talk inside against the small ones outside, Language writing focuses on the talk itself so that inside and outside become shifting features of how the poet rearranges speech textures. But simply to say this is to lump all Language writing together. I want to isolate two strands within that writing, each of which tends to emphasize one of these two basic principles, so that I can trace its specific transformations of Objectivist values. By stressing relatively radical transformations, we can then recognize what is at stake in more muted and perhaps more subtle extensions of Objectivism attempted by other poets.

Lyn Hejinian provides a superb example of the first of these strands because in her poems the ideal of sincerity comes to demand a self-consciousness so intricate and mobile that it forces poetry to a sense of discontinuities, gaps, and readerly participatory differences quite foreign to the original Objectivist project. Here, for example, is her analysis of the poet's responsibilities to avoid closure:

> What then is the fundamental necessity for openness? Or, rather, what is there in language itself that compels and implements the rejection of closure?
>
> I perceive the world as vast and overwhelming; each moment stands under an enormous vertical and horizontal pressure of information, potent with ambiguity, meaning-full, unfixed and certainly incomplete. What saves this from becoming a vast undifferentiated mass of data and situation is one's ability to make distinctions. . . . The open text is one which both acknowledges the vastness of the world and is formally differentiating.[1]

Poetry acknowledges that vastness by radicalizing its own sense of process, then utilizing all the elements of language to create the counter-pressure of the poet's power to develop and extend those distinctions. Form has to "make the primary chaos (i.e. raw material unorganized information, uncertainty, incompleteness, vastness) articulate without depriving it of its capacious vitality, its generative power" ("Rejection," *Poetics Journal* 137). So even the very notion of form has to be displaced from the realm of objects into that of psychological processes. Form, for Hejinian, is continually negotiated in the ways that readers construct tracks through the play of presences and shadows comprising the poem. Poetry can only be defined as a process of making and finding gaps and connections charged with the mind's awareness of a life not reducible to any other less intense, combinatory mode.

These abstractions should take on substance if we turn even briefly to her actual poetic work. This is the fifth poem in Hejinian's *The Cell:*

O observation!
What I see
And it's the little lyric
    of recessed sociability
The subconscious is close
There is an impersonal history
    of it
Any hour is my anxiety
    in space
The aesthetic room
Outdoors the clouds pour shape
    and stability into myopic interstices
These
Those—between seeing and believing
Individualism inspires an individual which
    disbelieves
The chamber on the rug
    which disbelief believes
The viscera
I can see it with
    shift and vicissitudes
The walls were thought at
    fault, interior
Loss of labor, isolation, love
But one finds it just
    as one's curious concept of
    experience exhibits oneself (*The Cell* 12)[2]

Sincerity here consists in an absolute refusal to let closure emerge in any way that might give the appearance of letting self-consciousness relax its scrutiny, or its delight in the mind's intricate shifts of attention. As Hejinian puts it elsewhere in *The Cell,* lyric self-consciousness presents "a person decomposing the unity / of the subjective mind by / dint of its own introspection" (157). Here the introspection begins by recognizing the temptation to high lyric apostrophe, so that the poem has to shift quickly to the unadorned subject of seeing and then back (motivated largely by internal rhyme) out to self-consciousness of the literary questions involved in the opening contrast. Where Oppen had been able to focus on a clear opposition between inside and outside, Hejinian finds herself driven to decompose observation into the competing elements of seeing and believing, which then become the principal dynamic psychological and cultural forces that the poem has continually to keep in balance.

This commitment to decomposition recasts the entire process of balancing as an activity that prevents postulating any overall structural resolution.[3] Probably no single reading can capture the range of leaps and suggestions that drive the poem, since for Hejinian observing observation opens into the various voices and echoes that allow belief to form within our visual scenarios. Even when she brings her poem to a kind of conclusion, the witty closing lines will not sit still for any one observing position. "Just" modulates beautifully between temporal, visual, and moral registers. And the aura of precision in the final lines ironically works against stability. Clearly the personal has to surrender dominance: it consists only in what becomes exhibited as and through one's concepts. But what does it mean for concepts to "exhibit oneself"? Does the self emerge simply as an effect of those concepts, or does the very notion of "oneself" depend on this promise and progress of exhibition, a final twist on seeing in order to believe? In other words, these final lines complete the introspective undoing of unity, but win from that undoing a strong sense of the many ways in which the personal is exhibited and distributed within this unpacking and regathering of how seeing and believing refuse to coincide.

Charles Bernstein's "Poem" presents a very different tone. Here the poet's genius consists in the ways it deflects the urgencies driving Hejinian's version of sincerity, while in the process guiding us to reexamine what is embodied in the spaces that poetic attention composes. I cite the opening and closing lines:

> here. Forget.
> There are simply tones
> cloudy, breezy
> birds & so on.
> Sit down with it.
> It's time now.
> There is no more natural sight.

Anyway transform everything
silence, trees
commitment, hope
. . . .

hang
a bulk of person
"ascending", "embodied". (*Shade* 3, 5)

I love this opening. The initial "here" invokes all the immediacy staged by the romantic lyric and recast in the Objectivist's stress on sincerity as a condition of writing. But all that actually flows from the uncapitalized "here" is an enigmatic imperative to forget. Where we might have expected some urgent state of attention to emerge, we get only the sly presence of a composing intelligence insisting on its right to replace the evocation of presence with imperatives organized from within the writing. Is this "forget" telling us what writers need from their audience as the precondition for their remaking the world, or does it remind readers of what they are in fact seeking when they try to identify with the "here" that the poem seductively holds out to them?

This dense opening line suffices to indicate to an audience that it has to operate here primarily in terms of a second-order self-consciousness concerned less with what words refer to than with the social and psychological functions they perform. Then we realize that the poem expands simply as a repository of elements and worries that go into the writing of poems, now all a part of some kind of meta-poem. But this meta-poem is not Mallarmé's comprehensive Book. Rather, it is an ironically self-emptying site, with each element partially deprived of any direct emotional reference by the virtual quotation marks (or citationality) that writing as reprocessed language cannot avoid. Yet as poetry is ironized, its "here" begins to take on a new strangeness as the one place where we can enjoy hearing those quotation marks and trying out the combinatorial possibilities that emerge when expressions lose the urgency of that other "here" where choices are constrained by circumstance. As the poem puts it, "The distance positively entrances," even when that "positively" makes us wonder if we do better to treat "entrances" as a verb made from a noun which makes the positive simply a matter of what can enter the poem.

Bernstein's way of materializing language by dematerializing its referents takes us a long way from Objectivist ideals of the material substance that art becomes. But the genealogy is not hard to locate—first in the general sense of having the poem stress the materiality of its building blocks, as in Oppen, and second in the disjunctive efforts to enhance the internal properties of language that one finds in Zukofsky. Indeed, one can almost hear late Zukofsky in the air that circulates through the disjunctive elements and in the strange sense of substance that stems from our learning to replace the order of reference by attention to qualities directly exhibited by the expressions. But what matters in those material qualities is very different in Bernstein.

Where Zukofsky stresses musicality, Bernstein stresses rhetoricity. For Bernstein these isolated phrases do not so much echo in any one harmonic register as lead out to the voices that might speak them and the ideologies that govern the practices where such speech has material effects. So with Bernstein what for Zukofsky had been a poetics devoted to meditative composure instantly becomes one forcing us to recognize the degree to which even our lyrical projections are caught up in the ideological structures betrayed by what we cannot quite forget in what we hear. Perhaps working with quotation marks provides a richer means of engaging the real than the modes of assertion relied upon by traditional lyrics, since in Bernstein we directly engage the social rather than attempting to forget it. And maybe poetry now is more useful if it no longer tries to purify the language of the tribe but teaches us to hear the various tribes whose values the demotic language simultaneously expresses and exposes.

Bernstein offers a more eloquent and precise summary of the values at stake here than I can. For him composition is no longer a matter of Olson's "breath" but of how the poet makes "the structures of meaning in language more tangible and in that way allowing for the maximum resonance of the medium" (*Content's Dream* 35).[4] What for Hejinian is a density of information becomes for Bernstein a plenitude of combinatorial possibilities no longer anchored in anything so situated as a person's breathing:

> By rotating sentences within a paragraph (a process analogous to jump cutting in film) according to principles generated by and unfolding in the work (rather than in accordance with representational construction patterns) a perceptual vividness is intensified for each sentence since the abruptness of the cuts induces a greater desire to savor the tangibility of each sentence. . . . The text operates at a level that not only provokes projections by each sentence but by the sequencing of the sentences suggests lines or paths for them to proceed along. At the same time, circumspection about the nature and meaning of the projections is called forth. The result is both a self-reflexiveness and an intensification of the items/conventions of the social world projected/suggested/provoked. A similar process can also take place within sentences and phrases and not

> only intersententially. Syntactic patterns are composed which allow for this combination of projection and reflection in the movement from word to word. (*Content's Dream* 36–37)

Clearly the transformations worked by poets like Hejinian and Bernstein give objectivist principles new theaters—at one pole by providing a fuller phenomenology of consciousness engaging itself simultaneously as subject and as object; at the other pole by linking objectivist materiality to a self-reflexiveness that Bernstein calls an "intensification of the items/conventions of the social world projected/suggested/provoked" by literary composition. But no advance is without its price, and hence without its internal gaps, tensions, and sense of limitations that provoke constant need for self-modification. By attending to the roles Objectivism played in providing ideals that proved fundamental to this new writing, I think we can be fairly precise in locating some of the more central gaps, tensions, and limitations that younger writers are likely to explore as they work to transform what is now their heritage of experimental possibilities.

An objectivist critique of this heritage would focus on statements like Hejinian's locating the demands on poetry in an "enormous vertical and horizontal pressure of information, potent with ambiguity, meaning-full, unfixed and certainly incomplete." For it is difficult to understand how any structure of information per se can on its own provide a sufficient basis for showing how poetry seeks out cultural pressures in order to demonstrate what powers it affords a given cultural moment. Conversely, the same line of critical thinking would find Bernstein's poetics even more disturbing because his resistance to representation of all kinds makes the question of pressure become very difficult even to formulate. Bernstein's emphasis is entirely on the writer's compositional freedom to elaborate "syntactic patterns . . . which allow for this combination of projection and reflection in the movement from word to word." This emphasis, I hasten to add, is sufficient to make him deeply concerned with how writing reaches out toward the world without succumbing to the scenic mode that representational ambitions now find it very difficult to avoid. And his work intricately develops a range of voices and ideological crossing reminding us how much of our values are reflected in our language uses. But Bernstein's poetics does not foreground the situation from which the experiments derive; nor does it dramatically stage poetry as an interpretation of specific situations or even of ways of interpreting situations. Where Hejinian constantly risks collapsing the agent and world into the immediacies of a mind attempting to negotiate the flow of information, Bernstein expands the composing agency to the point that there is very little room for working out how that agency might be tested by the world.

Probably the easiest way to measure what seems missing in Hejinian's version of pressure (and Bernstein's non-version) is to make comparisons with Wallace Stevens's vision of poetry establishing a counter-pressure to the pressure of reality. But for my purposes it is better to insist on the limitations of Stevens's position because these highlight what is distinctive about the Objectivist versions of lyric agency. Hence the contrast may help indicate what contemporary writing may be able to learn from that Objectivist work. Objectivist poets have to reject Stevens's schema as too abstract: his sense of pressure remains philosophical and therefore invites interpretations of the world rather than acts within it. Objectivism can preserve Stevens's overall model of poetry as counter-pressure, but only by adding a demand that this pressure manifests itself within the concrete situations that specific poems project as underlying the work of poetic composition. Only then will aesthetic choice be inseparable from existential choice, and poetry literally take on immediate ethical force.

For example, even though Oppen's "Eclogue" is quite abstract in its contrasts, the poem sets a clear emotional problem to which the writing must pose a partial answer—not as an interpretation or smug resolution, but as the testing of how an evocation of the small ones outside might provide a means of adjusting to the sense of emptiness produced by version of talk with which the poem begins. The sense of agency produced is by no means a conventional one, since we have to be able to imagine ourselves dwelling in an imaginative space where "flesh and rock and hunger" occupy the same plane, and where being born is inseparable from a stark sense of self as learning to bear its alienation. However Oppen's innovations remain grounded in projected situations that provide both test and reward for the powers of concentration and precise reserve that the poetry elaborates. Without its strong sense of the demands on it, Objectivist poetry's resistance to the lyric ego would not be nearly as compelling or as convincing as it often is.

I cannot argue that all poetry has to have the foregrounding of composing agency which Objectivism so richly separates from self-reflexive egocentricity. One cannot dismiss the forms of intensity and intelligence that poets like Hejinian and Bernstein produce. And one cannot ignore the ways that modern writing has taken on itself the challenge to decompose and reconfigure our conventional views of subjective agency. Yet it is important that we at least notice some of the consequences of what for contemporary experimental poetry has become a road less taken, if only because such noticing helps appreciate just how humanly rich the earlier Objectivist work is.

The most important concrete contrast between Objectivist poetry and the new poetries consists in the ways that writerly agency is handled. Objectivism insists on clear connections between the effort to establish a style and the exemplifying of existential commitments to pursue lives self-reflexively worth living. "Sincerity" combines an effort at clarity and measure inseparable from ethical ideals that entail standing by one's words and submitting that life to assessments of how well this taking of responsibility keeps social relations in dynamic balance. Because objectivist poetics resists the distance involved in traditional allegorical versions of interpretation, it forces writing to take on ethical obligations that cannot be satisfied by noble pronouncements offering opinions about the good. It wants nobility earned by the measures poetry composes.

This model of responsibility then generates two basic concrete differences from the values central to Hejinian and Bernstein—in how readers are engaged and in how poetry can establish possible political projections. Almost all contemporary experimental writing has insisted on its commitment to a poetics of participation that transforms the reader from passive witness to an authorial performance into an active co-creator of whatever meanings the texts can be said to possess. I find this view objectionable on many counts—not the least being the psychology of agency that underlies equating active readerly participation with generating individual readerly meanings. But here I want simply to point to how attributing this participation to readers follows necessarily from the ways that these poets envision the structures of demand from the world that poetry must engage. If the demand is to appreciate the density of emotional fields as the poem creates a texture of differentiations, or if it is to hear the range of embeddings that language carries, then there is no specific pressure on what we might call the quasi-ethical dimension of the authorial performance. Composing intelligence need not establish provisional exemplars for imaginative emotional economies, and texts are not quite tests of how certain attitudes might provide measures within typical situations. Correspondingly, readers need neither try identifications with the agency dramatized nor make demands that the performance afford terms by which we might explore the values and limitations of such identifications. The co-creative, participatory reader posited by Language writing may pay for that freedom by surrendering the opportunity to try out different selves and to explore specific emotional configurations that insist we surrender our petty individualisms, as well as our perhaps equally petty postmodern absolutizing of sheer mobility as our basic orientation toward the world.

Bernstein or Hejinian might reply that I am purchasing a sense of the dramatic force of poetry by pushing it back into representational straitjackets. And

I would have to admit that I certainly risk that. But the danger can be substantially modified if we distinguish among ways of bringing representational content to bear, or, better, among ways of being representative. At one pole there is conventional realism, definable by a demand structure calling for specific representational illusions that become representative by providing types; at the other pole there are various modernist experiments emphasizing the capacity of texts to foreground authorial actions by projecting their possible exemplary roles in the world. Objectivist writing managed to use the second orientation to justify a radical version of the first, wherein representation is not a matter of types but of quite specific denotations. For the emphasis remains on how the particular authorial performance finds a language capable of measure that does not impose the lyrical ego, and how that language can establish a means of taking responsibility for one's own political commitments.

There is no compelling reason that a contemporary poetry so directly take on specific political concerns. But Bernstein's, Andrews's, and Silliman's early theorizing made the capacity to engage politics a basic virtue of their poetics. Their concentration on language as medium seemed to afford fresh access to the political, since they were not bound to the constant process of just setting one set of ideological slogans against others. And, more important, they would no longer suffer from the contradictory position in which the most radical political poetry tended to be formally the most conservative, so that any change in ideas would still depend on overall models of person and language that simply repeated at our most fundamental levels of self-understanding the very notions that sustained the now dominant social powers. For the Language writers, change would only come if we could shift our focus from the content of political stances to the specific relations of signification shaping our very ideas of content. Language writing could be political because it disrupted the syntactic forms by which hegemony is maintained. Such work would lead us to recognize the ideological structures inherent in the languages we use in our practical lives; and it would exemplify modes of release and of pleasure that might emerge if we invested our imaginative lives in working against that hegemony.

These are not insignificant ideals. But, as I have argued elsewhere, it is questionable whether they deserve to be called political, since they do not directly affect any of the agendas we pursue in public life or the specific commitments we make to actual political communities.[5] There is, in other words, no concrete demand for specific responsibilities or for bearing witness to concrete political values. My argument need not be taken as a call for a renewed socialist poetry, although that might not be a bad thing. I simply want to recall the powerful sense of witness in Reznikoff, in Oppen, and, somewhat differently, in

Niedecker. If we compare these writerly attitudes to the politics of action writing, we have to be struck by how vague these contemporary stances have to be because the need they respond to is so pervasive and unfocused. The contemporaries want to base politics on resistance to the entire structure of representation. But politics may be a practice that only makes sense within some form of representation, some form of showing how positive claims might be both warranted and representative. Poetry may matter most for and as politics when it takes on the task of working out specific equations between responsiveness and responsibility as the ultimate measure of art.

Afterword to this Afterword

Both of the press readers for this book in manuscript expressed some dismay that this book ends with my insisting that we best honor Objectivism now by seeing it contrastively positioned in relation to some of the theoretical values governing contemporary experimental poetry. For them this was too oppositional and not sufficiently affirmative. I have to admit that they are at least partially right. But I will not alter the overall argument of my essay, so I cannot suddenly develop an entirely positive contemporary extension of objectivist values—a fact that says something more negative about contemporaries than about the Objectivists. I can, however, modify my argument in three ways.

First, I should be more explicitly positive about a legacy that has the power not only to generate the transformations we have been tracing but also to remind us of what these transformations fail to accomplish. And I should make it more clear that there is in contemporary experimental writing a substantial gulf between what the writing accomplishes and what the theory proposes. My quarrel is strictly with the poetics that these poets develop to justify their work. The work, represented here by Hejinian and Bernstein, continues to make transformations of the objectivist values of sincerity and expressive materiality vital for late-twentieth-century contexts.

My second modification cannot be simply a clarification but entails an apology. Because I wanted to trace how contemporaries directly engaged the two basic principles of Objectivist writing, I ignored the degree to which contemporary poetry has also been substantially affected by another, more general objectivist ideal—that of poetry as the force of witness based on careful and impersonal attention to socially expressive particulars. Once we do attend to this tradition of witnessing, we will recognize it influencing a wide range of contemporary experiments in using poetry as a sensitive instrument for historical documentation. Sincerity provides a direct social value for the work of warding off the lyrical ego, and objectivity establishes a demand that such poetry not merely refer to history but somehow capture its rhythms and tones and even the effect of its silences.

One could distinguish three quite different ways that objectivist principles give depth and resonance to the ideal of documentation. From Williams and Oppen it is not a large leap to Gary Snyder's intensely focused particulars at once situating the mind in the details of a life and dramatizing how the mind lives in its own self-objectification as part of that concrete world. Beverly Dahlen and Rachel Blau DuPlessis seem to me to share Snyder's ideal of rendering subjectivity in terms of those concrete modes of attention defining its care for particulars, but their focus is more on the mobility and complexity of that subject, as if placement in poetry were primarily a matter of coming to accept one's own subjective energies as dynamic objects within experience. And finally, what Reznikoff, Oppen, and Rakosi do as documenters of their contemporary lives, Susan Howe and Rosmarie Waldrop seek from dense historical research. Emerging out of a contemporary America for the most part entirely alienating to that moral imagination, Howe and Waldrop turn their documentary attention to historical settings where we might at least begin to understand the forces shaping us, and promising alternative fields of imaginative energy.

The last modification of my essay is more difficult because it involves evaluative questions about how we can best use aspects of our literary heritage. For there is now some quite interesting work by young poets that in part directly invokes Objectivist discipline and resources without pursuing the transformations that I have been tracking. Perhaps these poets make such direct connections as a means of engaging what are now emerging as limitations in the radical poetics developed by Bernstein, Hejinian, and their peers. Whatever the cause, the best poems in this vein deserve celebrating, but for me not without a somewhat nostalgic modernist resistance to the nostalgia that seems to pervade any effort to recuperate a literary mode without transforming it. I am not at all sure that my criticism is warranted, since part of the objectivist spirit is the call for creations that become timeless through the particularity of their perceptions and structure of internal relations. Yet work that is too timeless or which too much bears marks of repeating other fantasies of timelessness may just not be contemporary enough. So now insistent opposition has to yield to uneasy confusion.

To spell out the positive possibilities of this return, and hence to make the competing pulls compelling, I need a very fine contemporary poem in the objectivist mode. Jean Day's *The Literal World* provides the necessary example:

> The quiet quieted down more quietly
> and the shade was overcast more darkly

in the shadow of her obedience
to the habitual devices of instrumentation
human noise displays. We ticked off the names
of the lover: the flat, the free, and the brave
but these could not inhibit
her pleasant habitation of intellectual time
where the soul continues like a faucet
or ambles so the floorboards shake
and plants fall over backward
in a time of maximum coincidence
the fog rolls in rolls over and the mind
is bright with verses. (47)

This is by no means the only style that Day's volume explores.[6] And the turn to Objectivism brings into play two quite different strands of that orientation. While the poem as a whole takes on the task of producing an intense physicality that makes the mind seem inseparable from an affective embodiment in sensations, its concluding lines also bring into play echoes of Pound's interest in thin, clear, distinct sounds which for him echo Greek lyric modes.

The insistence on physicality is brilliantly rendered in Day's opening lines. The poem manages simultaneously to avoid any sense of description, of being merely a representation, and to evoke a dense sense of being placed within concrete experience. And, like the best Objectivist work, the resulting elemental consciousness itself begins to take on a double valence. It remains rooted in detail, but it also works so elementally that the details take on a strange literalness within the mind, as if the speaker's own psychic states could take on a material presence analogous to that of things. One powerful way of gaining that effect is to have the opening of the poem drenched in repetition, as if that were the condition of entering a fully material setting. Yet all the repetition soon also provides an anchor for a contrasting process where the poem's syntax gorgeously opens up to become an emblem for what the poem calls "a time of maximum coincidence."

This time of coincidence requires a close attention to space, since coincidence brings physical aspects of the scene into close conjunction. And indeed the fog that "rolls in rolls over" the scene provides the poem's basic figure for absorbing this sense of time within a feel for spatial relations. More important, this emblem for conjunction within the scene prepares the way for a more capacious emblematic sense that the entire poem manages literally to become in itself testimony to the overall state it refers to. Noise modulates into a lyrical play that literally instantiates the "pleasant habitation of intellectual time." For at one pole latinate multisyllabic words make habitation a strangely verbal affair; at the other the very pleasures that wording brings become themselves conditions releasing within habitation an enticing playfulness.

The poem begins in darkness and ends in brightness. Such contrasts are conventional, and as such usually banal. But Day does not proceed by elaborating the contrasts. Instead we become aware of them only with the apparently sudden emerging of the mind as "bright with verses" not because it somehow conquers the darkness but because it manages to participate fully in the time that opens out of the noises of habitation. Poetic syntax then becomes the actual fundamental force of that mind. It allows the mind to be "bright" with verses almost as if it were with child—not the lonely originator of mysterious song but the simple bearer of verses that become extensions of the forms of exhilarated freedom afforded by this relation to time and to space.

Perhaps we can read Day's return to Objectivism in the same spirit. There need be no opposition between past and present because the orientation called for does not work on the level of such oppositions. Here the poem lives in the qualities of participation it brings to the scene, or better, to the scenes provided on one hand by contemporary life, on the other by literary history. Inhabiting both so fully ought certainly to suffice, and teach us to be content with such sufficiency. And yet even "the mind . . . bright with verses" may not be content.

Notes

Introduction

1. With thanks to Claude Royet-Journoud and Simon Smith for providing this text.

2. Zukofsky's comment, in a question-and-answer session in 1969 at the American Embassy in London, may be a deliberate echo of Oppen (with a shift from "we" to "I"): "When I was a kid I started the Objectivist movement in poetry. There were a few poets who felt sympathetic towards each other and Harriet Monroe at the time insisted, we'd better have a title for it, call it something. I said, I don't want to. She insisted; so, I said, alright, if I can define it in an essay, and I used two words, *sincerity* and *objectification,* and I was sorry immediately. But it's gone down into the history books; they forgot the founder, thank heaven, and kept the terms, and, of course, I said *objectivist,* and they said *objectivism* and that makes all the difference" (*Prepositions* 170–71).

3. While the use or non-use of the quotation marks by both poet and critic might call for particular attentiveness and critical analysis, we shall now drop them as the poetics to which they refer has become larger than the conjunction or original moment articulated by Zukofsky.

4. All the Objectivists tried to enact a concept of poetry as critical knowledge, cognition, and ethics, something honored, not incidentally, in Lyn Hejinian's meditations on Oppen's work in "Reason," in her collected essays, *The Language of Inquiry.*

5. For discussion of the relations between Zukofsky and Williams during this period, see Quartermain, *Disjunctive Poetics* chapter 5.

6. In an illuminating chapter on Zukofsky as a Jewish poet, Stephen Fredman identifies the choice with which *Menorah Journal* was once confronted (1930) between the age-mates Zukofsky and Lionel Trilling as upcoming young Jewish intellectuals; to Zukofsky's disgruntlement, they chose Trilling (Fredman, *Between*).

7. The fact that the completion of the poems in 1931 predates the essay is not a

problem in this case. Oppen's *Selected Letters* (82) state clearly that the ideas in Zukofsky's essays were talked out between the two young men; Oppen remarks that the essays did not have anything new for him because the ideas had circulated between the poets in conversation.

8. The letter probably dates from her surrealist period; Ozenfant's book was published in 1931. The letter is signed "Lorine Hartwig"; this dates it between 1928, when she married Frank Hartwig, and 1942, when they divorced. Mentions of Zukofsky, with whom she corresponded from 1931 and whom she met in late 1933, indicate a time in the mid- to late 1930s, because the ideas the two were discussing suggest a maturing and mutually intense intellectual relationship, rather than its early stages. The letter also mentions a loan by Hoard to Niedecker of materials by Virginia Woolf. This letter is among the materials Gail Roub possesses relating to Niedecker.

9. Nuances of Zukofsky's relation to Jewish culture are illuminated in a chapter, alluded to above ("Sincerity and Objectivism: The Jewish Contexts of an American Poetic Movement"), in Fredman's *Between*. In addition, Zukofsky's "The" is set in the context of semiticized discourses in DuPlessis, *Entitled New*.

10. As Irving Howe suggests, this poetry was fundamentally the product of "a wonderful interregnum in the life of the Jews: the period of *Yiddishkayt*, in which the opposing impulses of faith and skepticism stand poised, locked in opposition, yet sharing a community of culture" (Howe and Greenberg 12). A number of the translations in *A Treasury of Yiddish Poetry*, it is worth noting, are by Marie Syrkin, Reznikoff's wife. In this rich tension between assimilation/secularization and maintenance of Jewish particularism emerge several generations of Yiddish poetry and such practitioners as Yehoash [Solomon Bloomgarden] (1872–1927) and Abraham Reisen (1876–1953) in a first generation, Mani Leib (1883–1953) and Moishe Leib Halpern (1886–1932) in a second generation (Die Yunge), and Jacob Glatshteyn (1896–1971) and others of a third generation (the In Zich poets).

11. "Testimony" occurs in two interesting usages in Exodus (King James version) in which the Covenant itself is said to be a "testimony" and God instructs: "And thou shalt put into the ark the testimony which I shall give thee" (Exodus 25:16). At a parallel place of early instruction, the Ark of the Covenant itself (containing the Torah scrolls, elegantly wrapped, a holy of holies in Judaism) is called "the Testimony" and a piece of manna is deposited in it (Exodus 16:34) as a permanent witness of God's intervention in human time.

Chapter 2

1. In putting quotation marks around this word, Zukofsky underscores the arbitrary, "as if" character of the label—as he titled his long poem, not *A*, but "*A*". And Zukofsky also deliberately chose the adjectival form, "Objectivists," for he did not want to found an "ism." Subsequent critical practice has varied. Michael Heller, in the only book to date on this group of poets, scrupulously avoids any reference to "Objectivism," but he omits the quotation marks around "Objectivist," while Jenny Penberthy uses both the adjectival and the nominal forms, without quotation marks. While it might be worth following Zukofsky's practice, in part to distinguish the poetic filiations here un-

der discussion from Ayn Rand's philosophic Objectivism, for this volume I have allowed the editors to remove the quotation marks.

2. But the generational boundaries tend to blur. Williams sometimes saw himself not as a forerunner of the Objectivists but as a member of the group; and indeed, Zukofsky included a Williams poem in the special issue of *Poetry.* In his later years, furthermore, Zukofsky sometimes suggested that his own poetic practice had influenced Pound and Williams, rather than vice versa.

3. In his later years, Zukofsky tried to distance himself from this early influence too. In preparing his collected critical essays, *Prepositions,* he discarded the extended discussion of Reznikoff's poetry that forms the central thread of the "Sincerity and Objectification" essay, as printed in the February 1931 *Poetry.* Zukofsky saved only the general theoretic statements from this essay, collaging them together to form the first part of "An Objective," the second essay in *Prepositions.*

4. Rexroth got more pages in *An "Objectivists" Anthology* than any other single poet; but he vigorously disavowed the label, and the discursive poetics that he adopted in the late 1930s diverges sharply from the practice of the other Objectivist poets.

5. In this respect I follow most recent critical practice, while casting a relatively wide net. In the notable 1969 issue of *Contemporary Literature* devoted to the Objectivist poets, L. S. Dembo groups Reznikoff, Zukofsky, Oppen, and Rakosi under this rubric—thus ignoring Niedecker, although at the time she was living not far from Madison, Wisconsin, home base of that journal. In *Conviction's Net of Branches,* the only book on the Objectivist poets to date, Michael Heller focuses on Reznikoff, Zukofsky, Oppen, Rakosi, and Niedecker. In his preface, Heller mentions Bunting as another poet whose work is grounded on objectivist principles. He has excluded Bunting, he says, only because "my subject here is American poetry" (xii).

6. In *Prepositions* 12, Zukofsky reprints this definition, but without the reference to "Military use."

7. The former imagists whom Zukofsky admired all eventually criticized this movement as tending toward subjectivism. By 1916, for example, Pound was dismissing F. S. Flint and John Gould Fletcher, two erstwhile imagists, as essentially impressionists. And for Williams, imagism lacked any structural necessity, any external resistance to the mind's self-aggrandizing gestures. As for Zukofsky, it is significant that Amy Lowell and Carl Sandburg are notably absent from his list of forebears, as is H.D., whose poetry of the 1920s veered decisively toward a visionary idealism.

8. This objection may be why Zukofsky excluded the work of Tyler and Ford from the collection of poems that forms the body of the special issue, exiling them instead to the appended symposium.

9. The poem was probably written in the late 1940s or 1950s. However, Robert Bertholf's editorial procedures in *From This Condensery* make it very difficult to date Niedecker's work.

10. I am here invoking Heidegger, who deeply affected Oppen's thinking. For Heidegger, metaphysical thought begins the moment we ask, "Why is there anything at all, rather than nothing?" (*Metaphysics* 1).

11. Indeed, most of them were only incidentally interested in philosophical questions as such. In his note to Tyler and Ford, Zukofsky says that the question of whether

the object exists "in the mind or *per se* is perhaps not a problem for poets to worry about" (in *Poetry* 37.5 [February 1931]: 288). Some decades later, however, Zukofsky would devote a massive volume, *Bottom: On Shakespeare,* to the destruction of epistemology.

12. Within the Communist Party, Lenin's confidence in the power of the mind to grasp objective reality would rigidify into the dogma that the "party line" was scientifically correct, so that anyone who diverged from this line was not only mistaken but unwilling or unable to perceive reality—thus either willfully perverse or insane.

13. During the last few decades, two quite distinct Pounds have emerged within the critical literature. On the one hand, we have the poet whom Michael North, for example, sees as dedicated to the erection of poetic monuments, and as the "fascist" coeval of the "nationalist" Yeats and the "conservative" Eliot—all in various ways cultural reactionaries. On the other hand we have the "indeterminate" Pound of Marjorie Perloff, heir of Rimbaud and progenitor of John Cage (*Poetics of Indeterminacy*). It is of course possible that Pound was both a political reactionary and a poetic revolutionary. The question is which of these two Pounds we are principally interested in—and how we choose to use "our" Pound. Zukofsky's Pound is an indeterminate Pound, an innovator opening up the possibility of a new processual poetics. Indeed, Zukofsky may fairly be credited with discovering (the skeptic may say "inventing") this "other" Pound, in his 1929 essay on the elder poet's work ("Ezra Pound" in *Prepositions*).

14. The correspondence between Pound and Zukofsky shows that the two enjoyed a particularly close relationship, but many of the other Objectivists were also touched by the influence of the older poet. Bunting lived for a time with Pound in Rapallo, and throughout his life he acknowledged Pound as his principal poetic master. And Pound himself acknowledged a special relationship to Zukofsky and Bunting by dedicating his *Guide to Kulchur* to them. Oppen too visited Pound in Rapallo, and Pound wrote a warmly affirmative introduction to Oppen's first book. Reznikoff declared that reading Pound's imagist principles in *Poetry* galvanized him into a new poetic idiom and continued to inform his poetic practice throughout his life. Rakosi, on the other hand, seems relatively untouched by Pound's influence. Instead his earlier poetry often echoes Eliot and Stevens, and after 1930 Williams becomes an important influence. For Niedecker, Marianne Moore is clearly an early and persistent influence, along with Zukofsky himself. But Pound also affects her work, primarily through Zukofsky.

15. I hope this essay will suggest some reasons why these Jewish poets were drawn to Pound, despite his anti-Semitism. But clearly this affiliation deserves fuller study.

16. As my comments here may suggest, I read Derridian deconstruction as a "Jewish" critique of a "Christian" logocentrism.

17. In recent years other stigmatized groups have sought to rename themselves in proudly affirmative terms, but the Jews have been doing so for at least two millennia.

18. Unfortunately, Pound often forgot this hard truth, dreaming that he himself could, by the sheer power of his ego, return the poet to his proper role as adviser of the prince—thus his delusions concerning Mussolini. That fantasy led finally toward madness. But this delusion does not mean that Pound was wrong about what was happening in commercial publishing. In the special issue of *Poetry,* Zukofsky echoes with approval

Pound's insistence that "The small magazines are to be praised for standing on their own against the business of the publishing racket" (271).

19. This kind of poetry lingered on, even among writers acknowledged as serious poets, into the 1920s and 1930s. Edna St. Vincent Millay, for example, was one of the two or three most admired and most popular American poets of these decades:

O world, I cannot hold thee close enough!
Thy winds, thy wide gray skies!
Thy mists, that roll and rise!
Thy woods, this autumn day, that ache and sag
And all but cry with color! That gaunt crag
To crush! To list the lean of that black bluff!
World, world, I cannot get thee close enough! (Monroe and Corbin Henderson 382)

Chapter 3

1. For important studies that contribute to this aspect of the Objectivist movement, see Altieri, "Objectivist Tradition"; Hatlen, "Zukofsky"; Heller, *Conviction's Net;* and Perloff, "Barbed-Wire."

2. For a clear summary of the modernist assumptions concerning the function of language in relation to the immediacy of things, see Hatlen's discussion of what he calls the "late Imagist" "poetics of presence," in "Zukofsky."

3. Zukofsky makes a similar point in Dembo and Podrom (223) when he discusses how the "clear physical eye" sees, suggesting that the way to prevent "abstraction" from becoming whole-making generalization is to insist, in Zukofsky's own words, that "the abstract idea is particular, too."

4. In his response to a question concerning Francis Ponge and what Sartre calls the "crisis of language," Zukofsky uses the "assassin" metaphor in a similar way when he points out that "one of the nice statements Ponge makes is that the poet who falsifies the object is an assassin; instead of calling the object what it is, this kind of poet develops grand metaphors and all the 'baroque' curlicues" (Dembo and Podrom 231).

5. See Macann 40. In his discussion of symbolist and Objectivist poetics in terms of the poet's feeling in relation to the object, Rakosi makes the similar argument, pointing out that the symbolist adopts what Dembo calls an "*a priori*" approach, that is, "An object was simply an occasion for him to project this feeling," while the Objectivist, an "*a posteriori*" one: "He let his feelings depend upon the object and was faithful to the object." See Dembo and Pondrom 201.

6. *Against Epistemology,* as Adorno claims, is not intended to be a thorough, systematic, and complete analysis of Husserl's philosophical thinking. Aiming across Husserl's work, Adorno concentrates, instead, on "the possibility and truth of epistemology in principle," for which "Husserl's philosophy is the occasion and not the point of this book" (1). Especially pertinent to Rakosi's Objectivist poetics are Adorno's discussions and critique of what might be called an anthropomorphic phenomenology.

7. Adorno uses this metaphor in his critique of the Husserlian concept of "atti-

tude." As the translator's footnote points out, the word "attitude" also means, as a verb in German, "to focus," which Husserl, Adorno believes, may have borrowed from the language of photography (*Against Epistemology* 196). In contrast to the "natural attitude," which is the "unreflective acceptance of the 'general thesis of the world' in its spatio-temporality" (195), Husserl's "phenomenologically reduced attitude," as Christopher Macann summarizes, refers to a "positional consciousness [that] becomes an explicitly intentional consciousness, that is, an implicitly or explicitly reflective consciousness 'of.' In other words, it is not the object itself so much as the intentional relation to the object which now becomes the focus of attention" (33).

8. The recent philosophical reflections and critique of Western culture share very much the same rhetoric. In his analysis of the form of knowledge acquisition in the seventeenth century, Michel Serres, for instance, makes a similar argument, though from a different perspective, pointing out that "knowledge is a hunt. To know is to put to death" (28).

9. The chronological order of the poems gathered in *The Collected Poems of Carl Rakosi* is a subject beyond the scope of this paper. Rakosi himself makes it clear, in his interview with Evans and Kleinzahler, that he has "arranged them all, not according to when they were written but what their sense and climate are" (240). And this "sense and climate" seems to have been crystallized—not without irony, of course—in the section of "Adventures of the Head," in a probe into the subject-object relationship, thus granting a justification for the choice of poems under discussion in this study.

10. Rakosi's implied argument is shared by other critics. Though Jeffrey Peterson's reading of "The Romantic Eye" emphasizes the tension between two "authoritative modes of vision," romantic and scientific, which "are undercut at the expense of one another," he also points out that "the scientific and the romantic are copresent, reciprocal in magnified seeing" (163). Similarly, in *The Cosmic Web* Katherine Hayles asserts that "These twentieth-century epistemological assumptions have more in common with Romanticism. . . . Modern science is not renouncing Romanticism, only changing its emphases" (18).

11. Rakosi often uses the term "subject" to mean "topic"; in my use it refers to the speaking subject.

12. Rakosi's training in psychology and his longtime working experience as a social worker would be an important topic yet to be studied. For a partial treatment of this issue, see Peterson.

13. See also Hatlen, "Carl Rakosi," in which he points out that in Rakosi there is this "constant, unresolved struggle between Ego and Object, With the Ego infusing meaning into the Object, and with the Object serving as a necessary limit-point to the pretensions of the Ego" (139).

14. Ovid, *Metamorphoses* 106:

On all sides, through the fields, along the highways,
He saw the forms of men and beasts, made stone
By one look at Medusa's face. He also
Had seen that face, but only in reflection
From the bronze shield his left hand bore.

15. I am grateful to Peter Quartermain and Rachel Blau DuPlessis for suggesting this connection.

16. The term "demilitarize" is John Cage's. In his "Preface" to "Writing for the Second Time through *Finnegans Wake*," Cage writes, "Due to N. O. Brown's remark that syntax is the arrangement of the army, and Thoreau's that when he heard a sentence he heard feet marching, I became devoted to nonsyntactical 'demilitarized' language" (*Empty Words* 133). With its denotations, connotations, as well as its corresponding image, this term, as such, is consistent with those of the Medusa's glance as a weapon used to conquer the object. See also "Foreword," *M* x.

17. See Matthew 7:3–5 and Luke 6:41–42.

18. Adorno, *Minima Moralia* 50, and the translator's footnote.

Chapter 4

1. As one measure of the degree to which both Oppen's work and that of the Objectivists generally has been overlooked, I would note its absence (until very recently) from poetry anthologies, textbook anthologies of American literature, and historical overviews of American poetry. Until 1994, Oppen appeared in not a single one of the major classroom anthologies of American literature; then seven of his poems were published in the fourth edition of the *Norton Anthology of American Literature.* (Rachel Blau DuPlessis notes that six Oppen poems were to be included in the first *Norton Anthology of Modern Poetry* [1973], but finally they were left out. Meanwhile Zukofsky, included in this first edition, was dropped from the second [Oppen, *Selected Letters* 364 n. 9]). The *Columbia History of American Poetry* (1993) contains a few pages on Oppen himself but nothing on the Objectivists as a group. The *Columbia Literary History of the United States* (1988) contains four sentences on the Objectivists in its 1,199 pages of text. Hyatt Waggoner's *American Poets: From the Puritans to the Present* (1984), promoted on its dust jacket as "the most comprehensive and acute survey available of the course of American poetry," mentions neither the group nor any individuals associated with it. The list could go on.

2. This erasure extends to Margaret Dickie's *On the Modernist Long Poem.* Peter Baker, who does discuss Zukofsky, mentions Oppen in one footnote, though not as a writer of serial poems (*Obdurate Brilliance*).

3. For a contrary opinion on Oppen's tone and rhetorical stance, see Jonathan Galassi, who often finds Oppen "openly, even severely didactic" (167), a poet-teacher who sees it as his role to speak for others, not just for himself. Oppen himself, however, claims that he tries to avoid didacticism, even at those points where it might be expected: "Very few of those poems that touch on the social-political ethic exhort" (Oppen and Oppen, "Conversation" 46). In "Of Being Numerous" he writes, "I don't mean that much can be explained" (*Collected Poems* 162)—hardly the stance of a didact. To place Oppen's tone, which he calls "impoverished" (213), accurately, one might contrast it with that of those two arch-didacts Pound and Olson.

Noting that to "include history" for Oppen is more than a matter of breadth and scale, Henry Weinfield summarizes the ambiguous relationship that "Of Being Numerous" has to the modernist long poem tradition: "'Of Being Numerous' . . . is a poem that 'includes history' with greater depth than any we have had in recent years. Thus, although it makes no such claims for itself but even questions the validity of such a claim for poetry in the present, it carries the burden of the modernist version of epic, serving as both a continuation and a corrective to that tradition" (379).

4. In questioning the usefulness of Miller's and Gardner's work for reading Oppen, I do not intend to deny Whitman's presence in Oppen's poetry. One could speculate that Whitman, inventor of the American serial poem and the first poet to write a language of New York, provided Oppen with one powerful precedent (among others) in American poetry for exploring the relationship between individual and society. On this point, "Myself I Sing" is an important transitional poem between Oppen's early work (especially "Party on Shipboard," which Oppen quotes in "Myself I Sing") and "Of Being Numerous." The title's allusion suggests that Oppen's concerns in the poem will recapitulate Whitman's in his famous lines: "One's-self I sing, a simple separate person, / Yet utter the word Democratic, the word En-Masse" (165). Oppen begins, however, by using his characteristic literalism to ironize the Whitmanesque stance: "Me! he says, hand on his chest. / Actually, his shirt" (*Collected Poems* 35). Despite Oppen's interest in Whitman, then, he does not model the style, voice, setting, scope, or vision of his own serial poems on *Leaves of Grass.* In fact, Bernard Waldrop, reviewing *The Materials,* contrasts the two poets, noting how in Oppen one finds "no rambling catalogs of things, no ranting that he is part of the whole universe" (51). George Monteiro reads "Night Scene" (*Collected Poems* 118), which depicts a drunk about to attempt suicide by jumping into the Hudson River, as offering "wry commentary on romantic notions such as that of Walt Whitman's 'man in the open air'" (227).

5. I read the tone of this letter rather differently from Rachel Blau DuPlessis, for whom "the end of the letter seems to claim that Oppen is another kind of confessional poet" (Oppen, *Selected Letters* 414 n. 14).

6. For the modernist period especially, this canon remains largely predictable and, for some critics, actually constitutive of modernism; referring to *The Waste Land, The Bridge, Paterson,* and *The Cantos,* Margaret Dickie argues that "together, the compositions of these poems compose the history of Modernism" (17). The discussions that I have cited so far also remain overwhelmingly centered on male writers, with only minor exceptions: Conte's half-chapter on Niedecker, Rosenthal and Gall's chapters on Dickinson and on Plath and Sexton, and their brief mentions of Riding, Rukeyser, Rich, and H.D. (though not of *Trilogy* or *Helen in Egypt*). In *Obdurate Brilliance,* Peter Baker devotes a half-chapter to Stein and a few pages to Bernadette Mayer. Otherwise, critical work on the long poem and on serial poems has largely excluded women's writing in these forms.

While it focuses on poems written by women since 1970, Lynn Keller's *Forms of Expansion: Recent Women's Long Poems* provides a valuable corrective to the largely phallocentric history of criticism and theorizing on the long poem. Keller discusses work by Sharon Doubiago, Judy Grahn, Brenda Marie Osbey, Rita Dove, Marilyn Hacker, Susan Howe, Beverly Dahlen, and Rachel Blau DuPlessis. For other discussions of the long poem that address the relationship between gender and genre, see Susan Stanford Friedman's essays "Craving Stories," "Gender and Genre Anxiety," and "When a 'Long' Poem Is a 'Big' Poem," and Keller, "The Twentieth-Century Long Poem."

7. Ron Silliman's distinction between what he calls the serial poem as "formally contained" and the series as "potentially infinite" parallels Conte's between the finite and infinite series. For Silliman, the difference is partly one of imagined scale (either potential or actual), a difference between the poem conceived "as a book or tale" and the poem "taken as a lifework" ("Sentences" 15–16). Conte reiterates the argument of *Unending Design* in compressed form in his 1992 essay "Seriality and the Contemporary Long Poem."

8. Unlike Olson's and Williams's, Oppen's sense of place is rarely celebratory. He investigates "the meaning / Of being numerous" (*Collected Poems* 151) in the face of what he describes to Charles Amirkhanian and David Gitin as "the increasing meaninglessness or uselessness of New York City" and its loss of "even the historical meaning that it had" ("Conversation" 21). In this same interview Oppen describes San Francisco, his home in his later years and the setting for another serial poem, "Some San Francisco Poems," as "much too clever a city and a very strange city," generating "a sense of isolation" from its location on "the bare edge of the continent and simple space beyond" (22). Oppen's use of place in his poetry, then, is generally willed. As Constance Hunting puts it, "Oppen's eye adjusts itself to geography not automatically but through willed effort. He makes the geography; it does not make him" (54).

9. Ezra Pound considered the feasibility of the imagist long poem as early as 1916 in this note from *Gaudier-Brzeska:* "I am often asked whether there can be a long imagiste or vorticist poem. The Japanese, who evolved the hokku, evolved also the Noh plays. In the best 'Noh' the whole play may consist of one image. I mean it is gathered about one image. Its unity consists in one image, enforced by movement and music. *I see nothing against a long vorticist poem*" (94; emphasis added).

10. As he says in his working papers, Oppen sees syntax as a means to separate as much as to connect words. It involves, for him, "a careful packing of a poem . . . to avoid destroying a word by its relationships" ("Adequate Vision" 29); "each WORD MUST BECOME SOLITARY" (27). One virtue of "little" words, Oppen says to Kevin Power, is that "they remain attached to the object" and "can be separated from each other" (Oppen and Oppen, "Conversation" 47). Similarly, he sees one function of the poetic line "as separating the connections of the progression of thought" (Dembo and Pondrom 180). Many critics note in passing the disjunctions that result from this view of syntax and the line; Perloff ("Shape"), Berry, and Oderman offer useful and sustained discussions of the issue.

11. This is Oppen's explication of the image in a letter to June Oppen Degnan, 27 September 1963: "Ouroboros of course is . . . the closed universe, the closed self" (223).

12. Compare Pound's description of *The Waste Land,* in a 24 December 1921 letter to Eliot, as "the longest poem in the Englisch langwidge" (quoted in Cox and Hinchcliffe 22).

13. Two particularly helpful articles discuss this feature of Oppen's work in more detail than I am able to here: see DuPlessis, "George Oppen," and Hatlen, "Opening Up the Text." Of the "five linguistic processes"—"interrogation, negation, repetition, interruption, and dialogue" (265)—that Hatlen uses to describe the movement of "Of Being Numerous," negation resembles most closely what I have called reversal and contradiction.

14. In the final selection of his *Collected Poems,* Oppen seems to see the simultaneous proximity and distance between people in the world as an organizational model for his poetry: "the people standing at a little distance / from each other, or in small groups // would be the poem." That he had "Of Being Numerous" specifically in mind is suggested by the fact that he quotes a prominent phrase from the earlier poem, "bright light of shipwreck" (255).

15. Any claim for a connection specifically between *Of Being Numerous* (1968) and *Pieces* would be untenable because Creeley wrote most of *Pieces* between November 1967 and August 1968. At the same time, he would have had access to *This In Which* (1965), containing "A Narrative" and "A Language of New York," and presumably to *Discrete Series.* And after the publication of *Of Being Numerous,* he continued his own work in serial form beyond *Pieces* into *A Daybook* and, more ambiguously since they are printed as separate poems, *Thirty Things.*

16. Robert Grenier, editor of Creeley's *Selected Poems* for Scribner's and one of the early practitioners and theorists of what came to be called Language writing, connects his work *Sentences* to *Pieces* specifically on the basis of this attention to "writing," to the materials of language. He describes his work as that of a "generation speaking back (different results from similar premises—a toast, as much of my work to date might be—you'd think there were compatriots and tradition) and demonstrating further workings deriving from precedents in Stein and Zukofsky, particularly correlating to that apparently largely neglected and misunderstood second period of Creeley's development, the stuff in *Pieces,* . . . where the primary interest is language process/energy released by an intensity of perception given closeup to the elements of language (letters, syllables, words) in the process of their self-formation" (422). Such a reading of *Pieces* as anticipating certain preoccupations of Language writing is reinforced by numerous comments from Creeley himself: "Words are the material of writing," for instance, or "writing is primarily the experience of language" (*Tales* 59, 103).

17. Oppen seems, however, to have felt less commitment to this common processual poetics than Creeley, remarking in a 1975 interview that he had confidence "neither in the language nor in the accident of my own voice like Creeley" ("Interview" 15).

18. Commentary on the relations between prosody and presence in Objectivist writing is characterized mainly by its multiple contradictions. Eleanor Berry and Marjorie Perloff agree on associating certain prosodic features with a prosody of presence. They disagree on where these features appear, which explains why Berry's Oppen sounds like Perloff's Williams. (Berry also makes more distinctions than Perloff between Oppen's 1960s writing and his early and late work.) Berry associates the frequent syntactic regularity and coincidence of line with syntactic unit in Oppen's 1960s work with his celebration of "a world of solidities and edges," a poetics of naming and praising (310, 315); for Perloff, "the presence of the moment is made manifest" in Williams through similar prosodic means ("Shape" 229). Perloff explicitly *distinguishes* Oppen's prosody, with its "curious disruptiveness" by which "the text itself is . . . called into question" (229), from Williams's. Bernstein echoes Perloff in arguing that Oppen's prosody leans away from effects of presence; yet their Oppen sounds like Hatlen's Williams, in whom we are asked to associate "syntactic dislocations" with attention to "sensory particulars." Curiouser and curiouser, as Alice said.

Bernstein's metaphor of the hinge for Oppen's line break recalls Creeley's sense of his own line break as a "pivot" ("Interview" with David Elliott 58), and indeed Bernstein suggests Oppen's "use of the line as hinge" as one possible aspect of his influence ("Hinge" 242). In a 1968 interview (before the publication of *Pieces*), Oppen expressed reservations about Creeley's line: "A lot of the worst of modern poetry, and it would be true of some quite good poetry, such as Creeley's, uses the line-ending simply as the end of a line, a kind of syncopation or punctuation" (Dembo and Pondrom 180).

19. In a January 1966 letter, Oppen writes that "Of Being Numerous" has "been a harrowing work for me, partly for the difficulty, a difficulty I suppose of courage or of honesty in permitting the imperfect to appear imperfect, and the difficulty of distinguishing that decency from the indecency of permitting mere sloppy work, a different kind of faking—. Imperfect, but I think it has to be" (*Selected Letters* 128–29).

Chapter 5

1. I have taken this opportunity to revise—effectively, to rethink—the chapter on "Objectivists and Communists" from *American Writers and Radical Politics, 1900–39*, incorporating some primary material that was unavailable at the time it was written in the mid-1980s. There seemed then little room for the Objectivists in the "story" of American poetry, or indeed on the cultural Left; there are a few signs now, and *The Objectivist Nexus* might be taken as one of them, that things are changing.

2. Margaret Anderson had written with considerable enthusiasm about Goldman, and had contributed to Goldman's journal, *Mother Earth:* see "The Challenge of Emma Goldman" and "Emma Goldman in Chicago."

3. Michael Gold, "White Hope of American Drama," new magazine section of the *Daily Worker* 26 February 1927: 8. See "Does New York Want a Proletarian Theatre? 'Reflect American Life with Robust Carelessness,' Says John Howard Lawson," new magazine supplement to the *Daily Worker* 26 March 1927: 8; John Dos Passos's "Towards a Revolutionary Theatre," *New Masses* 3 (December 1927): 20. His *Airways, Inc.* was staged by the New Playwright's Theatre at the Grove Street Theatre in 1929. It ran for four weeks, as Dos Passos recalled, "before an audience made up largely of empty seats." Charles Yale Harrison wrote the NPT obituary, "The New Playwrights Give Up the Struggle," *New York Evening Post* 27 April 1929 (clipping in Box 9, Charles Yale Harrison Manuscripts Collection, Butler Library, Columbia University).

4. Founded as a workers' school by the Socialist Party in 1906, and funded by a bequest of $200,000 from Carrie Rand, the Rand School in New York and its related Camp Tamiment in rural Pennsylvania were at the heart of Socialist and workers' education in New York City.

5. Gold to Sinclair, n.d. [1931], Lilly Library, Indiana University. Gold's tormentors were led by Melvin P. Levy, who had reviewed *Jews Without Money* in the *New Republic* on 26 March 1930, a review that greatly displeased Gold. Philip Rahv, E. A. Schachner, and Conrad Komorowski were also young leftists then emerging in the John Reed Clubs. The lines of allegiance and conflict were often twisted and confusing. A. B. Magil, who led the attack on Rahv's leftism in 1932 ("Pity and Terror," *New Masses* 7 [December 1932]: 16–19), had also clashed with Gold at the Kharkov conference in 1930.

6. Cf. Max Eastman, "To Nicolai Lenin," *Liberator* 1 (November 1918): 17; and Witter Bynner, "Shame on You, Lenin!" in *May Days: An Anthology of Verse from "Masses-Liberator,"* ed. Genevieve Taggard (New York: Boni & Liveright, 1925), 208.

7. See also Zukofsky to Kenneth Burke, Isidor Schneider, and Edwin Berry Burgum, 1 March 1936, in the Schneider Papers, Butler Library, Columbia University. Zukofsky knew the jargon of the Left, all the moves.

8. Philip Rahv, "For Whom Do You Write? Replies from Forty American Writers," *New Quarterly* 1 (Summer 1934): 12.

9. Despite Williams's settled distaste for socialism and Marxism, the Left maintained a generally friendly attitude toward him in the 1930s: see Michael Gold in the *Daily Worker* 12 October 1933; Milton Howard's review of Williams's *Collected Poems* in *Daily Worker* 10 February 1934; and Edwin Seaver's review of *White Mule* in *Daily Worker* 28 July 1937.

10. Rakosi's autobiographical account of his years in Madison strongly emphasizes the estrangement a "poor little Jewish boy" felt amidst the "blond young Babbitts of North European stock" who made up his fellow students at the University of Wisconsin in the 1920s. See Rakosi's "Scenes from My Life," *Collected Prose* 85–104.

11. Academic interest in the Objectivists was aroused in 1969 by L. S. Dembo, who edited a special issue of *Contemporary Literature* on their work. Two decades later, in a book both learned and deeply sympathetic to the Left, *Repression and Recovery,* Cary Nelson's sole reference to Oppen is: "Other poets associated with Objectivism include George Oppen (1908–1984) and Lorine Niedecker (1903–1970), both notable for their exquisite craft" (176–77).

12. The publication of Pound and Zukofsky, *Pound/Zukofsky: Selected Letters,* adds significant examples of Pound's efforts to manipulate the younger poets, and of their struggle (especially young Jewish poets') to keep Pound's favor and benefit from his patronage, all the while maintaining a healthy distance from his fascism and anti-Semitism. Correspondence from this volume is quoted by date.

13. Zukofsky reported Rakosi's departure to Texas in a letter to Pound on 5 February 1931.

Chapter 6

This is a revised version of "Poetry and Politics in the 1930s: Basil Bunting's Other History," in Caddel, *Sharp Study* 98–113. I would like to thank Richard Caddel, John Lucas, Martin Priestman, Denise Riley, and, especially, Andrew Crozier for their helpful comments on drafts of that essay.

1. "You can't grip years, Postume" was published in the *Sunday Times,* 14 December 1969. Substantial sections of *Villon* appeared in George Steiner's *Penguin Book of Modern Verse Translation* (1966). *The Spoils* was published entire in Edward Lucie-Smith's *British Poetry since 1945* (1970). And his work was represented in a number of other anthologies—in, for instance, John Matthias, *23 Modern British Poets* (1971).

2. Leavis continued to point the finger at the institutions of literary production and distribution in England: "the contemporary literary world is controlled by a system of personal and institutional relations, that, pursuing its own ends, is inevitably

hostile to the play of criticism and to the emergence and recognition of the new and significant" ("Mr Pryce Jones, the British Council and British Culture'" [1951–52], *Selection* 1: 181).

3. For a searching analysis of Pound's anti-Semitism see Casillo.

4. Bunting's obituary of Pound ("Prince of Poets ") studiously omits any mention of politics.

5. Basil Bunting to Anne Tibble, 19 April 1965, Durham University Library: Bunting Archive, MS 95.

6. Reviewing this often unintentionally funny book, Leavis commented: "any competent reviewer knowing nothing of the author would have been bound to deduce from the book that, of all professions, the literary was one for which he was certainly not intended by nature" ("Keynes, Spender, and Currency-Values," *Selection* 1: 185).

7. One of the examiners at Peterhouse, with remarkable prescience, explained to Bunting's headmaster: "It was felt that there was a possibility of brilliance in him, but that his work was as yet too uneven" (H. J. Edwards to [Evans], 16 February 1916, Bunting Archive).

8. For a thorough account of this poem see Kenneth Cox, "A Commentary" 20–36.

9. See also Bunting, "Preface" to *Joseph Skipsey.*

10. Sounding like a premature disciple of Paul de Man, he also told Zukofsky in 1934: "Follow up any abstraction a little way and it will commit suicide" (quoted in Makin 295).

11. Louis Zukofsky, *A Workers Anthology,* typescript dated 8 March 1935 in Bunting Archive, MS 54.

12. Basil Bunting to Barry Redfern, undated letter of March 1980, Bunting Archive, MS 115.

13. For a discussion of the relation of politics and poetry in the work of Oppen see Seed, "Living the Storm."

14. This uncharacteristic piece of writing has been usefully examined by Caddel, "Acknowledged Land."

15. Basil Bunting to Michael Butler, 2 September 1968, Bunting Archive, MS 112/1. The letter deals with the experience of the generation of post–World War II writers in England but specifically relates it to the previous war, which was, he says, felt even more severely.

16. Jan Montefiore looks at the way in which the invention of "the Auden generation" has excluded women poets in "'Undeservedly Forgotten.'"

17. For instance: Frances Scarfe, *Auden and After;* Robin Skelton, ed., *Poetry of the Thirties;* A. T. Tolley, *Poetry of the Thirties;* Samuel Hynes, *The Auden Generation;* V. Cunningham, *British Writers of the Thirties.* For two books that do raise some interesting questions about the received picture of the literature of the period see Lucas, *The 1930s,* and Caesar, *Dividing Lines.*

Chapter 7

1. See my discussion on "An Objective" and on Objectivist poetics in general as one of "workability" in *Conviction's Net of Branches.*

Chapter 8

An earlier, shorter version of this article appeared in the *Journal of American Studies* 31 (1997): 2, 203–18, published by Cambridge University Press, to whom acknowledgments are made.

1. Information about Niedecker's life is relatively limited. For a helpful account of the relations between Niedecker's life and work see Jenny Penberthy, *Niedecker and the Correspondence with Zukofsky.* The discussion of Niedecker's career as a choice is in the essay by Rachel Blau DuPlessis in *Lorine Niedecker: Woman and Poet,* which also contains a wide range of material on Niedecker's life and work.

2. It was published in 1955. "She rose to His Requirement" was slightly altered by the early editors in addition to the omission of dashes, primarily in the final stanza, which now reads "It lay unmentioned—as the Sea / Develop Pearl, and Weed, / But only to Himself—be known / The Fathoms they abide—" (*Selected Poems* 359).

Chapter 10

1. *By the Well of the Living and Seeing* (1969), first poem; *Complete Poems* 2: 91 (the *Complete Poems* are hereafter abbreviated *CP*). The story of the destruction of his grandfather's poetry is part of his mother's narrative in "Early History of a Seamstress" (1929) (published as part of *Family Chronicle*), and is repeated in his 1930 novel *By the Waters of Manhattan,* whose first half recasts "Early History"—less successfully to my reading—into the third person, leaving the rest almost entirely unchanged. Reznikoff alludes to the burning of his grandfather's "bulky" manuscript again a few pages before the end of the novel.

2. These three works were brought together as *Family Chronicle*—a masterpiece of historical autobiography (a genre more commonly presented today as oral history). First published in England under this title by Norman Bailey & Co., it was published by Universe Books, New York, in 1971, with a perfunctory introduction by the Jewish chronicler and humorist Harry Golden.

3. Sharp 206. Hindus, *Man and Poet,* reprints the *Poetry* version of the essay, 377–88.

4. Syrkin had first read Reznikoff in 1920, while a college student at Cornell. "My particular friend at Cornell was Laura Reichenthal, later Laura Riding, and I had already been exposed to strains of modernist verse. But the culture had not taken. My first reaction to Charles's verse was negative" (Syrkin 37). The Reznikoff-Riding connection, albeit oblique, is fascinating.

5. *The Manner Music* 128. Prose versions of Reznikoff's poems can be found beginning on 15, 19, 25, 27, 28, 58, 60, 77, and 115.

6. *Inscriptions: 1944–1956,* #23 (excerpt); *CP* 2: 76. This poem is also quoted below in section 8. In the Poetry Center reading, Reznikoff called this poem, and #21, discussed below, his "platform as a writer of verse."

7. "Aphrodite Vrania" in *Poems,* 1920, #25; *CP* 1: 36.

8. *Inscriptions,* #23; *CP* 2: 76. The final stanza of this three-stanza poem is quoted immediately below.

9. What makes the poems disjunctive is that they are not, in fact, threaded together by the use of such conjunctions as "meanwhile" and "at the same time," which smooth over the synaptic break between units, that allow for the syncopation of cubo-seriality. The use of such hinges as "meanwhile" is particularly favored by John Ashbery, a device that apparently makes the marvelous incongruities of his work appealing to some critics who dislike the more textually disruptive practices described here. Note also that biblical and Homeric parataxis employs frequent conjunctions to link elements, a feature that distinguishes this older form of parataxis from modernist collage and montage. A fuller discussion of this issue would need to account for the structurally related use of parallelism in analphabetic poetries.

10. Conte, *Unending Design* 20. Conte defines the form of the serial poem as "both discontinuous and capable of recombination." He notes that the discontinuity of the elements of the serial poem "—or their resistance to a determinate order—distinguishes the series from thematic continuity, narrative progression, or meditative insistence that often characterizes the sequence. . . . The series demands neither summation nor exclusion. It is instead a combinative form whose arrangements admit a variegated set of materials." In contrast, the sequence relies on "mechanic or imposed organization"—for example, the temporal progression of the seasons (21).

11. In *Disjunctive Poetics,* Peter Quartermain links the paratactic prosody of Zukofsky with Bunting and Pound and back to Whitman. See especially 127–33. Conte makes the distinction between seriality and proceduralism: "Serial works are characterized by the discontinuity of their elements and the centrifugal force identified with an 'open' aesthetic. Procedural works, on the other hand, are typified by the recurrence of elements and a centripetal force that promises a self-sustaining momentum" (*Unending Design* 42).

12. Wittgenstein's *Philosophical Investigations* and *Zettel* exemplify the distinction between intrinsic and extrinsic order. *Zettel* is made up of over seven hundred slips found together in a file box. These slips were mostly cut from extensive typescripts of Wittgenstein's, and many of the fragments were subsequently reworked. In addition, it appears that some of the remarks were written originally as part of this series. The editors remark that "now we know that his method of composition was in part to make an arrangement of such short, almost independent, pieces." For our investigation here, it is striking that some of the sections of *Zettel* were cut out of "one or two total rearrangements of *Investigations* and other material"; the fact that Wittgenstein made such recombinations underscores the serial nature of his major philosophical work. See the "Editor's Preface," *Zettel.* Serial forms are particularly valuable for both philosophy and criticism, despite the fact that they are almost never employed.

13. Linda Simon provides these quotes in a useful synopsis of the responses to Reznikoff in her "Annotated Bibliography." Milton Hindus's laudatory review of *Family Chronicles* is representative of the "giving up the baby with bathwater" or "weak" response to Reznikoff's detractors, even though Hindus is not here talking about the poems (Simon 426). The work is difficult, Hindus argues, not because of the presence of avant-garde defamiliarizing devices "but because of its seemingly absolute and artless and primitive simplicity. . . . He studiously and purposefully *flattens* . . . every incident. . . . Reznikoff consistently subdues all the highlights in his pictures and produces a

monochromatic effect which demands the utmost effort and attention from the reader" (Simon 426). One wants to immediately add here what Jerome Rothenberg wrote of tribal primitivism: *primitive means complex.* Still, it is the picture of Reznikoff as "artless and unassuming," as Carl Rakosi describes him (Simon 429), that underplays how very artful and assuming this work is.

14. "Introduction" to *Man and Poet* 22.

15. *Inscriptions,* #21; *CP* 2: 75. As previously noted, Reznikoff calls this poem, and #23, his "platform as a writer of verse"; #21 is also cited in sections 2 and 29.

16. Gershom Scholem, in *Major Trends,* notes that "the doctrine of God's immanence in all things" has earlier roots "among the great Jewish mystics and Kabbalists. To me, not the doctrine seems new, but rather the primitive enthusiasm with which it was expounded and the truly pantheistic exhilaration evoked by the belief that God surrounds everything and pervades everything" (347–48).

17. *Inscriptions,* #20; *CP* 2: 75. This is the sense of paradise I hear in Ron Silliman's *Paradise* and Lyn Hejinian's "The Guard."

18. These are the last words in Sarah Reznikoff's "Early History of a Seamstress," *Family Chronicle* 99.

19. *Jerusalem the Golden,* #1; *CP* 1: 107. In the talk with Dembo, Reznikoff responds to a question about "a personal sense of isolation or exile" in this poem: "I don't think 'isolation' is the word. I don't feel isolated in English; it's just that I'm missing a lot in not knowing Hebrew. Incidentally, Havelock Ellis in one of his books, as I remember it, points out the tendency in a writer to use characteristics of the speech of his ancestors, even a speech he no longer knows" (104).

20. *Inscriptions,* #21; *CP* 2: 75. Reznikoff's "platform."

21. In "On Reznikoff and 'Talking Hebrew,'" John Martone writes that "Central to Reznikoff's objectivism is the poet's subordination of the self to the material at hand. The poetic subject and not the poet as subject is the center of the work. The sincerity, Zukofsky said about Reznikoff's work, is in the details. And all Reznikoff's books . . . direct our attention not so much to an experiencing authorial self as to a detailed, profoundly historical world of experience. Reznikoff is the first American poet to 'decenter' the subject on so massive a scale. . . . Revolutionary in the context of American poetry, [this decentering] is a basic feature of the Talmud and a given in traditional Jewish hermeneutics" (72).

22. #XXIV, immediately following the adjacent poem; emphasis added.

23. "Autobiography: Hollywood"; *CP* 2: 39. Compare Oppen's "And the pure joy / Of the mineral fact // Tho it is impenetrable // As the world, if it is matter, / Is impenetrable" (*Collected Poems* 148).

24. "Early History of a Writer"; *CP* 2: 172. Reznikoff mentions this anecdote, identifying Kittredge's Shakespeare course at Harvard, which is not mentioned in the poem ("Talk with Dembo" 103).

25. William Carlos Williams, "Between Walls," *Collected Poems* 1: 453: what shines in this poem is "the broken": that which is damaged or destroyed and that which has been cast aside, but, at the same time, the fragment, the shard of ineffable worth. "Actual Word Stuff, Not Thoughts for Thoughts" is the title of Quartermain's essay on Williams and Zukofsky in *Disjunctive Poetics;* the quote is from a 1928 letter from Williams to

Zukofsky. One might imagine Stein's project as a radical extension of seriality to the level of syntax, so that not only sentences or phrases or details but also individual words are permuted.

26. Pointlessness is a typical charge made against radical modernist discontinuity and fragmentation. Thus, Reznikoff's poems are "essentially insignificant" and "incidental and decorative" according to a 1934 review; while Hayden Carruth, reviewing *Testimony,* speaks of Reznikoff's "cold, neutral language" as "uninteresting" and "lifeless," and Robert Alter refers to the "seeming impassivity . . . flatness, and numbing pointlessness" of different Reznikoff works. See Simon. In contrast, John Martone is right when he calls *Testimony* "the most difficult of the modernist long poems. . . . No grandiose mythopoetic vision distracts us from the commonplace, from the [often brutal] circumstances of everyday life" (79).

27. In "First, There Is the Need" Reznikoff writes, "Clarity, precision, order, but the answer is intensity: with intensity we have compression, rhythm, maybe rhyme, maybe alliteration. The words move out of prose into verse as the speech becomes passionate and musical instead of flat" [5]. Reznikoff also talks about prose not having the "intensity that I wanted" in #17 of "Early History of a Writer" (*CP* 2: 171).

28. My own reading of Reznikoff began with *Testimony,* which for some time overshadowed my reading of his other poems. I see these remarks as a commentary on how to approach, how to interpret, Reznikoff's great anti-epic. The best account of the composition of *Testimony* is Shevelow, "History and Objectification."

29. *Poems* (1920), #22; *CP* 1: 35. The quotation in section 52 is the last stanza of this poem.

30. Williams, "Spring and All" ("To Elsie"), *Collected Poems* 1: 217; William Blake, "Introduction" to his indelible series *Songs of Experience.*

31. This letter was originally published, in a translation by Jean-Paul Auxeméry, in *a.b.s.: poètes à royaumont* no. 3 (1990), along with Auxeméry's original letter to me.

Chapter 11

This essay first appeared in the *Journal of American Studies* 31 (1997): 153–70. I am grateful to Cambridge University Press for permission to reprint it here.

1. See *Selected Letters* xiv, and Mary Oppen, *Meaning.*

2. The contrast is proposed in McGann, "Contemporary Poetry" 624–47. Perelman (*Marginalization* 40) also notes that in the seventies "The Objectivists were still active and were in fact a much stronger presence than they had been in prior decades."

3. For the counter-view, that Zukofsky's practice "exposes the object-status of the poem as a delusion," see Davidson, "Dismantling 'Mantis'" 522. I have suggested a qualification to Davidson's argument in Nicholls, "Lorine Niedecker" 199–200.

4. See, for example, Oppen, *Selected Letters* 249–50: " . . . that the Cantos would benefit as poetry thru excision as drastic as Pound's editing of the Waste Land—emerges as obviously true[.] I suspect we all admit to ourselves—or I will admit *for* myself that I read the Cantos in fragments as fragments. Despite the challenges of the scholars."

5. Hatlen, "Not Altogether" 326: "Oppen's later poetry represents, I believe, a sys-

tematic attempt to body forth certain political commitments (Oppen today calls his political position 'populism') in and through an uncompromisingly modernist poetic method."

6. Cf. Agamben 86: "What the State cannot tolerate in any way . . . is that the singularities form a community without affirming an identity, that humans co-belong without any representable condition of belonging (even in the form of a simple presupposition)."

7. In an unpublished note, Oppen writes: "Numerous: not only that I could not see the individual merged in 'humanity,' but that I saw humanity no less helpless [deletion] than the individual." Quoted from the George Oppen Papers, Box 13, Folder 8, by kind permission of the Mandeville Special Collections Library, University of California at San Diego, and Linda Oppen.

8. See "An Adequate Vision" 17: "But Numerous actually takes more space for a simpler undertaking than *This In Which.* The relationship between things—the relationship between people; What it is rather than That it is. Surely simpler tho it is consciously played out against the background That it is. Which is of course why the poem could not be satirical." For a gloss on the title of *This In Which,* see Oppen in Dembo, "The 'Objectivist' Poet" 163: "the nouns do refer to something; that it's there, that it's true, the whole implication of these nouns; that appearances represent reality, whether or not they misrepresent it: that this in which the thing takes place, this thing is here, and that these things do take place."

9. Referring to Maritain's *Creative Intuition in Art and Poetry,* Oppen remarks: "the word *presentness:* central to me too" (*Selected Letters* 311). The prose section that concludes this first poem recalls Mary Oppen talking about Yves Bonnefoy's *On the Motion and Immobility of Douve* (see *Selected Letters* 129).

10. For Oppen's negative view of "narrative," see, for example, *Selected Letters* 19: "If the novel is dead it seems likely to me that people just can't bear narrative, with its implication of the incomprehensibility of time, of the non-existence of what's past, and such." See also 55–56: "Narrative, which is everyone's art, and everyone's comfort, is wearing out. There is no fact more obvious than that every life ends badly."

11. See *Selected Letters* 254: "The 'Marxism' of Discrete Series is, was felt as, the struggle against the loss of the commonplace." The last phrase was borrowed from Michael Heller (see *Selected Letters* 252–53).

12. The phrase, from Heidegger's *Introduction to Metaphysics,* is used as an epigraph to Oppen's *This In Which* (1965). The matter of Oppen's interest in Heidegger, dating back to at least 1929, merits further attention. Some useful points are made in Chilton.

13. See, for example, Ziarek 28: "Being covers itself with beings, and in its retreat it becomes indistinguishable from beings, almost a being itself. This retreat is visible in the 'language of Being,' which continually missays and unsays Being, unable to escape describing it in the same syntactical and grammatical terms as entities."

14. See Oppen, *Collected Poems* 141: "Tho I had hoped to arrive / At an actuality / In the mere number of us / And record now / That I did not."

15. Cf. Nancy, "Finite History" 169: "History is not a narrative or a statement, but the announcement of a 'we' (history is writing in this sense)."

16. Cf. Derrida, "Living On" 167: "The word 'and' is to be understood in each case

as a conjunction that does not join logically, for example in contradiction, nor according to chronology, succession or absolute simultaneity, nor according to some fundamental ontology."

17. Cf. Rexroth, *Reverdy* vi: "Eliot works in *The Waste Land* with fragmented and recombined arguments; Pierre Reverdy with dismembered propositions from which subject, operator and object have been wrenched free and re-structured into an invisible or subliminal discourse which owes its cogency to its own strict, complex and secret logic." See also Nicholls, "Lorine Niedecker" 199.

18. *The Cantos,* 546. In an unpublished note, Oppen writes: "pull down they [*sic*] vanity etc It's a remarkably bombastic ant / but the wasp, whose head or tip . . . I think it is the great moment in Pound's writing, the great moment of the cantos." Quoted from the George Oppen Papers, Box 13, Folder 20, by kind permission of the Mandeville Special Collections Library, University of California at San Diego, and Linda Oppen.

19. Oppen tended to reject "ethics" (meaning, for him, moralism) in favor of "ontology." See, for example, *Selected Letters* 118, where Oppen notes of "Of Being Numerous" that there "I speak of the ontological not the ethical problem." See also 119: "Atrocity becoming ordinary—worldly—despite the secular ethic, despite our fear of the disappearance of an ethic which is not based on an ontology and an eschatology. This is the meaning of 'crisis.'" In his interview with Oppen, Dembo observes that "for all your desire merely to report your feelings and to repudiate an ethical aim for your poetry, you do have strong ethical convictions to express. But, as you've said, the important thing is that the ethic be felt and not merely constructed" ("The 'Objectivist' Poet" 174).

20. See, for example, Derrida, *Writing* 111: "Ethics, in Levinas's sense, is an Ethics without law and without concept, which maintains its non-violent purity only before being determined as concepts and laws. This is not an objection: let us not forget that Levinas does not seek to propose laws or moral values, does not seek to determine *a* morality, but rather the essence of the ethical relation in general."

Chapter 12

1. Note that the original version of Reznikoff's poem in the 1931 Objectivist issue read "A girder, itself among the rubbish" (252). The word "still" was introduced when the poem was reprinted in *Jerusalem the Golden* (1934).

2. Christopher Beach describes one counter to Bloom, a "poetic 'fathering' of the self . . . that does not involve an Oedipal child/father relationship—a 'repression' of the self or of the father—but rather an opening of the psyche to additional sources through the re-creation of new fathers. [Robert] Duncan provides here an alternative metaphor to that of 'mis-reading': poetic growth as 're-creation'" (139).

3. Oppen's otherwise uncollected poem is on the rear cover of volume 2 of the *Complete Poems of Charles Reznikoff,* published in 1977.

4. "Characteristically," Lawrence Lipking states, "the *tombeau* incorporates many reminiscences of the poet it memorializes—style, verse forms, images, specific lines—and it may even try, eerily, to impersonate his voice" (140).

5. See Joanne Feit Diehl.

6. Niedecker was not alone in her observation. Writes Phillip Lopate in reference to his encounters with Reznikoff during the 1960s, "I imagined I saw in him traces of bitterness and disappointed ambition, which he fiercely suppressed behind a set of gentle shrugs" (201–2).

7. Writing of such poets as Pound and Dickinson, Lipking says, "Their contempt for 'official' poetry and 'heroic' careers implies a reverse ambition: a self-consuming devotion to craft. Indeed, one might argue that resistance to orthodox definitions of greatness and public careers itself constitutes a career ideal" (xii–xiii). Dickinson's life, he says, "was given dramatic shape by her consciousness of the public poetic destiny she would not engage. The idea of a career enables the idea of an anti-career" (131).

8. Atypical response, however, occurs occasionally. In a letter to Cid Corman, Niedecker offers a stinging comment on Eliot: "This morning I took the route thru the park to the branch library (the box by its door) to take back T. S. Eliot's Murder in the Cathedral and Edith Sitwell's Taken Care of. Such things I read. Ugh! This was at 6:30, the sun hardly over the horizon, frosty air but I'm always warm after oatmeal. Well, I decided there were books I could read that would give me a healthy and lovely feeling. So I came home and read all nine of your books" (Faranda 74). Niedecker later complains to him about Zukofsky's unwillingness to write an introduction or publicity blurb for her 1966 collection *T & G*. "You can understand what I feel," she writes to Corman. "Says he does this kind of thing for nobody now" (80).

Chapter 13

1. I mean both that commercial publication first made some of their work generally accessible (Oppen, *The Materials,* 1962; Reznikoff, *By the Waters of Manhattan: Selected Poems,* 1962; Zukofsky, *All: The Collected Shorter Poems,* 2 vols., 1964, 1965; Rakosi, *Amulet,* 1967) and that they were subject to group configuration: see, for example, *Contemporary Literature* 10.2 (Spring 1969) Special Number: The "Objectivist" Poet.

2. For Zukofsky's opinion of Hughes's anthology, see "American Poetry 1920–1930."

3. For convenience of reference the reader may consult the versions of these essays in Zukofsky's *Prepositions,* with the caution that there "Sincerity and Objectification" appears as Part II of "An Objective" and has been purged of reference to Reznikoff.

4. It seems unlikely that Zukofsky would have taken note of Taupin's book were the author (who taught French at Columbia) not personally known to him. The notion that modern poetry in English should go to school in France has been around at least since the 1890s (cf. Arthur Symons, *The Symbolist Movement in Literature,* 1899; and also the cases of Stuart Merrill and Francis Vielé-Griffin); its attraction for American modernists (most amiably stated by Harold Rosenberg, "French Silence") no doubt owes much to the denial of any umbilical link to English culture. But although Taupin provided Zukofsky with "American Poetry" as a cultural entity, he more usefully afforded him two points of theoretical resistance: influence as a category of literary history, and Imagism as the content of the decade 1910–20. For Zukofsky's opinion of Taupin's book see "Imagisme."

5. Rakosi had also published four poems in *Exile* 2 (Autumn 1927).

6. This is not the place to go into the details of Pound's relations with Zukofsky and other "younger poets," but it is worth noticing that by 1933 Pound had qualified his enthusiasm for Zukofsky's project. "A whole school or shoal of young American writers seems to me to have lost contact with language as language . . . in particular Mr Zukofsky's Objectivists seem prone to this error" ("Notes" 253; Pound nevertheless included Zukofsky and Oppen in *Active Anthology*). Pound (unlike Williams, however) seems to have been determined to keep poets of the younger generation at arm's length, and to have assigned to Zukofsky the role of convening them; this did not accord with Zukofsky's notions (a) that individual members of a generation could develop and (b) that relations between generations were concretely relations between contemporaries. The thesis of my essay is that Zukofsky used the term "Objectivists" to refer to poets of both Pound's generation and his own, and that his editorial work was intended to make just this connection.

7. The slightly different form of words used for the headnote statement of principles in *Poetry* was as follows. "*An Objective: (Optics)—The lens bringing the rays from an object to a focus. (Military use)—That which is aimed at. (Use extended to poetry)—Desire for what is objectively perfect, inextricably the direction of historic and contemporary particulars.*"

8. Zukofsky read the Everyman's Library edition of the *Ethics,* translated by A. Boyle (I am indebted to Mark Scroggins for this information), and would have found the terms "natura naturata" and "natura naturans" rendered as "passive nature" and "active nature." Such interpretation obscures the finer verbal distinction by grammatical inflection of the Latin, which is more successfully brought across into English by Spinoza's contemporary, Dryden, in the preface to *Annus Mirabilis* (1667). "*Wit writing,* (if you will give me leave to use a school-distinction), is no other than the faculty of imagination in the writer. . . . *Wit written* is that which is well defined, the happy result of thought, or product of imagination" (14). The distinction was first made in the twelfth century by Averroes in his commentary on Aristotle, *De Caelo* (for medieval scholastic philosophy Aristotle was *the* philosopher, and Averroes his most important commentator), but for Dryden it was a commonplace to be turned to witty advantage (note the pun on "school"). Spinoza appears to have revived it briefly in order to establish the proper relation of intellect to nature ("that which is contained in the intellect objectively must of necessity be granted in nature," *Ethics,* I, Prop. XXX) by attributing the intellect to "natura naturata" (I, Prop. XXXI). Romantic theory used the distinction somewhat differently; Coleridge, for example, refers to "the essence, *natura naturans,* which presupposes a bond between nature in the higher sense and the soul of man" (*Biographia Literaria* 1: 257). Epistemologically Spinoza is closer to Locke than to such romantic notions of the creative powers of the imagination, but in considering Zukofsky's use of Spinoza we would do well to bear in mind that historically such ideas stood between him and Spinoza.

9. Translator's note, *Ethic,* trans. White 30.

10. White's note draws attention to the need to distinguish between God and his creation, creator and created. But Spinoza's definition of God as "a being absolutely infinite" (*Ethics and "De Intellectus Emendatione"* 1) incorporates everything with God in

a way that sidelines theological disputes about limitation of God's power by reason or free will. Santayana, in his introduction to the translation Zukofsky read, makes clear that Spinoza was considered dangerous because he removed moral sanction from religion. "The scandal consisted in the fact that Spinoza denied final causes, or purposes at work in nature, and that, in their ordinary sense, he denied the immortality of the soul, free-will, and moral responsibility. What came to turn these doctrines (which might have passed for simple materialism) into positive blasphemy was that he identified nature with God, and taught that all things, whether in the eyes of men they were good or evil, mean or noble, were integral parts of the divine being" (vii).

11. My editors suggest that I explain. The appeal of the *Communist Manifesto* to the workers of the world that they should unite to cast off their chains was, of course, a message of secular hope: the workers had *nothing* to lose and a world to win. But this is not quite what I have in mind when I use the phrase "the hope of the communist." For Western communists in the 1920s and 1930s the Soviet Union was both a cause to be defended and a beacon of hope: Soviet industrial development bore out Marx's account of the contradictions of capitalism, as did—closer to home—the depression. The hope of the communist appears, therefore, as a disposition projected in a positive mode ("I have seen the future, and it works"—Lincoln Steffens) and with strong negative reinforcement when setbacks occurred. Thus later in the 1930s the note of hope in communist representations of the popular struggle against fascism (André Malraux, *L'espoir*, for example, or Montagu Slater, *Haunting Europe*) is likely, by its historical innocence, to strike the contemporary reader as pathos. These are European examples, and may be without American equivalents; indeed, it may be that the element of hope detectable in Zukofsky's sense of *direction* may set him apart from other American communists. The contrast I have in mind is with the American communist cult of proletarian literature (a blatant case of theoretical backwardness), which, whatever hopeful premises underwrote its politics, involved tactical deployment of themes of abjection, misery, and squalor.

12. For further remarks on the performativity of poetic language in Zukofsky's theory, see my "Paper Bunting."

Chapter 15

1. This essay is a revision and expansion of remarks made at the conference on American Objectivists, which was organized by Emmanuel Hocquard at the Centre Littéraire de la Fondation Royaumont, from 29 September to 1 October 1989. The essay was published a year later in *Action poétique* (number 120), and was subsequently reprinted in di Manno, *Tribu Perdue*. For this translation, the author has revised and expanded some of the endnotes. The essay was translated by Rachel Blau DuPlessis, with Peter Quartermain and Yves di Manno.

2. Emmanuel Hocquard's *Bibliothèque* is a short essay on contemporary poetry in which the author insists, among other topics, on the importance to him of Reznikoff's *Testimony* (1965) and *Holocaust* (1977) both as a "technique" and as an example of "neutralism"—a depersonalized or distancing stance—in modern verse.

3. Blaise Cendrars's *Kodak* (first published in 1924, later, because of threats by the

Kodak Company, retitled *Documentaires*) is a fifty-page poem entirely composed of statements "extracted" and put into verse form from a pulp novel by Gustave Le Rouge called *Le mystérieux docteur Cornélius.*

4. Paul Nougé (1895–1967) was the leader of the Belgian surrealists. The thirty-page-long poem *Un miroir exemplaire de Maupassant* (1966), "written" in the fifties, consists entirely in the putting into verse of sentences or short paragraphs from Maupassant.

5. To understand this, one must go all the way back to the symbolist generation, that is to say, to the moment when this split began. However, to do so would deflect us from this discussion.

6. Saint-John Perse (1887–1975): his first book (*Eloges*) appeared in 1911; the second one (*Anabase*) was translated by T. S. Eliot (into English), Giuseppe Ungaretti (into Italian), and Walter Benjamin (into German). Arthur Cravan (1887–1918): a pioneer of French modernism; his magazine *Maintenant* appeared in 1912. He married the poet Mina Loy just before his death. Victor Segalen (1878–1919); the first edition of *Stèles* (1987) appeared in Beijing in 1912.

7. Pierre Reverdy (1889–1960) was associated ca. 1910–20 with the cubist painters in Paris. Along with that of Apollinaire and Cendrars, his poetry of the period (1945, 1991) was the first French attempt to enter the modern era and to invent a new ("free") verse.

8. Tristan Tzara (1896–1963), Max Jacob (1876–1944), Robert Desnos (1900–1945), Pierre Albert-Birot (1876–1967), and Francis Picabia (1879–1953) were well-known French poets of the first half of the century, mainly acquainted with early modernism and/or surrealism (Auster, *Twentieth-Century French Poetry*).

9. As for the history of poetry written in French, our preferences are again increasingly complicated. Let's just say that we are much more moved nowadays by Maurice Scève's *Délie* than by his *Microcosme,* more moved by Jean de Sponde than by D'Aubigné—so far as the sixteenth century is concerned.

10. To translate "les pages encores vierges de ce futur Livre ouvert," the translator has cited the words of H.D. from *Trilogy* (570), since di Manno's phrase, also interestingly trumping Mallarmé, irresistibly suggested this option.

Chapter 16

1. I take the quotation in the first paragraph from the version of Hejinian's "Rejection of Closure" in Perelman, *Writing/Talks* 271. This version, however, is more restrained in its claims about her poetry, so my quotation in the next paragraph is from the original version of the essay in *Poetics Journal* (1984), 137.

2. I am indebted to Faith Barrett for my appreciation of this poem.

3. The poem does offer a basic statement of its thematic concerns at precisely its midpoint, but far more than Oppen, Hejinian has to let this center also seem caught up in the poem's constant wobbling—there is no effort to isolate two or three competing organizational frameworks.

4. Let me also use this note to comment on differences between the Objectivist notion of material form and the formal site composed by Bernstein's way of giving tan-

gibility to the projective force of sentences proceeding along different paths. Bernstein's theorizing does return to contemporary writing a sense of the relation between citation and siting basic to modernism. By making the poem abstract, one can also offer new ways of its taking on a material force in terms of how its elemental properties relate to each other, so that we can appreciate poems as distinctive kinds of objects or even ontological sites with their own independent imaginative physicality. Bernstein's version of synthetic composition, in fact, may take on its fullest resonance if we link its treatment of folds and textures to the ways that synthetic cubism defined a complex interface between the precision of attention and the dense otherness of what would become surreal speculative space. But from the point of view of Objectivist poetics, Bernstein's spaces may be too verbal, too exclusively a matter of layering textual properties, without sufficient attention to the kinds of push-and-pull tensions that a more referential language might evoke. Compare the layering folds of Bernstein's "Poem" to the work done by the two structural patterns we observed in Oppen's "Eclogue." Oppen's materiality is not simply a matter of folds but also of concrete forces held in considerable dynamic tension—in my view more like Picasso's and Braque's analytic work from 1909 to 1911 than like synthetic cubism. So if we were now to heed examples like Oppen's, poets might explore more elemental conflicting structures as ways of extending not only the play of intellect but its very phenomenological status as it takes on material forms.

5. I have discussed these problems in the political claims of Language writing at greater length in my essay "Without Consequences Is No Politics" in von Hallberg, *Politics and Poetic Value.* This volume also has interesting responses to my argument by Jerome McGann and Jed Rasula.

6. For Day's relation to the experimental tradition see "In a fit of knowledge" (*Literal World* 71).

Works Cited

Abrams, M. H. *The Mirror and the Lamp: Romantic Theory and the Critical Tradition.* New York: Norton, 1958.

Adorno, Theodor W. *Against Epistemology: A Metacritique.* Trans. Willis Domingo. Cambridge: MIT P, 1982.

———. *Minima Moralia: Reflections from Damaged Life.* Trans. E. F. N. Jephcott. London: Verso, 1974.

Agamben, Giorgio. *The Coming Community.* Trans. Michael Hardt. Minneapolis: U of Minnesota P, 1993.

Allen, Donald M., ed. *The New American Poetry, 1945–1960.* New York: Grove, 1960.

Alter, Robert. "Charles Reznikoff: Between Present and Past." *Defenses of the Imagination.* Philadelphia: Jewish Publication Society, 1977. 119–35.

Altieri, Charles. *Enlarging the Temple: New Directions in American Poetry during the 1960s.* Lewisburg, PA: Bucknell UP, 1979.

———. "From Symbolist Thought to Immanence: The Ground of Postmodern American Poetics." *Boundary 2* 1.3 (Spring 1973): 605–41.

———. "The Objectivist Tradition." *Chicago Review* 30.3 (Winter 1979): 5–22.

———. "The Unsure Egoist: Robert Creeley and the Theme of Nothingness." *Contemporary Literature* 13 (1972): 162–85.

———. "Without Consequences Is No Politics: A Response to Jerome McGann." von Hallberg 301–8.

Anderson, Margaret. "The Challenge of Emma Goldman." *Little Review* 1 (May 1914): 5–9.

———. "Emma Goldman in Chicago." *Mother Earth* 9 (December 1914): 320–24.

———. *My Thirty Years' War: An Autobiography.* New York: Knopf, 1930.

Andrews, Bruce. "Poetry as Explanation, Poetry as Praxis." *Paradise and Method: Poetics and Praxis.* Evanston: Northwestern UP, 1996. 49–71.

Antin, David. "Modernism and Postmodernism: Approaching the Present in American Poetry." *Boundary 2* 1.1 (Fall 1972): 98–133.

Aragon, Louis. "The Red Front." Trans. E. E. Cummings. *Contempo* 3.5 (February 1933): 4–5, 8.

Auster, Paul. "The Decisive Moment." Hindus, *Man and Poet* 151–65.

——, ed. *The Random House Book of Twentieth-Century French Poetry.* New York: Random House, 1982.

Austin, J. L. *How to Do Things with Words.* Ed. J. O. Urmson and Marina Sbisà. 2nd ed. Cambridge: Harvard UP, 1975.

Baker, Peter. *Obdurate Brilliance: Exteriority and the Modern Long Poem.* Gainesville: U of Florida P, 1991.

——, ed. *Onward: Contemporary Poetry and Poetics.* New York: Peter Lang, 1996.

Barthes, Roland. *The Rustle of Language.* Trans. Richard Howard. New York: Hill and Wang, 1986.

Beach, Christopher. *ABC of Influence: Ezra Pound and the Remaking of the American Poetic Tradition.* Berkeley: U of California P, 1992.

Benét, William Rose. "The Phoenix Nest." *Saturday Review of Literature* 24 March 1934: 580.

Benjamin, Jessica. *The Bonds of Love: Psychoanalysis, Feminism, and the Problem of Domination.* London: Virago, 1990.

Benjamin, Walter. "N [Re The Theory of Knowledge, Theory of Progress]." Trans. Leigh Hafrey and Richard Sieburth. *Benjamin: Philosophy, Aesthetics, History.* Ed. Gary Smith. Chicago: U of Chicago P, 1989. 43–83.

——. "Theologico-Political Fragment." *Reflections: Essays, Aphorisms, Autobiographical Writings.* Trans. Edmund Jephcott. Ed. Peter Demetz. New York: Harcourt Brace Jovanovich, 1979. 312–13.

——. "Theses on the Philosophy of History." *Illuminations.* Trans. Harry Zohn. Ed. Hannah Arendt. New York: Schocken, 1968. 253–64.

Bernstein, Charles. *Content's Dream: Essays, 1975–1984.* Los Angeles: Sun & Moon, 1986.

——. "Hinge, Picture." *Ironwood* 26 (1985): 240–44.

——. "Reznikoff's Nearness." *Sulfur* 32 (1993): 6–38.

——. *Shade.* College Park: Sun & Moon, 1978.

——. *The Sophist.* Los Angeles: Sun & Moon, 1987.

Bernstein, Charles, and Bruce Andrews. "Repossessing the Word." *The L=A=N=G=U=A=G=E Book.* Ed. Bruce Andrews and Charles Bernstein. Carbondale: Southern Illinois UP, 1984. ix–xi.

Bernstein, J. M. *Recovering Ethical Life: Jurgen Habermas and the Future of Critical Theory.* London: Routledge, 1995.

Bernstein, Michael André. *The Tale of the Tribe: Ezra Pound and the Modern Verse Epic.* Princeton: Princeton UP, 1980.

Berry, Eleanor. "Language Made Fluid: The Grammetrics of George Oppen's Recent Poetry." *Contemporary Literature* 25 (1984): 305–22.

Blackmur, R. P. *The Double Agent.* New York: Arrow, 1935.

Blanchot, Maurice. *The Writing of the Disaster.* Trans. Ann Smock. Lincoln: U of Nebraska P, 1986.

Bloch, Ernst. "Marxism and Poetry." Eagleton and Milne 84–90.

Bloom, Harold. *Poetics of Influence.* New Haven: Schwab, 1988.

———. "The Sorrows of American-Jewish Poetry." *Figures of Capable Imagination.* New York: Seabury, 1976. 247–62.

———. *Wallace Stevens: The Poems of Our Climate.* Ithaca: Cornell UP, 1977.

Bosworth, Patricia. *Diane Arbus: A Biography.* New York: Knopf, 1984.

Boyarin, Daniel. *Unheroic Conduct: The Rise of Heterosexuality and the Invention of the Jewish Man.* Berkeley: U of California P, 1997.

Boyarin, Jonathan. "Voices around the Text: The Ethnography of Reading at Mesivta Tifereth Jerusalem." *The Ethnography of Reading.* Ed. Jonathan Boyarin. Berkeley: U of California P, 1993. 212–37.

Bruns, Gerald L. "Dialogue and the Truth of Scepticism." *Religion and Literature* 22.2–3 (1990): 85–91.

Bunting, Basil. "Basil Bunting: Taken from Two Interviews by Paul Johnstone, recorded in April 1974 and April 1975." *Meantime* 1 (April 1977): 67–80.

———. "Carlos Williams's Recent Poetry." *Westminster Magazine* 23.2 (Summer 1934): 649–54.

———. *Complete Poems.* Oxford: Oxford UP, 1994.

———. "English Poetry Today." *Poetry* 39.5 (February 1932): 264–71.

———. Letter to Zukofsky, 27 April 1934. Tls at Beinecke Library, Yale University.

———. "Marvellous Moscow." *Outlook* 27 August 1927: 283–84.

———. "Mr T. S. Eliot." *New English Weekly* 8 September 1932: 499–500.

———. "A Note on Briggflatts." Durham: Basil Bunting Poetry Archive, 1989, n.p.

———. "Observations on Left-Wing Papers." Caddel, *Sharp Study* 44–47.

———. "Pound and 'Zuk.'" *Paideuma* 7 (1978): 373–74.

———. Preface. *Joseph Skipsey: Selected Poems.* Ed. Basil Bunting. Sunderland, England: Ceolfrith, 1976. 7–14.

———. "Prince of Poets." *Sunday Times* [London] 12 November 1972: 38.

———. "The Roots of the Spanish Revolt." *Spectator* 24 July 1936: 138.

Butterick, George F. *A Guide to* The Maximus Poems *of Charles Olson.* Berkeley: U of California P, 1978.

Caddel, Richard. "Acknowledged Land: A Biography of 'They Say Etna' and a Debate between Bunting and Pound." *Ezra Pound and Europe.* Ed. R. Taylor and C. Melchior. Amsterdam: Rodopi, 1993. 69–79.

———. "Consider: Lorine Niedecker and Her Environment." Penberthy, *Woman and Poet* 281–86.

———, ed. *Sharp Study and Long Toil: Basil Bunting Special Issue.* Durham: *Durham University Journal* (March 1995).

Caesar, A. *Dividing Lines: Poetry, Class, and Ideology in the 1930s.* Manchester: Manchester UP, 1991.

Cage, John. *Empty Words.* Middletown: Wesleyan UP, 1979.

———. *M: Writings '67–'72.* Middletown: Wesleyan UP, 1973.

Casillo, Robert. *The Genealogy of Demons: Anti-Semitism, Fascism, and the Myths of Ezra Pound.* Evanston: Northwestern UP, 1988.

Cavell, Stanley. *This New Yet Unapproachable America: Lectures after Emerson after Wittgenstein.* Albuquerque: Living Batch, 1989.

Cendrars, Blaise. *Documentaires: Complete Poems.* Trans. Ron Padgett. Berkeley: U of California P, 1992.

Chilton, Randolph. "The Place of Being in the Poetry of George Oppen." Hatlen, *George Oppen* 89–112.

Coleridge, Samuel Taylor. *Biographia Literaria*. Ed. J. Shawcross. 2 vols. London: Oxford UP, 1907.

Conroy, Jack. Letter to V. J. Jerome, 2 August 1933. V. J. Jerome Papers, Sterling Memorial Library, Yale University.

Conroy, Jack, and Ralph Cheyney, eds. *Unrest: The Rebel Poets Anthology, 1929*. London: Stockwell, 1929.

——. *Unrest: The Rebel Poets Anthology, 1930*. London: Braithwaite and Miller, 1930.

Conte, Joseph M. "Seriality and the Contemporary Long Poem." *Sagetrieb* 11.1–2 (1992): 35–45.

——. *Unending Design: The Forms of Postmodern Poetry*. Ithaca: Cornell UP, 1991.

Corman, Cid. "The Transfigured Prose." *Paideuma* 7 (1978): 447–53.

Cox, C. B., and Arnold P. Hinchcliffe, eds. *T. S. Eliot: The Waste Land—A Casebook*. Nashville: Aurora, 1970.

Cox, Kenneth. "A Commentary on Bunting's 'Villon.'" *Agenda* 16.1 (1978): 20–36.

Crane, Hart. *Complete Poems and Selected Letters and Prose*. Ed. Brom Weber. Garden City, NY: Doubleday Anchor, 1966.

Creeley, Robert. *The Collected Poems of Robert Creeley, 1945–1975*. Berkeley: U of California P, 1982.

——. "Interview: Robert Creeley." With Ekbert Faas. *Towards a New American Poetics: Essays and Interviews*. Ed. Ekbert Faas. Santa Barbara: Black Sparrow, 1978. 165–98.

——. "An Interview with Robert Creeley." With David L. Elliott. *Sagetrieb* 10.1–2 (1991): 45–65.

——. *Tales Out of School: Selected Interviews*. Ann Arbor: U of Michigan P, 1993.

——. *Was That a Real Poem and Other Essays*. Ed. Donald Allen. Bolinas: Four Seasons Foundation, 1979.

Crozier, Andrew. "Paper Bunting." *Sagetrieb* 14.3 (1995): 45–74.

Cunningham, V. *British Writers of the Thirties*. Oxford: Clarendon, 1988.

Davidson, Michael. "Dismantling 'Mantis': Reification and Objectivist Poetry." *American Literary History* 3.3 (1991): 521–41.

——. *Ghostlier Demarcations: Modern Poetry and the Material Word*. Berkeley: U of California P, 1997.

Davie, Donald. *The Poet in the Imaginary Museum: Essays of Two Decades*. Manchester: Carcanet, 1977.

Day, Jean. *The Literal World*. Berkeley: Atelos, 1998.

Dembo, L. S. "The Existential World of George Oppen." *Iowa Review* 3.1 (1972): 64–91.

——. *The Monological Jew*. Madison: U of Wisconsin P, 1988.

——. "The 'Objectivist' Poet: Four Interviews." *Contemporary Literature* 10 (1969): 155–219.

Dembo, L. S., and Cyrena N. Pondrom. *The Contemporary Writer: Interviews with Sixteen Novelists and Poets*. Madison: U of Wisconsin P, 1972.

Dent, Peter, ed. *The Full Note: Lorine Niedecker*. Budleigh Salterton, England: Interim, 1983.

Derrida, Jacques. "Living On: Borderlines." *Deconstruction and Criticism*. Ed. Harold Bloom et al. London: Routledge and Kegan Paul, 1979. 75–176.

———. "Structure, Sign, and Play in the Discourse of the Human Sciences." *Writing and Difference.* Trans. Alan Bass. Chicago: U of Chicago P, 1978. 278–93.

———. *Writing and Difference.* Trans. Alan Bass. London: Routledge, 1978.

Dewey, John. *The Quest for Certainty.* New York: Putnam, 1960.

Dickie, Margaret. *On the Modernist Long Poem.* Iowa City: U of Iowa P, 1986.

Dickinson, Emily. *The Poems.* Ed. Thomas H. Johnson. 3 vols. Cambridge: Belknap Press of Harvard University Press, 1955.

———. *Selected Poems.* New York: Dover, 1990.

di Manno, Yves. *La Tribu Perdue (Pound vs. Mallarmé).* Paris: Java, 1995.

Dorman, Robert L. *Revolt of the Provinces: The Regionalist Movement in America, 1920–1945.* Durham: U of North Carolina P, 1993.

Doyle, Charles. *Richard Aldington: A Biography.* London: Macmillan, 1989.

Dryden, John. "Preface to *Annus Mirabilis.*" *Essays.* Ed. W. P. Ker. Oxford: Clarendon, 1900. 10–26.

dubois, Page. *Sappho Is Burning.* Chicago: U of Chicago P, 1995.

Dufrenne, Mikel. *Language and Philosophy.* Trans. Henry B. Veatch. Bloomington: Indiana UP, 1963.

Duncan, Robert. "The H.D. Book. Part Two: Nights and Days. Chapter 9." *Chicago Review* 30.3 (Winter 1979): 37–88.

———. *The Opening of the Field.* New York: Grove Press, 1960.

DuPlessis, Rachel Blau. *Genders, Races, Religious Cultures in Modern American Poetry, 1904–1934.* New York: Cambridge UP, 2000.

———. "George Oppen: 'What Do We Believe to Live With?'" *Ironwood* 5 (1975): 62–77.

———. "Lorine Niedecker, The Anonymous: Gender, Class, Genre, and Resistances." Penberthy, *Woman and Poet* 113–37.

———. "Manifests." *Diacritics* 26.3–4 (1996): 31–53.

———. "Objectivist Poetics and Political Vision: A Study of Oppen and Pound." Hatlen, *George Oppen* 123–48.

———. "On the Island." *Sagetrieb* 3.1 (1984): 113–18.

Eagleton, Terry, and Drew Milne, eds. *Marxist Literary Theory.* Oxford; Blackwell, 1996.

Evans, George, and August Kleinzahler. "An Interview with Carl Rakosi." *Conjunctions* 11 (1988): 220–45.

Faranda, Lisa Pater, ed. *"Between Your House and Mine": The Letters of Lorine Niedecker to Cid Corman, 1960 to 1970.* Durham: Duke UP, 1986.

Feit Diehl, Joanne. "'Come Slowly—Eden': An Exploration of Women Poets and Their Muse." *Signs* 3 (1978): 572–87.

Felstiner, John. *Paul Celan: Poet, Survivor, Jew.* New Haven: Yale UP, 1995.

Fenollosa, Ernest. *The Chinese Written Character as a Medium for Poetry.* Ed. Ezra Pound. San Francisco: City Lights, 1964.

Finkelstein, Norman. "The Dialectic of *This In Which.*" Hatlen, *George Oppen* 359–73.

———. "Jewish-American Modernism and the Problem of Identity: With Special Reference to the Work of Louis Zukofsky." Scroggins, *Upper Limit Music* 65–79.

———. *The Ritual of New Creation.* Albany: SUNY P, 1992.

Forde, Victoria M. "The Odes." Terrell, *Basil Bunting* 125–44.

Foucault, Michel. *The Archeology of Knowledge.* London: Tavistock, 1972.

Fraser, G. S. "Sound before Sense." *Times Literary Supplement* 5 May 1978: 496.

Fraser, Kathleen. "The Tradition of Marginality" (1985). *Where We Stand: Women Poets on Literary Tradition.* Ed. Sharon Bryan. New York: Norton, 1993. 52–66.

Fredman, Stephen. *Between Judaism and Modernism: Charles Reznikoff, Objectivism, and the* Menorah Journal. Forthcoming.

——. "Call Him Charles." *Sagetrieb* 13.1-2 (1994): 55–81.

Freedman, Jonathan. *Professions of Taste: Henry James, British Aestheticism, and Commodity Culture.* Stanford: Stanford UP, 1990.

Freeman, John, ed. *Not Comforts/But Vision: Essays on the Poetry of George Oppen.* Budleigh Salterton, England: Interim, 1985.

Freeman, Joseph. *An American Testament.* New York: Farrar & Rinehart, 1938.

——. "Four Poems." *Partisan Review* 1 (February–March 1934): 44–46.

——. "Ivory Towers—White and Red." *New Masses* 11 September 1934: 20–24.

——. "Love at Dawn." *Liberator* (April 1922): 12.

Friedman, Susan Stanford. "Craving Stories: Narrative and Lyric in Contemporary Theory and Women's Long Poems." *Feminist Measures: Soundings in Poetry and Theory.* Ed. Lynn Keller and Cristanne Miller. Ann Arbor: U of Michigan P, 1994. 15–42.

——. "Gender and Genre Anxiety: Elizabeth Barrett Browning and H.D. as Epic Poets." *Tulsa Studies in Women's Literature* 5 (1986): 203–28.

——. "When a 'Long' Poem Is a 'Big' Poem: Self-Authorizing Strategies in Women's Twentieth-Century 'Long Poems.'" *LIT* 2 (1990): 9–25.

Galassi, Jonathan. "Determined Forms." *Poetry* 129 (1976): 164–70.

Gardner, Thomas. *Discovering Ourselves in Whitman: The Contemporary American Long Poem.* Urbana: U of Illinois P, 1989.

Géfin, Laszlo. *Ideogram: History of a Poetic Method.* Austin: U of Texas P, 1982.

Gilman, Sander L. *Jewish Self-Hatred: Anti-Semitism and the Hidden Language of Jews.* Baltimore: Johns Hopkins UP, 1986.

Ginsberg, Allen. *Collected Poems, 1947–1980.* New York: Harper & Row, 1984.

Gold, Michael [Irwin Granich]. "Towards Proletarian Art." *Liberator* 4 (February 1921): 20–25.

Greenblatt, Stephen. *Renaissance Self-Fashioning: From More to Shakespeare.* Chicago: U of Chicago P, 1980.

Gregory, Horace. "A Barrel of Poets." *American Mercury* 33 (1934): 382–83.

Grenier, Robert. "A Packet for Robert Creeley." *Boundary 2* 6.3/7.1 (1978): 422–41.

Grice, H. P. "Logic and Conversation." *Speech Acts.* Vol. 3 of *Syntax and Semantics.* Ed. P. Cole and J. Morgan. New York: Academic P, 1975. 41–58.

Gruber, Ruth. "An Interview/Conversation with Ted Berrigan, George Oppen, and Marvin Cohen, June 11th 1973." *Poetry Information* 20–21 (Winter 1979–1980): 110–12.

H.D. *Trilogy. Collected Poems, 1912–1944.* Ed. Louis L. Martz. New York: New Directions, 1983.

Harari, Josue V., and David F. Bell. "Introduction: *Journal à plusieurs voies.*" Serres, *Hermes* ix–xl.

Hatlen, Burton. "Art and/as Labor: Some Dialectical Patterns in 'A'-1 through 'A'-10." *Contemporary Literature* 25 (Summer 1984): 205–34.

——. "Carl Rakosi and the Re-Invention of the Epigram." Rakosi, *Collected Prose* 125–44.

———. "'Feminine Technologies': George Oppen Talks at Denise Levertov." *American Poetry Review* 22.3 (1993): 9–14.
———. "From Modernism to Postmodernism: Zukofsky's 'A'-12." Scroggins, *Upper Limit Music* 214–29.
———, ed. *George Oppen: Man and Poet.* Orono, ME: National Poetry Foundation, 1981.
———. "'Not Altogether Lone in a Lone Universe': George Oppen's *The Materials.*" Hatlen, *George Oppen* 325–57.
———. "Objectivism in Context: Charles Reznikoff and Jewish-American Modernism." Presented at the Annual Meeting of the Modern Language Association, New York, 1992.
———. "Opening Up the Text: George Oppen's 'Of Being Numerous.'" *Ironwood* 26 (1978): 263–95.
———. "Zukofsky, Wittgenstein, and the Poetics of Absence." *Sagetrieb* 1.1 (1982): 63–93.
Havelock, Eric. *The Muse Learns to Write: Reflections on Orality and Literacy from Antiquity to the Present.* New Haven: Yale UP, 1986.
Hayles, N. Katherine. *The Cosmic Web: Scientific Field Models and Literary Strategies in the Twentieth Century.* Ithaca: Cornell UP, 1984.
Hazlitt, William. "On Consistency of Opinion" (1821). *Selected Writings.* Ed. J. Cook. Oxford: Oxford UP, 1991.
Hegel, G. W. F. *The Phenomenology of Mind.* New York: Harper and Row, 1966.
Heidegger, Martin. *An Introduction to Metaphysics.* Trans. Ralph Manheim. Garden City, NY: Anchor Books, 1961.
———. *Poetry, Language, Thought.* Trans. Albert Hofstadter. New York: Harper and Row, 1975.
Hejinian, Lyn. *The Cell.* Los Angeles: Sun & Moon Press, 1992.
———. "The Guard." *The Cold of Poetry.* Los Angeles: Sun & Moon, 1994, 11–37.
———. *The Language of Inquiry.* Berkeley: U of California P, 1999.
———. "The Rejection of Closure." Perelman, *Writing/Talks* 270–91.
———. "The Rejection of Closure." *Poetics Journal* 4 (May 1984): 134–43.
———. "Two Stein Talks." *Temblor* 3 (1986): 128–39.
Heller, Michael, ed. *Carl Rakosi: Man and Poet.* Orono, ME: National Poetry Foundation, 1993.
———. *Conviction's Net of Branches: Essays on the Objectivist Poets and Poetry.* Carbondale: Southern Illinois UP, 1985.
———. "Oppen and Stevens: Reflections on the Lyrical and Philosophical." *Sagetrieb* 12.3 (1993): 13–32.
Heymann, C. David. *Ezra Pound: The Last Rower—A Political Profile.* New York: Seaver, 1976.
Hill, Geoffrey. *The Lords of Limit: Essays on Literature and Ideas.* London: Deutsch, 1984.
Hindus, Milton. *Charles Reznikoff: A Critical Essay.* Santa Barbara: Black Sparrow, 1977.
———, ed. *Charles Reznikoff: Man and Poet.* Orono, ME: National Poetry Foundation, 1984.
Hocquard, Emmanuel. *La Bibliothèque de Trieste.* Royaumont: Éditions Royaumont, 1988.

Homberger, Eric. *American Writers and Radical Politics, 1900–39: Equivocal Commitments.* Basingstoke: Macmillan, 1986.
——. *The Art of the Real: Poetry in England and America since 1939.* London: Dent, 1977.
Hoover, Paul, ed. *Postmodern American Poetry: An Anthology.* New York: Norton, 1994.
Howe, Irving, and Eliezer Greenberg, eds. *A Treasury of Yiddish Poetry.* New York: Holt, Rinehart and Winston, 1969.
Howe, Susan. *My Emily Dickinson.* Berkeley: North Atlantic, 1985.
Hunting, Constance. "'At Least Not Nowhere': George Oppen as Maine Poet." *Paideuma* 10 (1981): 53–58.
Husserl, Edmund. *Ideas: General Introduction to Pure Phenomenology.* Trans. W. R. Boyce Gibson. London: Collier, 1962.
Hynes, Samuel. *The Auden Generation: Literature and Politics in the 1930s.* London: Bodley Head, 1976.
I'll Take My Stand: The South and the Agrarian Tradition. New York: Harper, 1930.
Johnson, Barbara. "Metaphor, Metonymy, and Voice in *Their Eyes Were Watching God.*" *Zora Neale Hurston.* Ed. Harold Bloom. New York: Chelsea House, 1986. 157–73.
Judd, A. *Ford Madox Ford.* London: Collins, 1990.
Judovitz, Dalia. "Vision, Representation, and Technology in Descartes." Levin 63–86.
Keller, Lynn. *Forms of Expansion: Recent Women's Long Poems.* Chicago: U of Chicago P, 1997.
——. "The Twentieth-Century Long Poem." *Columbia History of American Poetry.* Ed. Jay Parini. New York: Columbia UP, 1993. 534–63.
Kenner, Hugh. *The Art of Poetry.* Chicago: Chicago UP, 1959.
——. *A Homemade World: The American Modernist Writers.* New York: Morrow, 1975.
——. *The Pound Era.* Berkeley: U of California P, 1971.
Langer, Elinor. *Josephine Herbst.* Boston: Little, Brown, 1984.
Laughlin, James. "Pound's Economics." *Ezra Pound: The Legacy of Kulchur.* Ed. M. Smith and W. A. Ulmer. Tuscaloosa: U of Alabama P, 1988. 67–85.
Leavis, F. R. "Retrospect 1950." *New Bearings in English Poetry.* London: Penguin, 1963.
——, ed. *A Selection from "Scrutiny."* 2 vols. Cambridge: Cambridge UP, 1968.
Lenin, V. I. *Materialism and Emperio-Criticism.* Peking: Foreign Languages Press, 1972.
Lentricchia, Frank. "Lyric in the Culture of Capital." *Subject to History: Ideology, Class, Gender.* Ed. D. Simpson. Ithaca: Cornell UP, 1991. 191–216.
Levertov, Denise. "Poetry, Pure and Complex." *New Leader* 18 February 1963: 26–27.
Levin, David Michael, ed. *Modernity and the Hegemony of Vision.* Berkeley: U of California P, 1993.
Levine, George, ed. *Aesthetics and Ideology.* New Brunswick: Rutgers UP, 1994.
Lewis, Wyndham. *Blasting and Bombardiering.* London: Calder and Boyars, 1967.
Lipking, Lawrence. *The Life of the Poet: Beginning and Ending Poetic Careers.* Chicago: U of Chicago P, 1981.
Lopate, Phillip. "The Pen on Foot: The Literature of Walking Around." *Parnassus* 18.2–19.1 (1993): 176–212.
Lucas, J. "Edgell Rickword." *Moderns and Contemporaries: Novelists, Poets, Critics.* Brighton: Harvester, 1985. 144–50.
——, ed. *The 1930s: A Challenge to Orthodoxy.* Hassocks: Harvester, 1978.

Lucie-Smith, Edward. "A Man for the Music of Words." *Sunday Times* [London] 25 July 1965: 33.

Lyotard, Jean-Francois. *The Differend: Phrases in Dispute.* Trans. Georges Van Den Abbeele. Manchester: Manchester UP, 1988.

Macann, Christopher. *Four Phenomenological Philosophers: Husserl, Heidegger, Sartre, Merleau-Ponty.* New York: Routledge, 1993.

MacLeish, Archibald. "Nevertheless One Debt." *Poetry* 38 (July 1931): 208–16.

Makin, Peter. *Bunting: The Shaping of His Verse.* Oxford: Clarendon, 1992.

Mallarmé, Stephen. *Selected Prose, Poems, Essays, and Letters.* Ed. Bradford Cook. Baltimore: Johns Hopkins UP, 1956.

Martone, John. "On Reznikoff and 'Talking Hebrew in Every Language Under the Sun.'" *Sagetrieb* 7.2 (1988): 71–80.

Matthias, John, ed. *23 Modern British Poets.* Chicago: Swallow, 1971.

McAleavey, David. "Clarity and Process: Oppen's 'Of Being Numerous.'" Hatlen, *George Oppen* 381–404.

McGann, Jerome J. "Contemporary Poetry, Alternate Routes." *Critical Inquiry* 13 (1987): 624–47.

———. *The Textual Condition.* Princeton: Princeton UP, 1991.

Messerli, Douglas, ed. *From the Other Side of the Century: A New American Poetry, 1960–1990.* Los Angeles: Sun & Moon, 1994.

Middleton, Peter. *The Inward Gaze: Masculinity and Subjectivity in Modern Culture.* London: Routledge, 1992.

Miller, James E., Jr. *The American Quest for a Supreme Fiction: Whitman's Legacy in the Personal Epic.* Chicago: U of Chicago P, 1979.

Monroe, Harriet. "The Arrogance of Youth." *Poetry* 37.6 (March 1931): 328–33.

[Monroe, Harriet]. "Notes." *Poetry* 37.5 (February 1931): 294–95.

Monroe, Harriet, and Alice Corbin Henderson, eds. *The New Poetry: An Anthology of Twentieth-Century Verse in English.* New ed. New York: Macmillan, 1934.

Montefiore, Jan. "'Undeservedly Forgotten': Women Poets and Others in the 1930s." *P. N. Review* 95 (January–February 1994): 25–29.

Monteiro, George. "George Oppen's Hudson River 'Night Scene.'" *Sagetrieb* 9.1-2 (1990): 225–27.

Morrison, Blake, and Andrew Motion, eds. *The Penguin Book of Contemporary British Poetry.* Harmondsworth: Penguin, 1982.

Morse, Jonathan. *Word by Word: The Language of Memory.* Ithaca: Cornell UP, 1990.

Mottram, Eric. "Conversation with Basil Bunting on the Occasion of His 75th Birthday." *Poetry Information* 19 (1975): 3–10.

Nancy, Jean Luc. "Finite History." *The States of "Theory": History, Art, and Critical Discourse.* Ed. David Carroll. New York: Columbia UP, 1990. 149–72.

———. *The Inoperative Community.* Trans. Peter Connor. Minneapolis: U of Minnesota P, 1991.

Naylor, Paul. "The Pre-position 'of.'" *Contemporary Literature* 32 (1991): 100–151.

Nelson, Cary. *Repression and Recovery: Modern American Poetry and the Politics of Cultural Memory, 1910–1945.* Madison: U of Wisconsin P, 1989.

Nicholls, Peter. *Ezra Pound: Politics, Economics, and Writing.* London: Macmillan, 1984.

———. "Lorine Niedecker: Rural Surreal." Penberthy, *Woman and Poet* 193–217.

——. *Modernisms: A Literary Guide.* Berkeley: U of California P, 1995.
Niedecker, Lorine. "Extracts from Letters to Kenneth Cox." Dent, ed. 36–42.
——. *From This Condensery: The Complete Writings of Lorine Niedecker.* Ed. Robert J. Bertholf. Highlands: Jargon, 1985.
——. *The Granite Pail: Selected Poems.* Ed. Cid Corman. San Francisco: North Point Press, 1985.
——. Letter to Charles Reznikoff, 23 November 1959. Charles Reznikoff Papers. Archive for New Poetry, Mandeville Department of Special Collections. U of California, San Diego.
——. Letter to Clayton Eshleman, 18 November 1967. Clayton Eshleman Papers, Library, New York U.
——. Letter to Gail Roub. *Origin* 4th ser. 16 (July 1981): 42.
Nielsen, Aldon Lynn. *Reading Race: White American Poets and the Racial Discourse in the Twentieth Century.* Athens: U of Georgia P, 1988.
North, Michael. *The Political Aesthetic of Yeats, Eliot, and Pound.* Cambridge: Cambridge UP, 1991.
Nougé, Paul. *Un miroir exemplaire de Maupassant* in *L'expérience continue.* Bruxelles: Les Lèvres Nues, 1966.
Oderman, Kevin. "Earth and Awe: The One Poetry of George Oppen." *Sagetrieb* 3.1 (1984): 63–73.
Olson, Charles. *The Collected Poems of Charles Olson.* Ed. George F. Butterick. Berkeley: U of California P, 1987.
——. *Collected Prose.* Ed. Donald Allen and Benjamin Friedlander. Berkeley: U of California P, 1997.
——. *Human Universe and Other Essays.* Ed. Donald M. Allen. New York: Grove, 1967.
——. *Muthologos: The Collected Lectures and Interviews.* Ed. George F. Butterick. Vol. 1. Bolinas: Four Seasons, 1978.
Olson, Charles, and Robert Creeley. *The Complete Correspondence.* Ed. George F. Butterick. Vols. 1 and 2. Santa Barbara: Black Sparrow, 1980.
Oppen, George. "An Adequate Vision: A George Oppen Daybook." Ed. Michael Davidson. *Ironwood* 26 (1985): 5–31.
——. *Collected Poems.* New York: New Directions, 1975.
——. "A Conversation with George Oppen." With Charles Amirkhanian and David Gitin. *Ironwood* 5 (1975): 21–24.
——. Foreword. *Poems, 1937–1975: Volume 2 of the Complete Poems of Charles Reznikoff.* Ed. Seamus Cooney. Santa Barbara: Black Sparrow, 1978. 7.
——. George Oppen Papers, MSS 16. Mandeville Special Collections Library, UCSD.
——. "Interview with George Oppen [1975]." With Reinhold Schiffer. *Sagetrieb* 3.3 (1984): 9–23.
——. "Letters to Andy Meyer." *Ironwood* 26 (1985): 104–10.
——. "Letters to June Oppen Degnan." *Ironwood* 26 (1985): 215–36.
——. "Letters to Rachel Blau DuPlessis." *Ironwood* 24 (1984): 119–38.
——. Letter to Charles Reznikoff, ca. 1962. Charles Reznikoff Papers. Archive for New Poetry, Mandeville Department of Special Collections. University of California, San Diego.
——. *The Materials.* New York/San Francisco: New Directions/San Francisco Review, 1962.

———. "The Mind's Own Place" (1963). *Montemora* 1 (Fall 1975): 132–37.
———. "A Morality Play: Preface." *Nothing Doing in London* 2 (January 1968): n.p. [81–83].
———. "Oppen on His Poems: A Discussion." With L. S. Dembo. Hatlen, *George Oppen* 197–213.
———. "Poetry and Politics: A Conversation with George and Mary Oppen." With Burton Hatlen and Tom Mandel. Hatlen, *George Oppen* 23–50.
———. *Primitive.* Santa Barbara: Black Sparrow, 1978.
———. *Seascape: Needle's Eye.* Fremont, MI: Sumac, 1972.
———. *Selected Letters.* Ed. Rachel Blau DuPlessis. Durham: Duke UP, 1990.
———. "Statement on Poetics." *Sagetrieb* 3.3 (1984): 25–27.
———. "Three Oppen Letters with a Note." Ed. Serge Fauchereau. *Ironwood* 5 (1975): 78–85.
———. "Three Poets." *Poetry* 100.5 (1962): 329–33.
Oppen, George, and Mary Oppen. "Conversation with George and Mary Oppen, May 25, 1975." With Kevin Power. *Texas Quarterly* 21.1 (1978): 35–52.
Oppen, Mary. *Meaning a Life: An Autobiography.* Santa Barbara: Black Sparrow, 1978.
Ovid. *Metamorphoses.* Trans. Rolfe Humphries. Bloomington: Indiana UP, 1983.
Palmer, Michael. "Active Boundaries: Poetry at the Periphery." (1990). Baker, *Onward* 265–86.
———. "On Objectivism." *Sulfur* 26 (Spring 1990): 117–26.
Pearce, Roy Harvey. *The Continuity of American Poetry.* Princeton: Princeton UP, 1961.
Pearce, T. M. "What Is a Folk Poet?" *Western Folklore* 12 (1953): 242–48.
Penberthy, Jenny, ed. *Lorine Niedecker: Woman and Poet.* Orono, ME: National Poetry Foundation, 1996.
———, ed. *Niedecker and the Correspondence with Zukofsky, 1931–1970.* Cambridge: Cambridge UP, 1993.
———. "'The Very Variant': Lorine Niedecker's Manuscript Collection." *Library Chronicle of the University of Texas at Austin* 22.1–2 (1992): 113–47.
Perelman, Bob. *The Marginalization of Poetry: Language Writing and Literary History.* Princeton: Princeton UP, 1996.
———, ed. *Writing/Talks.* Carbondale: Southern Illinois UP, 1985.
Perloff, Marjorie. "'Barbed-Wire Entanglements': The 'New American Poetry,' 1930–1932." *Modernism/Modernity* 2.1 (1995): 145–75.
———. *The Dance of the Intellect: Studies in the Poetry of the Pound Tradition.* Cambridge: Cambridge UP, 1985.
———. *Poetic License: Essays on Modernist and Postmodernist Lyric.* Evanston: Northwestern UP, 1990.
———. *The Poetics of Indeterminacy: Rimbaud to Cage.* Princeton: Princeton UP, 1981.
———. *Radical Artifice: Writing Poetry in the Age of Media.* Chicago: U of Chicago P, 1991.
———. "'Shape of the Lines': Oppen and the Metric of Difference." Hatlen, *George Oppen* 215–29.
———. "The Shipwreck of the Singular: George Oppen's 'Of Being Numerous.'" *Ironwood* 26 (1985): 193–204.
Peterson, Jeffrey. "'The Allotropes of Vision': Carl Rakosi and the Psychology of Microscopy." Heller, *Carl Rakosi* 119–91.

Pound, Ezra. *The Cantos.* London: Faber and Faber, 1986.

———. *Gaudier-Brzeska: A Memoir.* New York: New Directions, 1970.

———. *Guide to Kulchur.* New York: New Directions, 1970.

———. *The Letters of Ezra Pound, 1907–1941.* Ed. D. D. Paige. New York: Harcourt, Brace and World, 1950.

———. *Literary Essays of Ezra Pound.* Ed. T. S. Eliot. London: Faber and Faber, 1954.

———. "Notes on Particular Details." *Active Anthology.* Ed. Ezra Pound. London: Faber, 1933. 253–55.

———. Preface. *Discrete Series.* By George Oppen. Rpt. *Paideuma* 10 (1981): 13.

Pound, Ezra, and James Laughlin. *Ezra Pound and James Laughlin: Selected Letters.* Ed. David M. Gordon. New York: Norton, 1994.

Pound, Ezra, and Marcella Spann, eds. *Confucius to Cummings: An Anthology of Poetry.* New York: New Directions, 1964.

Pound, Ezra, and Louis Zukofsky. *Pound/Zukofsky: Selected Letters of Ezra Pound and Louis Zukofsky.* Ed. Barry Ahearn. New York: New Directions, 1987.

Power, Kevin. "An Interview with George and Mary Oppen." *Montemora* 4 (1978): 187–203.

Prunty, Wyatt. "Emaciated Poetry and the Imaginative Diet." *Sewanee Review* 93 (1985): 78–94. Rpt. *"Fallen from the Symboled World": Precedents for the New Formalism.* New York: Oxford UP, 1990. 57–88.

Prynne, J. H. "English Poetry and Emphatical Language." *Proceedings of the British Academy* 74 (1988): 135–69.

Quartermain, Peter. *Basil Bunting: Poet of the North.* Durham: Basil Bunting Poetry Archive, 1990.

———. *Disjunctive Poetics: From Gertrude Stein and Louis Zukofsky to Susan Howe.* New York: Cambridge UP, 1992.

Rabinbach, Anson. "Between Enlightenment and Apocalypse: Benjamin, Bloch, and Modern German Jewish Messianism." *New German Critique* 34 (Winter 1985): 78–123.

Rainey, Lawrence. "The Creation of the Avant-Garde: F. T. Marinetti and Ezra Pound." *Modernism/Modernity* 1.3 (1994): 195–219.

Rakosi, Carl. *Collected Poems.* Orono, ME: National Poetry Foundation, 1986.

———. *Collected Prose.* Orono, ME: National Poetry Foundation, 1983.

———. *Ex Cranium, Night.* Los Angeles: Black Sparrow Press, 1975.

———. "A Note on the 'Objectivists.' Feb. 8, 1969." *Stony-Brook Poetics Journal* 3/4 (1969): 36–37.

———. *Poems, 1923–1941.* Ed. Andrew Crozier. Los Angeles: Sun & Moon, 1995.

———. *Selected Poems.* Norfolk: New Directions, 1941.

———. "A Word about the Objectivists." *To Magazine* 2.1 (Spring 1994): 63–66.

Reagan, Dale. "Basil Bunting: Obiter Dicta." Terrell, *Basil Bunting* 229–74.

Renwick, Roger de V. *English Folk Poetry: Structure and Meaning.* London: Batsford, 1980.

"Resolution on *Monde.*" *Literature of the World Revolution.* Special Number 1931 (Reports, Resolutions, Debates of the Second International Conference of Revolutionary Writers).

Reverdy, Pierre. *Plupart du Temps, 1915–1922.* Paris: Gallimard, 1945.

———. *Selected Poems of Pierre Reverdy.* Selected by Mary Ann Caws. Trans. John Ashbery, Mary Ann Caws, and Patricia Terry. Winston-Salem: Wake Forest UP, 1991.

Rexroth, Kenneth. *American Poetry in the Twentieth Century.* New York: Herder & Herder, 1971.

———, intro. and trans. *Pierre Reverdy: Selected Poems.* New York: New Directions, 1969.

Reznikoff, Charles. *By the Waters of Manhattan.* New York: Boni, 1930.

———. *By the Waters of Manhattan: Selected Verse.* Intro. C. P. Snow. New York/San Francisco: New Directions/San Francisco Review, 1962.

———. *Family Chronicle.* New York: Universe, 1971.

———. "First, There Is the Need." *Sparrow* 52 (January 1977): [unpaginated].

———. *Holocaust.* Santa Barbara: Black Sparrow, 1975.

———. Letter to Albert Lewin, 17 September 1933. Albert Lewin Papers. Special Collections. U of Arizona.

———. Letter to George Oppen, 15 December 1959. George Oppen Papers. Archive for New Poetry, Mandeville Department of Special Collections. U of California, San Diego.

———. *The Manner Music.* Santa Barbara: Black Sparrow, 1977.

———. "A Memoir." *Ironwood* 5 (1975): 29.

———. *Poems, 1918–1936: Volume 1 of the Complete Poems of Charles Reznikoff.* Ed. Seamus Cooney. Santa Barbara: Black Sparrow, 1976.

———. *Poems, 1937–1975: Volume 2 of the Complete Poems of Charles Reznikoff.* Ed. Seamus Cooney. Santa Barbara: Black Sparrow, 1977.

———. *Separate Way.* New York: Objectivist Press, 1936.

———. "A Talk with L. S. Dembo." Hindus, *Man and Poet* 97–107.

———. *Testimony: The United States (1885–1915) Recitative.* 2 vols. Santa Barbara: Black Sparrow, 1978, 1979.

———. *Testimony: The United States 1885–1890, Recitative.* New York/San Francisco: New Directions/San Francisco Review, 1965.

Richards, I. A. *Principles of Literary Criticism.* 1925. New York: Harcourt, Brace & World, n.d.

Rosenberg, Harold. "French Silence and American Poetry." *The Tradition of the New.* New York: Horizon, 1969. 87–95.

Rosenberg, Joel. "Jeremiah and Ezekiel." *The Literary Guide to the Bible.* Ed. Robert Alter and Frank Kermode. Cambridge: Harvard UP, 1987. 184–206.

Rosenthal, M. L., and Sally Gall. *The Modern Poetic Sequence: The Genius of Modern Poetry.* New York: Oxford UP, 1983.

Ross, Andrew. "The New Sentence and the Commodity Form: Recent American Writing." *Marxism and the Interpretation of Culture.* Ed. Cary Nelson and Lawrence Grossberg. Basingstoke: Macmillan, 1988. 361–80.

Scarfe, Francis. *Auden and After: The Liberation of Poetry, 1930–1941.* London: Routledge, 1942.

Schappes, Morris U. "Historic and Contemporary Particulars." *Poetry* 41.6 (March 1933): 340–43.

———. "Objectivists Again" [Letters from Schappes and Louis Zukofsky]. *Poetry* 42.2 (May 1933): 117–18.

Schneider, Isidor. "Toward Revolutionary Poetry." *Comrade: Mister: Poems.* New York: Equinox Cooperative Press, 1934. 42.

Scholem, Gershom. *Major Trends in Jewish Mysticism.* New York: Schocken, 1961.
———. "Toward an Understanding of the Messianic Idea in Judaism." Trans. Michael A. Meyer. *The Messianic Idea in Judaism.* New York: Schocken, 1971. 1–36.
Schor, Naomi. *Reading in Detail: Aesthetics and the Feminine.* New York: Methuen, 1987.
Schulberg, Budd. *Moving Pictures: Memories of a Hollywood Prince.* New York: Stein & Day, 1981.
Scroggins, Mark. "The Revolutionary Word: Louis Zukofsky, *New Masses,* and Political Radicalism in the 1930s." Scroggins, *Upper Limit Music* 44–64.
———, ed. *Upper Limit Music: The Writing of Louis Zukofsky.* Tuscaloosa: U of Alabama P, 1997.
Seed, John. "Living the Storm: George Oppen's 'Songs of Experience.'" Freeman, *Not Comforts* 10–25.
Segalen, Victor. *Stèles.* Trans. Michael Taylor. Santa Monica: Lapis, 1987.
Seidman, Hugh. "Louis Zukofsky and the Polytechnic Institute of Brooklyn (1958–61)." Terrell, *Louis Zukofsky* 97–102.
Serres, Michel. *Hermes: Literature, Science, Philosophy.* Ed. Josue V. Harari and David F. Bell. Baltimore: Johns Hopkins UP, 1982.
Shapiro, Harvey. "Remembering Charles Reznikoff." Hindus, *Man and Poet* 85–87.
Sharp, Thomas Frederick. "'Objectivists' 1927–1934: A Critical History of the Work and Association of Louis Zukofsky, William Carlos Williams, Charles Reznikoff." Diss. Stanford U, 1982.
Shechner, Mark. *After the Revolution: Studies in the Contemporary Jewish American Imagination.* Bloomington: Indiana UP, 1987.
Shevelow, Katherine. "History and Objectification in Charles Reznikoff's Documentary Poems, *Testimony* and *Holocaust.*" *Sagetrieb* 1.2 (1982): 290–306.
Shoemaker, Steve. "Between Contact and Exile: Louis Zukofsky's Poetry of Survival." Scroggins, *Upper Limit Music* 23–43.
Shoptaw, John. "Lyric Incorporated: The Serial Object of George Oppen and Langston Hughes." *Sagetrieb* 12.3 (1993): 105–24.
Silliman, Ron. "I Wanted to Write Sentences: Decision Making in the American Long-poem." *Sagetrieb* 11.1–2 (1992): 11–20.
———. *The New Sentence.* New York: Roof Books, 1987.
———. *Paradise.* Providence: Burning Deck, 1985.
———. "Third Phase Objectivism." *Paideuma* 10 (1981): 85–89.
Simon, Linda. "An Annotated Bibliography of Works about Charles Reznikoff: 1920–1983." Hindus, *Man and Poet* 411–40.
Skelton, Robin, ed. *Poetry of the Thirties.* London: Penguin, 1964.
Spector, Herman. *Bastard in the Ragged Suit: Writings with Drawings.* Ed. Bud Johns and Judith S. Clancy. San Francisco: Synergistic Press, 1977.
Spender, Stephen. *World Within World: The Autobiography.* London: Hamilton, 1951.
Spiller, Robert E., et al., eds. *Literary History of the United States.* 3rd ed. New York: Macmillan, 1963.
Spinoza, Benedict. *Ethic.* Trans. William Hale White. 4th ed. London: Oxford UP, 1923.
———. *Ethics and "De Intellectus Emendatione."* Trans. A. Boyle, intro. George Santayana. London: Dent (Everyman's Library), 1910.
Steiner, George. "Postscript." *Language and Silence: Essays on Language, Literature, and the Inhuman.* New York: Atheneum, 1967. 155–68.

Stevens, Wallace. *Collected Poems.* New York: Knopf, 1961.

———. *The Necessary Angel.* New York: Vintage, 1965.

———. *Poems.* Selected by Samuel French Morse. New York: Vintage, 1954.

Stieglitz, Alfred. "Ten Stories." *Twice-a-Year* 5–6 (1940–41): 135–63.

Sullivan, J. P., ed. *Ezra Pound: A Critical Anthology.* London: Penguin, 1970.

Syrkin, Marie. "Charles: A Memoir." Hindus, *Man and Poet* 37–67.

Taggard, Genevieve, ed. *May Days: An Anthology of Verse from "Masses-Liberator."* New York: Boni & Liveright, 1925.

Taggart, John. "Deep Jewels: George Oppen's *Seascape: Needle's Eye.*" *Ironwood* 26 (Fall 1985): 159–68.

———. "George Oppen and the Anthologies." *Ironwood* 26 (Fall 1985): 252–62.

Taupin, Rene. *L'Influence du Symbolisme français sur la Poésie américaine (de 1910 à 1920).* Paris: Champion, 1929.

Taylor, Charles. *Sources of the Self: The Making of the Modern Identity.* Cambridge: Cambridge UP, 1989.

Terrell, Carroll F., ed. *Basil Bunting: Man and Poet.* Orono, ME: National Poetry Foundation, 1981.

———, ed. *Louis Zukofsky: Man and Poet.* Orono, ME: National Poetry Foundation, 1980.

Thompson, Stith. "Problems in Folklore." *An Introduction to Research in English Literary History.* Ed. Chauncey Sanders. New York: Macmillan, 1952. 253–76.

Tolley, A. Trevor. *The Poetry of the Thirties.* London: Gollancz, 1975.

Tomlinson, Charles. "An Introductory Note on the Poetry of George Oppen." *Ironwood* 5 (1975): 12–18.

———. *Some Americans: A Personal Record.* Berkeley: U of California P, 1981.

von Hallberg, Robert, ed. *Politics and Poetic Value.* Chicago: U of Chicago P, 1988.

Waldrop, Bernard. "George Oppen." *Burning Deck* 1 (1962): 51.

Walker, Jeffrey. *Bardic Ethos and the American Epic Poem: Whitman, Pound, Crane, Williams, Olson.* Baton Rouge: Louisiana State UP, 1989.

Watten, Barrett. "The Bride of the Assembly Line: From Material Text to Cultural Poetics." *The Impercipient Lecture Series* 1.8 (October 1997): 1–37.

———. *Total Syntax.* Carbondale: Southern Illinois UP, 1985.

Watten, Barrett, et al. "for *Change.*" *In the American Tree.* Ed. Ron Silliman. Orono, ME: National Poetry Foundation, 1986. 484–90.

Weaver, Mike. *William Carlos Williams: The American Background.* Cambridge: Cambridge UP, 1971.

We Gather Strength: Poems by Herman Spector, Joseph Kalar, Edwin Rolfe, Sol Funaroff. Intro. Michael Gold. New York: Liberal Press, 1933.

Weinfield, Henry. "'Of Being Numerous' by George Oppen." Hatlen, *George Oppen* 375–79.

Werner, Marta. *Emily Dickinson's Open Folios: Scenes of Reading, Surfaces of Writing.* Ann Arbor: U of Michigan P, 1995.

Whiting, Cécile. *Antifascism in American Art.* New Haven: Yale UP, 1989.

Whitman, Walt. *Complete Poetry and Collected Prose.* Ed. Justin Kaplan. New York: Library of America, 1982.

Whittemore, Reed. *William Carlos Williams: Poet from Jersey.* Boston: Houghton Mifflin, 1975.

Williams, Jonathan, ed. *Epitaphs for Lorine.* Penland, NC: Jargon, 1973.

Williams, Raymond. *Culture.* London: Fontana, 1981.

———. *Marxism and Literature.* Oxford: Oxford UP, 1977.

Williams, William Carlos. *Autobiography.* New York: New Directions, 1951.

———. *Collected Poems, Vol. 1, 1909–1939.* Ed. A. Walton Litz and Christopher MacGowan. New York: New Directions, 1986.

———. *Collected Poems, Vol. 2, 1939–1962.* Ed. Christopher MacGowan. New York: New Directions, 1986.

———. *The Embodiment of Knowledge.* Ed. Ron Loewinsohn. New York: New Directions, 1974.

———. Letter to Louis Zukofsky, 7 May 1929. Louis Zukofsky Papers. Harry Ransom Humanities Research Center, U of Texas at Austin.

———. "The New Poetical Economy." *Poetry* 44 (July 1934): 220–25.

———. Rev. of *An "Objectivists" Anthology,* ed. Louis Zukofsky. *Symposium* 4.1 (January 1933): 114–17.

———. *Selected Letters.* Ed. John C. Thirlwall. New York: McDowell Obolensky, 1957.

Wilson, Edmund. *The Thirties: From Notebooks and Diaries of the Period.* Ed. Leon Edel. London: Macmillan, 1980.

Wittgenstein, Ludwig. *Philosophical Investigations.* Trans. G. E. M. Anscombe. Oxford: Blackwell, 1958.

———. *Zettel.* Ed. G. E. M. Anscombe and G. H. von Wright. Trans. G. E. M. Anscombe. Berkeley: U of California P, 1967.

Works Progress Administration. *Wisconsin: A Guide to the Badger State.* Madison: Wisconsin Library Association, 1941.

Writers Take Sides: Letters about the War in Spain from 418 American Authors. New York: League of American Writers, 1938.

Yeats, W. B. *The Collected Poems.* London: Macmillan, 1952.

Yerushalmi, Yosef Hayim. *Zakhor: Jewish History and Jewish Memory.* Seattle: U of Washington P, 1982.

Young, Dennis. "Conversation with Mary Oppen." *Iowa Review* 18.3 (1988): 18–47.

Ziarek, Krzysztof. *Inflected Language: Towards a Hermeneutics of Nearness.* Albany: SUNY Press, 1994.

Zukofsky, Louis. *"A".* Berkeley: U of California P, 1978.

———. *All: The Collected Short Poems, 1923–1964.* New York: Norton, 1965.

———. "American Poetry, 1920–1930." *Symposium* 2 (1931): 60–84.

———. *Bottom: On Shakespeare.* Austin: Ark Press, 1963.

———. "The *Cantos* of Ezra Pound." *Criterion* 10 (April 1931): 424–40.

———. *Complete Short Poetry.* Baltimore: Johns Hopkins UP, 1991.

———. "Imagisme." *New Review* 1.2 (May–July 1931): 160–61.

———. Letter to Charles Reznikoff, 9 November 1949. Charles Reznikoff Papers. Archive for New Poetry, Mandeville Department of Special Collections, U of California, San Diego.

———. "Objectivists Again" [Letters from Morris U. Schappes and Zukofsky]. *Poetry* 42.2 (May 1933): 117–18.

———, ed. *An "Objectivists" Anthology.* Le Beausset, France, and New York: To Publishers, 1932.

———, ed. *Poetry: A Magazine of Verse* 37.5 (February 1931). Special "Objectivists" issue.

———. "Preface—'Recencies' in Poetry." *An "Objectivists" Anthology.* Ed. Louis Zukofsky. Le Beausset: TO Publishers, 1932. 9–25.

———. *Prepositions: The Collected Critical Essays.* Expanded edition. Berkeley: U of California P, 1981.

———. "Program: 'Objectivists' 1931." *Poetry* 37.5 (February 1931): 268–72.

———. "Sincerity and Objectification with Special Reference to the Work of Charles Reznikoff." *Poetry* 37.5 (February 1931): 272–85.

———. "Statement." *The Case of Ezra Pound.* Ed. Charles Norman. New York: Bodley, 1948. 55–57.

———. *A Test of Poetry.* New York: Jargon/Corinth, 1964.

———, ed. *A Workers Anthology.* Typescript. Basil Bunting Poetry Archive, University of Durham. MS 54.

Contributors

CHARLES ALTIERI teaches English literature at University of California, Berkeley. He is the author of six books and numerous essays. The books include *Canons and Consequences, Painterly Abstraction in Modernist American Poetry, Act and Quality,* and *Self and Sensibility in Contemporary American Poetry.* His *Subjective Agency* appeared in 1994. He was born in 1942 in New York City, which his accent still honors.

CHARLES BERNSTEIN's newest collections are *My Way: Speeches and Poems* (University of Chicago) and *Republics of Reality: 1975–1995* (Sun & Moon); he is editor of *Close Listening: Poetry and the Performed Word* (Oxford). Bernstein is David Gray Professor of Poetry and Letters at SUNY-Buffalo, where he teaches in the Poetics Program.

ANDREW CROZIER was educated at Cambridge, SUNY-Buffalo, and Essex. He is the author of twelve books of poetry collected in *All Where Each Is* (1985), and "Selected Poems" in *Ghosts in the Corridor* (with Donald Davie and C. H. Sisson) (1992). He has written essays on George Oppen, Carl Rakosi, Roy Fisher, Donald Davie, the New Apocalypse, and postwar British poetry. He was the editor (with Tim Longville) of *A Various Art* (1987), of Carl Rakosi's *Early Poems, 1923–41,* and of John Rodker, *Poems and Adolphe 1920.* Crozier teaches at the University of Sussex.

YVES DI MANNO is a French writer and translator, born in 1954. He has published ten books of his poetry, including *Champs* (Flammarion, 1984–87),

Le Méridien (Unes, 1987), and *Kambuja* (Flammarion, 1992), and translated Williams's *Paterson,* Pound's *Chinese Cantos* and *Guide to Kulchur,* and three books by Oppen. Since 1994 he has been the editor of the poetry series at Flammarion. His controversial essay about Pound's poetics, *La tribu perdue (Pound vs. Mallarmé),* including an "Objectivist" section, was published by Java Press in 1995.

Rachel Blau DuPlessis's most recent books are *Genders, Races, Religious Cultures in Modern American Poetry, 1904–1934* (Cambridge, 2000) and *Drafts 15–XXX, The Fold* (Potes & Poets, 1997). Her long poem project also appears in *Tabula Rosa* (1987) and *Drafts 3–14* (1991), and her essays in *The Pink Guitar: Writing as Feminist Practice* (1990). She edited *The Selected Letters of George Oppen* (1990), and co-edited *The Feminist Memoir Project: Voices from Women's Liberation* (1998). DuPlessis is a Professor of English at Temple University.

Norman Finkelstein is the author of a collection of poems, *Restless Messengers* (Georgia, 1992), and two volumes of criticism, *The Utopian Moment in Contemporary American Poetry* (Bucknell 1988, 1993) and *The Ritual of New Creation: Jewish Tradition and Contemporary Literature* (SUNY, 1992). He is completing a book on Jewish-American poetry, parts of which have appeared in *Contemporary Literature* (on Jerome Rothenberg) and *Upper Limit Music: The Writing of Louis Zukofsky* (Alabama, 1997). He is a Professor and Chair of the English Department at Xavier University.

Robert Franciosi is Associate Professor of English at Grand Valley State University in Michigan, where he teaches American literature and culture. His publications range from studies of modern poetry to essays on teaching. Currently he is writing on American literary responses to the Holocaust.

Stephen Fredman is Professor of English at the University of Notre Dame. His books include *Poet's Prose: The Crisis in American Verse* (Cambridge UP, 2nd ed. 1990) and *The Grounding of American Poetry: Charles Olson and the Emersonian Tradition* (Cambridge UP, 1993). He has completed work on a new book, *Between Judaism and Modernism: Charles Reznikoff, Objectivism, and the* Menorah Journal.

Alan Golding is the author of *From Outlaw to Classic: Canons in American Poetry* (U of Wisconsin P, 1995) and of numerous essays on writers in the Objectivist, Black Mountain, and post–New American Poetry traditions. Most recently he has published articles on the editing of *The New American Poetry,* on avant-gardist anthologies, and on Bruce Andrews. He is currently working on two parallel series of essays, on issues in the sociology of poetry and on individual Language writers. He teaches American literature at the University of Louisville.

BURTON HATLEN is Professor of English at the University of Maine, where he also serves as Director of the National Poetry Foundation. He is the editor of *Sagetrieb,* a journal devoted to scholarly and critical work on poetry in the imagist and Objectivist traditions. He has published a book of his own poetry, *I Wanted to Tell You,* and has published many articles on Shakespeare, Renaissance poetry, modernist and postmodernist poetry, and literary theory in such journals as *College English, English Literary Renaissance, Contemporary Literature, Twentieth Century Literature, American Poetry Review,* and *Paideuma.*

MICHAEL HELLER's poetry and criticism have appeared in numerous magazines and anthologies. His most recent volume of poetry is *Wordflow: New and Selected Poems* (Talisman House, 1997); others include *Knowledge* (1979) and *In the Builded Place* (Coffee House Press, 1990). He edited *Carl Rakosi: Man and Poet* (National Poetry Foundation) and is the author of *Conviction's Net of Branches* (Southern Illinois UP, 1985), the first critical book to focus solely on the Objectivist poets.

ERIC HOMBERGER was educated at the University of California, the University of Chicago, and Cambridge University. Currently Reader of American Literature, University of East Anglia, he has been visiting professor of American literature at the University of Minnesota and the University of New Hampshire. He is the editor of *Ezra Pound: The Critical Heritage* (1972), co-editor of *John Reed and the Russian Revolution* (1992) and *The Troubled Face of Biography* (1988), and author of *Scenes from the Life of a City: Corruption and Conscience in Old New York* (1994), *American Writers and Radical Politics, 1900–39* (1986), and *The Art of the Real: Poetry in England and American since 1939* (1977), among other books.

MING-QIAN MA received his Ph.D. in English from Stanford University, writing his dissertation on Language poetries. He is an Assistant Professor of English at University of Nevada, Las Vegas, and has published a number of articles on contemporary avant-garde poetry and poetics. He is currently writing a book on the philosophy of method in Language poetry.

Peter Middleton is the author of *The Inward Gaze: Masculinity and Subjectivity in Modern Culture* and many articles on contemporary poetry. His essay on poetry readings was recently published in Charles Bernstein's *Close Listening.* His *Writing to be Heard: American Avant-Garde Poetry and the Public Sphere, 1950–1990* was published by Northwestern University Press. He has a book forthcoming with Tim Woods on the representation of history in postwar writing. He is a senior lecturer in English at the University of Southampton, England.

Peter Nicholls is Professor of English and American Literature at the University of Sussex. He is the author of *Ezra Pound: Politics, Economics, and Writing* (Macmillan, 1984), *Modernisms: A Literary Guide* (University of California Press, 1995), and numerous essays on twentieth-century literature and theory. He is currently completing a book about contemporary American poetry.

Peter Quartermain is the author of *Disjunctive Poetics: From Gertrude Stein and Louis Zukofsky to Susan Howe* (Cambridge UP, 1992), and editor, with Richard Caddel, of the anthology *OTHER British and Irish Poetry since 1970* (Wesleyan UP, 1998). He edited the *Dictionary of Literary Biography: American Poets 1880–1945* (Gale Research, 1986) in four volumes, and has published extensively on American, British, and Canadian poets in articles appearing in *Boundary 2, Conjunctions, Paideuma, Parnassus, Chicago Review,* and elsewhere. He was the first Mountjoy Lecturer at Durham University (1990) with *Basil Bunting: Poet of the North.* He is a Professor of English at the University of British Columbia.

John Seed's most recent book of poetry is *Interior in the Open Air* (Reality Studios). He teaches history at the Roehampton Institute in London.

Index

Aboth. See *Pirke Aboth*
Abrams, M. H., 68
abstraction, 9, 11, 14, 32, 33, 36, 38, 59, 80, 92, 135–36, 154, 244, 292, 304, 323 (n. 3), 331 (n. 10), 341 (n. 4)
Abulafia, Abraham, 221
Active Anthology (edited by Pound), 128, 130, 137
Adams, Henry, 147, 284
adjacency, 218, 221, 249. *See also* seriality
Adonis, 202
Adorno, Theodor W., 56, 59, 60–62, 63, 66, 67, 71, 72, 77, 81, 82, 83, 323 (n. 6), 325 (n. 18)
aestheticism, 48, 59, 108, 122–23, 124, 146–47, 185–86
aesthetics, 20–21, 223–24, 243–44
Agamben, Giorgio, 336 (n. 6)
Akimov, Nicolai, 60
Albert-Birot, Pierre, 296, 341 (n. 8)
Aldington, Richard, 130
allegory, 43, 91–92
Allen, Donald M., 287
Altamira, 291
Alter, Robert: on Reznikoff, 196, 205, 335 (n. 26)
Altieri, Charles, 2, 6, 58–59, 81, 100
American-Jewish. *See* Jewish-American identity; Jewish-American poetry
"Amygism," 122
Anarchism, 108
Anderson, Margaret, 108, 329 (n. 2)
Andrews, Bruce, 102, 244, 302, 313
anthologies, 6, 111, 112, 115, 127, 128, 129, 130, 132, 136, 143, 162–63, 181, 186, 240, 265, 266, 278, 287, 325 (n. 1), 330 (n. 1), 339 (n. 6)
antifascism. *See* fascism
anti-Semitism, 5, 14–16, 44, 47, 115, 131, 228, 322 (n. 15), 330 (n. 12), 331 (n. 3)
Antin, David, 2, 31
Anvil, 124
apodeitic seeing (Husserl), 60, 63, 64, 71, 72, 73, 76, 77, 80. *See also* assertoric seeing; perception
Apollinaire, Guillaume, 136, 296, 341 (n. 7)
Aquinas, Thomas, 42
Aragon, Louis, 115, 296
Arbus, Diane, 119
Aristotle, 339 (n. 8)
Art of Poetry (edited by Kenner), 129
Ashbery, John, 29, 86, 333 (n. 9); "Europe," 221
assertoric seeing (Husserl), 60, 68, 73, 81. *See also* apodeitic seeing; perception
Auden, W. H., 129, 132, 142, 331 (n. 16); and Pound, 132; Bunting on, 132, 136
Auster, Paul: on Reznikoff, 204
Austin, J. L., 158
Auxemery, Jean-Paul, 237–38
avant-garde, 5, 54–55, 56, 109, 144, 153, 160–88, 242–43, 333 (n. 13)
Averroes, 339 (n. 8)

Baker, Peter, 325 (n. 2), 326 (n. 6)
Barbusse, Henri, 109, 114
Bar Kochba revolt (132–135 C.E.), 200–201
Barrett, Faith, 341 (n. 2)
Barthes, Roland, 65–66
Basshe, Am Jo, 109
Bataille, Georges, 217
Beach, Christopher, 17, 273, 337 (n. 2)
Becher, 109
Beckett, Samuel, 137, 247
Beethoven, Ludwig van, 171–72
Benét, William Rose, 116
Benjamin, Walter, 198, 204, 205, 341 (n. 6)
Berkeley Poetry Conference (1965), 290
Berkman, Alexander, 108
Bernstein, Charles, 18, 55, 83, 99, 101, 102, 197–98, 208, 252–53, 302, 312, 313, 314, 315, 335 (n. 28), 341 (n. 4); "Artifice of Absorption," 21; "Poem" ("here. Forget."), 307–10, 341 (n. 4); on Oppen, 253, 328 (n. 18); and Hejinian, 309–11
Bernstein, J. M., 184–85, 186
Bernstein, Michael, 85
Berrigan, Ted: "Tamborine Life," 221
Berry, Eleanor, 328 (n. 18)
Berryman, John, 86; *Dream Songs*, 91
Bertholf, Robert J., 221
Bible, 201, 220, 221, 246, 333 (n. 9). *See also names of individual books*
Blackburn, Paul: *Journals*, 88
Black Mountain poetry, 54, 127, 273, 287
Blackmur, R. P., 148
Black Sparrow Press, 215
Blake, William, 136, 181, 224
Blanchot, Maurice, 252
Blaser, Robin, 220
Bloch, Ernst: "Marxism and Poetry," 3–4, 9
Bloom, Harold, 17, 69–70, 191–93, 195, 196, 259–60, 273, 337 (n. 2); on Jewishness, 193–94
Bloomsbury Group, 132
Boas, Franz, 175
Bolshevism: Bunting on, 134
Bonnefoy, Yves: *On the Motion and Immobility of Douve*, 336 (n. 9)
Bowie, David, 222
Boyarin, Jonathan, 198–99
Boyle, Kay, 154
Braque, Georges, 341 (n. 4)
breath, 309–10
Bréton, André, 296
British Poetry since 1945 (edited by Lucie-Smith), 330 (n. 1)
Bromige, David, 215
Bronk, William, 291
Brooke, Rupert, 141
Brooklyn Polytechnic Institute: Zukofsky at, 260, 264
Brown, Norman O., 325 (n. 16)
Brown, Sterling, 210
Buchenwald, 291
Büchner, Georg: *Woyzeck*, 220
Bunting, Basil, 2, 4, 9, 37, 39, 40–41, 42, 53, 126–43, 210, 277, 321 (n. 5), 330 (n. 1), 331 (nn. 7, 10), 333 (n. 11); as outsider, 5, 47–48, 131; gaps in writing career, 5, 49, 128–29; politics, 130–37; reception, 126–30, 143; "Attis: Or, Something Missing," 137, 138; *Briggflatts*, 53, 126–27, 128, 129, 137, 142; *Caveat Emptor*, 128; *Chomei at Toyama*, 139–40, 143; "Observations on Left-Wing Papers," 14; *Poems 1950*, 129; *Redimiculum Matellarum*, 128; *The Spoils*, 129, 131, 143; "They Say Etna," 134, 137; *Villon*, 133; *The Well of Lycopolis*, 132, 138–39, 143; "The Word" (Ode 15), 41; on abstractions, 9, 14, 131; on Auden, 132, 136; on Bolshevism, 134; on Cummings, 136; on Eliot, 130; on English poetry, 131–32, 141–42; on rationalism, 135; and political poetry, 13–14; and Pound, 9, 41, 47, 130–31, 135, 322 (n. 14), 331 (n. 4); and Zukofsky, 13–14, 38, 120; Pound on, 143
Burke, Kenneth, 116, 213
Burns, Robert, 136, 181
Burnshaw, Stanley, 116
Butts, Mary, 4

Caddel, Richard, 161, 330
Cage, John, 240–41, 322 (n. 13), 325 (n. 16)
Cambridge University, 130, 133
Camus, Albert, 289
canonicity, 18, 20–21, 278–79, 281, 326 (n. 6). *See also* marginality, marginalization
Cantwell, Robert, 116
capitalism, 6, 48, 114, 340 (n. 11)
Carlyle, Thomas, 286
Carnevali, Emanuel, 120
Carruth, Hayden, 335 (n. 26)
Cavalcanti, 149
Cavell, Stanley, 218
Celan, Paul, 17, 288

Cendrars, Blaise: *Kodak* [a.k.a. *Documentaries*], 296, 340 (n. 3), 341 (n. 7)
Chambers, Whittaker, 4, 39
Champs Magnétiques (Breton and Soupault), 296
Chaplin, Charlie, 48
Chaucer, Geoffrey, 136
Cheyney, Ralph, 111
Christianity, 16, 45, 46–47
city. *See* Objectivist poetics: as urban
clarity, 9, 15–16, 71, 84, 162, 165–66, 167, 211, 223–25, 230–31, 232, 233–34, 252–53, 312, 335 (n. 27). *See also* difficulty; lucidity
class, 5, 13, 107–108, 109–110, 124, 135–37, 167–68, 207, 290. *See also* working class
closure, 7, 33, 59, 63–64, 91, 99, 251, 302, 305, 306–307; Hejinian on, 305, 341 (n. 1). *See also* open form
Cocteau, Jean, 10
cold war, 287
Cole, Norma, 3
Coleridge, Samuel Taylor: "Dejection: An Ode," 27–29, 339 (n. 8)
collage, 7, 31–32, 43–44, 193, 220–21, 333 (n. 9). *See also* montage
collectivity, 118, 158, 178–79, 198–99, 243, 245, 247, 299, 312, 328 (n. 14)
Columbia History of American Poetry, 325 (n. 1)
Columbia Literary History of the United States, 325 (n. 1)
Commentary, 262–63
communism, 4, 5, 48, 110, 112, 116, 135, 136, 154, 283, 287
Communist Manifesto, 340 (n. 11)
Communist Party, 5, 38, 39, 40, 45, 107, 109, 110, 111, 115, 124, 136, 240, 322 (n. 12)
community, 94, 178, 180, 223–24, 228, 243–45, 247–48, 250, 252, 299, 336 (nn. 6, 7, 8)
composition by field, 7
confessional poetry, 87, 258, 276, 326 (n. 5)
Confucianism, 243
connectivity, 7, 95–96
connotation, 26, 325 (n. 16)
Conroy, Jack, 111
constructivism, 7, 109, 305
Contact II (edited by Williams and West), 154
Conte, Joseph, 85, 87–88, 219, 220, 326 (n. 6), 327 (n. 7), 333 (nn. 10, 11)
conviction, 90, 99
Contemporary Literature, Objectivists issue, 55, 166, 321 (n. 5), 330 (n. 11), 338 (n. 1)
copula, 79
Corman, Cid, 3, 54, 161, 166, 169, 171, 172, 181, 263, 269, 338 (n. 8)
Corpus Juris, 214
Cowley, Malcolm, 112, 222
Cox, Kenneth, 11, 171
Crane, Hart, 31, 51, 86, 147–48; *The Bridge,* 88, 147–48, 149, 297, 326 (n. 6); "The Broken Tower," 148; "Modern Poetry," 147; Zukofsky on, 148
Cravan, Arthur, 296, 341 (n. 6)
Creeley, Robert, 17, 54, 97, 159, 287, 301, 302, 328 (n. 18); *A Daybook,* 328 (n. 15); "In London," 221; *Pieces,* 88, 96–98, 99, 100, 101, 102, 221, 328 (nn. 15, 16); *Selected Poems,* 328 (n. 16); "The sun will set again on," 102–103; *Thirty Things,* 328 (n. 15); *Words,* 221; on Duncan, 97; on Olson, 97; and Grenier, 328 (n. 16); and language poetry, 328 (n. 16); and Oppen, 97–101, 102–103, 328 (nn. 15, 17); Oppen on, 103, 328 (n. 18)
Criterion (edited by Eliot), 120, 128, 130
cubism, 219, 341 (n. 4)
cubo-serialism, 216, 218, 219–22, 333 (n. 9)
cultural poetics, 19, 20–22
Cummings, E. E., 261, 284, 285; *Is 5,* 281; Bunting on, 136

Dadaism, 296
Dahlberg, Edward, 116
Dahlen, Beverly, 315, 326 (n. 6)
Daily Worker, 112, 115
Dante, 30, 149, 181; *De vulgari elequentia,* 126; *Inferno,* 139
Darwin, Charles, 160
Davidson, Michael, 2–3, 13, 85, 215, 258–59, 335 (n. 3)
Davie, Donald, 126–27, 277
Day, Jean, 18, 342 (n. 6); *The Literal World,* 315–17
Degnan, June Oppen, 266
deixis, 75
de Man, Paul, 331 (n. 10)
Dembo, L. S., 2, 9, 55, 90, 196, 287, 321 (n. 5), 323 (n. 5), 330 (n. 11), 334 (n. 19), 337 (n. 19). See also *Contemporary Literature,* Objectivists issue
denotation, 26, 32, 325 (n. 16)

Derrida, Jacques, 59, 196, 322 (n. 16), 336 (n. 16), 337 (n. 20)
de Saussure, Ferdinand, 285
Descartes, René, 59
description, 28, 30, 31, 32, 64, 81, 101, 153, 222, 227, 252, 316. *See also* representation
desire, 25, 27, 28, 30, 32, 34, 35, 38–39, 42–43, 57, 66, 72, 74, 76, 78, 81, 82–83, 164–65, 174, 194–95, 198, 200, 242, 283
Desnos, Robert, 296, 341 (n. 8)
Deutcher, Isaac, 235
Dewey, John, 59
dialectical materialism, 40, 42
dialectics: in serial poem, 89–90, 116–17
Dickie, Margaret, 325 (n. 2), 326 (n. 6)
Dickinson, Emily, 48, 181, 220, 229–30, 274, 326 (n. 6); "She rose to his requirement," 186–87, 332 (Chap. 9, n. 2), 338 (n. 7); and Niedecker, 186–88
Die Yunge, 320 (n. 10)
difficulty, 232–33, 250. *See also* clarity
"Dixie," 146
Donne, John, 136, 181
Doolittle, Hilda. *See* H.D.
Dos Passos, John, 109, 329 (n. 3)
Doubiago, Sharon, 326 (n. 6)
Douglas, Major C. H., 144
Dove, Rita, 326 (n. 6)
Dryden, John: preface to *Annus Mirabilis*, 339 (n. 8)
duBois, Page, 20
Duchamp, Marcel, 223
Dufrenne, Mikel, 61
Duncan, Robert, 17, 35–36, 54, 86, 101, 159, 220, 275, 276, 292, 298, 302, 337 (n. 2); *The H.D. Book*, 35; *Passages*, 88, 297; Creeley on, 97
DuPlessis, Rachel Blau, 54, 66, 98–99, 102, 112, 161, 166, 207, 241–42, 271, 315, 325 (n. 1), 326 (n. 5), 326 (n. 6), 332 (Chap. 9, n. 1)
Dynamo, 113, 124

Échanges, 279
Eliot, T. S., 4, 10, 17, 30, 86, 109–10, 112, 120, 127, 128, 129, 130, 138, 146, 194, 227, 233, 242, 260, 262, 272, 278, 280, 281, 283, 285, 322 (n. 13), 322 (n. 14), 341 (n. 6); "Marina," 281; "Ash-Wednesday," 281; "The Hollow Men," 262; *Murder in the Cathedral*, 338 (n. 8); *The Waste Land*, 14–15, 94, 96, 126, 130, 138, 194, 217, 261, 281, 326 (n. 6), 327 (n. 12), 337 (n. 17); "What Is Minor Poetry," 266; and Oppen, 93–94, 96, 265–66; and Reznikoff, 263; Bloom on, 192; Bunting on, 130; Niedecker on, 338 (n. 8); Zukofsky on, 261, 263
Ellis, Havelock, 334 (n. 19)
empirical fact, 9
empiricism, 29, 42
Engels, Friedrich, 40
English as a second language, 5, 44, 46–47, 118–19, 194–95, 196–97, 210, 211, 226, 227–28, 334 (n. 19)
Enlightenment, 28–29, 30, 36, 184
Enslin, Theodore, 54
epic, 64, 85–86, 88–89, 94, 214, 217, 230–31, 233, 297–99, 325 (n. 3), 335 (n. 28)
epiphany, 183
epistemology, 3, 9, 13, 57–60, 66, 72, 80, 81–83, 89–90, 92, 226–27, 290, 292, 321 (n. 11), 324 (n. 10)
Eshleman, Clayton, 11
Ethical Culture Society, 45
ethics, 6, 9, 15–16, 39, 42–43, 44, 90, 166, 195, 205–206, 237–38, 240–53, 312, 337 (nn. 19, 20). *See also* Objectivist poetics: and ethics
Ethics of the Fathers. See *Pirke Aboth*
ethnicity. *See* race
Evans, George, 78
Exile (edited by Pound), 120, 121, 157, 208, 213, 281
existentialism, 17, 53, 289–90
expression, 33
Ezekiel, 202, 203

Faber Book of Modern Verse (edited by Roberts), 128
Fabian Socialism, 133, 135, 138
facticity, 62, 71, 197, 288–89
factuality, 16, 31, 297–98. *See also* truth
Farrell, James T., 116
fascism, 4, 107, 109, 115, 124, 131, 135, 144, 322 (n. 13), 330 (n. 12), 340 (n. 11)
Faulkner, William, 141
Fenollosa, Ernest: *Chinese Written Character as a Medium for Poetry*, 34; and Olson, 34
field. *See* poem as field
Finkelstein, Norman, 54, 93
Firdusi, 130
Flaubert, Gustave, 32; and Reznikoff, 223
Fletcher, John Gould, 321 (n. 7)
Flint, F. S., 321 (n. 7)
Flynn, Dallam, 129

folk, 11, 15, 169–70, 172–74, 176; definition, 174–75, 178–79
folklore, 161, 175–76, 178
folk poetry, 177, 178–80
folk speech, 170–71, 173, 176–78, 182, 184, 186. *See also* speech
Ford, Charles Henri, 40, 321 (nn. 8, 11)
Ford, Ford Madox, 133
form, 6, 9, 12, 25–26, 32, 33–34, 57, 90, 91, 92, 123, 126, 154, 217, 232–33, 246, 295–97, 305–306. *See also* Objectivism: and formalism
formalism, 13, 50–52, 124, 145, 162, 241–43, 277–78, 295, 302, 341 (n. 4)
Foucault, Michel, 22, 59
Franco, Francisco, 135
Frank, Waldo, 116, 147
Fraser, Kathleen, 3, 18
Frazer, Sir James G., 202
Fredman, Stephen, 203
Freeman, Joseph, 109–10, 111
Friedman, Susan Stanford, 326 (n. 6)
From Confucius to Cummings (edited by Pound and Spann), 129
From the Other Side of the Century (edited by Messerli), 240
Frost, Robert, 129, 233, 281
Fugitive poets, 144–46
Fulcrum Press, 127, 129
Funaroff, Sol, 112
futurism, 287

Galassi, Jonathan, 325 (n. 3)
Gall, Sally. *See* Rosenthal, M. L., and Sally Gall
Gardner, Thomas, 85, 86–87
Géfin, Laszlo, 85, 102
gematria, 221, 222
gender, 3, 11, 12, 18, 36, 47, 88–89, 107, 109, 112, 121, 132, 138, 163–66, 170, 177, 186–88, 233, 242, 243, 259–60, 268, 277, 303–304, 326 (n. 6), 331 (n. 16)
Genesis, 203
genre, 20–21, 326 (n. 6)
Gilman, Sander, 228
Ginsberg, Allen, 260; "Footnote to Howl," 224; Olson on, 88
Glatshteyn, Jacob, 16, 320 (n. 10)
God, 15, 16, 136, 224, 282–84, 320 (n. 11), 334 (n. 16), 339 (n. 10)
Gold, Mike, 43, 109, 111, 113, 119; *Jews Without Money,* 39, 329 (n. 5)
Goldman, Emma, 108, 329 (n. 2)
Gotham Book Mart, 118
Grahn, Judy, 326 (n. 6)
Graves, Robert, 127
Greenblatt, Stephen, 20, 21
Gregory, Horace, 18
Grenier, Robert, 102, 328 (n. 16); *Sentences,* 222, 328 (n. 16); and Creeley, 328 (n. 16)
Grosz, Georg, 109

Hacker, Marilyn, 326 (n. 6)
haiku, 181, 227, 269
halakah (the Way), 192
Halevi, Yehudah, 193–94, 195
Halper, 116
Halpern, Moishe Leib, 320 (n. 10)
Hannukah, 226
Hasidism, 223
Hatlen, Burton F., 2, 6, 12, 58, 64, 73, 99, 101, 219, 220, 243, 323 (n. 2), 324 (n. 13), 327 (n. 13), 328 (n. 18), 335 (n. 5)
Havelock, Eric A., 178
Hayles, Katherine, 324 (n. 10)
Hazlitt, William, 142
H.D., 36, 86, 211, 321 (n. 7); *Helen in Egypt,* 85, 326 (n. 6); *Trilogy,* 85, 285, 326 (n. 6), 341 (n. 10); Zukofsky on, 281
Heap, Jane, 108
Heath Anthology of American Literature, 6
Hebrew, 193–94, 210–11, 224, 227–28, 235, 334 (nn. 19, 21)
Hecht, S. Theodore, 39
Hegel, G. W. F., 83, 89, 135, 251, 304
Heidegger, Martin, 59, 267, 288–89; and Oppen, 247–48, 321 (n. 10), 336 (n. 12)
Heine, Heinrich, 211
Hejinian, Lyn, 3, 18, 83, 215, 249, 302, 305–307, 309–11, 312, 314, 315, 341 (n. 3); *The Cell,* 221, 306–307; *The Guard,* 334 (n. 17); on closure, 305, 341 (n. 1); and Bernstein, 309–11
Heller, Michael, 2, 54, 59, 66, 75, 81, 193–94, 320 (n. 1), 321 (n. 5)
Hemingway, Ernest, 242
Heraclitus, 291
Herbert of Cherbury, Lord, 163; "In a Glass-Window for Inconstancy," 164
Herbst, Josephine, 112, 116
Hermann, John, 112
hermetic tradition, 36
Herrick, Robert, 181
Heywood, Bill, 107–108, 109
Hill, Geoffrey: on Pound, 158

Hindus, Milton, 214, 223, 274, 333 (n. 13)
"historic and contemporary particulars" (Zukofsky), 2, 3, 9, 13, 25, 38–39, 43, 49, 52, 57, 267, 283–84
historical contingency, 6
historical process, 43, 83
history, 8, 13, 17, 26, 43, 85, 125, 140, 146, 153, 158, 193–95, 197, 198–99, 205, 236–37, 245, 248, 250, 278, 284, 286, 298, 314–15, 325 (n. 3), 327 (n. 8), 336 (n. 15). *See also* Objectivist poetics: and history
Hitler, Adolf, 135
Hoard, Mary, 10–11
Hocquard, Emmanuel, 340 (n. 1); *La Bibliothèque de Trieste,* 295–96, 340 (n. 2)
Hölderlin, Friedrich, 141, 220
Holocaust, 5, 6, 16, 17, 205–206, 250, 251, 288
Homberger, Eric, 91
Homer, 178, 221, 333 (n. 9)
Hoover, Paul, 240, 241
Hopkins, Gerard Manley, 130, 181
Horace, 146
Hound and Horn, 51, 279
House Unamerican Activities Committee (HUAC), 92
Howe, Irving, 320 (n. 10)
Howe, Susan, 83, 315, 326 (n. 6)
Hughes, Glenn, 278, 338 (n. 2)
Hughes, Langston, 18, 112, 210; *Montage of a Dream Deferred,* 221
Hulme, T. E., 284
humanism, 6
Hunting, Constance, 327 (n. 8)
Hurston, Zora Neale, 175–76, 188; *Their Eyes Were Watching God,* 175–76
Husserl, Edmund, 60, 61–62, 66, 81, 83, 323 (nn. 6, 7)
hypertext, 222
hypotaxis, 8, 233. *See also* parataxis

idealism, idealization, 39, 59, 304–305
ideogram, 7
ideology, 20, 38, 150, 152, 154, 162, 178, 197–98, 251, 309, 310, 313
Iliad, 154
I'll Take My Stand, 146
image, 9, 12, 122, 167, 195, 277–78, 284; Barthes on, 65–66
imagination, 9, 27–29
imagism, 3, 12, 30, 31, 32, 37, 53, 90–91, 99, 102, 117, 123, 151–52, 166–67, 201, 202, 226, 234, 246, 258–59, 262, 278, 280, 281, 287, 288, 312 (n. 7), 323 (n. 2), 327 (n. 9), 338 (n. 4). *See also* Objectivism: and imagism
Imagist Anthology 1930 (edited by G. Hughes), 278
implicature, 172
incoherence, 30
indeterminacy, 18, 53, 305
integrity, 64, 66, 71, 72, 74, 152, 205, 299, 329 (n. 19)
intensity, 89–90, 233, 310, 335 (n. 27)
intention, 81–82
internationalism, 162, 176
intersubjectivity, 179, 183, 186; in Niedecker, 171–72; in Williams, 174
In Zich poets, 15, 320 (n. 10)
Irigaray, Luce, 59

Jabès, Edmond, 17, 219, 226, 227–28
Jackson, Laura Riding. *See* Riding, Laura
Jacob, Max, 341 (n. 8); *Laboratoire central,* 296
James, Henry and William, 173
James, Jesse and Frank, 173
Jeffers, Robinson, 281
Jefferson, Thomas, 161
Jewish-American identity, 191–92, 196, 201–202, 203–205, 211, 218–19
Jewish-American poetry, 191–93, 194–97, 198–99
Jewish Frontier, 214–15
Jewish history, 196–209
Jewishness, 6, 14–16, 18, 46–47, 49, 107, 118–19, 194–96, 198–99, 207, 209, 210–39, 223–24, 227–29, 234–35, 236–37, 265, 320 (n. 11), 322 (nn. 14, 15), 329 (n. 5), 334 (nn. 16, 21); assimilationism, 5, 45, 194–96; Bloom on, 193–94. *See also* anti-Semitism
Jews, 5, 39, 44–45, 111, 118, 322 (n. 17), 330 (n. 12). *See also* Oppen; Rakosi; Reznikoff; Zukofsky
John Reed Clubs, 111–12, 124, 329 (n. 5)
Johnson, Barbara, 175–76
Jones, David, 143, 277
Joyce, James, 129, 130, 137, 233, 266, 280; *Ulysses,* 48
Judaism, 6, 16, 44–45, 125, 191–209. *See also* Messianism
Judovitz, Dalia, 60
Juvenal, 46

Kabbalah, 217, 221, 223–25, 334 (n. 16)
Kalar, Joseph, 112

Kant, Immanuel: *Critique of Judgment,* 184, 185
Keats, John, 163–64, 167, 170, 181, 286
Keller, Lynn, 326 (n. 6)
Kenner, Hugh, 2, 32, 75, 129, 141, 158, 288
Kharkov Conference (International Union of Revolutionary Writers) 1930, 111–12, 329 (n. 5); on Objectivism, 114
Kinnell, Galway, 86
Kittredge, G. L., 231, 334 (n. 24)
Kleinzahler, August, 78
Komarowski, Conrad, 329 (n. 5)

Lacan, Jacques, 177
language, 12, 16, 41–42, 43, 46, 49, 52–53, 57–60, 66, 68, 73, 75–76, 79–80, 83, 84, 92, 99, 102, 103, 151–52, 154, 158, 165–66, 179, 195, 224, 227–28, 229, 236, 248–49, 250, 252–53, 284–85, 305–306, 323 (n. 4), 328 (n. 17), 336 (n. 13)
language poetry, 3, 18, 54, 83, 102–103, 240, 244, 252–53, 273, 302, 305, 312, 313, 328 (n. 16), 342 (n. 5); and Creeley, 328 (n. 16). *See also names of individual writers*
Larkin, Philip, 127
Laughlin, James, 87, 124, 131
Lawson, John Howard, 109
League of American Writers, 115, 116
League of Professional Groups, 111
Leavis, F. R., 129, 330 (n. 2), 331 (n. 6); *New Bearings in English Poetry,* 130
Leib, Mani, 320 (n. 10)
Lenin, V. I., 12, 13, 39, 40, 112, 114, 133, 136; Zukofsky on, 42–43, 114, 322 (n. 12)
Lenowitz, Harris: *Gematria 27,* 222
Lentricchia, Frank, 130
Le Rouge, Gustave: *Le mystérieux docteur Cornélius,* 296, 340 (n. 3)
Levertov, Denise, 33, 54, 99
Levinas, Emmanuel, 251–52, 337 (n. 20)
Levine, George, 20
Levy, Melvin P., 329 (n. 5)
Lewin, Albert, 263
Lewis, C. Day, 132, 142, 143
Lewis, Wyndham, 242; *Blasting and Bombardiering,* 129
Liberator, 110
Lindsay, Vachel, 281
Lipking, Lawrence, 260, 271, 337 (n. 4), 338 (n. 7)
literary generations, 19, 257–60, 280, 286–93, 328 (n. 16), 339 (n. 6)
literary history, 7, 17, 19, 22, 163, 273, 286, 317, 330 (n. 2), 338 (n. 4)
literary movements, 19, 22, 286–87
literary tradition, 182–83, 206
Little Review, 108
Livy, 137
localism, 9, 14, 86, 89–90, 93, 23, 161–62, 165, 166, 169–71, 172, 175–78, 179–80, 181, 183–84, 185–86, 217, 219, 238, 268–69, 277
Locke, John, 339 (n. 8)
Loewinsohn, Ron, 31
Loewenthal, Jesse, 39
logopoeia, 177, 179, 285
London School of Economics, 133, 135
Lopate, Phillip, 338 (n. 6)
Lowell, Amy, 108, 122, 130, 281, 321 (n. 7)
Lowell, Robert, 87, 258, 260; *Notebook,* 91
Loy, Mina, 341 (n. 6); "Love Songs," 221
Lucas, John, 138
lucidity, 30, 188, 195. *See also* clarity
Lucie-Smith, Edward, 133, 330 (n. 1)
Luke, 325 (n. 17)
Lyotard, François, 251
lyric, lyricism, 26, 28, 35, 53, 57, 64, 84, 89, 94, 192–93, 196, 292, 297, 301, 302, 307, 309, 311, 313, 314, 316–17. *See also* song

Macann, Christopher, 323 (n. 7)
MacDiarmid, Hugh, 143, 277
Mackey, Nathaniel, 302
MacLean, Sorley, 143
MacLeish, Archibald, 10, 144
Macleod, Norman, 39
MacLow, Jackson, 33
MacNeice, Louis, 132, 142
Magil, A. B., 329 (n. 5)
Maintenant (edited by Cravan), 296, 341 (n. 6)
Mallarmé, Stephane, 18, 33, 34, 299, 308, 341 (n. 10)
Malraux, André, 340 (n. 11)
marginality, marginalization, 5–6, 15, 46–48, 55, 119, 127–28, 131, 143, 160, 167, 240, 265–67, 268, 269–71, 322 (n. 17)
Marinetti, F. T., 287
Maritain, Jacques: *Creative Intuition in Art and Poetry,* 336 (n. 9)
Martone, John, 334 (n. 21), 335 (n. 26)
Marx, Karl, 13, 39, 40, 43, 45, 89, 112, 125, 235, 340 (n. 11)
Marxism, 3, 4, 8, 12–13, 111, 120, 124, 135, 148–49, 150, 152, 207, 243, 283, 330 (n. 9), 336 (n. 11)

Marxist teleology, 3, 5; and Oppen, 9
Masefield, John, 132
Masters, Edgar Lee, 281
materialism, 40, 43
materialist practice, 4
materiality, 3, 7–8, 11, 39, 41, 69–71, 73, 81–83, 92, 99, 314, 341 (n. 4); of language, 14, 73, 92, 101, 151, 341 (n. 4). *See also* poem as object; word: materiality of
Matthew, 325 (n. 17)
Matthias, Jogn, 330 (n. 1)
Maupassant, Guy de, 296
Mayakovski, Vladimir, 109, 113
May Days: An Anthology of Verse from "Masses-Liberator" (edited by Taggard), 330 (n. 6)
Mayer, Bernadette, 326 (n. 6)
McAleavey, David, 95
McAlmon, Robert, 213, 261, 285; *North America*, 281
McCarthyism, 5. *See also* House Unamerican Activities Committee (HUAC)
McEvilley, Thomas: *4*, 222
McGann, Jerome, 19–20, 21, 335 (n. 2)
meaning, 7, 9, 28, 31–32, 51, 84, 90–91, 92, 99, 160, 171–72, 174, 177, 183, 217, 220–21, 223, 230, 231, 290, 309–310
measure, 32, 35
melopoeia, 277, 279
memory, 27, 197
Menorah Journal, 44, 319 (n. 6)
Merleau-Ponty, Maurice, 59
Merrill, James, 86
Merrill, Stuart, 338 (n. 4)
Messerli, Douglas, 240, 241
Messianism: Jewish, 194–95, 197, 198–99, 204–205. *See also* Judaism
metaphor, 26, 28–29, 30, 31, 34, 64, 66, 102, 169
metaphysics, 28–29, 292
metonymy, 225, 285
Midrash, 46
Millay, Edna St. Vincent, 281, 323 (n. 19)
Miller, James E., 85, 86
Milton, John, 29
modernism, 2, 5, 9, 13, 17, 28, 31, 36, 43, 48–50, 54, 59, 66, 85–87, 88, 103, 109, 110, 126, 129, 137, 138–39, 154, 161–62, 163, 168, 176, 179, 180, 183, 185–88, 192–95, 196–97, 200–201, 210, 222, 227, 231, 240–42, 244, 251–53, 262, 278–79, 285, 296–98, 300, 313, 315, 325 (n. 3), 326 (n. 6), 335 (n. 26), 341 (nn. 6, 7, 8), 341 (n. 4); and proletarian poetry, 112–13. *See also* avant-garde
Monde (edited by Barbusse), 114
Monroe, Harriet, 8, 37, 56, 120, 122, 136, 213, 241, 261, 262, 281
montage, 217, 221, 333 (n. 9). *See also* collage
Montefiore, Jan, 331 (n. 16)
Monteiro, George, 326 (n. 4)
Montgomery, Stuart, 129
Moore, Marianne, 2, 10, 37, 54, 141, 154, 166, 260, 280, 283, 284, 285, 322 (n. 14); *Observations*, 281
Morris, William, 48
Morrison, Blake, 143
Morse, Jonathan, 146
Moses, 203, 204
Mother Earth (edited by Goldman), 329 (n. 2)
Mother Goose, 181
Motion, Andrew, 143
Movement, The, 142–43
music, 8, 34, 52, 126, 154, 164, 165, 217, 223, 228, 231, 233–34, 271, 285, 309, 335 (n. 27)
Mussolini, Benito, 13, 135, 242, 322 (n. 18)
mysticism, 225
myth, 29, 30, 32, 35, 62, 74, 75–77, 86, 150, 243, 244–45, 248, 335 (n. 26); Zukofsky on, 29

naming, 157, 158, 203, 328 (n. 18)
Nancy, Jean Luc, 244–45, 247, 248–49, 251, 336 (n. 15)
narrative, 4, 92, 117, 126, 186, 221, 246, 248, 261–62, 263–64, 333 (n. 10), 336 (n. 10)
National Poetry Foundation, 2
National Socialism (Germany), 175. *See also* Nazism
natura naturans (Spinoza), 282–83, 339 (n. 8)
Nazism, 44, 144, 237–38, 290. *See also* National Socialism (Germany)
Negro spirituals, 18
Nelson, Cary, 110, 123, 330 (n. 11)
Nemerov, Howard, 119
New American Poetry, 17, 56, 275. *See also names of individual writers*
New American Poetry 1954–1960 (edited by Allen), 287
New Criticism, 97, 146, 196, 265, 302–303
New Directions, 214, 215, 266
New English Weekly, 130
New Masses, 109, 110, 111, 116, 119, 124, 199
New Mexico Quarterly, 173

New Playwrights' Theatre (New York), 109, 329 (n. 3)
New Republic, 329 (n. 5)
new sentence (Silliman), 221
New Testament, 178
New York School, 302
New York Times, 213
nexus, 2, 5, 6, 7, 15, 17–19, 21–22, 102, 167
Niedecker, Lorine, 2, 4, 6, 7, 10–12, 39, 53, 127, 159, 160–88, 221, 240, 259, 273, 277, 313, 321 (n. 5), 322 (n. 14), 326 (n. 6), 332 (Chap. 9, n. 1), 338 (n. 6); as outsider, 5, 47–48, 170–71, 268; reading in public, 171–72; reception, 171, 271, 330 (n. 11); recordings, 171–72; *Blue Chicory,* 241; "Darwin," 171; "For Paul," 173; *From This Condensery,* 221; "I rose from marsh mud," 186–88; *The Granite Pail,* 181; "LZ's," 41–42; *My Friend Tree,* 269; *New Goose,* 162, 178, 270, 271; "Remember my little granite pail," 181–85; "There's a better shine," 54, 162, 163, 166–67, 168; "The museum man!" 176–78; "Smile / to see the lake," 169–70; on Eliot, 338 (n. 8); on Objectivism, 10–12, 166–67; on Oppen, 167–69; on Sitwell, 338 (n. 8); on Zukofsky, 174, 181; and Dickinson, 186–88; and folk culture, 171–78, 180–81, 182; and Oppen, 12, 170–71; and Reznikoff, 268–73; and surrealism, 10–11, 12; and Williams, 173–74; and Zukofsky, 10–12, 38, 160, 161, 162, 163–65, 170–71, 172, 181, 185, 320 (n. 8); Zukofsky on, 260–61
Nielsen, A. L., 18
Nietzsche, Friedrich, 34
nomadism, 219
Nord-Sud (edited by Reverdy), 296
North, Michael, 322 (n. 13)
Norton Anthology of American Literature, 6, 325 (n. 1)
Norton Anthology of Modern Poetry, 325 (n. 1)
Norton Anthology of Postmodern American Poetry (edited by Hoover), 240
Nougé, Paul: *Un Miroir Exemplaire de Maupassant,* 296, 341 (n. 4)

objectification, 7–8, 9, 26, 32–34, 39, 40, 57, 81, 122, 154, 158, 241–43, 262, 266, 277, 282, 284, 295, 303
"objectism" (Olson), 34–35
Objectivism: definition, 3–8, 10, 29–32, 115, 120–23, 195, 226, 241, 276–78, 312, 319 (nn. 2, 3), 320 (n. 1); difficulty of definition, 1–3, 7, 21–22; early history, 4, 7, 10, 37–38, 56–57, 112, 116–17, 118–24, 212–14, 241, 261–62, 284–85, 319 (n. 2), 322 (n. 18); first stage, 4–5, 101–102; publication history, 2, 10, 118, 120, 121–22, 212–13, 241, 261, 338 (n. 1); reception, 2, 5–6, 7, 14, 17, 18, 54–55, 56–57, 85–88, 102–103, 110, 116, 118, 119–21, 126–27, 141, 160, 211, 215, 261, 271, 275–76, 325 (nn. 1, 2); and formalism, 3, 8, 13, 40, 241; Kharkov Conference on, 114; Rexroth on, 4, 37, 321 (n. 4); Royaumont Conference on, 215–16, 237–38; Spector on, 117. *See also Contemporary Literature,* Objectivists issue; *names of individual writers*
"Objectivist" issue of *Poetry* (February 1931), 1, 4, 7–8, 10, 12, 14, 37, 38, 40–41, 56, 121, 122, 213, 241, 257, 261, 279, 281, 287, 321 (nn. 2, 3), 322 (n. 18), 339 (n. 7)
Objectivist poetics: as urban, 5, 9, 47–48, 95, 118–19, 136–37, 139–40, 144, 154–56, 160–61, 168, 170–71, 175, 176–81, 195–96, 199–200, 201, 202–203, 204–205, 217, 231–33, 246–47, 260, 267, 271, 298; and ethics, 2, 6, 10; and history, 3, 6, 7, 86, 194–95; and imagism, 3, 8, 57, 59, 89, 122–23, 241, 283–85, 289, 321 (n. 7); and politics, 6, 8, 39–40, 107–25, 154, 243–44; and religion, 6, 39; and social observation, 3–4; and surrealism, 10–11. *See also* ethics; Jewishness; Judaism, and related headings; political poetry; *names of individual poets*
Objectivist Press, 116, 213, 262
Objectivist tradition, 32–36
"Objectivists" Anthology (edited by Zukofsky), 1, 4, 13, 37, 56, 114, 124, 128, 213, 279, 281, 282, 321 (n. 4); Schappes on, 114; Williams on, 115, 117
objectivity, 6, 7, 13, 16, 25, 35, 36, 39, 43, 49, 57–59, 63, 177, 227–28, 264, 283, 295, 314
objects, 25, 30, 32, 36, 37, 39, 41–43, 53, 57–59, 60–61, 62, 64, 66, 69–71, 78, 81, 90, 99, 162, 170, 242, 267, 269, 293, 323 (n. 2), 323 (n. 4), 323 (n. 5), 324 (n. 13)
Office of War Information, 288
Olson, Charles, 17, 25–26, 31, 33–35, 54, 86, 238, 240, 275, 276, 298, 309, 327 (n. 8); "As the Dead Prey Upon Us," 290; "Causal Mythology," 290; "In Cold Hell, In Thicket,"

(Olson, Charles, *continued*)
292; "The Kingfishers," 291; "La Préface," 290–91; *The Maximus Poems,* 85, 88, 290, 292, 297; "Projective Verse," 21, 25, 29, 287; "The Resistance," 289–90; on Oppen, 291–92; and Fenollosa, 34; and Oppen, 286–93, 325 (n. 3); and Pound, 287; Creeley on, 97; Oppen on, 89, 290, 292
open form, 32, 86, 98, 149, 250, 298–99, 305. *See also* seriality
Oppen, George, 1, 2, 3, 4, 5, 6, 11, 15, 16, 18, 31, 38, 39, 40, 54, 77–78, 84–103, 110, 115, 117–18, 119, 127, 136, 150–53, 175, 177, 195, 210, 213, 217, 240–53, 273, 277, 285, 298, 307, 308, 313, 315, 327 (nn. 10, 11), 328 (n. 18), 334 (n. 23), 336 (n. 10), 341 (n. 3); as existentialist, 289–90; as outsider, 5; gaps in writing career, 5, 38, 49, 141, 151, 153, 158–59, 213, 234, 240–41, 243, 265, 299; Jewishness, 5, 44–46, 118, 207–208, 258, 288; reception, 240, 265, 325 (nn. 1, 2), 330 (n. 11); "Animula," 92; *Discrete Series,* 7, 8, 53, 85, 88, 89–91, 92, 93, 94, 98–99, 102, 116–17, 118, 121, 151–53, 158, 213, 221, 240, 246, 328 (n. 15), 336 (n. 11); "Eclogue," 303–305, 311, 341 (n. 4); "A Language of New York," 85, 86, 92, 328 (n. 15); *The Materials,* 90, 240, 338 (n. 1); "In Memoriam Charles Reznikoff," 266–67; "The Mind's Own Place," 9; "Morality Play," 1; "A Narrative," 85, 92–93, 290, 328 (n. 15); "Night Scene," 326 (n. 4); "Occurrences," 92, 167–68, 249–50; *Of Being Numerous,* 84, 328 (n. 15); "Of Being Numerous," 87, 91, 93–96, 98–99, 100, 142, 201, 221, 236, 245–47, 248, 292, 325 (n. 3), 326 (n. 4), 327 (n. 13), 328 (n. 14), 329 (n. 19), 336 (nn. 7, 8), 337 (n. 19); "Party on Shipboard," 91, 247–48, 326 (n. 4), 326 (n. 6); "Psalm," 42, 84, 99; *Primitive,* 86, 100, 240, 241; "Route," 84, 99, 289–90; *Seascape: Needle's Eye,* 85, 100, 241, 249; "Seated Man," 167, 168; "Some San Francisco Poems," 85, 86, 91, 327 (n. 8); "Street," 168–69; *This in Which,* 84–85, 92, 93, 167, 328 (n. 15), 336 (n. 8), 336 (n. 12); on consciousness, 29; on Creeley, 103, 328 (n. 18); on Eliot, 93–94, 96, 265; on Ginsberg, 88; on Objectivism, 1–2, 6, 7, 8, 11; on Olson, 89, 290, 292; on Pound, 88–89, 267, 335 (n. 4), 337 (n. 18); on Reznikoff, 265–66; on Williams, 89, 170, 182; on Zukofsky, 9, 88–89; and communism, 5, 153, 243; and Creeley, 97–101, 102–103, 328 (nn. 15, 17); and ethics, 9; and Heidegger, 247–48, 321 (n. 10), 336 (n. 12); and Niedecker, 12, 170–71; and Olson, 286–93; and politics, 31, 120, 151, 207, 243–44, 325 (n. 3), 331 (n. 13), 335 (n. 5); and Pound, 208, 242–44, 245, 247, 248, 251–52, 322 (n. 14), 325 (n. 3), 339 (n. 6); and Reznikoff, 15, 207, 221, 257–59, 260, 265–68, 272; and sincerity, 9; and Whitman, 326 (n. 4); and Zukofsky, 120–21, 153, 169, 221, 240, 265, 319 (n. 2); Olson on, 291–92; Niedecker on, 167–69; Pound on, 240; Williams on, 116–17. *See also* ethics; integrity; intensity
Oppen, Mary, 112, 121, 213, 240, 258, 259, 265, 269, 288, 336 (n. 9)
organic form, 3, 192–93, 302
Origin (edited by Cid Corman), 54, 173, 181
Osbey, Brenda Marie, 326 (n. 6)
otherness, 45–46, 58, 70, 207–208, 242, 251–52, 341 (n. 4)
Ouroboros, 327 (n. 11)
Ovid, 67, 136, 324 (n. 14)
Oxford Book of Modern Verse (edited by Yeats), 128
Oxford Book of Twentieth-Century Verse (edited by Larkin), 127
Oxford University Press, 127
Ozenfant, Amedée: "Foundations of Modern Art," 11, 320 (n. 8)

Pagany, 124
Palmer, Michael, 3, 6, 18, 69, 77, 78, 215
paradise, 225
parataxis, 8, 218, 219, 221, 333 (nn. 9, 11). *See also* hypotaxis
Partisan Review, 116
Pater, Walter, 122
Pearce, Roy Harvey, 85, 86
Pearce, T. M., 178–79, 180, 181
Pearson, Ted: *Evidence,* 221
Penberthy, Jenny, 10, 161, 173, 174, 269, 320 (n. 1), 332 (Chap. 9, n. 1)
Penguin Book of Contemporary British Poetry (edited by Morrison and Motion), 143
Penguin Book of Modern Verse Translation (edited by Steiner), 330 (n. 1)
perception, 7, 8, 10, 11, 12, 22, 26, 26–28, 30, 31, 33–35, 38–39, 40, 42–43, 49–51, 57–59, 60, 64, 71, 81–82, 84, 90, 115, 117, 150–51, 153, 159, 174, 246, 249, 307, 323 (n. 3), 328

(n. 16). *See also* apodeitic seeing; assertoric seeing
Perelman, Bob, 102, 335 (n. 2)
perfection, 8, 25, 38–39, 43, 57, 66, 141, 265, 266, 283, 329 (n. 19). *See also* "totality of perfect rest" (Zukofsky)
Perloff, Marjorie, 2, 56, 59, 69, 85, 87, 192–93, 194, 245–46, 247, 322 (n. 13), 328 (n. 18)
Perse, Saint-John: *Éloges,* 296, 341 (n. 6)
Peterson, Jeffrey, 62, 324 (n. 10)
phanopoeia, 277, 279
phenomenology, 31, 59, 60–62, 81–82, 158, 162, 167, 310, 323 (nn. 6, 7)
Picabia, Francis, 296, 341 (n. 8)
Picasso, Pablo, 341 (n. 4)
Pierce, Charles Sanders, 166
Pirke Aboth (*Ethics of the Fathers*), 195, 218
Piscator, Erwin, 109
Plath, Sylvia, 326 (n. 6)
Poe, Edgar Allan, 87
poem as field, 26–27, 32, 35–36
poem as machine, 29
poem as mode of thought, 3, 6
poem as name, 156
poem as object, 3, 8, 9, 14, 18, 29, 33, 40, 116–17, 241, 242, 302, 303–304, 335 (n. 3), 341 (n. 4)
poetic line, 4, 100–101, 261, 292, 295–96, 300, 327 (n. 10), 328 (n. 18)
poetic sequence. *See* seriality
poetics of presence, 7, 13, 99–100, 101–102, 204, 245–46, 323 (n. 2), 328 (n. 18), 336 (n. 9)
poetics of resistance, 48
poetry: social meaning of, 3–4, 149–50, 245–48
poetry and politics. *See* political poetry
poetry as expressive, 10–11
Poetry (Chicago), 10, 13, 114, 120, 121, 128, 129, 131, 144, 162, 211, 262, 281. *See also* "Objectivist" issue of *Poetry* (February 1931)
Poetry New York, 287
political poetry, 12–13, 14, 16, 48, 110–25, 136–37, 149–54, 207, 243–44, 251, 273, 313, 331 (n. 4), 342 (n. 5)
politics, 9, 12, 31, 34, 55, 115, 123, 131, 134–37, 144–45, 228, 242–43, 313–14, 331 (n. 4), 336 (n. 6). *See also* Objectivist poetics: and politics
Ponge, Francis, 323 (n. 4)
Popular Front, 11, 14, 112, 135
populism, 11, 170, 175, 177, 182, 186, 247, 287, 335 (n. 5)
Porter, Katherine Anne, 112
postmodernism, 49, 56–57, 83, 87–88, 103, 159, 241, 244, 253, 312
poststructuralism, 2
Pound, Dorothy, 128, 131
Pound, Ezra, 2, 3, 4, 9, 12, 13, 14, 17, 18, 29, 30, 33, 35–36, 37, 40, 41, 42, 48, 49, 54, 86, 96, 109, 114, 115, 123, 124, 127, 128, 129, 130, 136, 137, 141, 154, 157–58, 194, 201, 207, 213, 224, 233, 241–42, 244, 249, 250, 252, 261, 262, 273, 275, 276, 279, 280, 281, 282, 287, 288, 298, 299, 316, 322 (n. 13), 322 (n. 18), 327 (n. 9), 327 (n. 12), 331 (n. 3), 333 (n. 11), 338 (n. 7); English reputation, 130–31; *The Cantos,* 31, 40, 43, 85, 88, 126, 153, 157–58, 202, 212, 217, 220, 242–43, 281, 284, 297–98, 326 (n. 6), 335 (n. 4), 337 (n. 18); *Guide to Kulchur,* 128, 242, 298; "Hugh Selwyn Mauberley," 31; *Lustra,* 117; "Papyrus," 51; "A Retrospect," 15, 99; on Bunting, 143; on Oppen, 240, 337 (n. 18); on Zukofsky, 339 (n. 6); and Auden, 132; and Bunting, 9, 41, 47, 130–31, 135, 322 (n. 14), 331 (n. 4); and objectivist poetics, 242–43; and Olson, 287; and Oppen, 208, 242–44, 245, 247, 248, 251–52, 322 (n. 14), 325 (n. 3), 339 (n. 6); and Rakosi, 121, 322 (n. 14); and Reznikoff, 208, 211, 218, 263, 322 (n. 14); and Zukofsky, 43–44, 51, 120–21, 131, 207–208, 277–78, 285, 321 (n. 2), 322 (nn. 13, 14), 330 (n. 12), 339 (n. 6); Bloom on, 192–93; Hill on, 158; Oppen on, 88–89, 267, 335 (n. 4)
Power, Kevin, 289, 327 (n. 10)
Pre-Raphaelites, 48
primitivism, 333 (n. 13)
Proensa, 297
process, 9, 245, 293, 305, 328 (n. 17)
Projectivism, 287, 292, 293
Proletcult, 109
proletarian: art, 109; poetry, 12, 15, 110, 340 (n. 11), and modernism, 112–13
Prunty, Wyatt, 97
Prynne, J. H., 168
psychoanalysis, 11, 111, 177

Quakerism, 133, 138
Quartermain, Peter, 319 (n. 5), 333 (n. 11), 334 (n. 25)

Rabinbach, Anson, 194
race, 18, 107, 111, 121, 207, 290
Rahv, Philip, 116, 329 (n. 5)
Raine, Craig, 143
Rainey, Lawrence, 287
Rakosi, Carl, 2, 4, 5, 18, 38, 39, 53, 59–83, 101, 115, 119, 127, 158, 213, 215, 240, 277, 285, 287, 299, 315, 323 (nn. 5, 6), 324 (nn. 9, 10, 11, 12, 13), 333 (n. 13); gaps in writing career, 5, 49, 141, 159, 234, 299; Jewishness, 44–46, 330 (n. 10); "Adventures of the Head," 62, 66, 69, 324 (n. 9); *Americana*, 48, 297; *Amulet*, 338 (n. 1); "Cenozoic Time," 69, 70–72; "Equations," 10; "Extracts from a Private Life," 281; *Ex Cranium, Night*, 59, 241; "How To Be with a Rock," 69, 73–77; "The Indomitable," 78–81; "Man Contemplating a Rock," 69, 72–73, 76–77, 82; "Objectivist Lamp," 67–69; "Riddle," 64–66; "The Romantic Eye," 62–64, 67, 68, 69, 72, 82; on Objectivism, 9–10, 78; and Pound, 121, 322 (n. 14); and Stevens, 10, 69–70; and Zukofsky, 38, 53, 123
Rand, Ayn, 320 (n. 1)
Rand School (New York), 109, 329 (n. 4)
Ransom, John Crowe, 51, 146
rationalism, 195, 198; Bunting on, 135
rationality, 165–66
Raworth, Tom: *A Serial Biography*, 221
realism, 13, 16, 18, 151, 174, 217, 222, 245, 313. *See also* socialist realism
realist practice, 3, 8, 9
reality, 4, 16, 17, 28, 31, 33, 35–36, 41–42, 71–72, 82–83, 157, 170, 241, 245, 289, 299, 336 (n. 8)
Rebel Poets, 111
"Red Front," 115
reference, 31, 58–59, 83, 99–100, 153, 157, 165–66, 236, 308–309, 341 (n. 4)
Reisen, Abraham, 320 (n. 10)
religion, 16, 30, 44–45, 99, 146
Renwick, Roger de V., 179, 181
representation, 57, 109, 157, 305, 310, 313–14, 316, 336 (n. 8). *See also* description
responsibility, 42, 44, 195, 312. *See also* ethics; integrity
Reverdy, Pierre, 296, 337 (n. 17), 341 (n. 7)
Rexroth, Kenneth, 337 (n. 17); on objectivism, 4, 37, 321 (n. 4)
Reznikoff, Charles, 2, 4, 5, 6, 8, 11, 14–16, 17, 18, 31, 37–38, 39, 40, 48, 78, 101, 108, 118–19, 121, 122, 123, 158, 159, 163, 181, 210–39, 240, 257–74, 277, 279, 281, 287, 295–96, 298, 313, 315, 334 (n. 21), 335 (nn. 26, 27, 28), 338 (n. 6); gaps in publishing career, 214, 264, 271; Jewishness, 44–46, 118–19, 125, 191–209; Poetry Center Reading (1974), 215–16, 218, 231, 234, 332 (n. 6); publishing history, 212–15, 258, 262, 264, 266, 269–70; reception, 213, 222–23, 233, 236, 259–60, 269–70, 335 (n. 26); reviewed by Spector, 113–14, 115; "Among the heaps of brick and plaster lies," 204–205, 257–59, 269, 337 (n. 1); *By the Waters of Manhattan: Selected Poems*, 215, 265, 272, 338 (n. 1); *By the Waters of Manhattan: An Annual*, 220, 332 (Chap. 10, n. 1); *By the Well of Living and Seeing*, 208–209, 210–11, 272; *Complete Poems*, 215, 237, 238; "Early History of a Seamstress," 211, 332 (Chap. 10, n. 1); "Early History of a Sewing Machine Operator," 211; "Early History of a Writer," 220, 231, 271; *Family Chronicle*, 332 (Chap. 10, nn. 1, 2), 333 (n. 13); *Five Groups of Verse*, 208, 212–13, 216–17; "from Jehuda Halevi's Songs to Zion," 193–94; "God and Messenger," 203–204; *Holocaust*, 205–207, 215, 220, 237–39, 241, 295, 340 (n. 2); "Hour after hour," 52; *Inscriptions 1944–1956*, 260, 264, 265, 268, 269, 272; *Jerusalem the Golden*, 201–202, 204–205, 220, 235, 337 (n. 1); "Jerusalem the Golden," 124–25, 234–35; "Karl Marx," 235; "Lament of the Jewish Women for Tammuz," 202–203; *The Manner Music*, 214, 215, 263–64; "Messianic," 199–200; "My parents were of a great company," 208; "Needle Trade," 211; "Night-Piece," 270, 272; *Nine Plays*, 213; *Poems*, 212; *Rhythms*, 212, 216, 217, 222; "Rooted among roofs," 201, 203; *Separate Way*, 115, 199; "The Shield of David," 235; "Spinoza," 235; "Te Deum," 273–74; *Testimony*, 15, 45, 115, 205, 213, 214, 215, 220, 226, 232, 234, 236, 238, 295, 297, 335 (n. 26), 335 (n. 28), 340 (n. 2); on Eliot, 263; on Pound, 263; and the Bible, 202–203; and Flaubert, 223; and Jewish history, 197–98, 200–201, 204, 205; and Niedecker, 268–73; and Oppen, 15, 207, 221, 257–59, 272; and Pound, 208, 211, 218, 263, 322 (n. 14); and serialism, 216; and Williams, 52–53, 196, 210, 214; and Yiddish, 18; and Zukofsky, 207, 220–21, 321 (n. 3);

Alter on, 196, 205; Auster on, 204; Bloom on, 192–93, 196; Dembo on, 196; Oppen on, 265–66; Zukofsky on, 14–15, 114. *See also* Zukofsky, Louis: "Sincerity and Objectification"
Reznikoff, Ezekiel (grandfather to Charles), 15–16, 208–209, 210–11, 214, 258, 332 (Chap. 10, n. 1)
Reznikoff, Sarah, 334 (n. 18)
rhetoric, 13, 135–36, 147, 150, 151, 152, 195, 222, 299, 302, 309
rhyme, 50, 52, 194, 208, 222, 269, 335 (n. 27)
Ricardo, David, 135
Rich, Adrienne, 326 (n. 6)
Richards, I. A., 94
Rickword, Edgell, 132, 138, 143
Riding, Laura, 210, 326 (n. 6), 332 (n. 4)
Rimbaud, Arthur, 322 (n. 13)
ritual, 196, 198–99, 298
Rivera, Diego, 12
Roberts, Michael, 128
Robinson, Edwin Arlington, 281
Rockwell, Norman, 233
Roeg, Nicholas: *The Man Who Fell to Earth,* 222
Roethke, Theodore, 86
Rolfe, Edwin, 112; "Kentucky—1932," 113, 117
romanticism, 28–29, 30, 31, 32, 35–36, 67–70, 76, 123, 129, 162, 168, 175, 181, 183, 192, 286, 301, 302, 324 (n. 10), 339 (n. 8)
Rosenberg, Harold, 338 (n. 4)
Rosenberg, Joel, 202
Rosenblum, Martin, 150
Rosenthal, M. L., and Sally Gall, 85, 87, 326 (n. 6)
Rosenzweig, Franz, 194
Rosh Hashanah, 236–37
Roskolenkier, Harry, 39
Ross, Andrew, 244
Roth, Henry: *Call It Sleep,* 116
Roth, Samuel, 212
Rothenberg, Jerome, 333 (n. 13); *Gematria 27,* 222; *Poland,* 297
Roub, Gail, 12, 166, 171
Rukeyser, Muriel, 326 (n. 6)
Russian Revolution (1917), 4, 283

Sacco and Vanzetti, 109
Sacred Edict of Kang H'sim, 243
Sage, Kay, 18–19
Sandburg, Carl, 321 (n. 7)
San Francisco Review (edited by Degnan), 266
Santayana, George, 339 (n. 10)
Sappho, 32
Sartre, Jean-Paul, 288, 323 (n. 4)
Scève, Maurice: *Délie,* 341 (n. 9)
Scalapino, Leslie, 302
Schachner, E. A., 329 (n. 5)
Schappes, Morris, 115; on *An "Objectivists" Anthology,* 114
Schechner, Mark, 207
Schelling, Felix, 157
Schneidau, Herbert, 32
Schneider, Isidor, 112
Scholem, Gershon, 194, 223, 224, 225, 229, 334 (n. 16)
Schor, Naomi, 233
Schulberg, Budd, 119
Schwartz, Delmore, 194
Schwerner, Armand, 54; *The Tablets,* 297
Scroggins, Mark, 13, 339 (n. 8)
Segalen, Victor: *Stèles,* 296, 341 (n. 6)
Seidman, Hugh, 54, 260
self, 32, 35, 45–46, 69, 100, 242, 246–47, 251–52, 307, 308, 313–14, 328 (n. 16), 334 (n. 21)
seriality, 4, 7, 18, 197, 219–22, 326 (n. 4), 327 (nn. 7, 8), 333 (nn. 10, 11), 334 (n. 25); in Creeley, 97–98, 101; in Dickinson, 220; in Oppen, 84–103, 230, 246–47, 325 (n. 2); in Reznikoff, 216–17, 219–20; in Wittgenstein, 333 (n. 12). *See also* adjacency; cubo-serialism; open form
serialogy, 98
Serres, Michel, 72–73, 324 (n. 8)
Sexton, Ann, 326 (n. 6)
Shakespeare, William, 136, 163, 164, 181; *Merchant of Venice,* 15; *Pericles,* 164–65, 186
Shapiro, Harvey, 87, 269
Shelley, Percy Bysshe, 269; "A Defense of Poetry," 21, 158; "Ode to the West Wind," 27–29
Shem, Israel Baal, 223
Shevelow, Katherine, 335 (n. 28)
"shipwreck of the singular" (Oppen). *See* Oppen, George: "Of Being Numerous"
Shoptaw, John, 18
silence, 172
Silliman, Ron, 3, 5, 54, 56, 59, 101, 102, 221, 302, 313, 327 (n. 7), 334 (n. 17)
Simon, Linda, 333 (n. 13)
Sinai, 203, 204

sincerity, 7, 8, 9, 10, 15, 18, 26, 29, 32–35, 38, 40, 58–59, 81, 122–23, 158, 241–42, 251–52, 262, 277, 282, 284, 302, 305, 306–308, 312, 314, 316, 334 (n. 21); Bunting on, 14
Sinclair, Upton, 108, 111
Sitwell, Edith: Niedecker on, 338 (n. 8)
Sitwell family, 132
Slater, Montague, 340 (n. 11)
Smiles, Samuel, 135
Snow, C. P., 215
Snyder, Gary, 315
Social Credit, 144
socialism, 15, 39, 45, 133, 144, 154, 175, 329 (n. 4), 330 (n. 9)
socialist realism, 5, 12, 43, 149, 313
song, 297–99, 300. *See also* lyric, lyricism
sound, 161, 165, 171–72, 277–78. *See also* music
Soupault, Philippe, 296
Soviet Union, 109, 114, 340 (n. 11)
Spanish Civil War, 135
Spann, Marcella, 129
Spectator (London), 135
Spector, Herman, 12, 112; "Saturday Eve, East Side," 112–13; on Objectivism, 117; on Reznikoff, 113–14, 115
speech, 46, 49, 52, 86, 160, 162, 169–70, 172, 184, 188, 194, 195, 248, 281, 284, 295, 298, 302, 334 (n. 19), 335 (n. 27). *See also* folk speech
Spender, Stephen, 132, 142, 143, 331 (n. 6)
Spengler, Oswald, 147, 148
Spicer, Jack, 220
Spinoza, Benedict, 125, 166, 235, 282–84; *Ethics,* 283, 339 (nn. 8, 10). See also *natura naturans*
Squire, J. C., 141
Stalin, Josef, 135
Stalinism, 5, 124
Steffens, Lincoln, 340 (n. 11)
Stein, Gertrude, 2, 4, 5, 14, 54, 223, 230, 231, 236, 326 (n. 6), 328 (n. 16), 334 (n. 25); *Tender Buttons,* 220
Steiner, George, 206, 330 (n. 1)
Stevens, Wallace, 2, 10, 29, 49, 54, 94, 156–57, 192, 213, 285, 311, 322 (n. 14); *Harmonium,* 281; "The Noble Rider and the Sound of Words," 156–57; "The Poems of Our Climate," 156; "The Rock," 69–70; and Rakosi, 10, 69–70
Stieglitz, Alfred, 107, 108
Strachey, John, 116
subjectivity, subject, subjective agency, 6, 9–10, 11, 57, 61–62, 64, 66, 71–72, 82, 123, 162, 192–93, 223, 245, 295, 307, 311, 315, 321 (n. 7), 324 (n. 9), 324 (nn. 11, 13), 334 (n. 21)
sublimity, 6, 28–31, 35–36
Sunday Times (London), 127, 330 (n. 1)
surrealism, 40, 295–96, 341 (nn. 4, 8); and Niedecker, 10–11, 161, 166–67; Zukofsky on, 11
symbol, 27, 28–29, 31–32, 40, 43, 168, 170, 211, 225, 234, 236
symbolism, 3, 6, 8, 26, 33–34, 53, 57, 69, 237, 323 (n. 5)
symbolist poetry, 48, 122, 341 (n. 5)
Symons, Arthur, 338 (n. 4)
syntax, 52, 53, 75, 79–80, 84, 91, 102, 152, 158, 174, 185, 228, 249, 250, 267, 292, 309–10, 313, 316, 317, 325 (n. 16), 327 (n. 10), 328 (n. 18), 333 (n. 9), 334 (n. 25), 336 (n. 13), 336 (n. 16). *See also* deixis; hypotaxis; parataxis
Syrkin, Marie, 212, 214, 238, 264, 273, 320 (n. 10), 332 (n. 4)

Taggard, Genevieve, 330 (n. 6)
Taggart, John, 89, 98, 102
Talmud, 195, 198, 334 (n. 21)
Tammuz, 202
Tate, Allen, 10, 51, 146, 281
Taupin, René, 280, 338 (n. 4)
Taylor, Charles, 183
Terrell, Carroll F., 2
testimony, 15–16, 32, 81, 158, 195, 200, 205–206, 226–27, 229, 235–39, 295–96, 312, 313–14, 316, 320 (n. 11). *See also* integrity; sincerity
textual transmission, 19–20, 21
theology, 27, 31
things. *See* objects
"thinking with the things as they exist" (Zukofsky), 8, 26, 40, 43, 49, 57, 58–59, 74, 195, 293
Thomas, Dylan, 143
Thompson, Stith, 176, 178, 179
Thoreau, Henry David, 325 (n. 16)
Times (London), 129
Times Literary Supplement (London), 129
To Publishers, 116, 213
Toller, Ernst, 109
Tomlinson, Charles, 2, 116, 156
Toomer, Jean, 210; *Cane,* 220

Torah, 45, 197, 208, 221, 320 (n. 11)
"totality of perfect rest" (Zukofsky), 8, 122, 158, 241, 266
tradition: Zukofsky on, 162–63
Transatlantic Review (edited by F. M. Ford), 133
transcendence, 6, 7, 30, 33–34, 61, 69, 99, 147, 223–26, 231, 244, 278, 335 (n. 26)
transition (edited by Jolas), 12
translation, 18, 193–94, 300
transparency of words. *See* reference
Tresca, Carlo, 40
Trilling, Lionel, 14, 319 (n. 6)
Trotsky, Leon, 133
truth, 9, 15–16, 30, 36, 41, 42, 49–50, 58–59, 60, 82, 195, 243–45, 249, 251
23 Modern British Poets (edited by Matthias), 330 (n. 1)
Tyler, Parker, 40, 321 (nn. 8, 11)
Tzara, Tristan, 296, 341 (n. 8)

Ungaretti, Giuseppe, 341 (n. 6)
universality, 6, 30, 51, 122–23, 165, 169–70, 175–76, 186, 278

Van Gogh, Vincent, 266
veracity, 8. *See also* truth
Vièle-Griffin, Francis, 338 (n. 4)
Villon, François, 133, 136
Vines, Sherard, 132
volk, 175

Waggoner, Hyatt, 325 (n. 1)
Waldrop, Rosmarie, 3, 315
Walker, Jeffrey, 88
Warren, Robert Penn, 146
Watten, Barrett, 3, 20, 54, 78
Webb, Beatrice and Sydney, 135
Weeks, Howard, 39
We Gather Strength, 112–13
Weil, Simone, 226
Weinfeld, Henry, 325 (n. 3)
Werner, Marta, 220
West, Nathanael, 154
Western Folklore, 178
"Western Wynd," 25, 26–27
Wheelwright, John, 37, 39
Whips and Scorpions (edited by Vines), 132
White, William Hale, 283, 339 (n. 10)
Whitehead, Alfred North, 34
Whitman, Walt, 48, 69, 86–87, 88, 96, 167, 224, 297, 333 (n. 11); and Oppen, 326 (n. 4)
Wilde, Oscar, 108
Williams, Jonathan, 173
Williams, Raymond, 179–80, 185
Williams, William Carlos, 2, 3, 5, 7, 10, 14, 17, 31, 33–34, 35–36, 37, 49, 54, 86, 90, 96, 101, 122, 127, 141, 151, 153–56, 157, 158, 163, 194, 201, 213, 217, 224, 231, 259, 261, 270, 275, 276, 280, 284, 288, 298, 299, 315, 322 (n. 14), 327 (n. 8), 328 (n. 18), 330 (n. 9), 339 (n. 6); as Objectivist, 321 (n. 2); *Autobiography,* 3; "Between Walls," 334 (n. 25); *Collected Poems 1921–1931,* 213, 262; *Paterson,* 85, 88, 126, 297, 326 (n. 6); "Perpetuum Mobile: The City," 154–56; "The Red Wheelbarrow," 170, 181, 182–83; *Spring and All,* 113, 155, 159, 220, 281; "This is just to say," 174; *The Wedge,* 174; on Objectivism, 3, 115; on *An "Objectivists" Anthology,* 115, 117; on Oppen, 116–17; on Reznikoff, 262; and Niedecker, 173–74; and Reznikoff, 52–53, 196, 210, 214, 272; and Zukofsky, 120, 154, 321 (n. 2), 334 (n. 25); Bloom on, 192–93; Oppen on, 89, 170, 182; Zukofsky on, 114
Wilson, Edmund, 111, 112
Winters, Yvor, 10, 51
Wisconsin: A Guide to the Badger State, 176, 177
Wishart, Laurence, 132
witness. *See* testimony
Wittgenstein, Ludwig, 158, 166, 232, 333 (n. 12); *Philosophic Investigations,* 232, 333 (n. 12); *Zettel,* 231, 333 (n. 12)
Wolfe, Humbert, 141
Woolf, Virginia, 320 (n. 8)
word: materiality of, 3, 41, 43, 51, 52, 83, 157, 308, 327 (n. 10), 341 (n. 4)
Wordsworth, William, 69
Worker's Anthology (edited by Zukofsky), 136
Workers' Art Theater (Moscow), 109
working class, 4, 137, 175, 176
World War II, 5, 17, 220, 287–92, 331 (n. 15)
WPA project, 161, 175, 176
Writers Take Sides, 115
writing careers, gaps in, 2, 4–5, 120, 124, 137. *See also names of individual writers*
Wylie, Elinor, 281

Yeats, William Butler, 30, 35, 128, 129, 131, 147, 178, 265, 322 (n. 13)
Yehoash (Solomon Bloomgarden), 320 (n. 10)
Yellow Book, 48

Yerushalmi, Yosef Hayim, 197
Yiddish, 14, 18, 44, 49, 119, 211, 261
Yiddishkayt, 14–15, 320 (n. 10)
Yiddish poetry, 15, 320 (n. 10)

Zen Buddhism, 32
Ziarek, Krzysztof, 336 (n. 13)
Zolinsky, Henry, 39
Zukofsky, Celia, 264
Zukofsky, Louis, 1, 2, 3, 4, 5, 6, 7, 10, 14–15, 16, 26, 29, 30, 31, 33–34, 35, 52, 75, 81, 83, 97, 101, 115, 119, 124, 127, 128, 135–36, 158, 162–63, 165–66, 167, 181, 183, 195, 201, 210, 213, 217, 230, 235, 240, 260, 268, 272, 273, 275–85, 287, 293, 296, 298, 309, 320 (n. 1), 323 (n. 3), 323 (n. 4), 328 (n. 16), 333 (n. 11), 335 (n. 3), 338 (n. 2), 338 (n. 4); as outsider, 5, 136; as political poet, 12–13, 123, 148–50; at Brooklyn Polytechnic Institute, 260, 264; gaps in writing career, 5, 141; Jewishness, 14–15, 16, 44, 46, 207–208, 320 (n. 9); politics, 136; reception, 325 (nn. 1, 2); *"A"*, 43, 85, 88, 114, 123, 141, 148–49, 220, 221, 235, 263, 264, 282, 297; *All*, 221, 338 (n. 1); "American Poetry 1920–1930," 279, 280–83, 284; *Bottom: On Shakespeare*, 148, 321 (n. 11); "Crickets' / thickets," 50–52; *80 Flowers*, 241; "Ezra Pound: His Cantos," 279; "Henry Adams: A Criticism in Autobiography," 279, 284; "Mantis," 9, 13, 51, 148–49, 168; "Mantis, An Interpretation," 13, 148, 149–50, 168; "Poem Beginning 'The'," 14–15, 208, 220–21, 281, 320 (n. 9); "Program: 'Objectivists' 1931," 2, 10, 14, 15, 38–39, 213, 261, 281–85, 287, 339 (n. 7); "'Recencies' in Poetry," 282; "Sincerity and Objectification," 7–8, 9, 11, 14–15, 25–26, 57, 59, 213, 241, 261–62, 279, 287; *A Test of Poetry*, 162–65, 167, 171, 174, 186; *A Worker's Anthology*, 136; on Crane, 148; on Eliot, 261, 263; on H.D., 281; on Lenin, 42–43, 114, 322 (n. 12); on myth, 29; on Niedecker, 260–61; on Objectivism, 319 (n. 2); on surrealism, 11; on Reznikoff, 14–15, 114 (*see also* Zukofsky, "Sincerity and Objectification"); on tradition, 162–63; on Tyler and Ford, 40; and Bunting, 13–14, 38, 136, 331 (n. 10); and Lenin, 42–43, 114; and Marx, 43–44, 148–49, 152, 340 (n. 11); and Niedecker, 10–12, 38, 161, 162, 163–65, 170–71, 172, 181, 185, 270, 322 (n. 14), 338 (n. 8); and Oppen, 120–21, 153, 169, 221, 240, 265, 319 (n. 2); and Pound, 43–44, 51, 120–21, 131, 207–208, 277–78, 285, 321 (n. 2), 322 (nn. 13, 14), 330 (n. 12), 339 (n. 6); and Rakosi, 38, 53, 123; and Reznikoff, 207, 213, 220–21, 260–65, 321 (n. 3); and Williams, 51, 120, 154, 321 (n. 2), 334 (n. 25); Niedecker on, 174, 181; Oppen on, 88–89. *See also* "historic and contemporary particulars" (Zukofsky)
Zukofsky, Paul, 264